THE HORGAN BROTHERS – THE IRISH LUMIÈRES

Na Lumière Gaelacha – Na Deartháireacha Uí Argáin

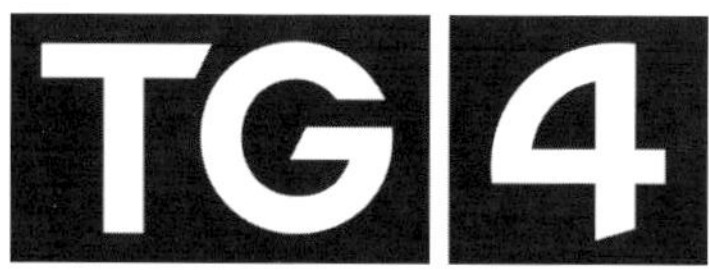

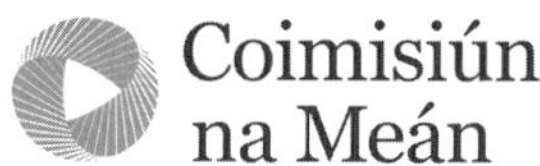

Coimisiún na Meán

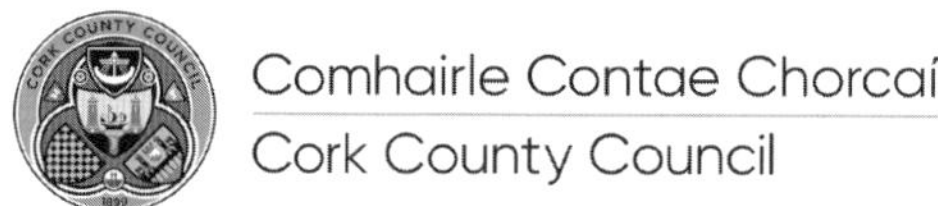

Comhairle Contae Chorcaí
Cork County Council

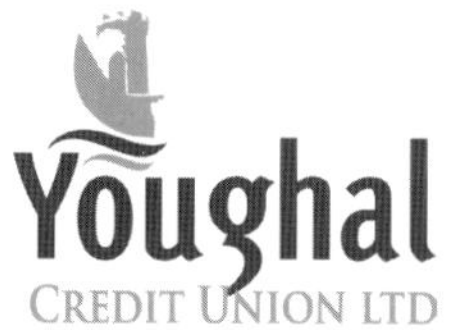

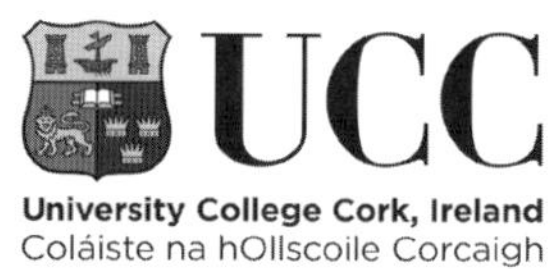

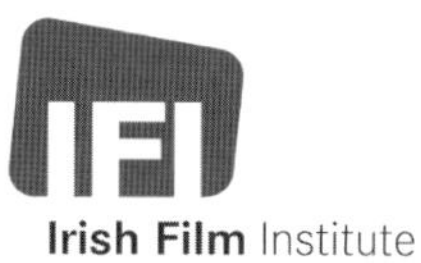

THE HORGAN BROTHERS
THE IRISH LUMIÈRES

Na Lumière Gaelacha – Na Deartháireacha Uí Argáin

A book to accompany the TG4 documentary
Leabhar le dul leis an gclár faisnéise ar TG4

DARINA CLANCY
with contributions from
JIM HORGAN AND PATRICIA HORGAN WHYTE

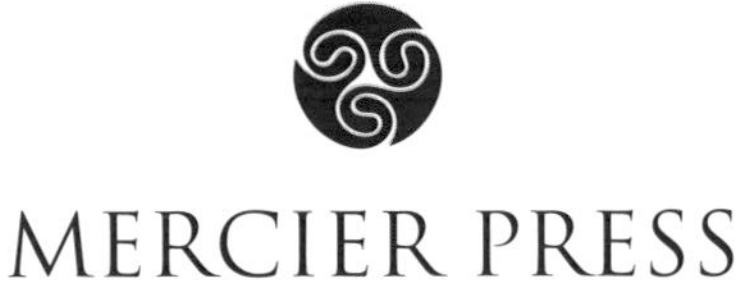

MERCIER PRESS

MERCIER PRESS
Cork
www.mercierpress.ie

ISBN 978-1-78117-844-7

Printed and bound in the EU.

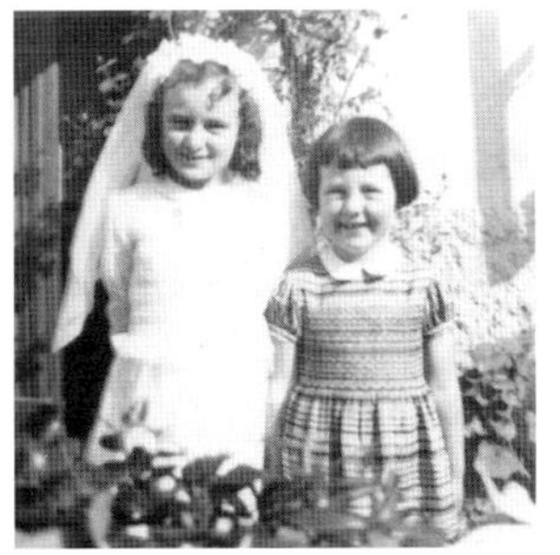
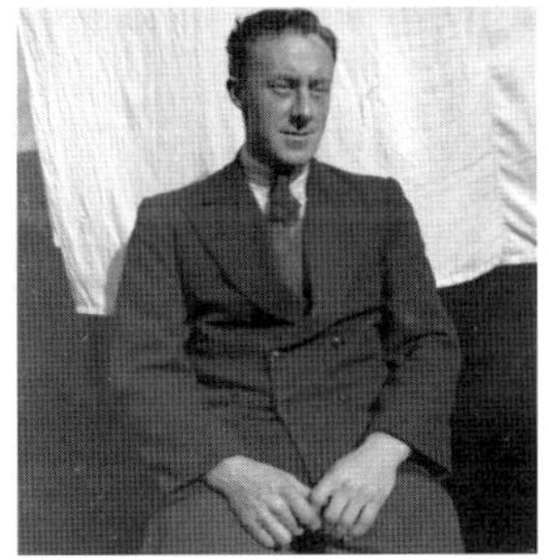
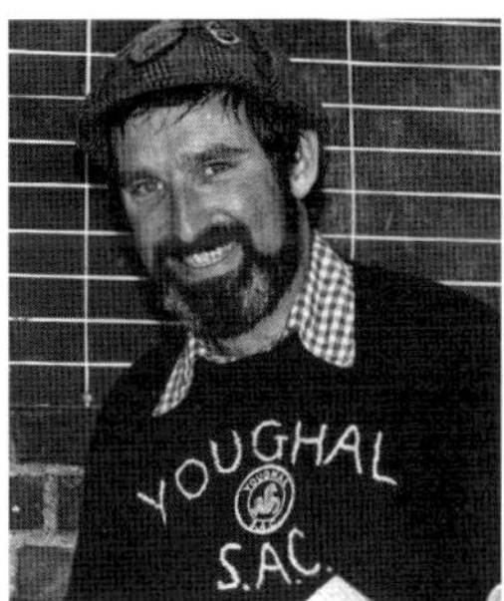

CONTENTS

Acknowledgements

With any project, it takes a village. This book could not have been completed without invaluable help from many sources.

In the first instance, Jim and Mary Horgan, Patricia and Michael Whyte, Mary McAuliffe, the family of Joan Collins, Conall Horgan and Niamh Horgan – all of whom shared their personal memories of their family with wonderful openness. Thanks to Jim for all his efforts over the years to reprint and save the Horgan photographs and films. To Patricia for researching and documenting the stories. Thanks to Ted Horgan and Carina Horgan for being great neighbours to my uncle and aunt, Myles and Mary Clancy. To Teresa Watkins, thank you for the beautiful paintings.

Thanks to Brian Whyte for his focused work on assembling and digitally improving the photograph collection and for representing the Horgan family throughout the creation of this book.

Thanks to the entire team at Mercier Press, an incredible Cork institution. I'm incredibly grateful for their patience and guidance, but especially for recognising the importance of publishing this book.

To the amazing professional, Orla Riordan, thanks for all your time and assistance (and company) during the composition of the book.

A huge thanks to all at Cork County Libraries, Cork County Archives, and Cork County Council for their work on the photographs and for continuing to support the memory of the Horgan Brothers. A special mention goes to Ian McDonagh in the Cork County Arts office. Rose Carroll and Sharon Conroy, thank you for your continued support.

Thanks to the entire TG4 commissioning team for their continuing support, especially to Laura Ní Cheallaigh, who understood and supported this story from the outset. Thanks also to the Sound and Vision scheme.

To my colleagues at Cormorant Films: Bailey Gavin, thank you for your stalwart support, sanity, and laughter. To Rupert MacCarthy Morrogh and Gearóid O'Sullivan, thank you for making the documentary look so beautiful that it inspired me to go further. To all the team that worked on it, thank you. As always, I owe a special word of thanks to the Hudsucker team for their incredible work and diligence.

Thanks to the Irish Film Archives and the Irish Film Institute for their continuing work in promoting and preserving the Horgan collection and the information provided for this book. Thanks to all the team in the IFI especially those who assisted in the filming of the Horgan camera and projector.

Thanks to Andy Kelly for his technical support and the incredible knowledge of the cameras and photographic styles of the time. Thanks to all those who shared their photographs, but especially to Michael Hackett and Maurice Cronin for keeping and scanning some of the photos that would otherwise have been lost. To Billy Field who shared the last remaining original Horgan Picture Theatre poster with us from Fields Printers in Youghal.

Thanks to Dr Ciara Chambers at UCC and her colleague Ellen Scally who have completed extensive research on the Horgan Brothers and were so generous with their findings and their time.

Thanks to Kieran Quinn at Youghal Credit Union for supporting Youghal stories and projects.

Deep gratitude to all the expert contributors to the documentary whose knowledge is distributed throughout this book.

Thanks to the Blackwater Kayaking Adventures group for identifying the location of some of the photographs across East Cork and West Waterford.

Finally, I want to thank my family, especially my son Diarmuid, for always just knowing, and my friends for their vital support.

To the descendants and friends of all the people captured in the Horgan Collection and who appear in this book, I do hope you enjoy it.

Foreword

This book is long overdue. With its publication, the Horgan brothers' story and their contribution to Irish cinema will at last get the attention they deserve. Until now, their importance to Irish cinema has been known only to a few people in the film industry here. Animators mostly. This is because, at the Galway Film Fleadh, the animation award for Best Irish Animation is called the James Horgan Award.

The award recognises the achievement of James Horgan in creating Ireland's first animation. In producing it, James made a model of the Youghal Clock Gate Tower come alive and dance through the streets of the town. Lost for many years, the film was coincidentally retrieved at the same time that the Galway Film Fleadh – the first Fleadh – was being held. More than a prodigal son returning to Irish animation, the news that six seconds of the Clocktower animation had survived was something like a cinematic spiritual resurrection, really. The Fleadh decided there and then that there must be an annual competition of Irish animation – again a first – and the prize should be called the James Horgan Award.

The Horgan brothers deserve yet more recognition. Their portfolio of documentary photography, their cinematic experiments, as well the very first animation, is no mere trifle, unsophisticated work from innocent amateurs to be passed by. This book will make you stop and take notice. It demonstrates that the brothers were major pioneers of European cinema. The period the brothers worked in was one of wonderful mechanical development: the aeroplane, the telephone and, of course, the camera. However, it was one thing to be filled with wonder, as most people were, by these machines, it is another thing to embrace them, and the brothers did more than embrace the early camera, they owned it.

Their enquiring minds and their creativity are parallel to better-known pioneers in cinema like J. Stuart Blackton or Alice Guy. They are our Irish Auguste and Louis Lumière. I am sure this homage to the Irish Lumières will bring the Horgans and their work beyond the animation sector to the entire Irish film industry and to the wider Irish public as well, giving them the respect they have earned. Perhaps on top of that, The Irish Lumières will begin the journey for the international recognition they also deserve.

STEVE WOODS*

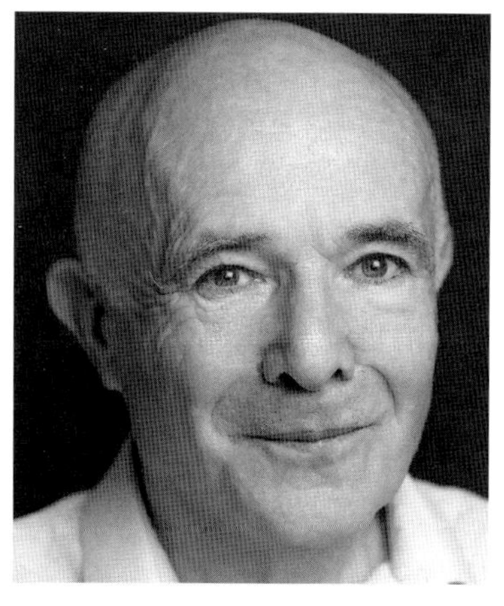

*Steve Woods has worked in film since 1988. His award-winning work encompasses animations, documentaries, dance films and experimental films.

A founder member of The Galway Film Fleadh, he programmed a showcase Irish animation at the Annecy International Animation Festival in 2012. Steve teaches Experimental Animation at the National Film School in IADT, Ireland. He is the author of *Drawing the Line* the first book written on Irish animation.

PREFACE

Often, when something is on your doorstep, it can be taken for granted as general knowledge and something that has always been known as fact. I've always known about the Horgan Brothers and, to this day, it's difficult to understand why they have not received the recognition they deserve on a national stage.

I first heard of the Horgan Brothers as I grew up in Youghal, County Cork, Ireland. My Dad filled me with stories of going to the 'pictures' at the Horgan Picture Theatre, and how he and his friends, after watching a western, would come running out of the cinema down the street firing cap guns when they could afford them, or when they couldn't, they simply used their fingers as guns. He went to the cinema as often as he could, as did most people from the area, with matinée screenings after school, and a lengthy evening programme of shorts and features. Films came and went from the Horgan's cinema – from their own local newsreels, at the very beginning of the concept of the cinema theatre, to the biggest studios and names. The film reels were delivered to Youghal by train and transported down Lighthouse Hill by a large wooden barrow to the cinema theatre on Friar Street, parallel to where Dad grew up.

The cinema brought a whole new world to the small town of Youghal at a time when Ireland was emerging from British colonialism to become an independent Republic. The films adjusted perspective in thinking, understanding and beliefs, not to mention introduced big, wild characters and places.

The Horgan Brothers, who ran the cinema, left a huge impression on the town of Youghal and its hinterland by capturing the area's social history and introducing images and films from all over the world. Almost every household locally has a photograph taken by the Horgan Brothers, and I recently stumbled across two in my grandmother's old Jacobs biscuit box, which is crammed with family photos.

As I grew up, I found out more about Horgan Brothers purely through word of mouth from locals. Very little information was available in the 1980s and at that time, I didn't quite have the courage to knock on doors. It wasn't until I moved to Dublin in the 1990s and saw the Horgan film collection showcased in the IFI, that the importance of the Horgan Brothers really hit home. Their film diaries alone give an account of the volume of films that were passing through the cinema on a weekly basis. However, it is their own films and photography that capture a time in Ireland in a way that very few other photographers have done, and certainly no other films or animations of that time have survived. Their films remain the oldest and most important indigenous films in Ireland.

Throughout my career, I have researched many photographic collections and the Horgan's is notably different from others. I know from working behind the camera for decades that it is a rare talent to work from that perspective and to be able to put people at ease – the Horgans did this with a remarkable level of vitality and levity. As a result, we see many people smiling and their eyes are shining in their photographs. People are enjoying themselves as they are being snapped living their lives. The Horgans documented life in rural Ireland with fun and magic at the core but were also there to document events that would otherwise be forgotten.

These brothers were adventurers, experimenters and entrepreneurs. They loved where they lived and captured the area in all its beauty. Their photographs of the Blackwater show so little has changed in that landscape in over a century.

Sometimes it takes time to find the right way to tell a story, and even more so with one that is very familiar. When I imagined a way to tell the story of the Horgan Brothers so that it would be accessible to all, I was delighted to meet with two of the grandchildren of James Horgan, Patricia Whyte and Mary McAuliffe. I wanted to do their story justice and bring the brothers' work to life to expose the magic, creativity and experimentation they had in abundance. It has been my honour as a woman from Youghal to tell their story and to bring it to an international stage.

This book focuses on the vast range of photographs that the Horgan Brothers captured as local Irish men, at a time when photographs would have been taken by people from another country. This book acts as an accompaniment to the documentary produced by Cormorant Films for TG4, *Na Lumière Gaelacha – Na Deartháireacha Uí Argáin (The Irish Lumières – The Horgan Brothers)*.

Darina Clancy
Managing and Creative Director, Cormorant Films

Introduction

This book brings the photographs of the Horgan Brothers together for the first time as a companion to the TG4 documentary *Na Lumière Gaelacha (Na Dearthảireacha Uí Argáin)*. It will bring you back to a world we have forgotten, a time when image capture was unique, experimental, exciting and unfamiliar. A time when things began to be seen from a different point of view – when magic, art and science mixed to bring us the contemporary art forms that we call photography, film and animation – forms the Horgan Bothers pioneered in Ireland, at a time when another set of brothers in France, the Lumière Brothers, were leading the way.

The Horgans were riding the crest of a wave, specifically in Ireland. They captured Irish culture through photography at a time when image manipulation was in its infancy. They developed their craft by using the backdrop of their small town while entertaining the townspeople. With these tools, they did something magical and were quietly at the forefront internationally of how image capture and manipulation would entertain and change the world.

They were trailblazers of their time artistically and technically and were pioneers of so many elements of the image-capturing business. The brothers were continuously creating and innovating. They moved from producing travelling light shows to developing a photography business touching up and manipulating their own photographs. They founded the concept of picture postcards and created a large catalogue of postcards for sale. They built drama and photographic sets filled with detail and fun. They experimented with cameras both technically and creatively, adapting them, discovering and pioneering different techniques. They filmed the first-ever newsreels in the world. They created the earliest record of animation in Ireland and ultimately opened their own cinema acquiring the first ever cinema licence in County Cork on 17 April 1910. All this showed their focus and interest in the medium as well as their entrepreneurship and tenacity in business. This business sense afforded them success in achieving other firsts in the town – they were the first to have electricity installed to run their cinema projector and owned one of the first motor cars, an Argyle car.

Their imaginativeness was evident from the outset in their approach to the technology they were using. They worked on photographs adding features, colourising them and writing on them. Their skills were so advanced that the Royal Irish Constabulary, or the RIC, often consulted the brothers for their expertise to distinguish if photographs had been doctored.

The Horgan brothers captured life in Youghal and its surroundings in a very natural and relaxed style. This came from the fact that they lived amongst the people, as well as their love of fun and pushing boundaries. Fun shines through continually in their images and especially in the experimentation with sets and costumes.

Their love of their local area is evident, especially in all aspects of marine life, in and on the water. They captured beaches, quaysides, all kinds of boats and long stretches of the river Blackwater. Youghal, as a large and busy port, has been visited by well-known names throughout history. Using their artistic skills, they recreated images of some of these visits, including Walter Raleigh and referenced the words of others, such as the poet Spencer. During their own lifetime, using their own community as their palette, the brothers captured key moments of national and international historical significance that may otherwise have been forgotten.

In the beginning, they operated from their own shoemaker's business on Brown Street, their mother would ask customers, 'is it Mr Horgan the shoemaker or Mr Horgan the photographer you'd like to see?' If the request was for the shoemakers, the brothers would arrive in leather aprons. If the request was for the photographers, they wore white coats. The business model the Horgan adopted was constantly evolving, largely to the credit of Thomas Horgan, who was recognised as the business mind in the family. The brothers tapped into the understanding that people liked to see themselves, photographing and filming people at large group events and enjoyed the profits from the magic of showing these images to large groups when developed, in local halls initially and eventually their own cinema. They recognised that landscapes were always appreciated, but those that featured people were more popular. They overcame technical and copyright challenges with resourceful and imaginative technical solutions and used their creations to fuel their growing business. They moved quickly with innovations and made advances of their own at a pace that followed rapidly in the footsteps of the Lumières in France.

What is very special in all their work is that the Horgan Brothers captured life at a time when Ireland was emerging from centuries of British rule through to the formation of the Republic. This was all captured through the lens of Youghal and its hinterland. Through that small geographic area and the community of people, the Horgan Brothers have left us with a significant historical record of rural Ireland. They captured people at work and play: Fishermen tending nets and the rope walk along the hill parallel to the Clock Gate, where families would work on the ropes for the fishermen. They courted kings and exotic travellers, farmers and worshipers. They also photographed important political and social events in local and world history, taking portraits of First World War soldiers who never returned home, volunteer camps, political and religious activities and activists. One notable photograph is the gates of Kam Tin. In an unusually early example of the return of colonial artefacts, Henry Arthur Blake appropriated the gates when he was the governor of Hong Kong, who when he retired erected them at his home, Myrtle Grove, in Youghal. The Horgan brothers captured a visit by a Chinese representative to Myrtle Grove, who brought the gates back to their original home in Kam Tin.

The brothers were amongst the embers of what is now an industry worth billions – the entertainment business. They fashioned magic lantern shows, travelling to the hinterlands of East Cork and West Waterford on their bicycles to village halls where people would come to have their portraits taken. They projected slides from all over the world during these shows, organised sing songs showing the lyrics on the screen and hosted a range of visiting acts such as magicians, jugglers, gymnasts and dancers. They later would show short films bought from the Lumières. Later still they adapted a projector to capture and show their own films which they called 'The Youghal Gazette', the very first newsreels anywhere in the world. The title card of their 'Youghal Gazette' newsreels was bespoke to their heritage, using shamrocks instead of the fleur de lys.

The development of modes of transport and communication are documented throughout their collection, from the donkey and cart to the horse and trap. They initially used bicycles to transport all their equipment from village to village for the magic lantern shows, eventually purchasing a car, one of only two in Youghal. This motor car allowed them to expand their reach even further into Cork and Waterford allowing the brothers to get to places and capture images that were extremely attractive to the public. They pioneered the postcard business in Ireland which developed into a vast, prolific collection of images that were sold and posted with messages, all over the world. It was one of their most lucrative enterprises which afforded them the opportunity to open their own photographic studio on Friar Street in Youghal.

This marked the beginning of yet another chapter for the brothers, whose innovation was infused into numerous enjoyable studio sets and backdrops. Many of the glass plates that remain depict the family dressed as characters, brandishing props against contemporary sets that are intricately designed, with fun at the heart of them all. This love for and enjoyment of their craft led them to create what is now recognised as Ireland's first example of animation in Ireland, the dancing Clock Gate, a building that was once the gateway to the walled town of Youghal and remains a key landmark.

Their love of film and entertainment ultimately led them to open a 600-seat cinema two doors down from the Photographic Studio on Friar Street, right next door to the already-established Regal Cinema. The film programmes featured screenings of multiple films throughout an evening or afternoon, all beamed onto the screen by rear projection as the theatre was so long. The projector and screen backed into the home of the Horgans on Strand Street, and the screen needed to be dampened before, and sometimes during, any screening to ensure the clarity of the image. One of the first films projected was the Pattern at St Declan's Well in Ardmore, County Waterford. The seating styles can be clearly seen in the photographs of the interior of the cinema, with a scaled cost depending on where you chose to sit.

Entertainment continued in the Horgan Picture Theatre, and music accompanied the silent movies. Masie Horgan from Cobh became their lead pianist and also played at the very popular Strand Palace. She later married Thomas Horgan's son, Timothy Horgan. The Horgans were excellent musicians and created their own orchestra which included many family members. The presence of a live orchestra meant that sing songs were part of the evening's entertainment, as well as accompanying films. However, live entertainment also meant that the Horgan's paid less tax due to a post-war live entertainment tax deduction.

As soon as sound came to accompany the pictures, the Horgans discovered that the length of their cinema caused an echo. One of the ways they alleviated this issue was to adorn the walls with James' artwork. The relief paintings were hung all along the walls of the cinema to absorb the sound. His artwork was also featured in the foyer of the picture theatre. The posters advertising the films from the opening of the cinema to its closure were printed locally in Youghal by Fields Printers, which has been operating for over two hundred years.

The cinema eventually closed in 1988, but not before the brothers handed over the baton to two Horgan women who ran it until then.

The Horgan Photographic Collection gives us a window into Irish heritage in all walks of life in rural Ireland at a time we'd otherwise need to imagine, but here we have life being lived, captured by the newest of cultural art forms. Many of the stories that accompany these photographs have come from the descendants of the Horgan Brothers and from local lore and word of mouth. Much work has taken place by the descendants to preserve the photographs. Here, we see the images as they are today in all their authenticity, sometimes showing cracks across the prints that now exist on the original glass plate negatives, or where broken sections of glass are missing. This is the first time their archive has been brought together in book form.

The documentary, *Na Lumière Gaelacha*, can be accessed on the TG4 player through the QR code at the front of the book.

If you have any extra information on any of the photographs, or wish to purchase printed photographs, please email Horganphotos@gmail.com.

More of the Horgan photographic collection can be found at https://cork digitalarchive.ie/collections/show/4

The Horgan 'Youghal Gazette' films can be viewed on the IFI Archive Player at www.ifiarchiveplayer.ie

The Horgan equipment and document collections are available to be viewed by appointment at the IFI, www.ifi.ie.

THE HORGAN BOYS AND THEIR PLAYGROUND

The story of the Horgan Brothers began in the late 1800s in Youghal, a seaside town in County Cork, Ireland, a country still under British rule. The country had suffered a devastating famine just thirty years before the eldest, Thomas Horgan, was born in 1875, James was born in 1877, and Philip, the youngest was born in 1879. The boys, along with their parents Timothy and Elizabeth Horgan, enjoyed a good life as they grew up in the town that would become the inspiration for much of their work, Youghal.

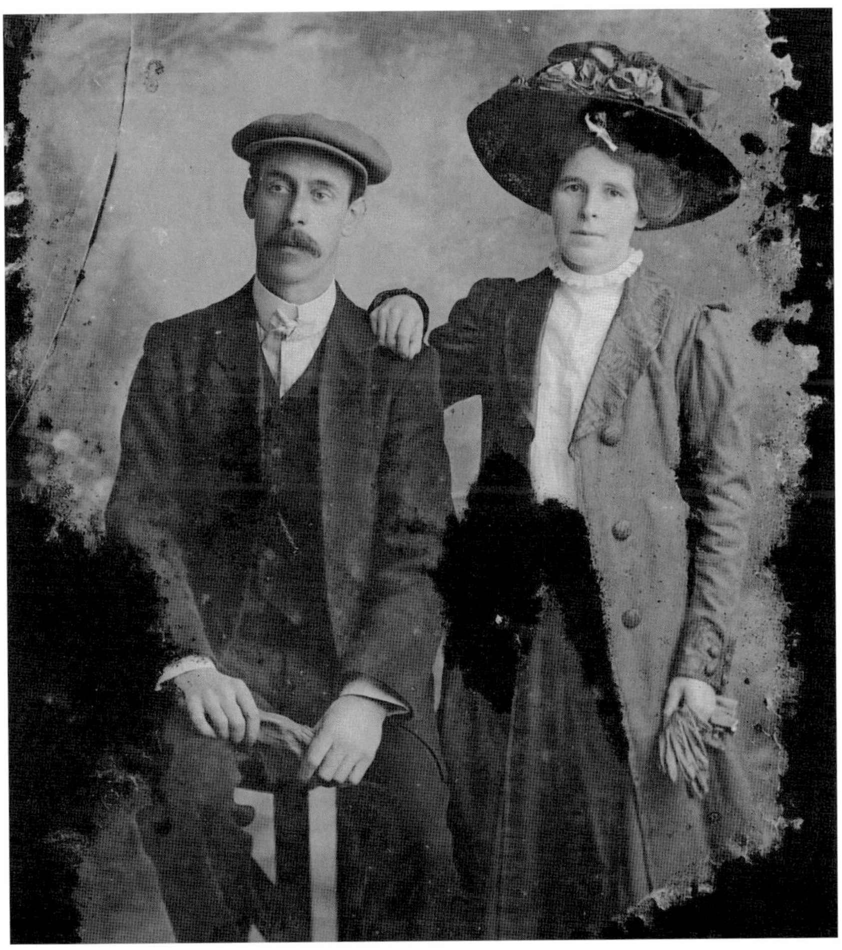

Thomas Horgan and his wife Nora.

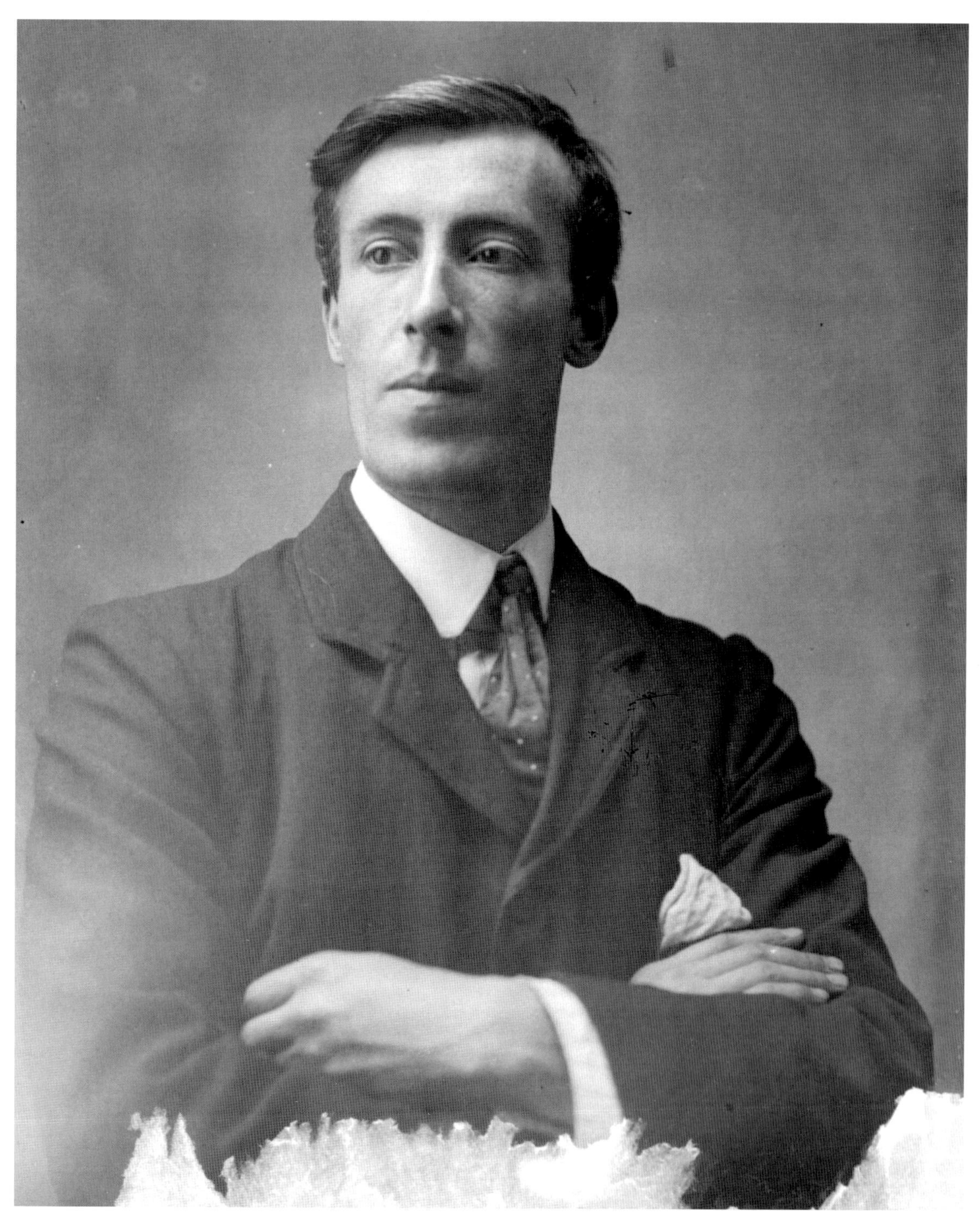

James Horgan.

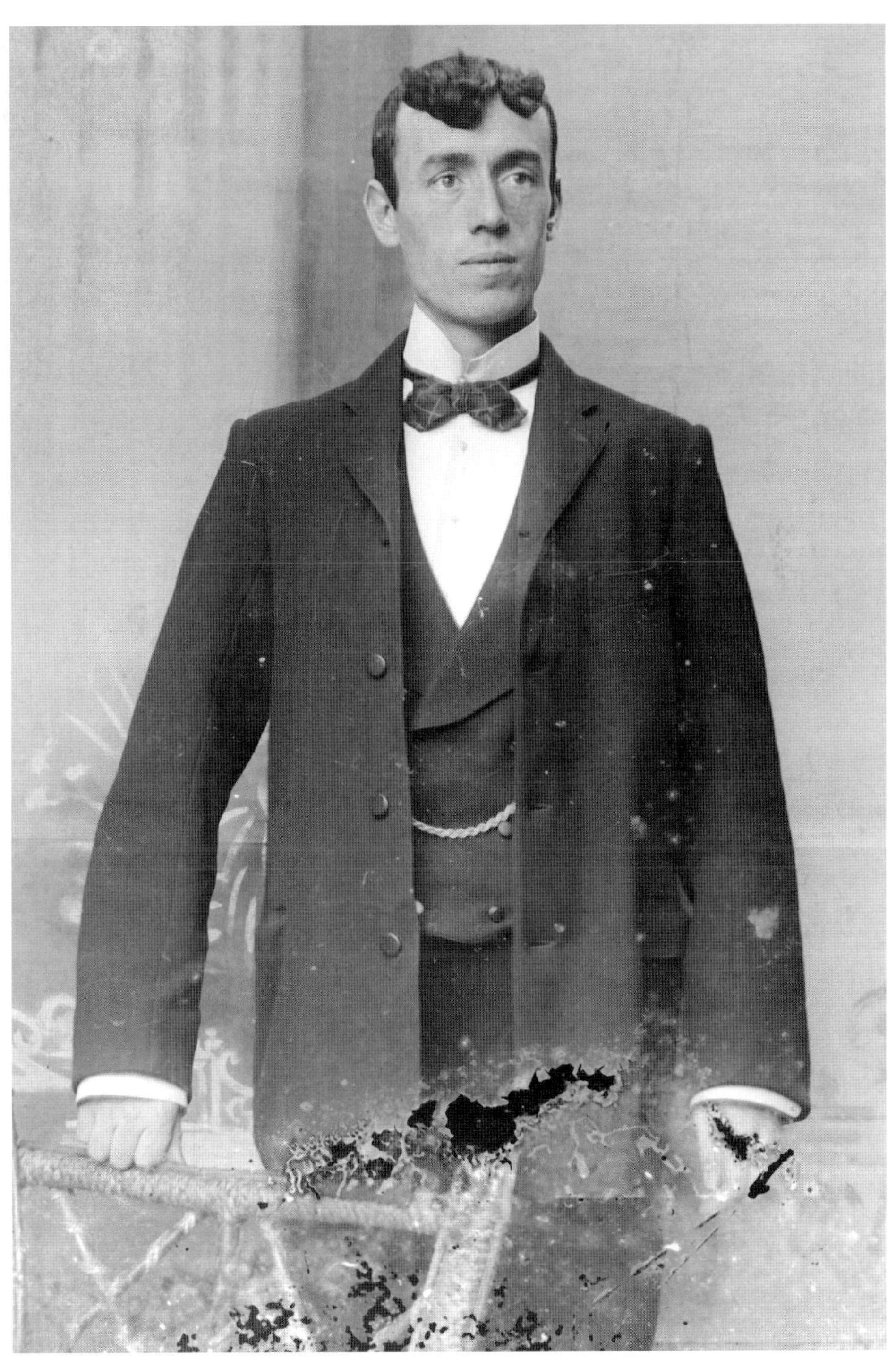

Philip Horgan.

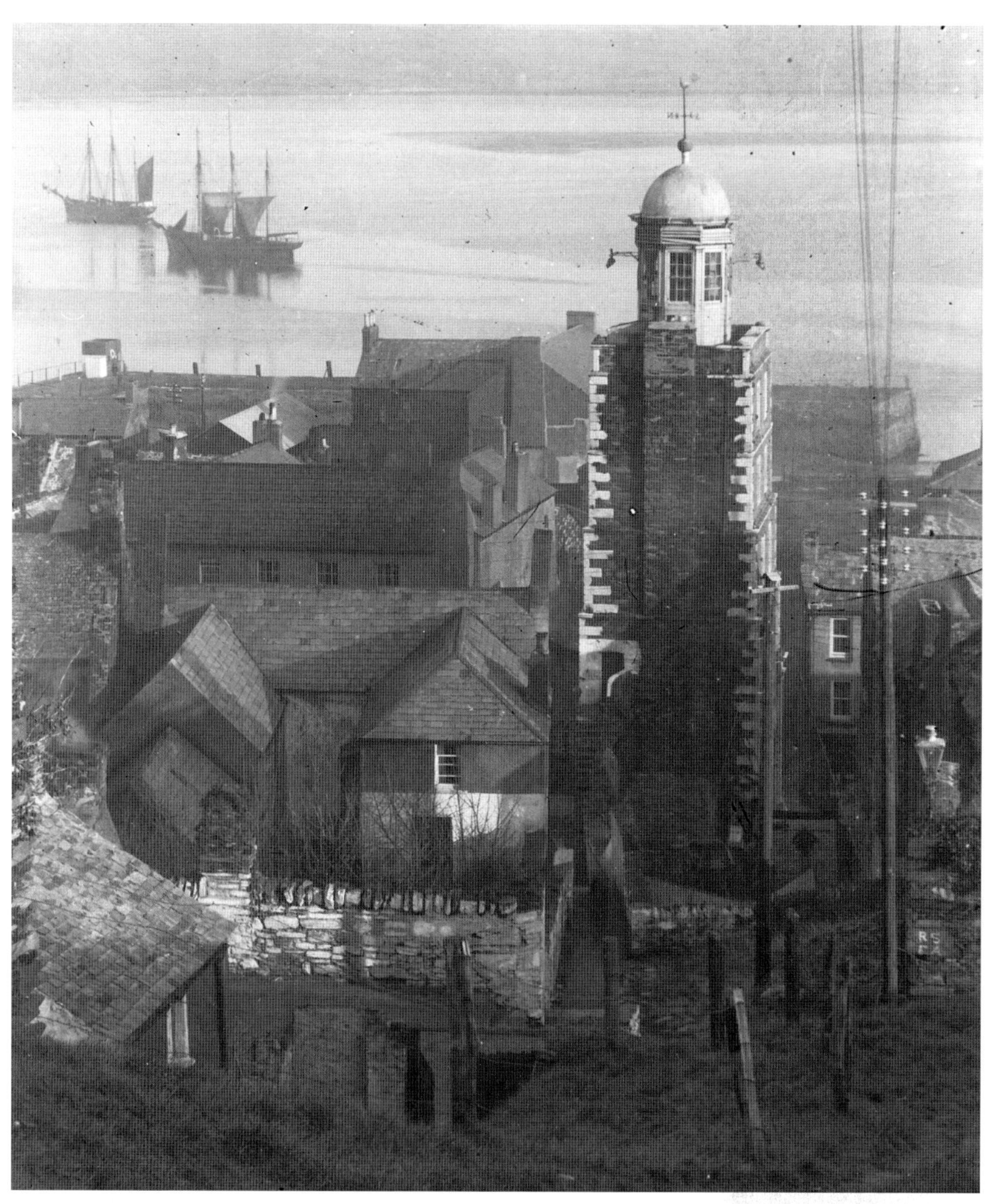

The Clock Gate Youghal from the Jail Steps
with the Blackwater estuary in the background.

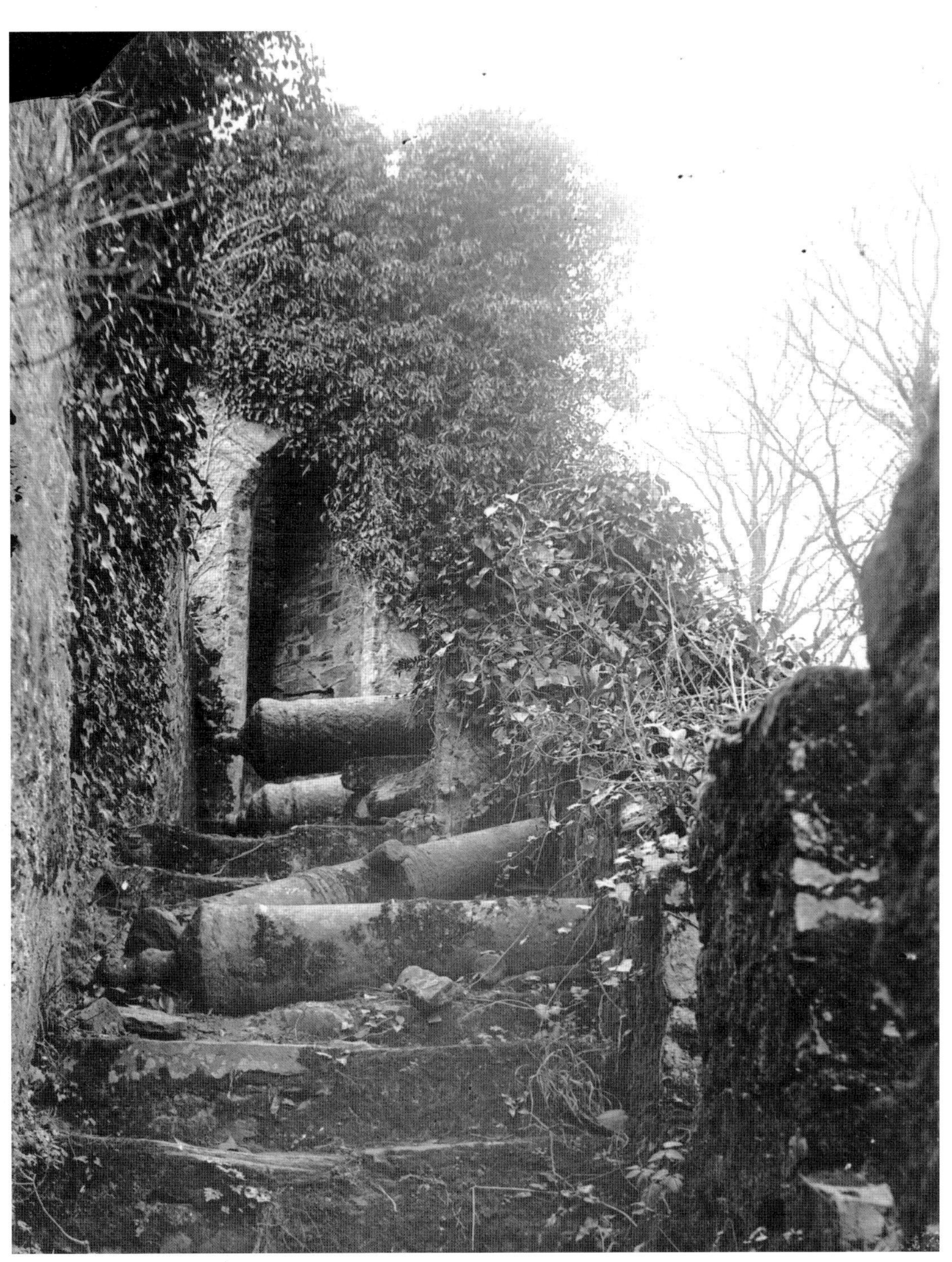

The old cannons on the town walls of Youghal.

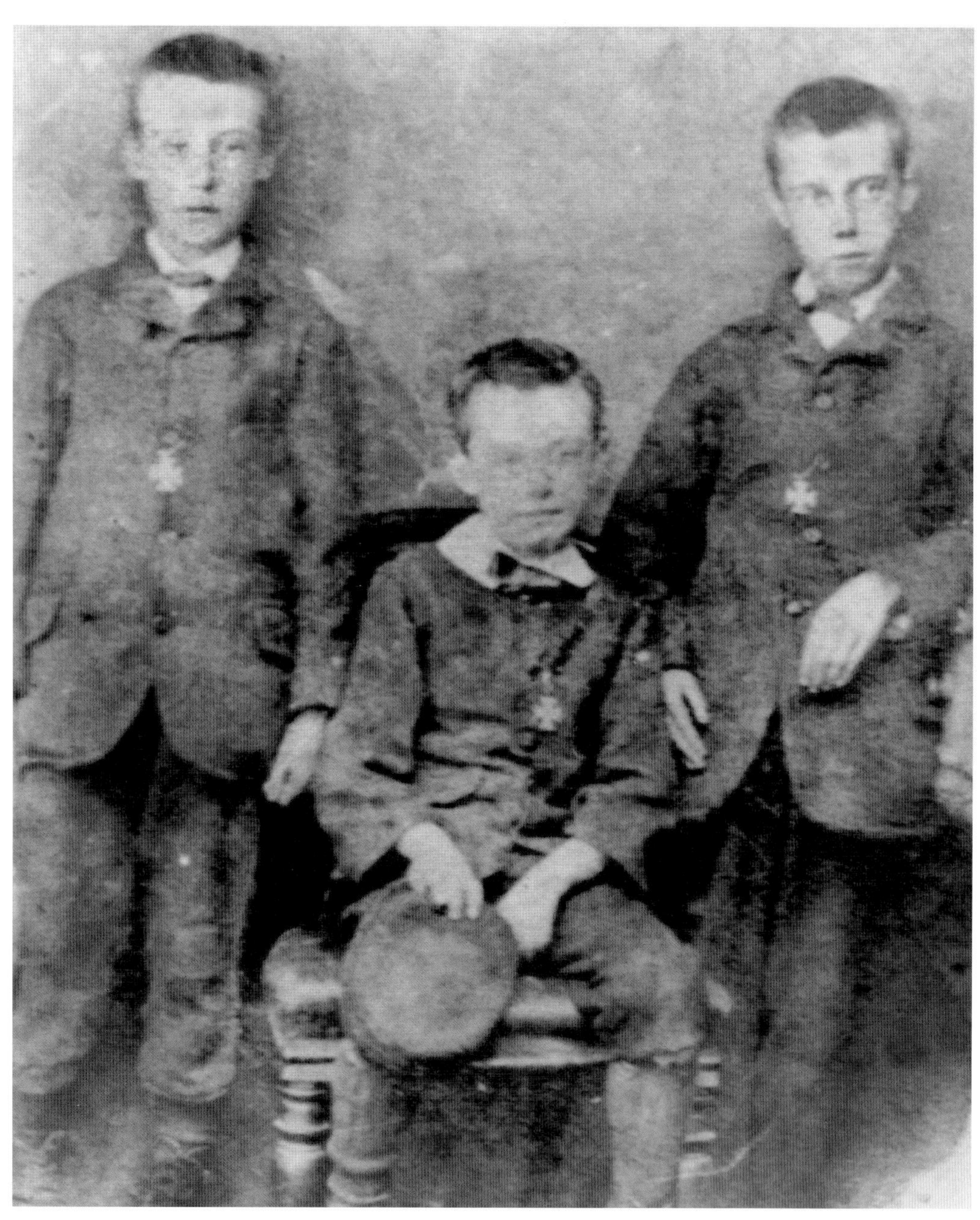

*The oldest existing picture of the Horgan brothers with
their confirmation pins taken with a pinhole camera.
Considering the age of the photograph we are lucky to have it.*

Timothy, the boys' father, was a shoemaker and according to accounts from descendants, he had a contract to make cavalry boots for the army, which gave the family a steady income. However, tragedy struck when their father died at just forty-two, from an asthma attack, when the boys were still young, leaving Elizabeth, just thirty-nine, a widow with no income. They had only been married for seven years. Elizabeth needed to secure a future for her boys, but money was running out. Poverty and hunger enveloped the family until, finally, three days had passed without any food. A sovereign that Timothy had saved was found on the third day of starvation and saved the family from being broken up and sent to the workhouse. Now on stable ground, the three boys had to have their communion and confirmation before Elizabeth could consider any apprenticeship for them.

The brothers developed their interest in photography as early as 1886. They took their first known picture with a pinhole camera from Merrick's store which is dated between 1887–1889.

A pinhole camera shines light through a tiny hole in the camera onto sensitised paper at the back of the camera. As light shines in a straight line, the light from the top shines on the bottom of the paper, the light from the left shines on the right of the paper, and the light from the right shines on the left – an upside-down mirror image.

The boys were dressed up, ready for the photo, with their confirmation badges on their left lapels in the usual way, when an argument broke out about how this would work out in terms of an upside-down mirror image. Some said it would come right when turned upright. Some said it would not and that the badges should be put on the right lapel to correct the image. Elizabeth had to intervene, and she put all the badges in the middle, and that is how they appear today.

The retrieval of the coin that her deceased husband had saved, enabled Elizabeth to secure an apprenticeship for her boys with a local shoemaker, Timothy Delacour, on south main street in Youghal. This photo was taken by Joseph William Lapham in 1886 and clearly shows the shop displaying a swinging boot shape of the shoemaker above the door of De la Cour.

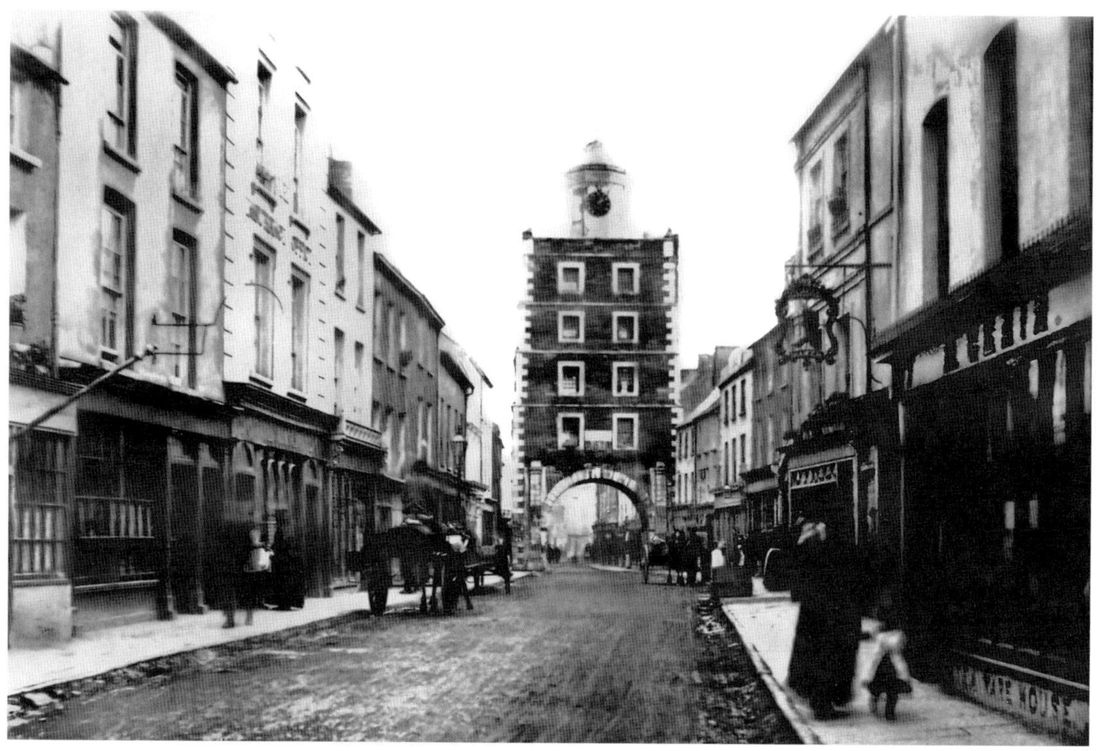

Delacour Shoemakers on the right of the picture.

Youghal was the landscape and set where the Horgans initially plied their trade, and the people of the town were their characters. The focal point for their work stemmed from the Clock Gate, the 1777 structure and the dividing gate of the walled town that straddles the main street between what is now North Main and South Main Street. Stemming from there, the brothers captured life on the streets out to the strand and the brickworks, and all the significant buildings in between.

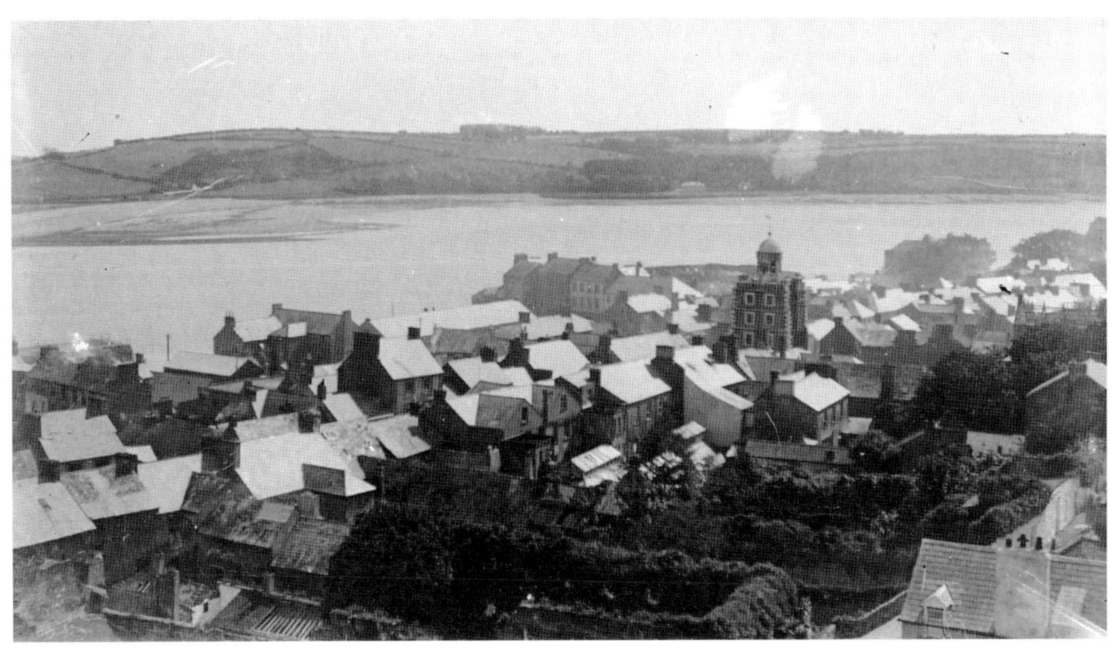

Youghal town with the Clock Gate standing out within the rooftops.

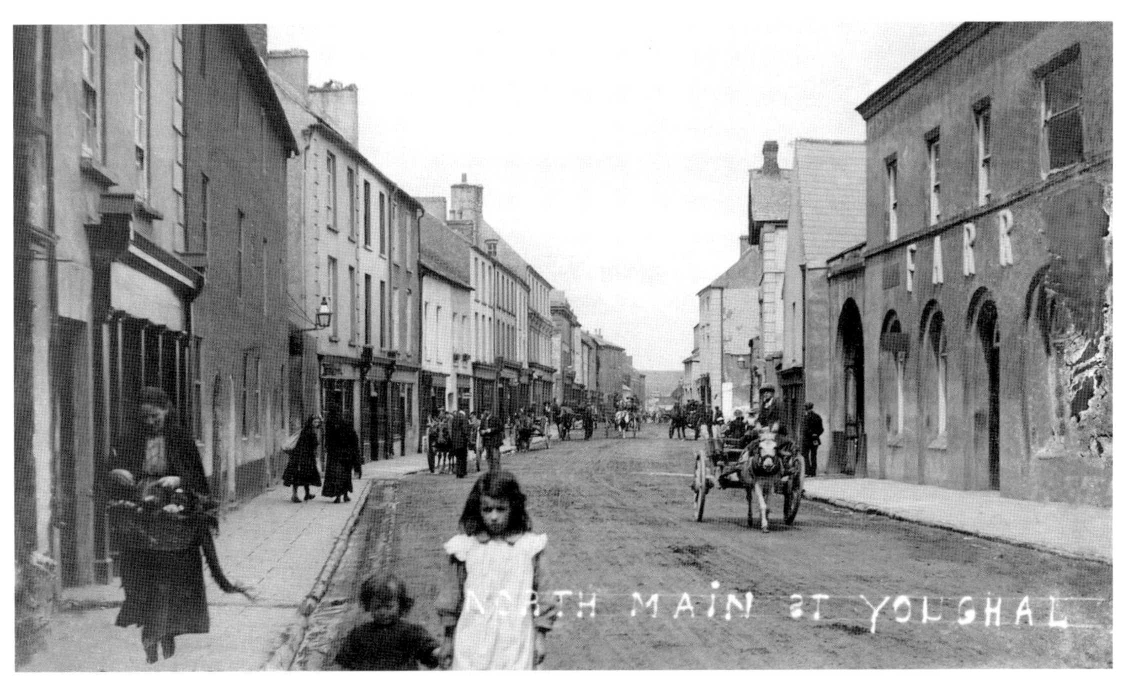

North Main Street, Youghal.

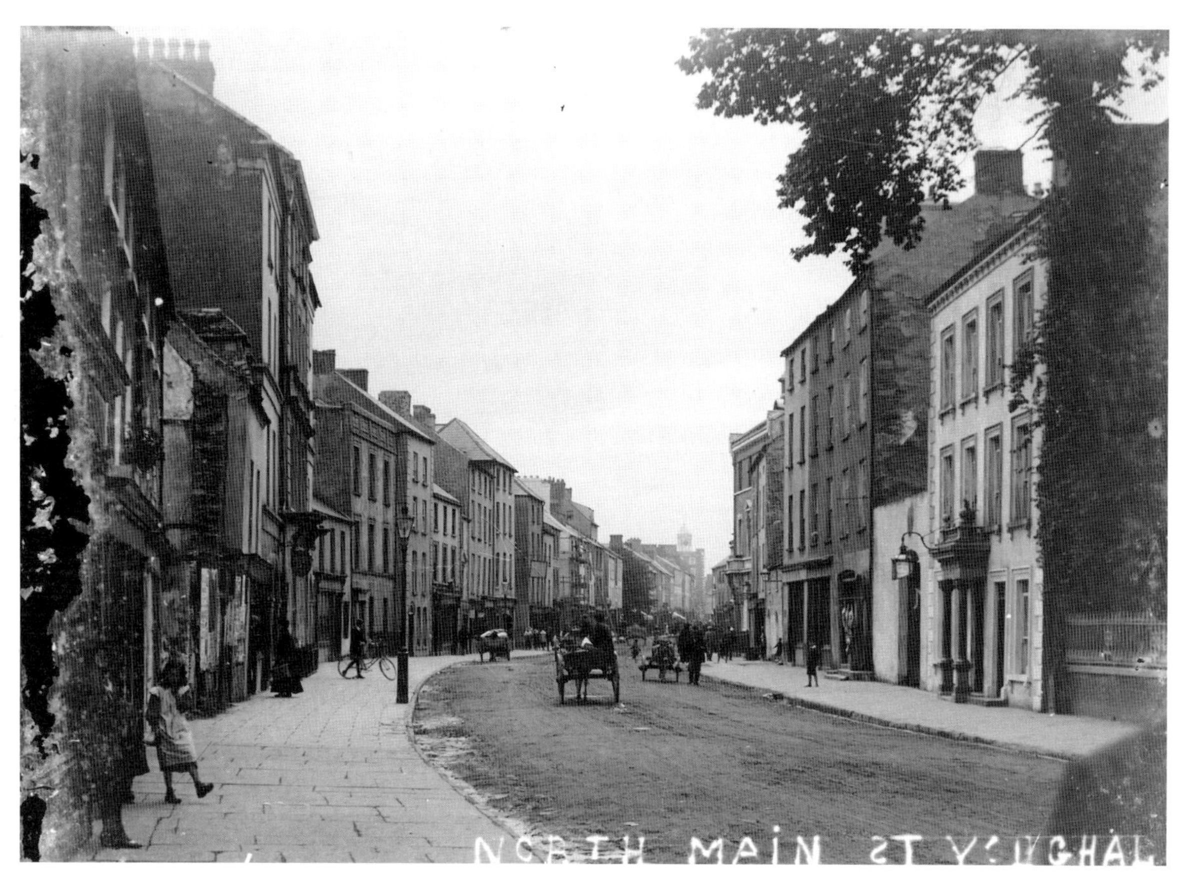

Another view of North Main Street, Youghal.

Across top right – *South Abbey Street, Youghal.*
Across bottom right – *Tallow Street, Youghal.*

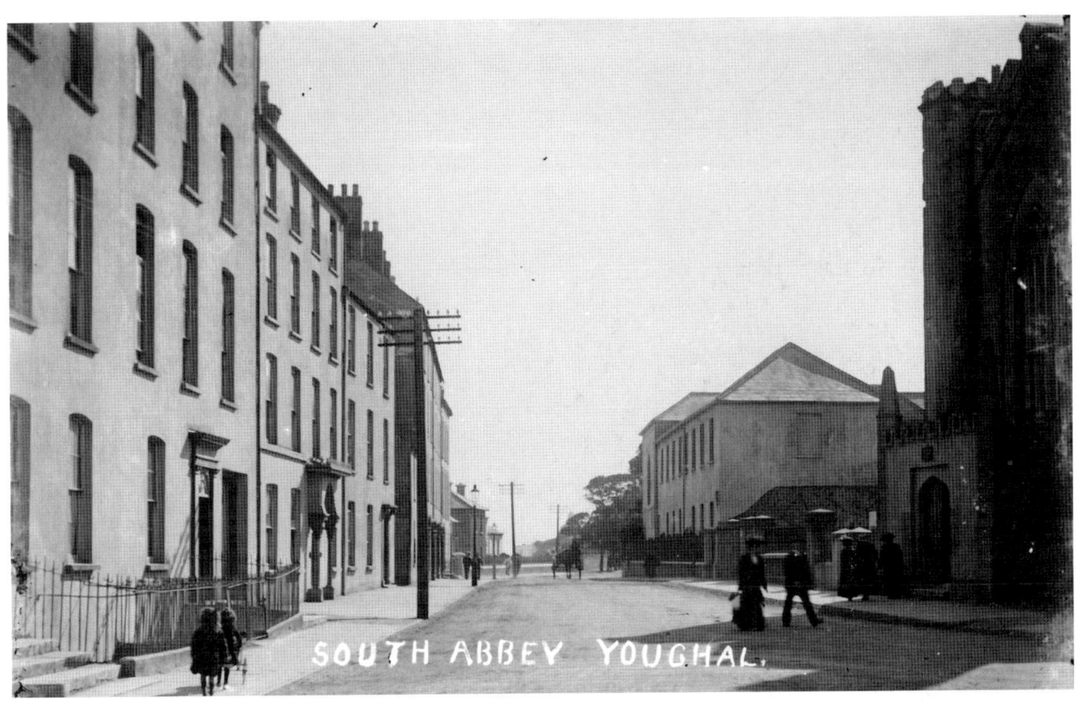

SOUTH ABBEY YOUGHAL.

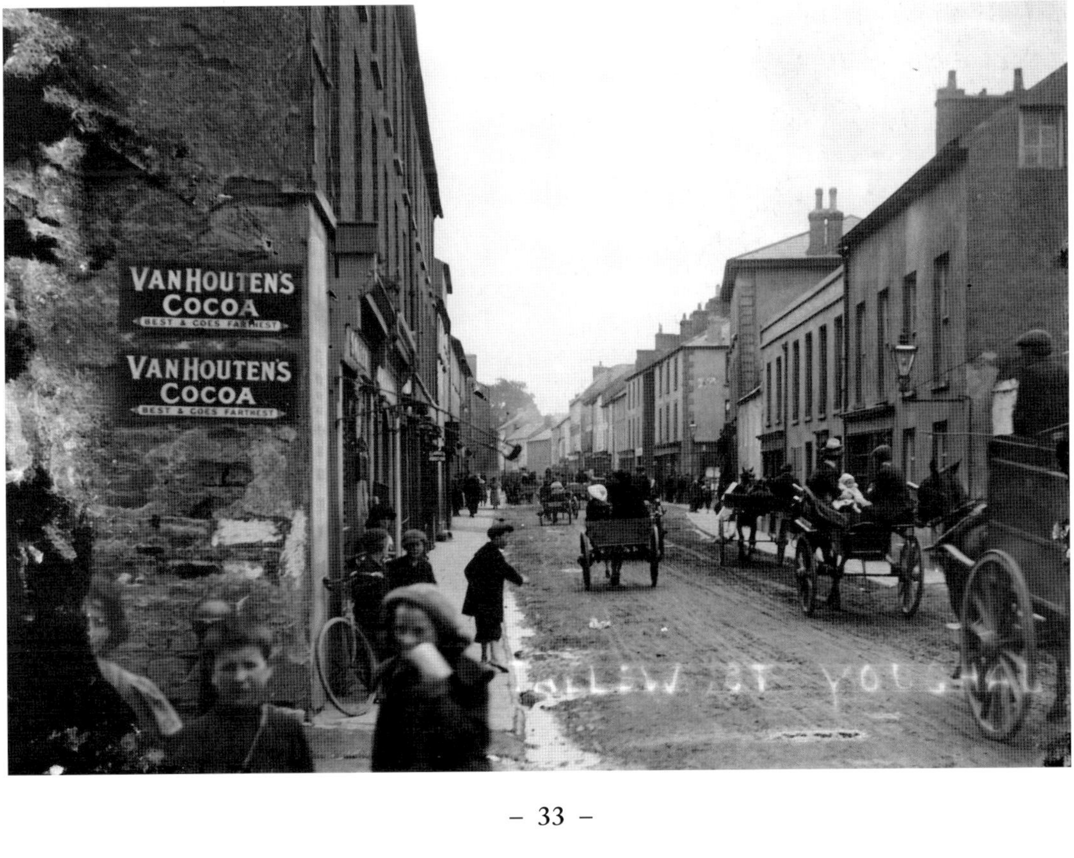

VAN HOUTEN'S
COCOA
BEST & GOES FARTHEST
VAN HOUTEN'S
COCOA
BEST & GOES FARTHEST
TALLOW ST YOUGHAL

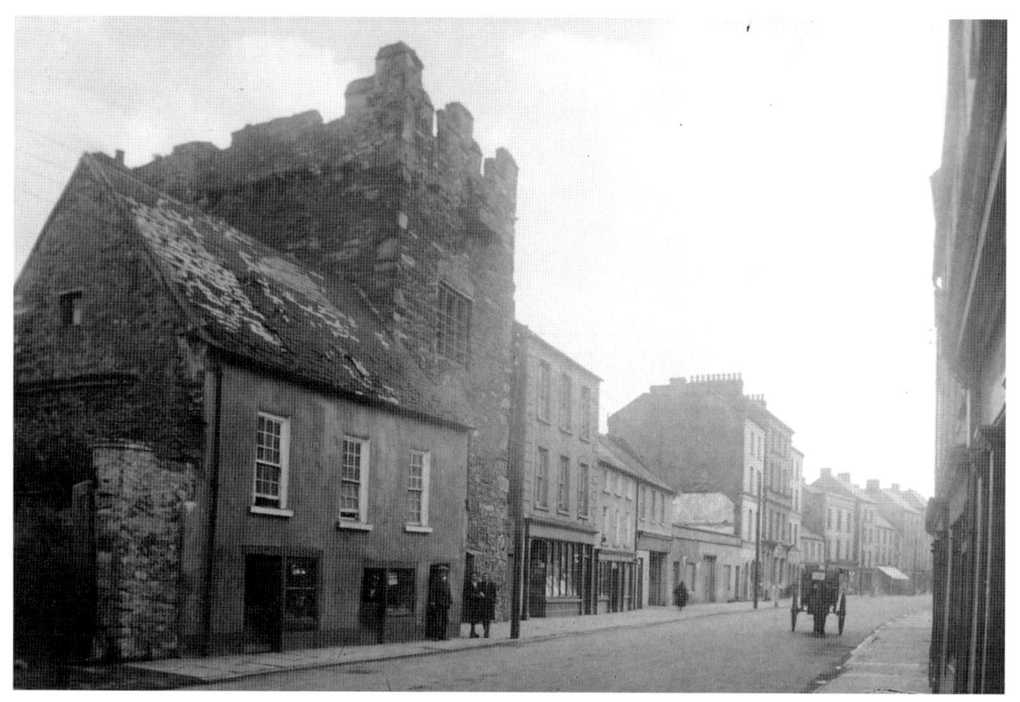

Tyntes Castle, North Main Street, Youghal.

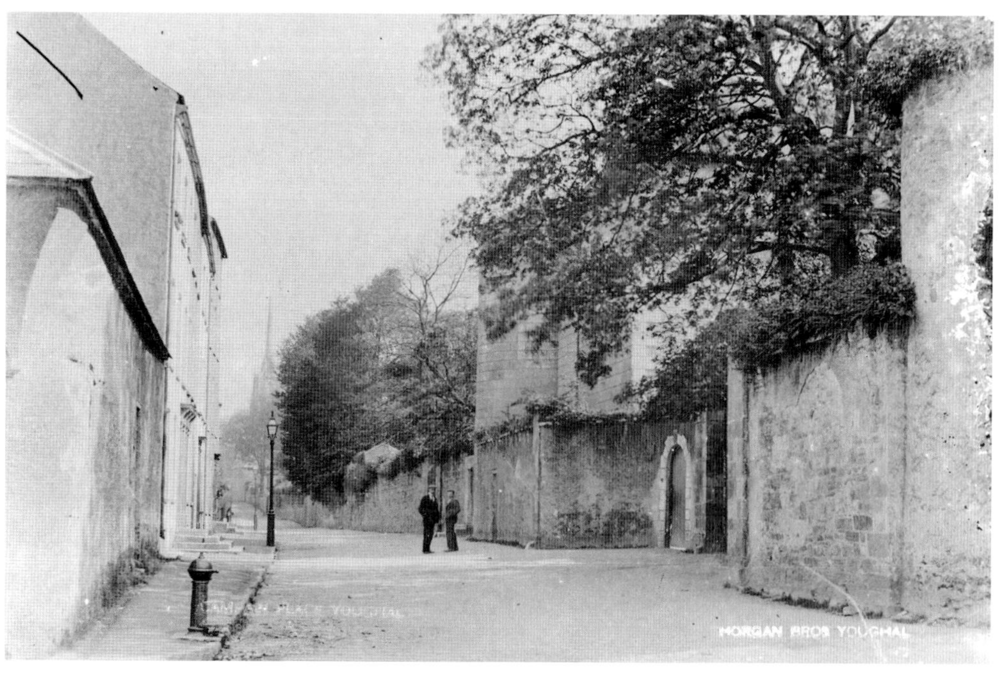

Emmet Place, Youghal.

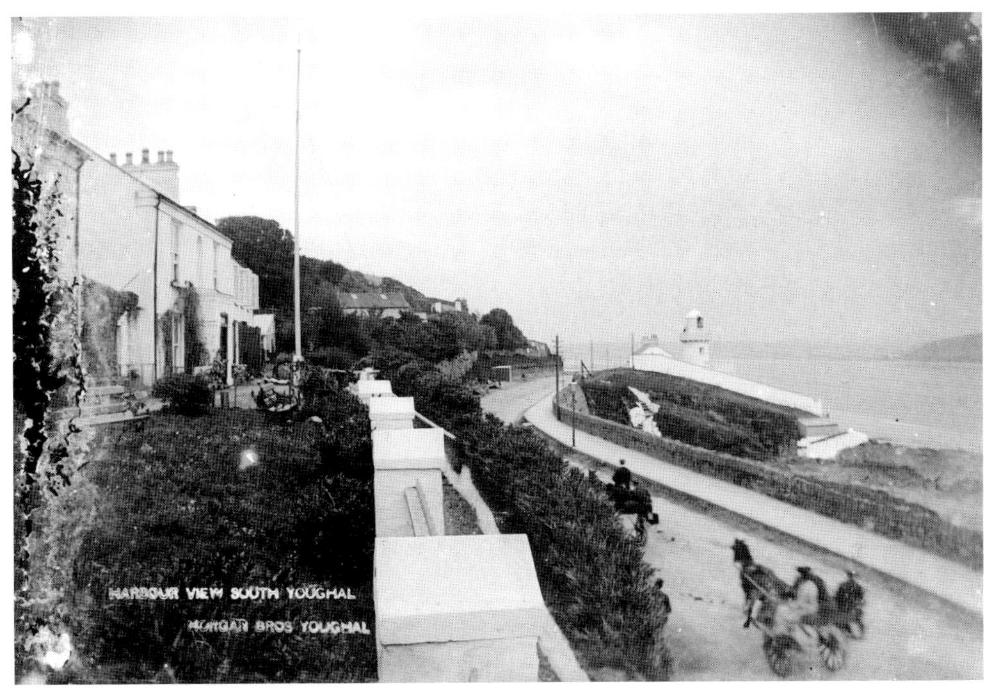

The lighthouse from Harbour View in Youghal.

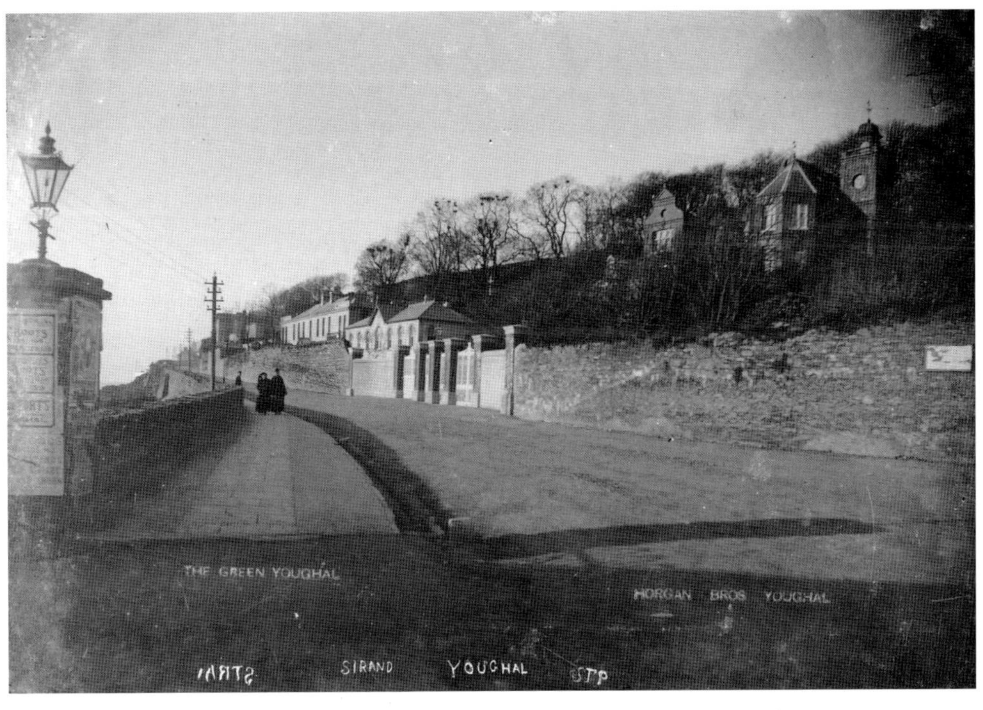

Ashton Court, later known as Loreto Convent.

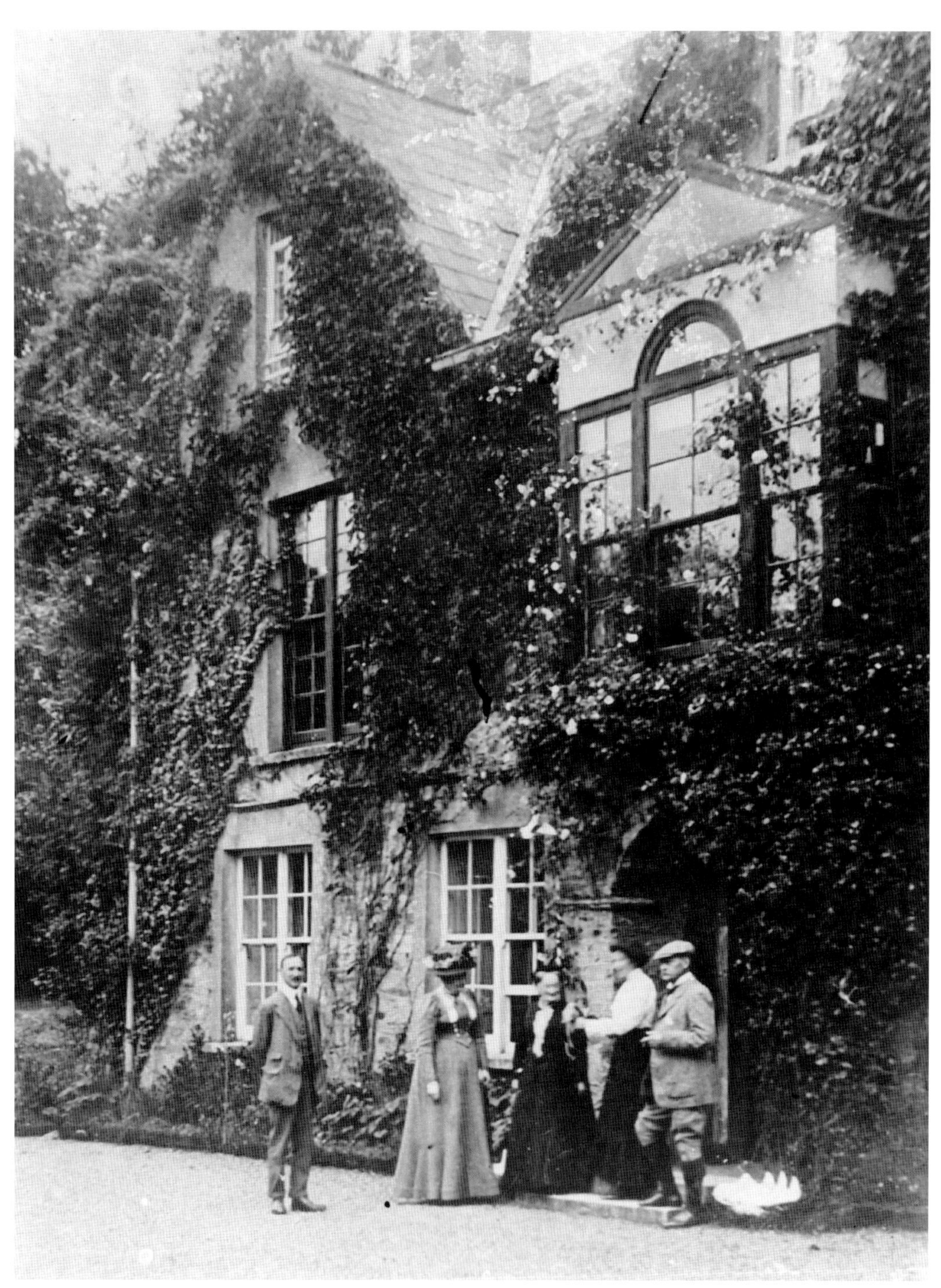

The Blake family at Myrtle Grove.

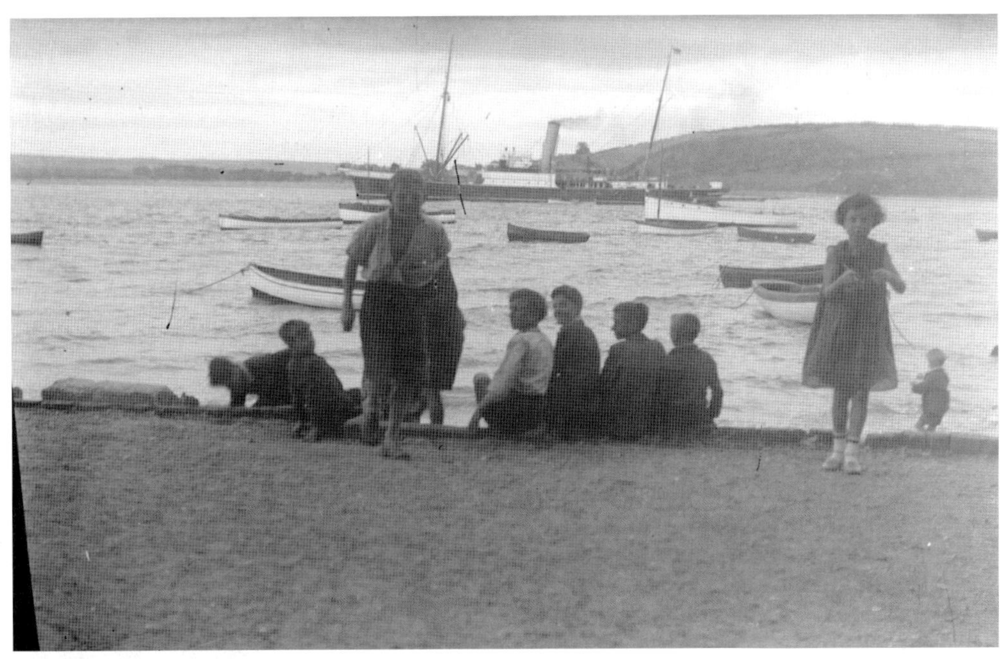

Children playing on the Mall beach, Youghal.

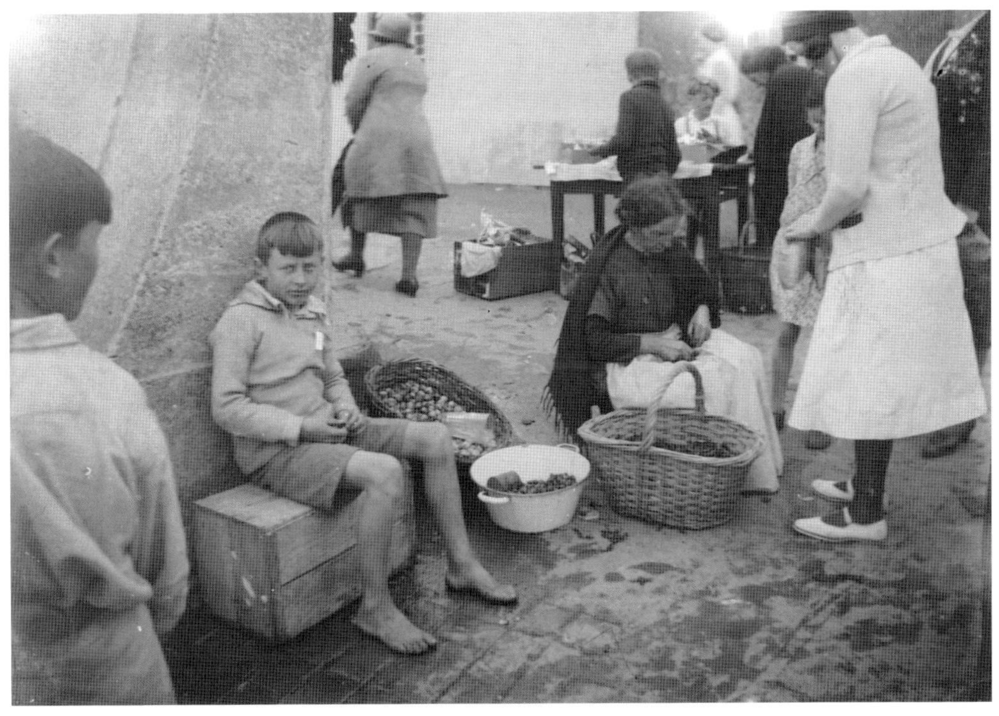

Selling cockles at the market.

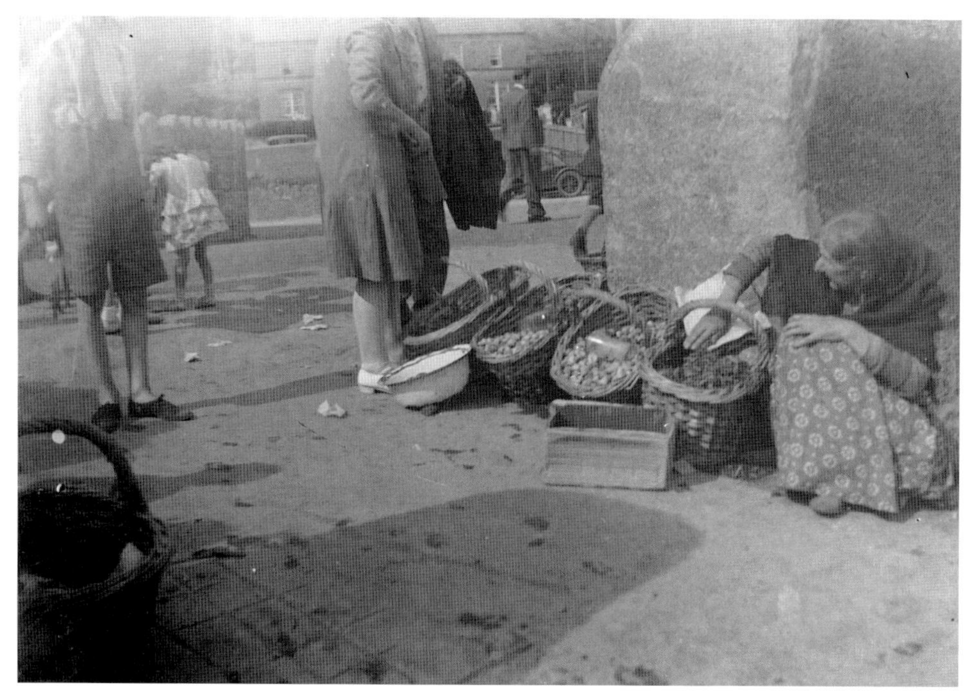

Old lady selling fare (above) and below a market at Youghal Strand.

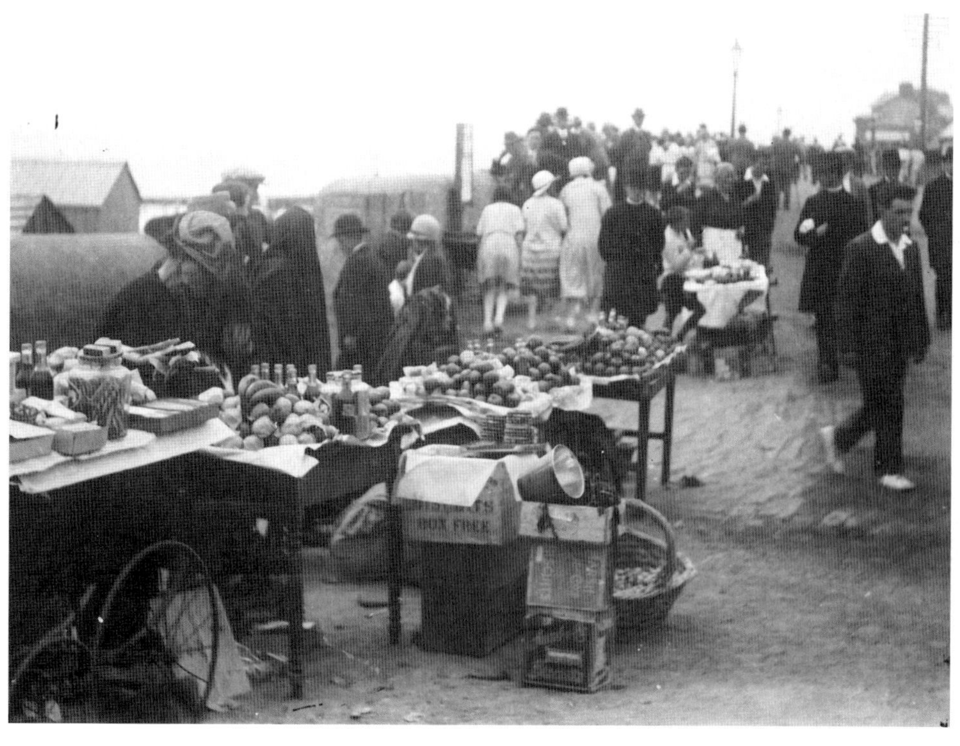

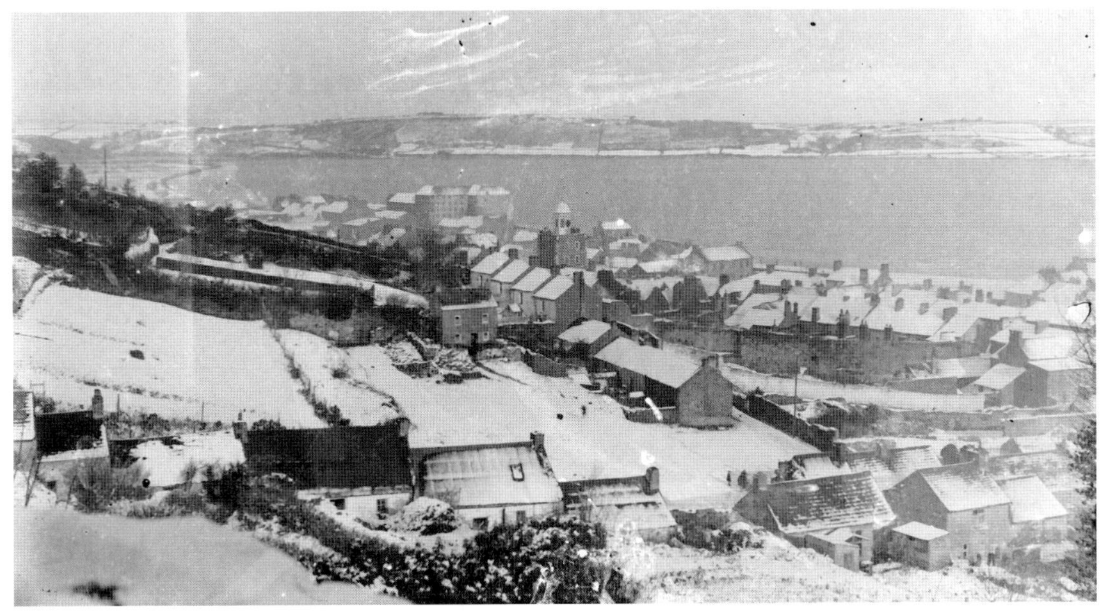

Snow on the rooftops of Youghal.

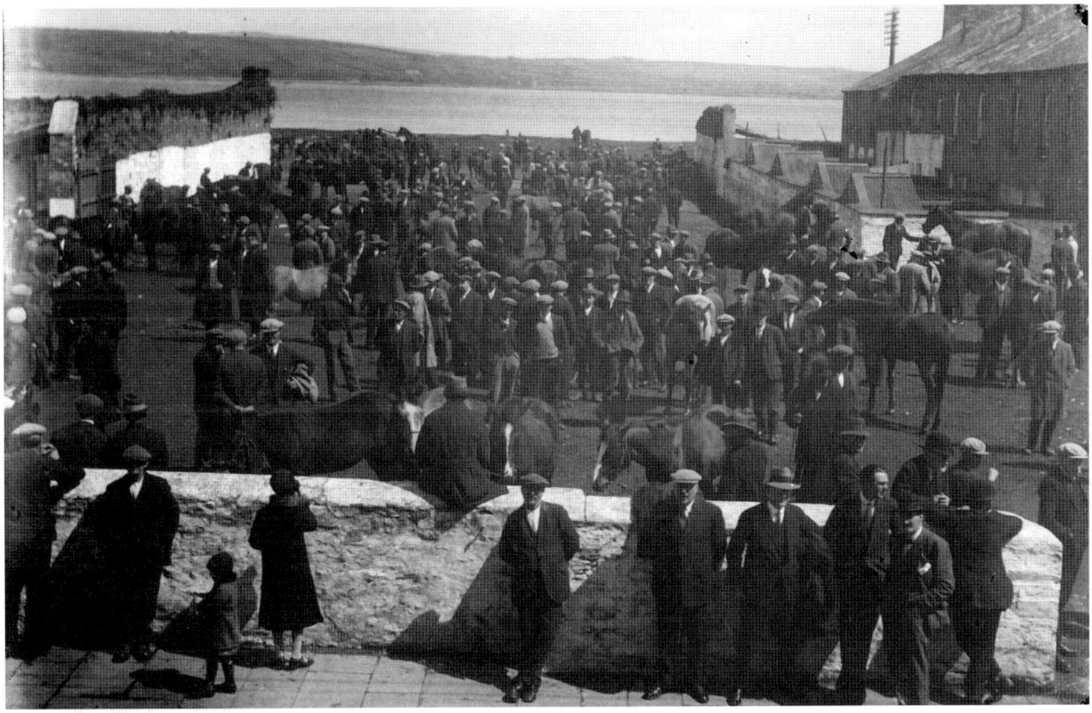

Fair day in Youghal.

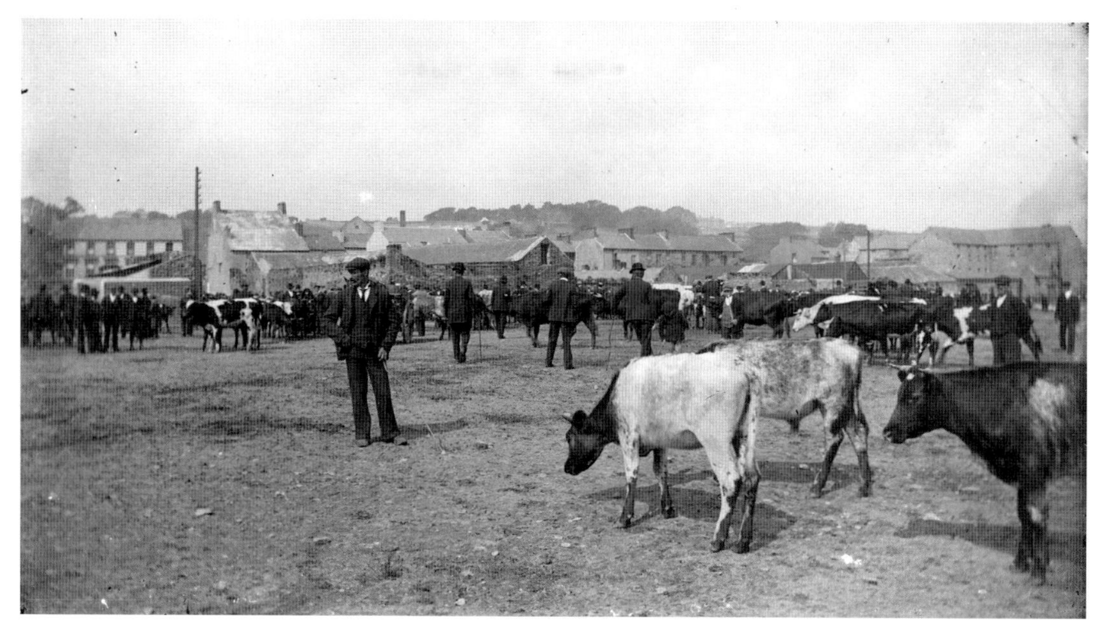

Livestock at fair day in Youghal.

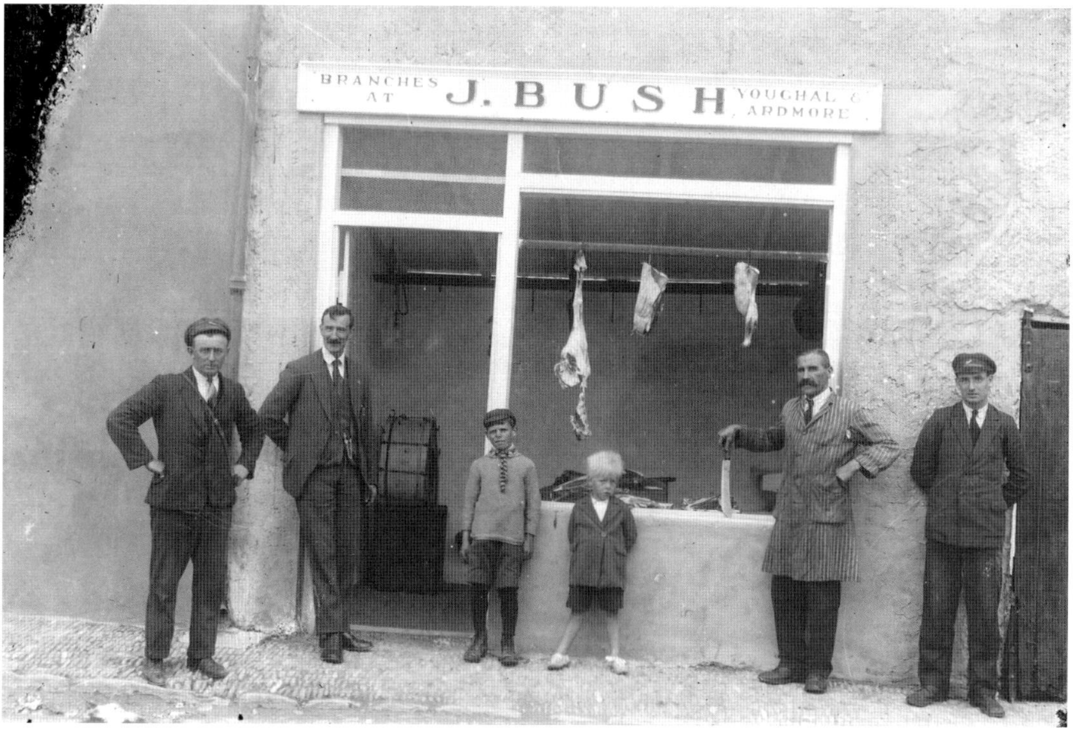

Bush butcher shop.

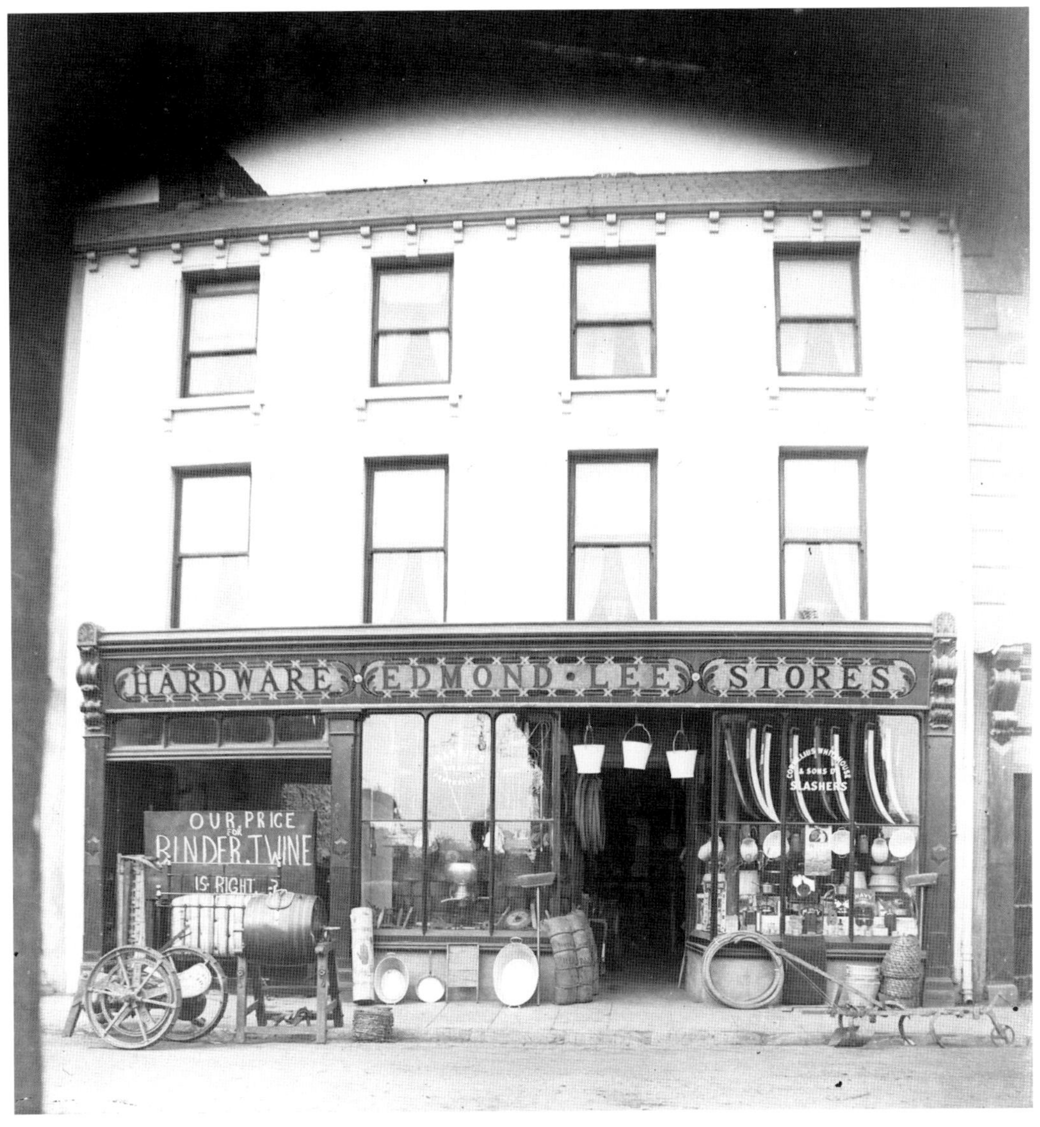

Lee Hardware Stores.

Portraits were an important part of their business and the Horgans captured important moments in locals lives – births, communions, marriages, confirmations and graduations. There are scores of portraits like these in the Horgan Collection on the Cork County Library website in the Local Studies Digital Archive section.

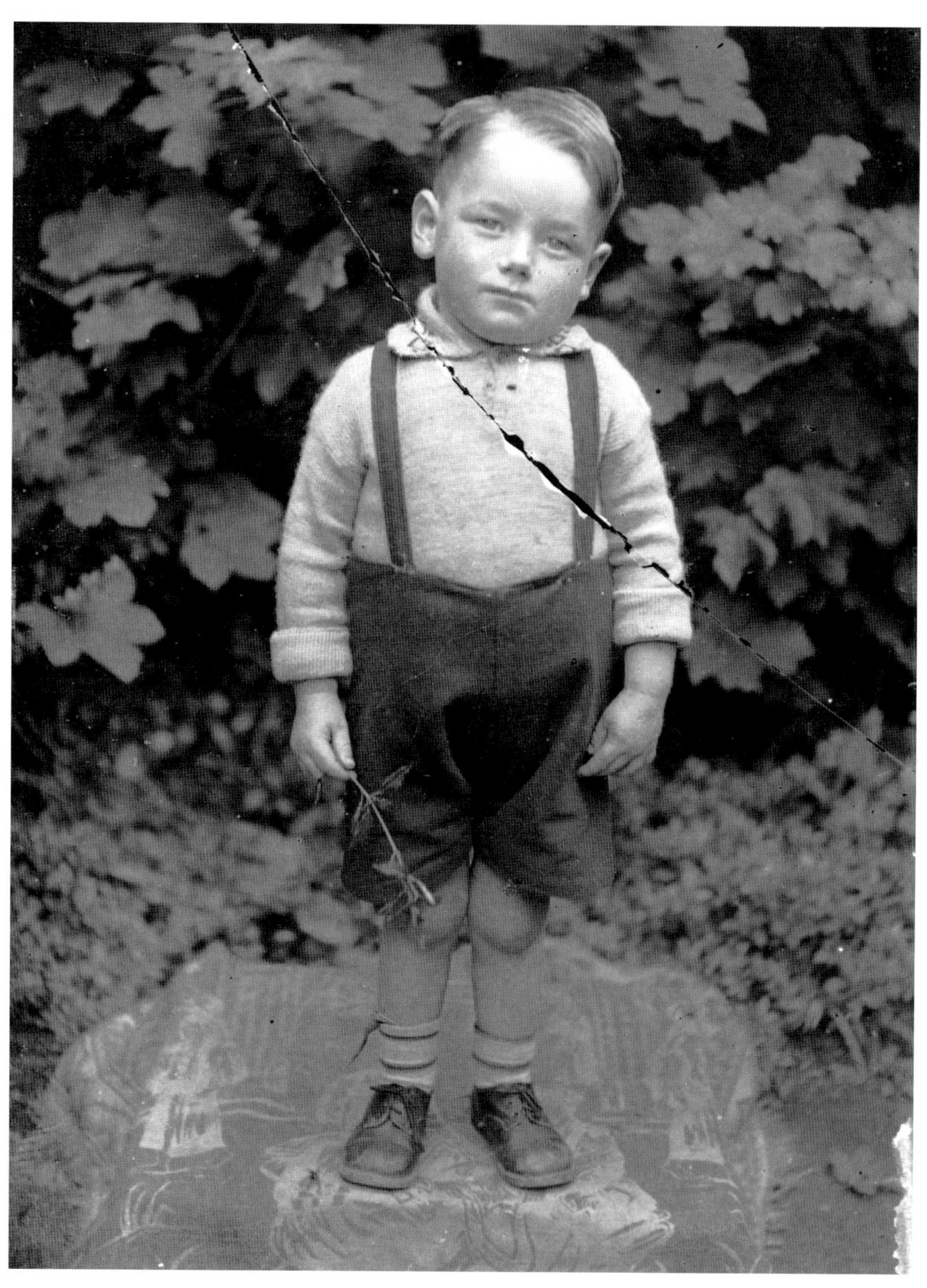

Outdoor portrait of a young boy from a glass negative.

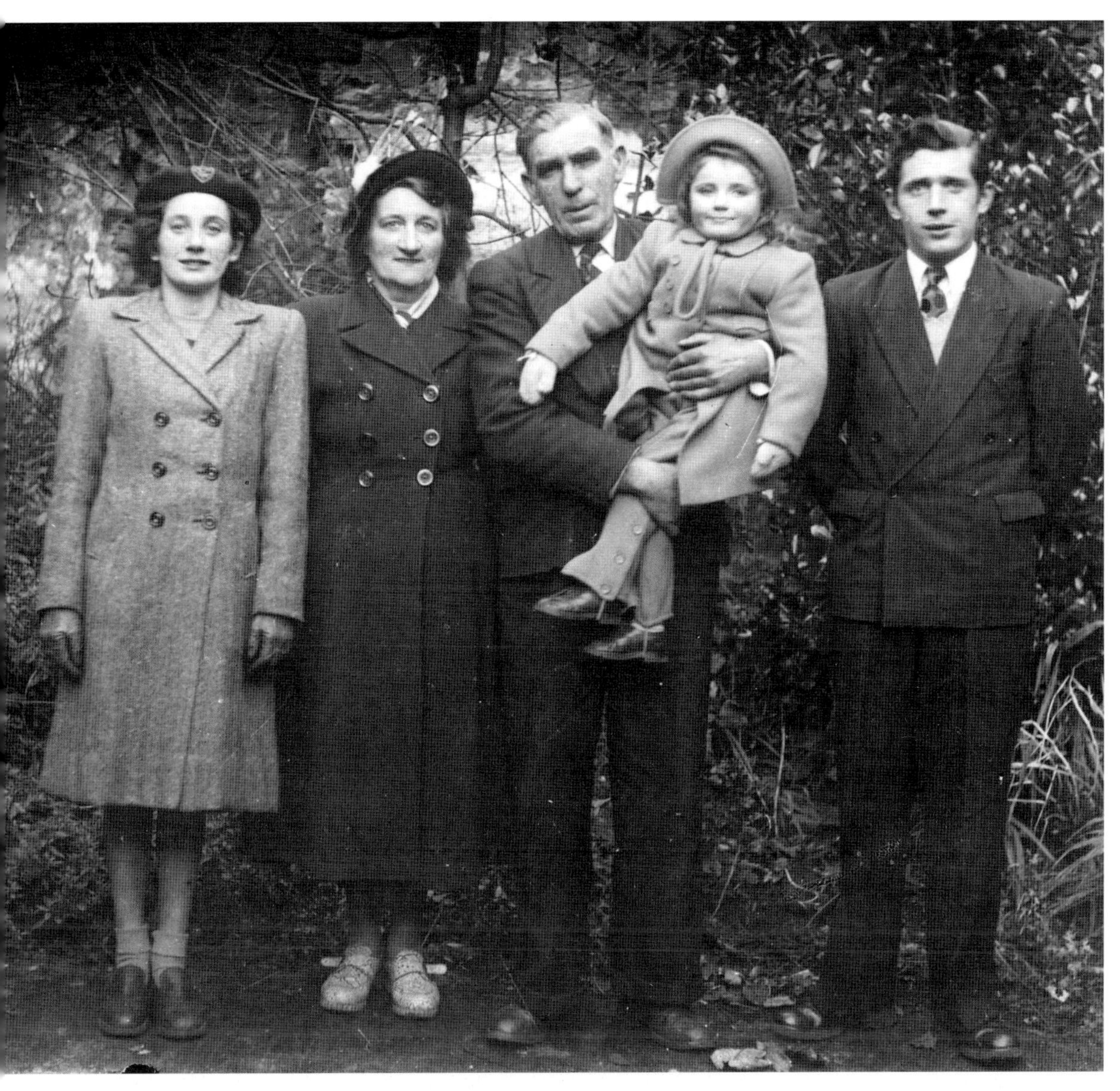

Outdoor portrait of a family.

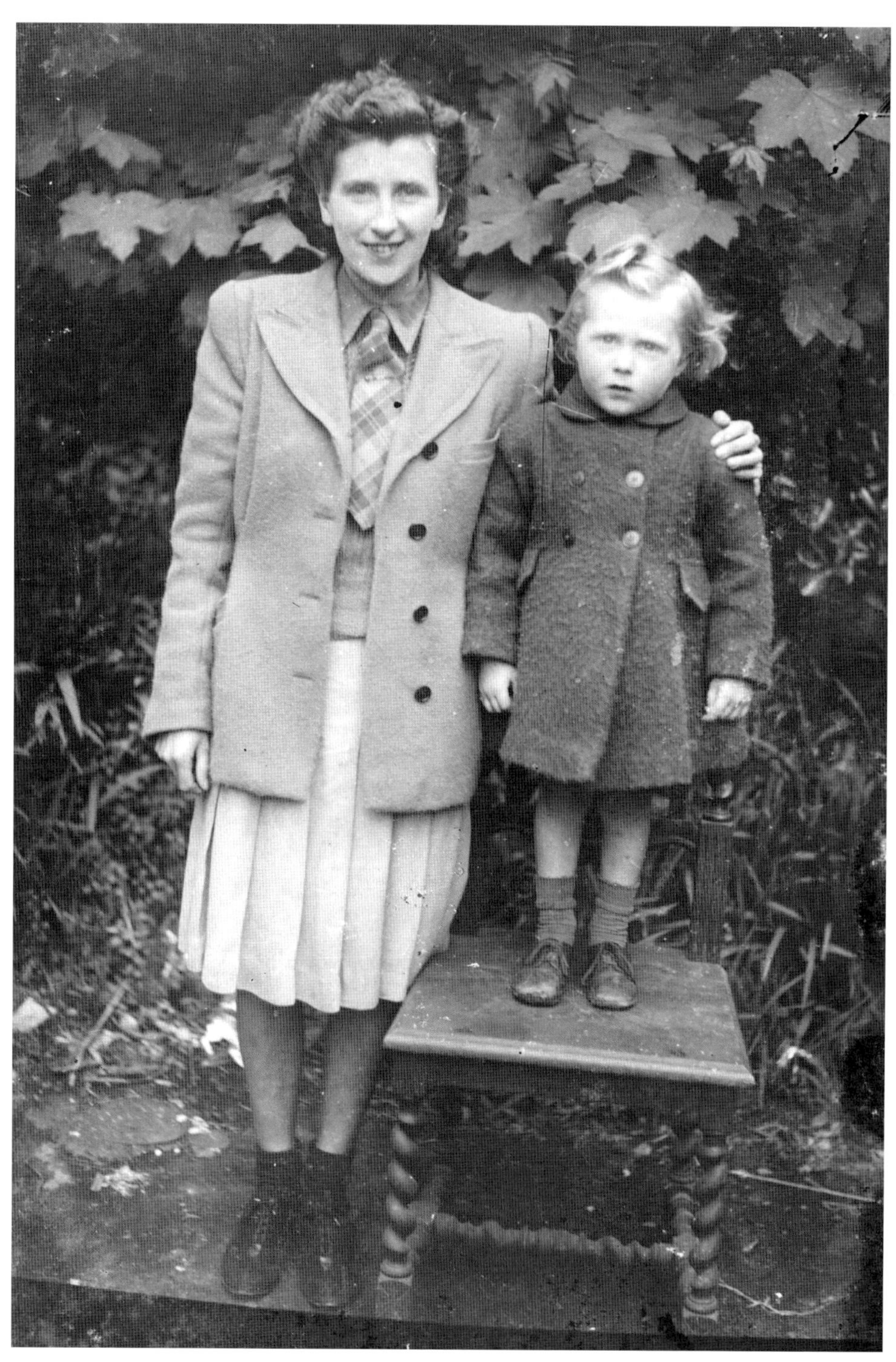

Outdoor portrait of a mother and child.

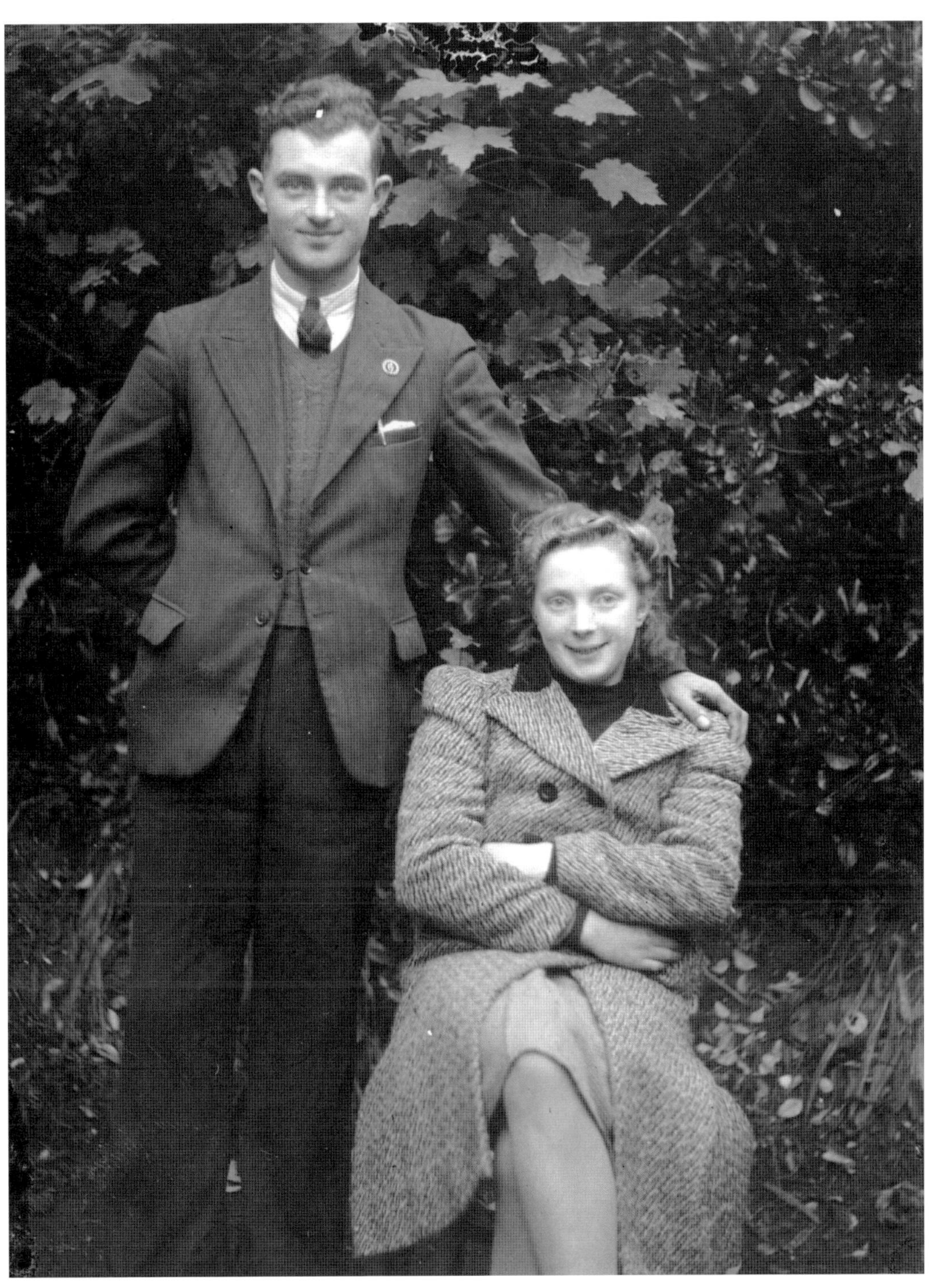

Outdoor portrait of a young couple.

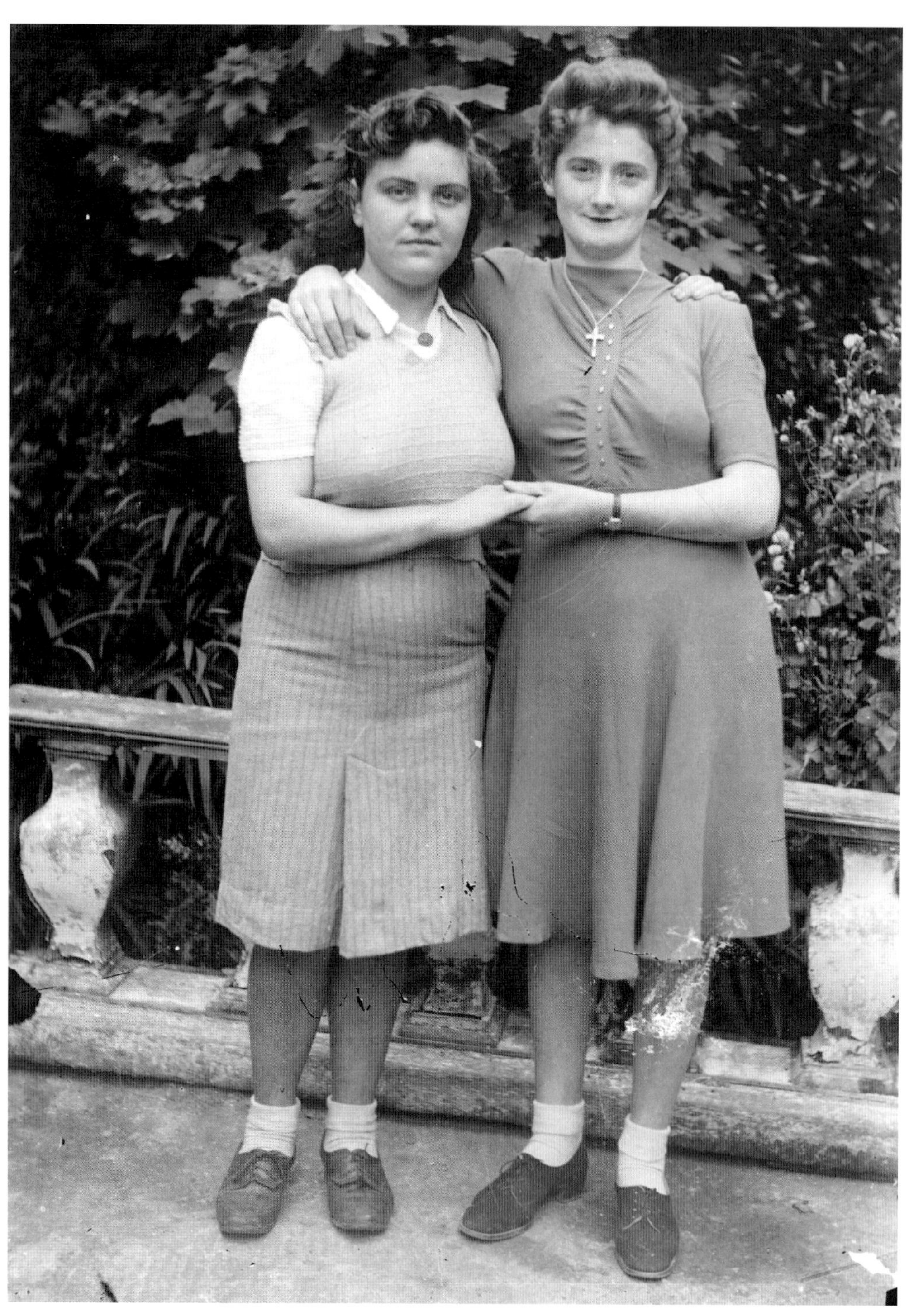

Outdoor portrait of sisters.

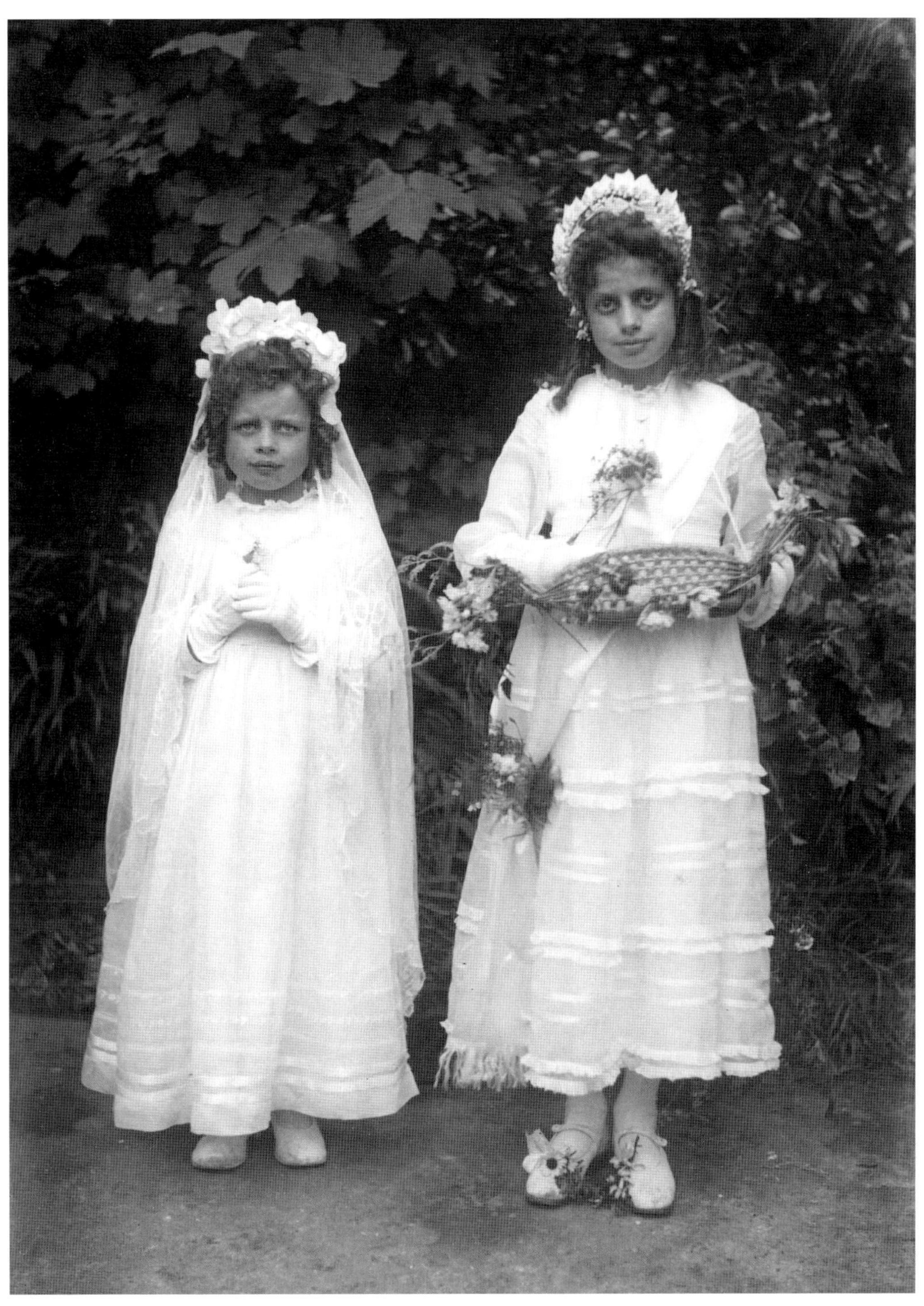

Two girls in their communion dresses.

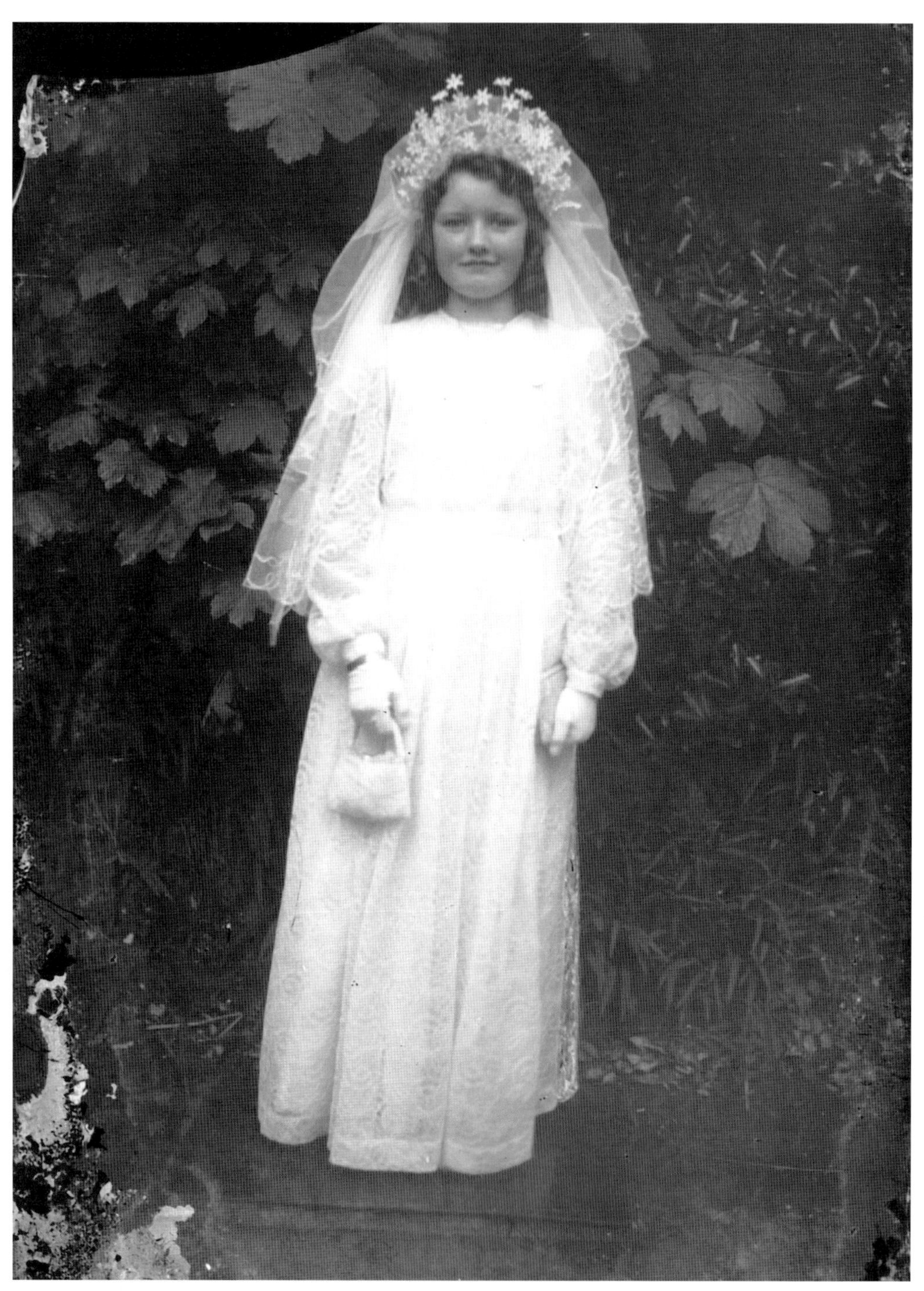

Communion portrait.

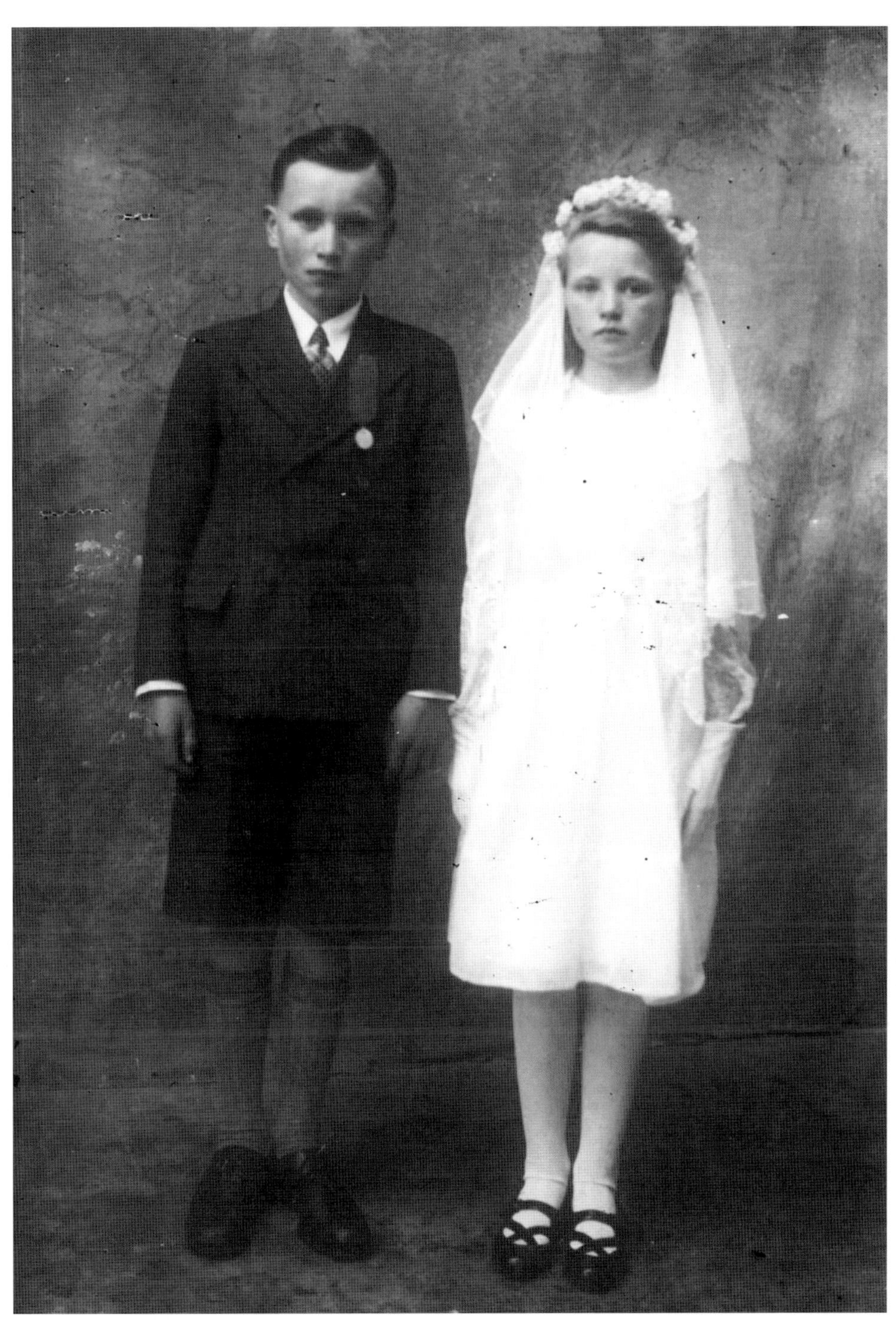

A boy and girl in their communion clothes.

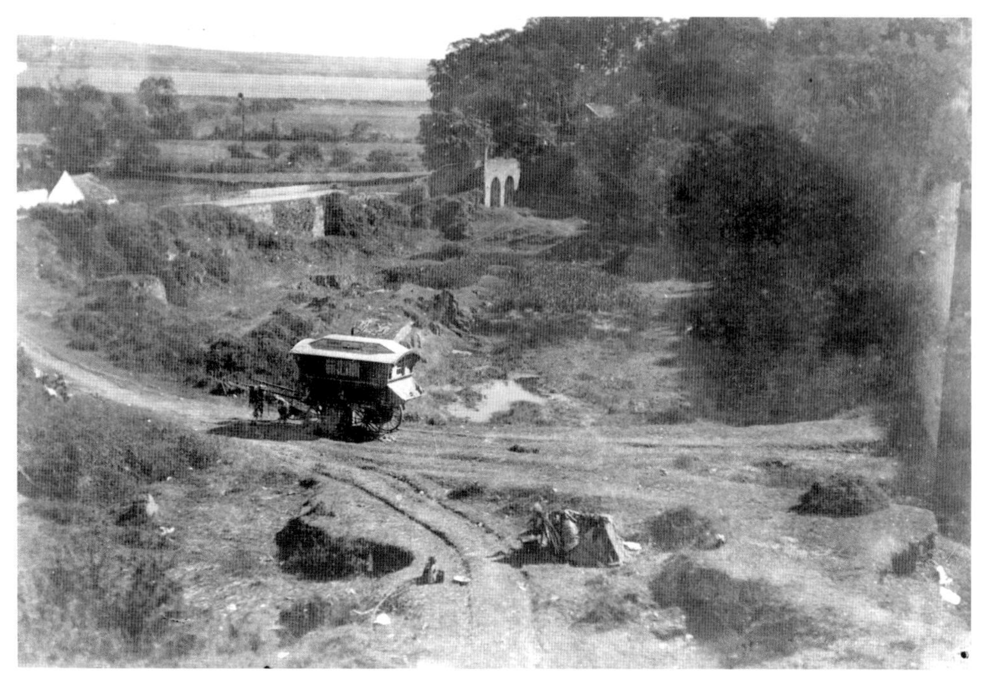

The quarry at Youghal with a caravan.

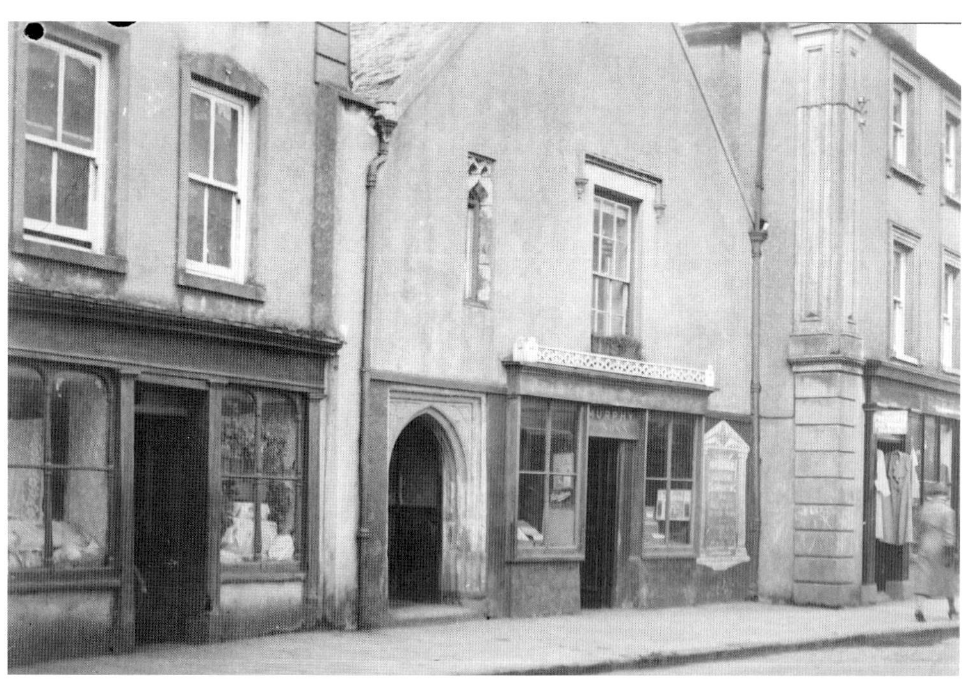

The priory building on North Main Street, Youghal.

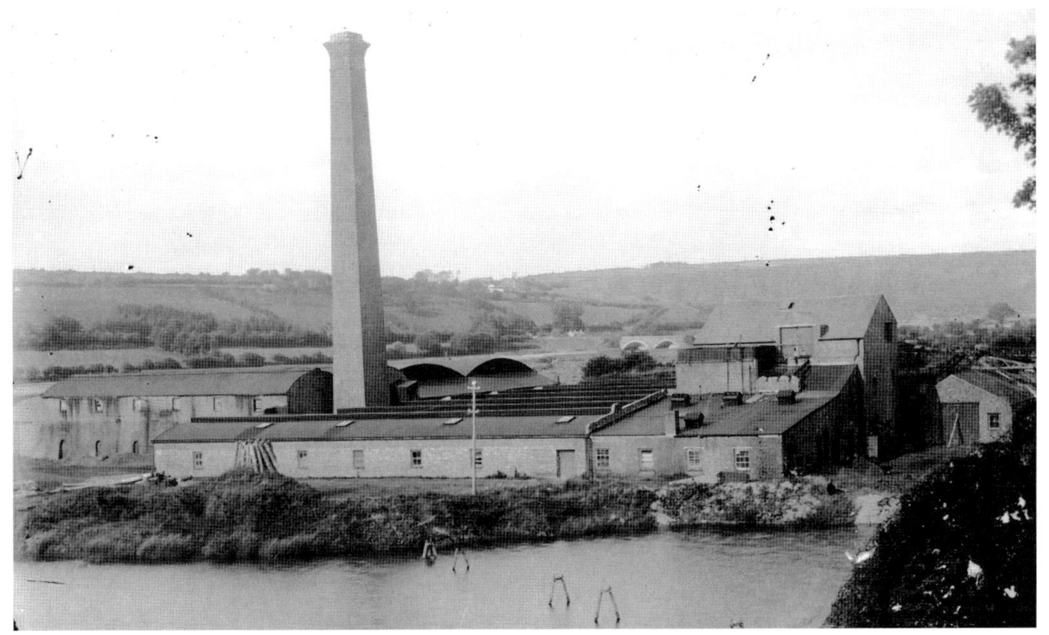

*Youghal Brickworks which can be seen near
the Rincrew roundabout on the bypass.*

The estuary of the river Blackwater flows by Youghal into the sea, where a vast strand stretches for kilometres. The Promenade and Claycastle have hosted many visitors for over one hundred years. The photographs have changed in style and transport across decades.

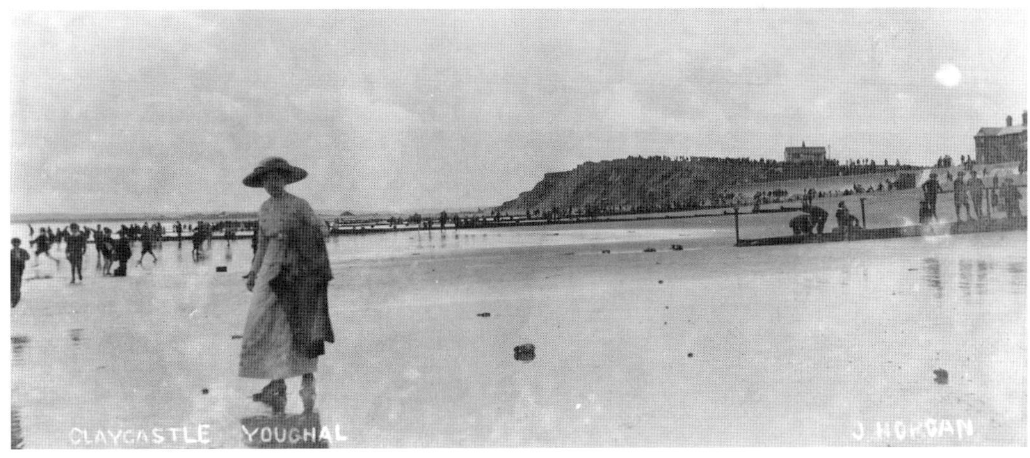

Mrs Hogdeboom, Marietta Horgan's mother, on Youghal Strand.

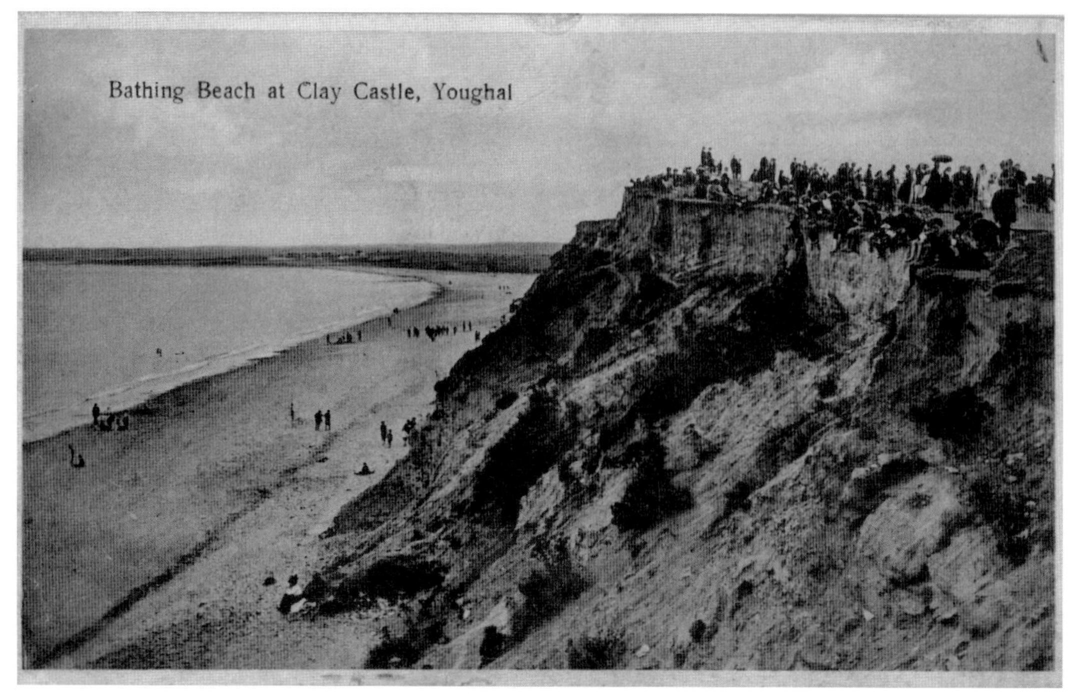

Claycastle beach.

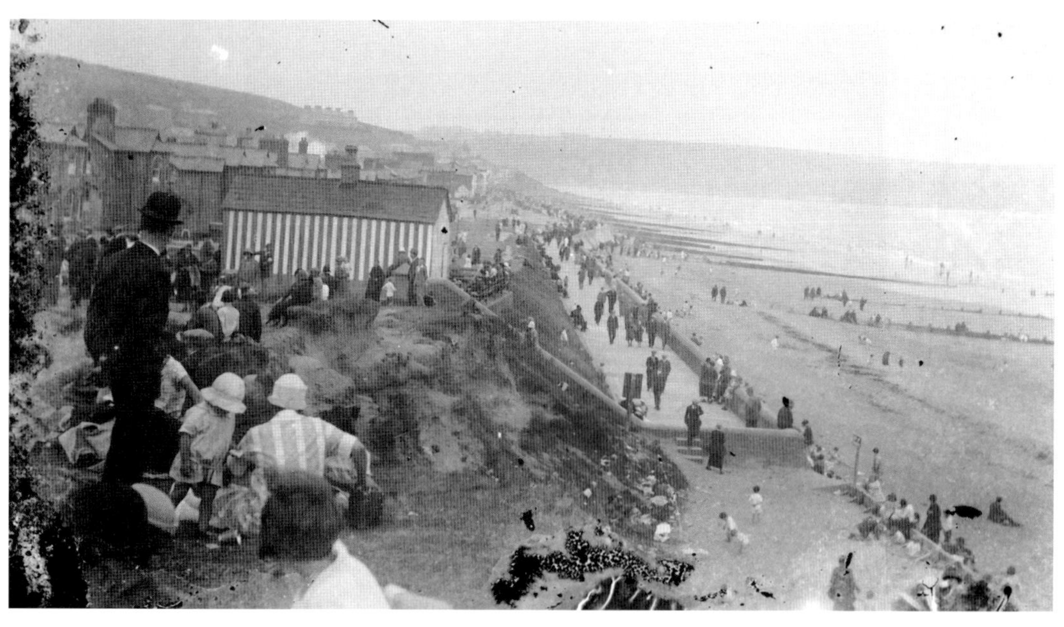

View of Youghal Front Strand from the top of Claycastle.

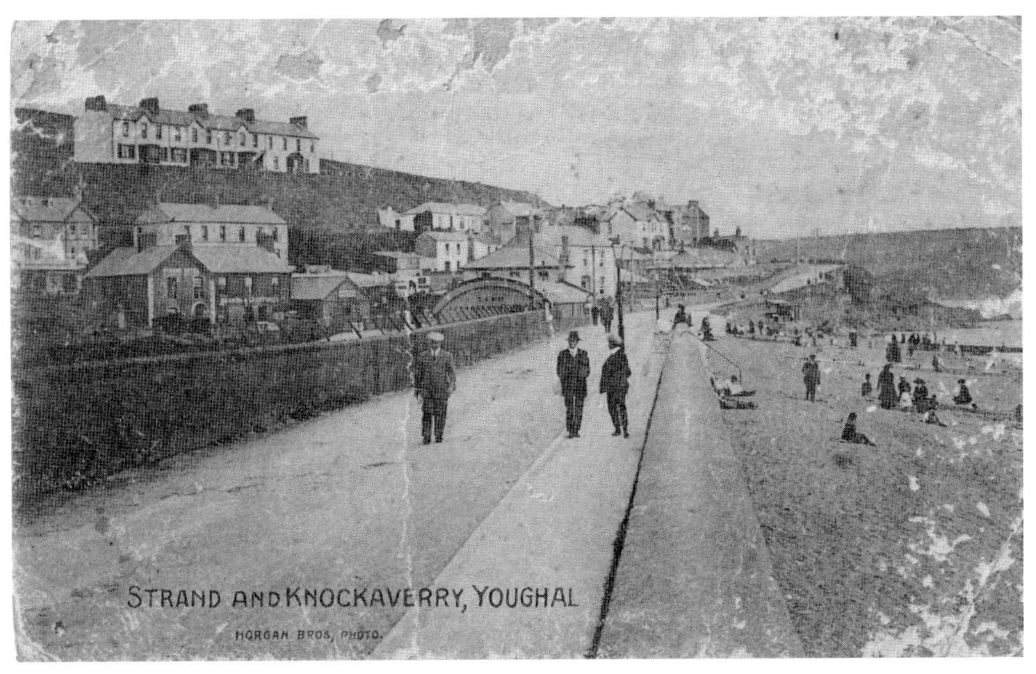

Front Strand and Knockaverry postcard.

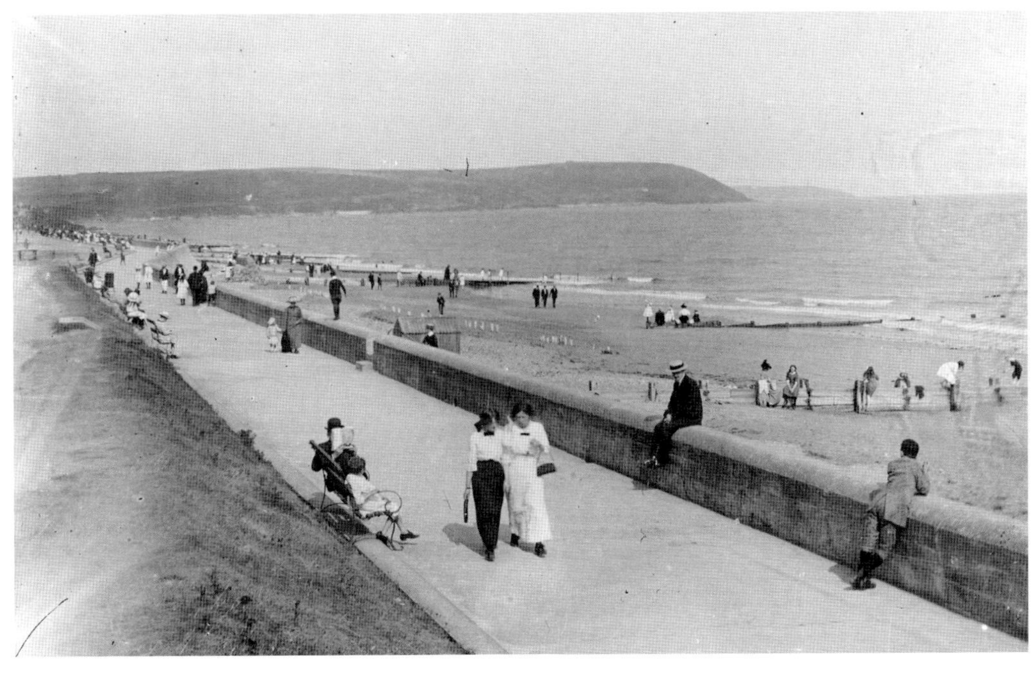

Promenade on the Front Strand, Youghal.

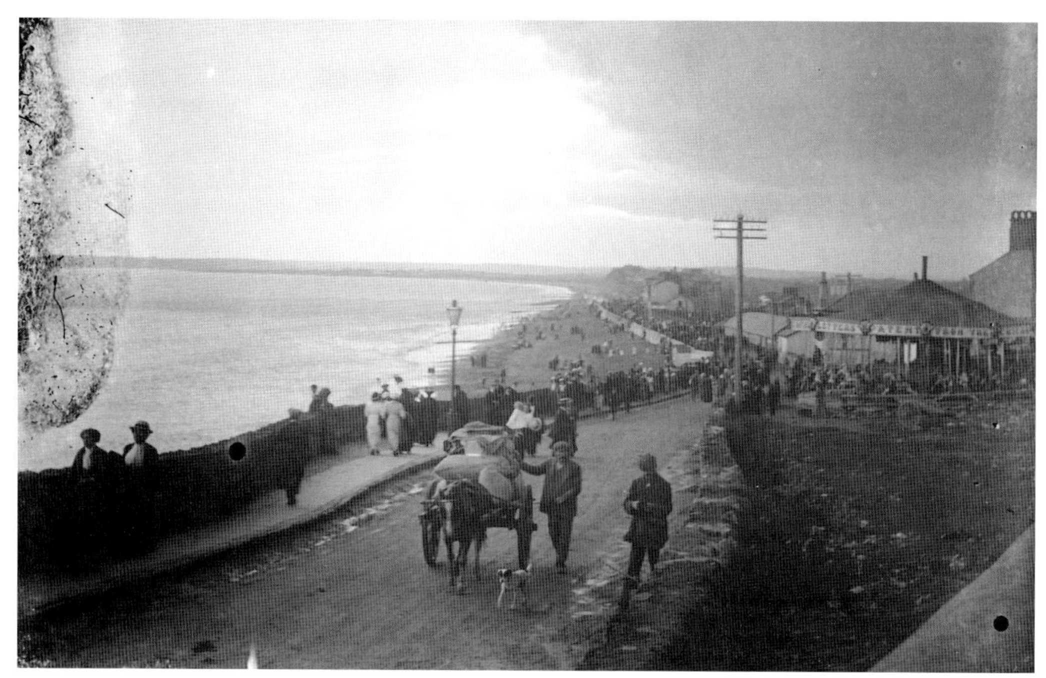

The strand from Moll Goggin's Corner.

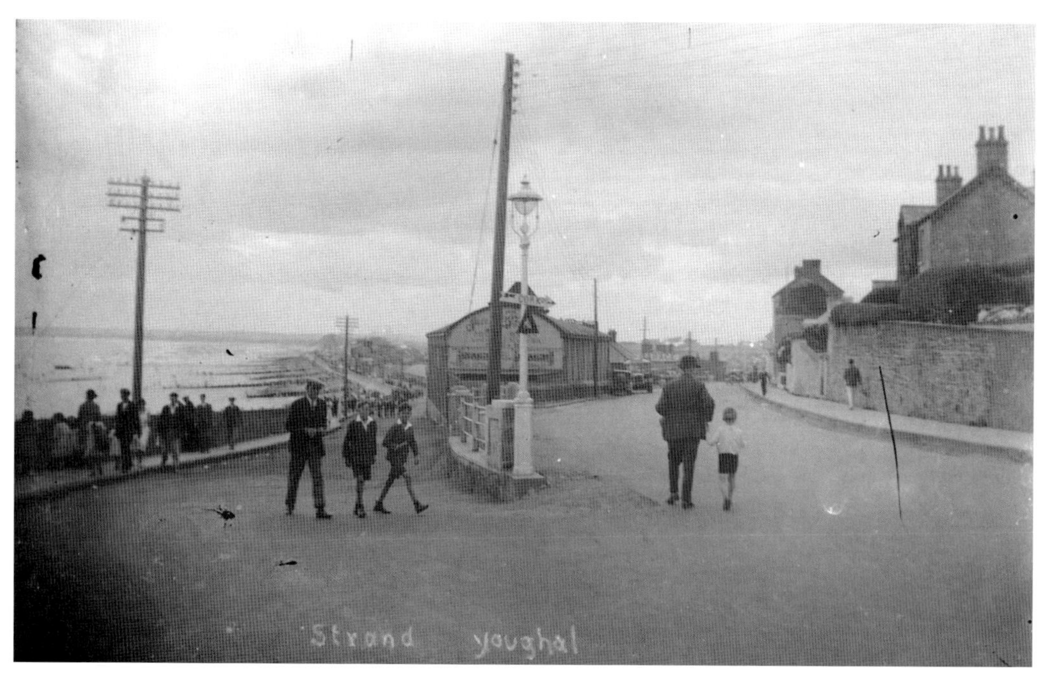

Front Strand Youghal.

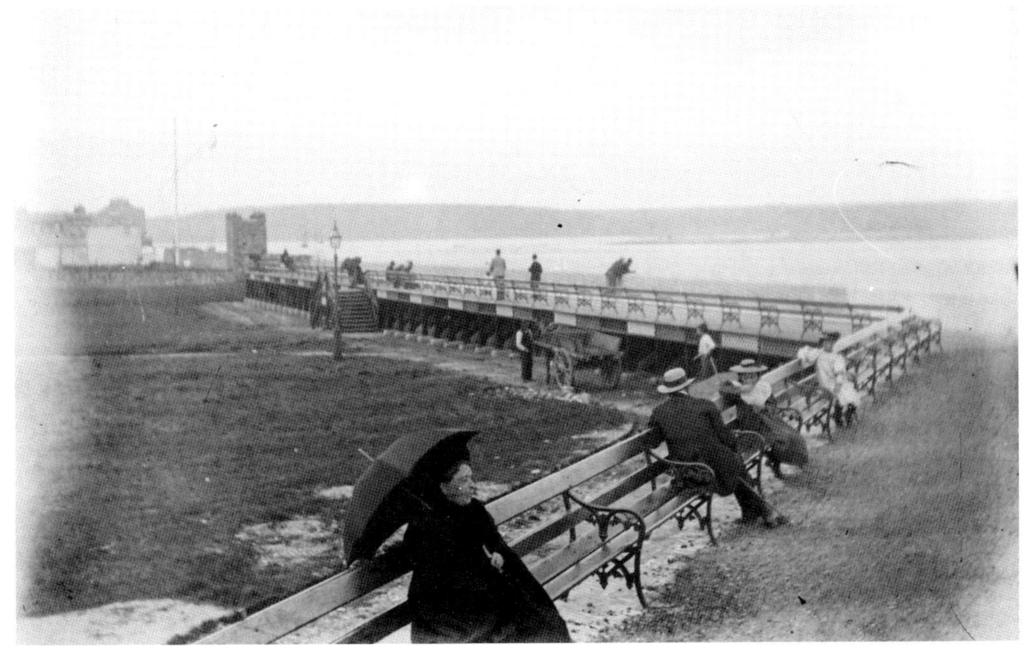

Green Park Promenade.

The evolution of transport in the late 1800s and early 1900s was swift. From the donkey and cart to the horse and trap, the bicycle to the modern motor car.

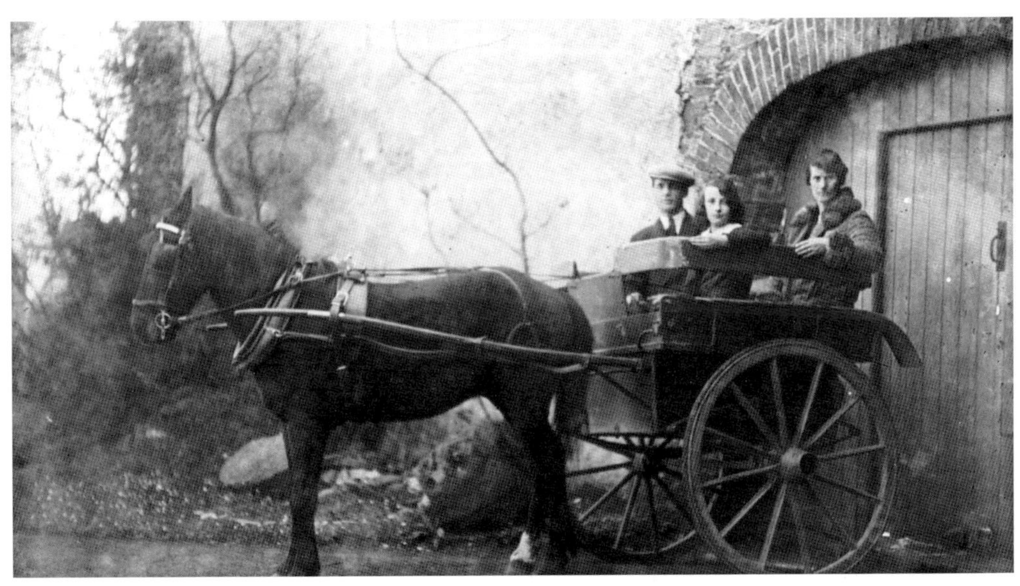

Family with their horse and trap.

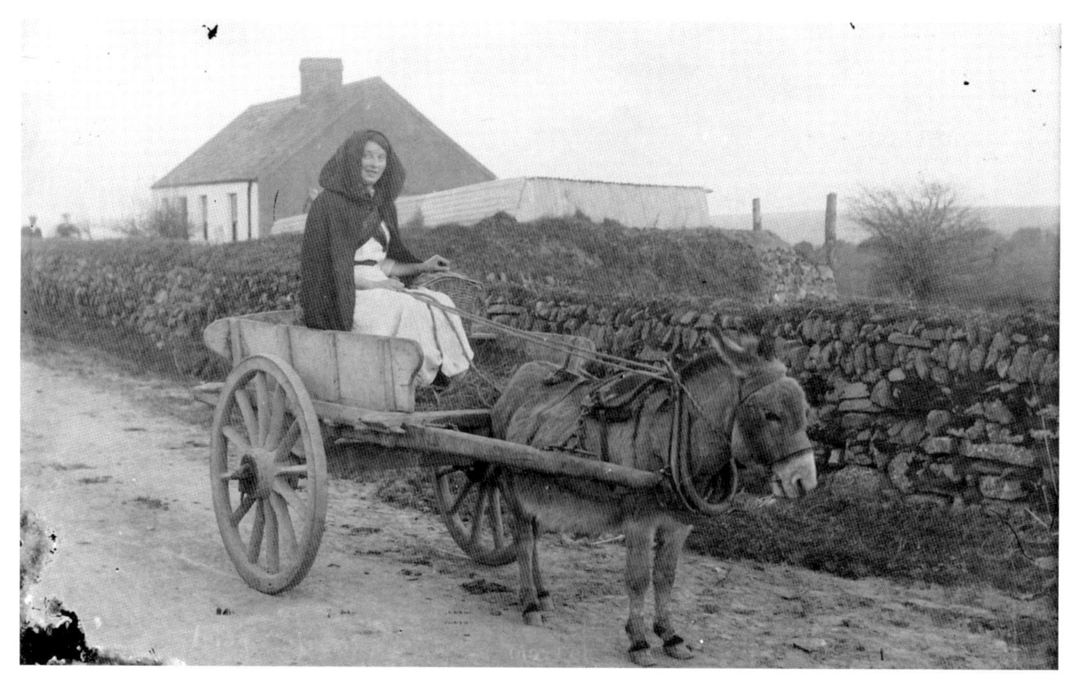

A woman on a donkey and cart.

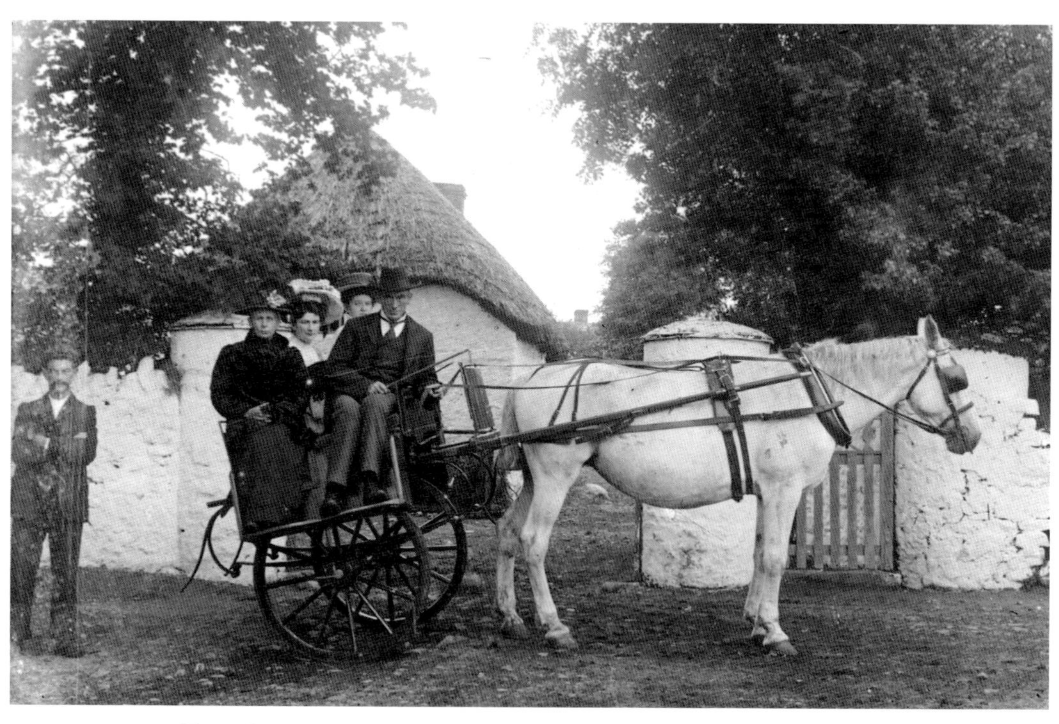

Family travel by horse and trap from their thatched home.

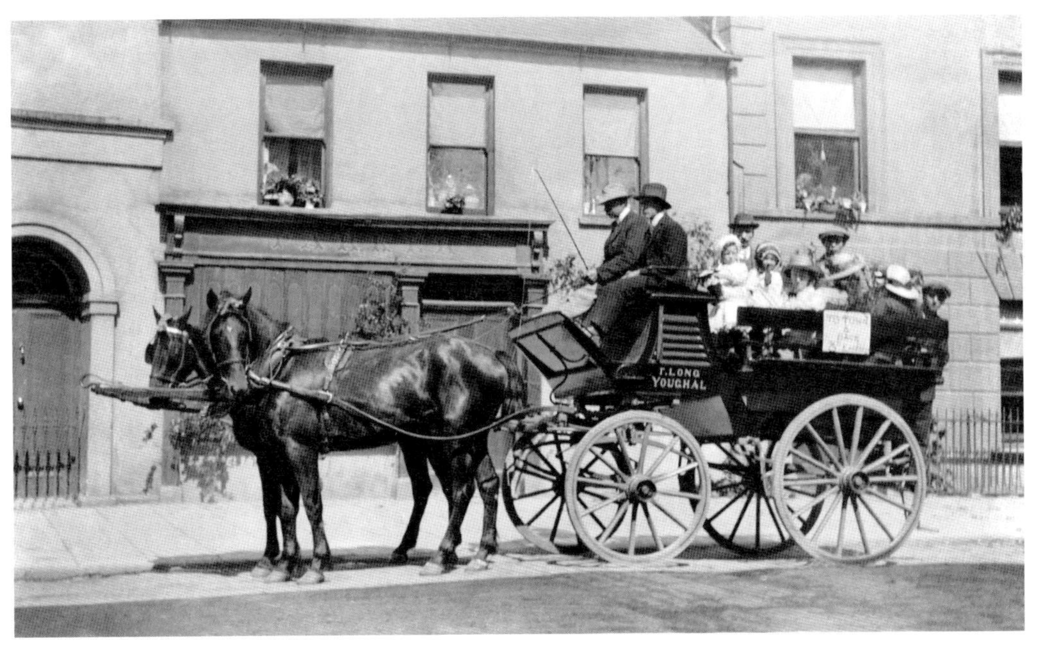

Youghal stagecoach.

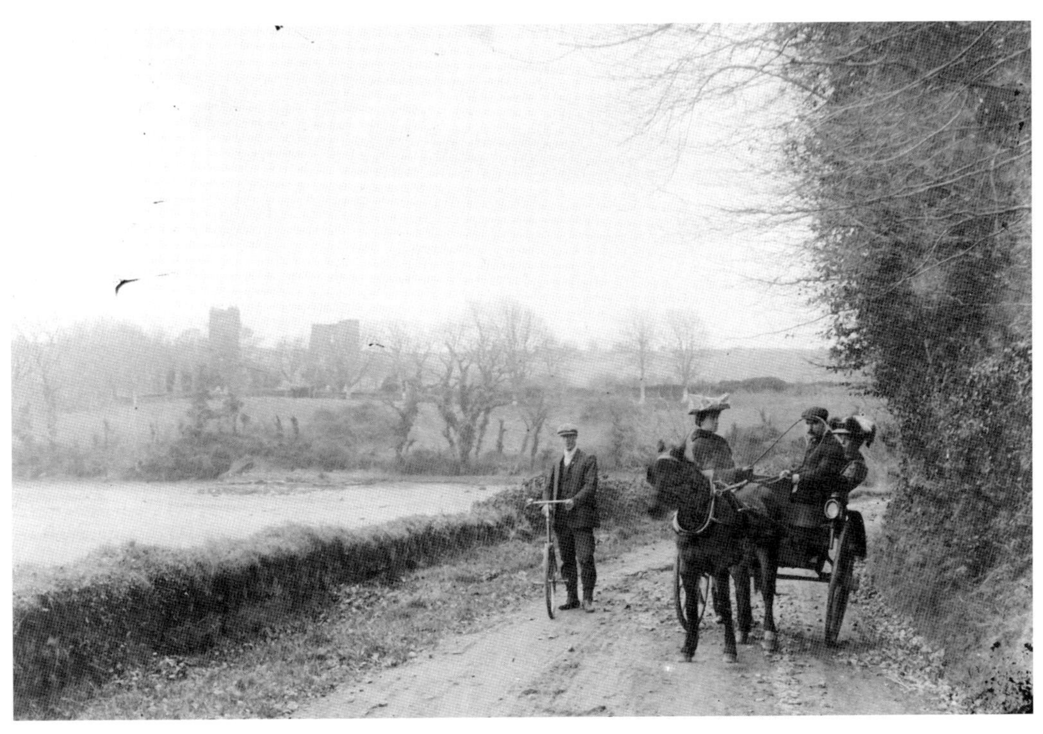

James with his bicycle beside a horse and trap.

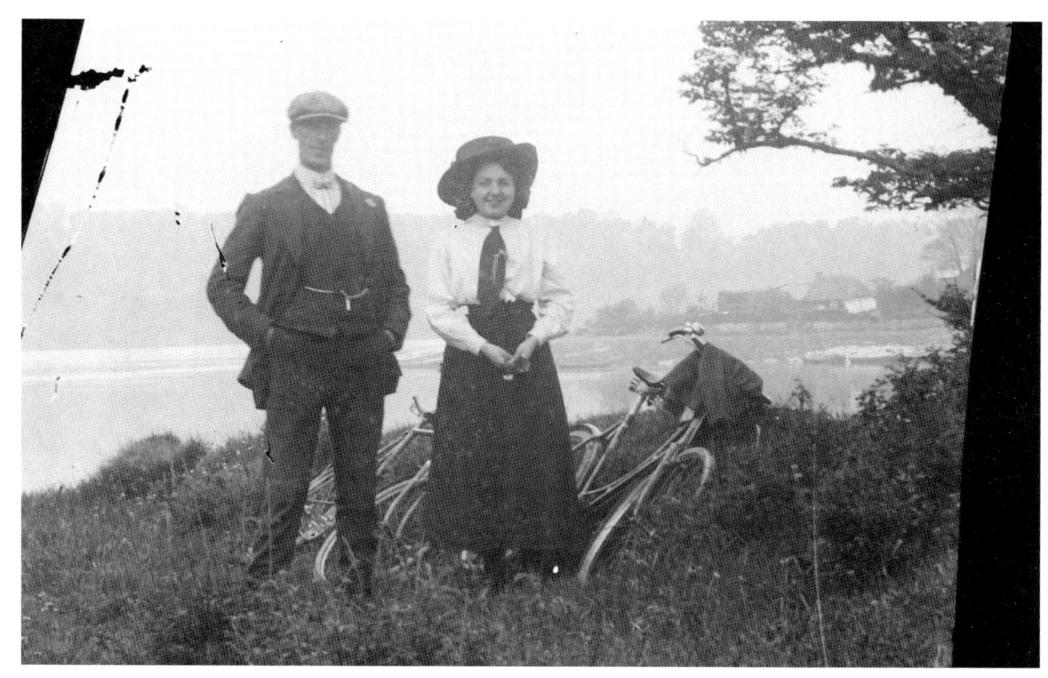

James and Marietta on an outing with their bicycles.

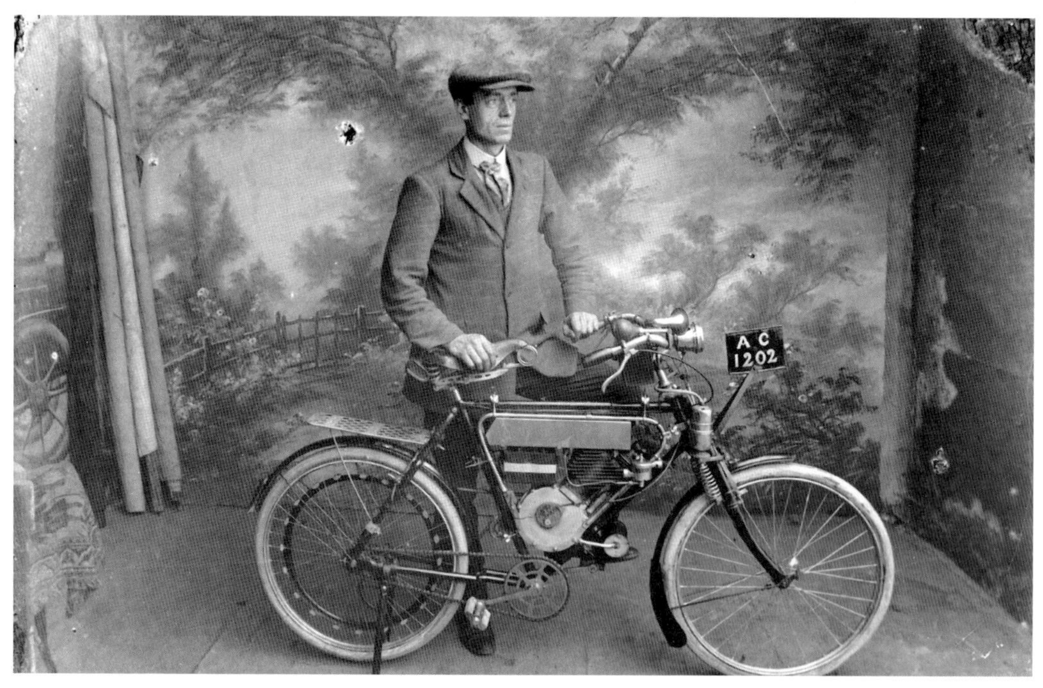

Philip Horgan posing with a motor driven bicycle.

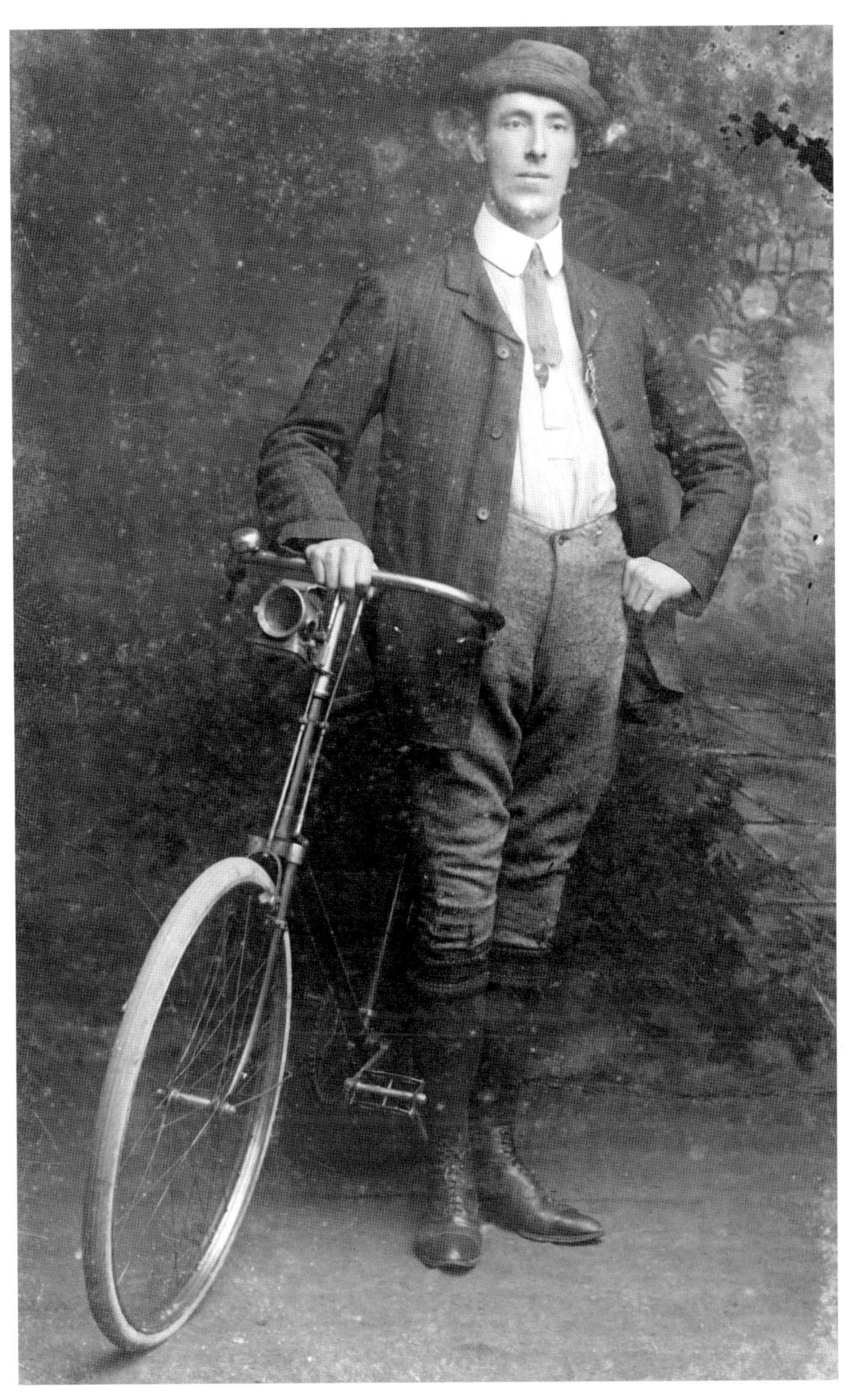

James Horgan posing in his studio with a bicycle.

Magic and Travelling Light Shows

The brothers developed travelling light shows, which featured magic lantern projectors, music, magic acts, and photography. These shows brought the sparkle and magic of the images and entertainment to very rural parts of East Cork and West Waterford. They initially travelled to the hinterlands of Youghal on their bicycles, packed to the gills with equipment. The brothers would set up their equipment and often invite other entertainers to accompany them. One of the highlights of the event was having your photograph taken.

These photographic sessions were spread over two weekends. On the first weekend, the brothers would set up a studio in a hotel or hall, for example, Tatton's Hotel in Killeagh. People came from all around to have their photographs taken and to view the intricate camera equipment. The Horgans would then take the glass negatives home to develop and print them.

The following weekend they would return and the locals came to collect the photographs. The climax of the day was the magic lantern show. Slides were shown, through a paraffin-fuelled projector depicting scenes of the Vatican, the skyscrapers in New York, Coney Island, tea growing in China and a whole range of educational, geographical and current affairs.

Their glass slides which they had captured with their own cameras were also projected such as Corpus Christi processions, political gatherings, scouts, weddings and even local characters. The projection of these images in small villages opened people up to a whole new world and way of viewing themselves and others.

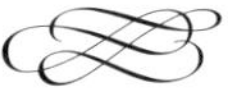

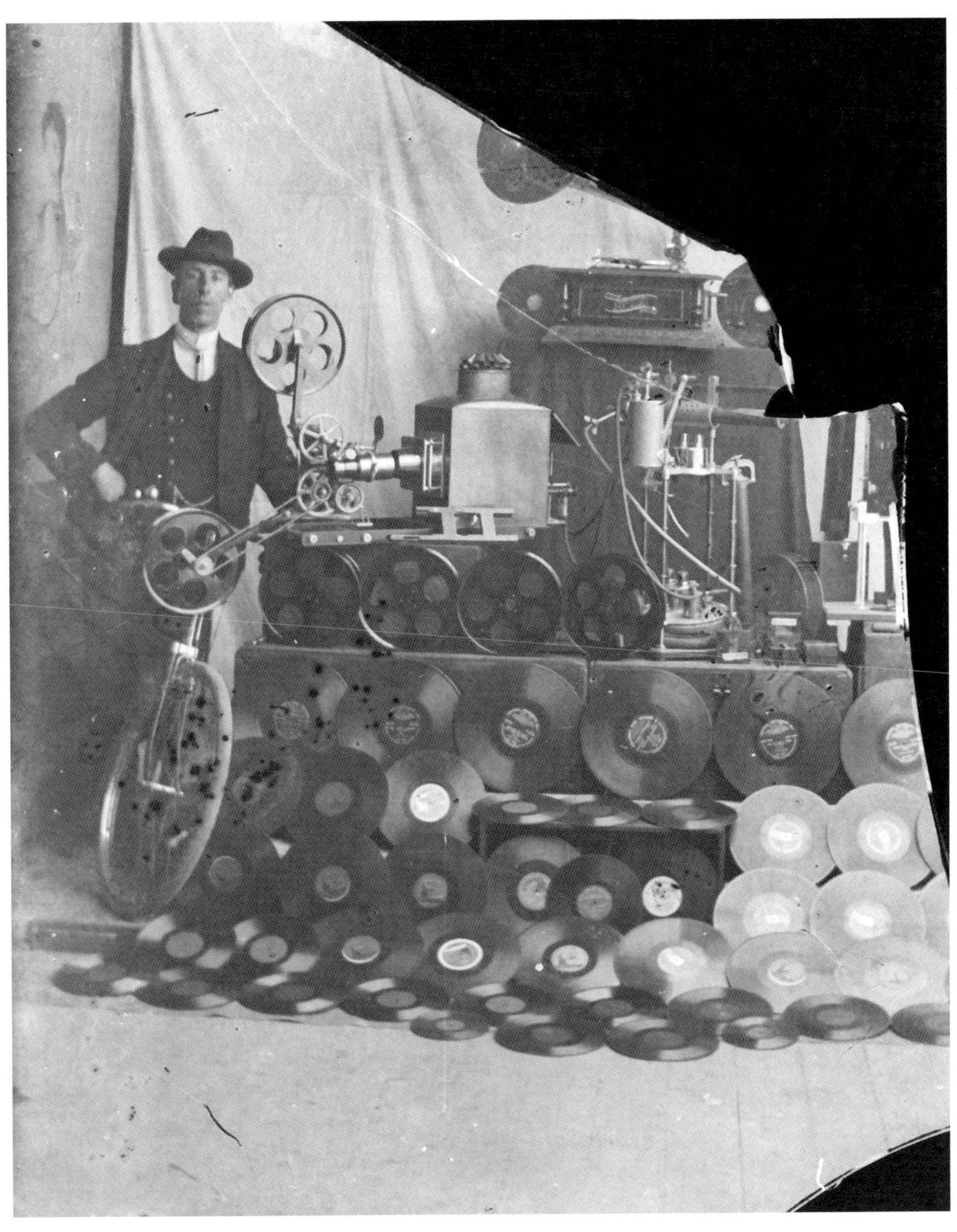

James Horgan with all the Travelling Light Show equipment, including a bicycle.

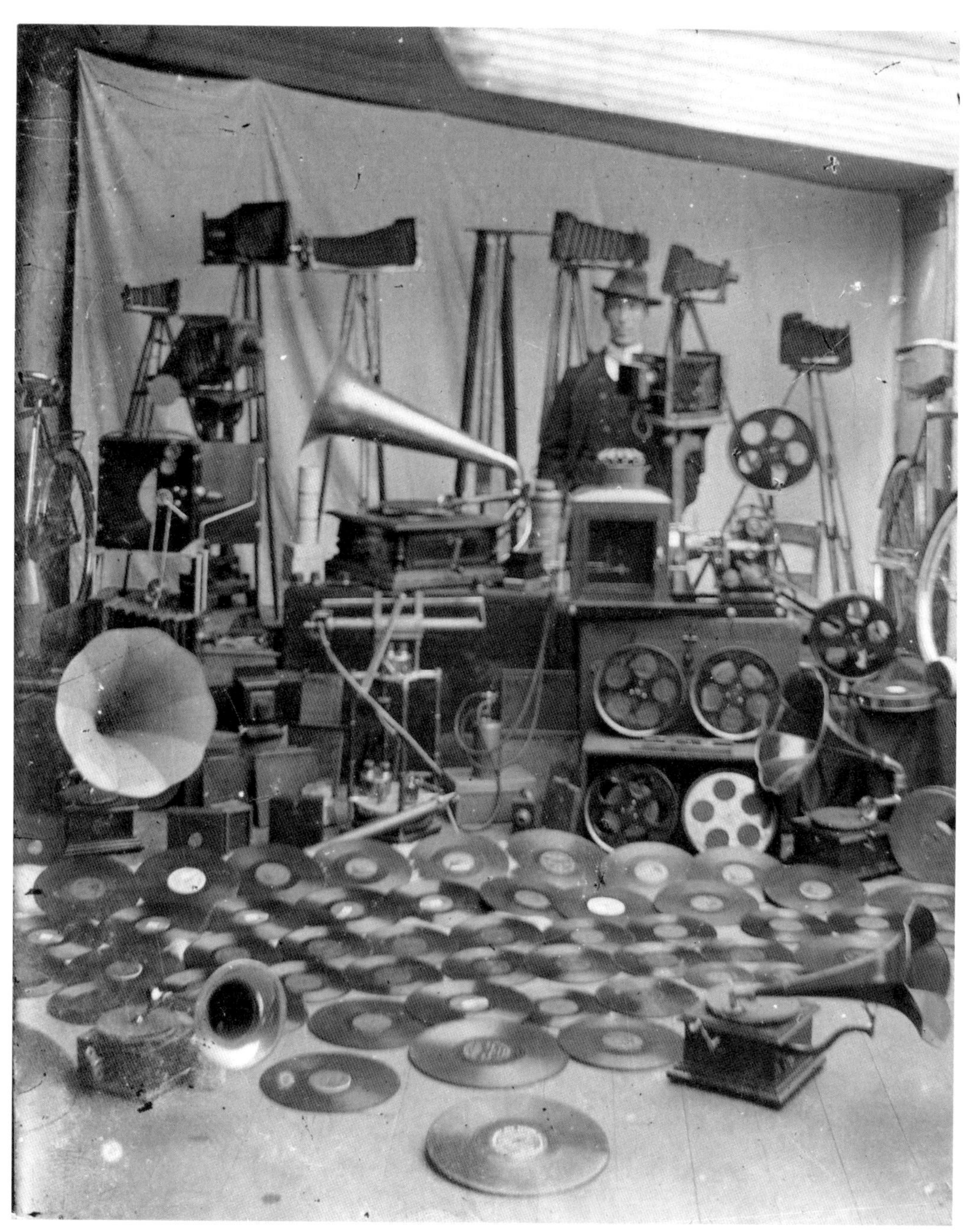

James Horgan with even more Travelling Light Show equipment.

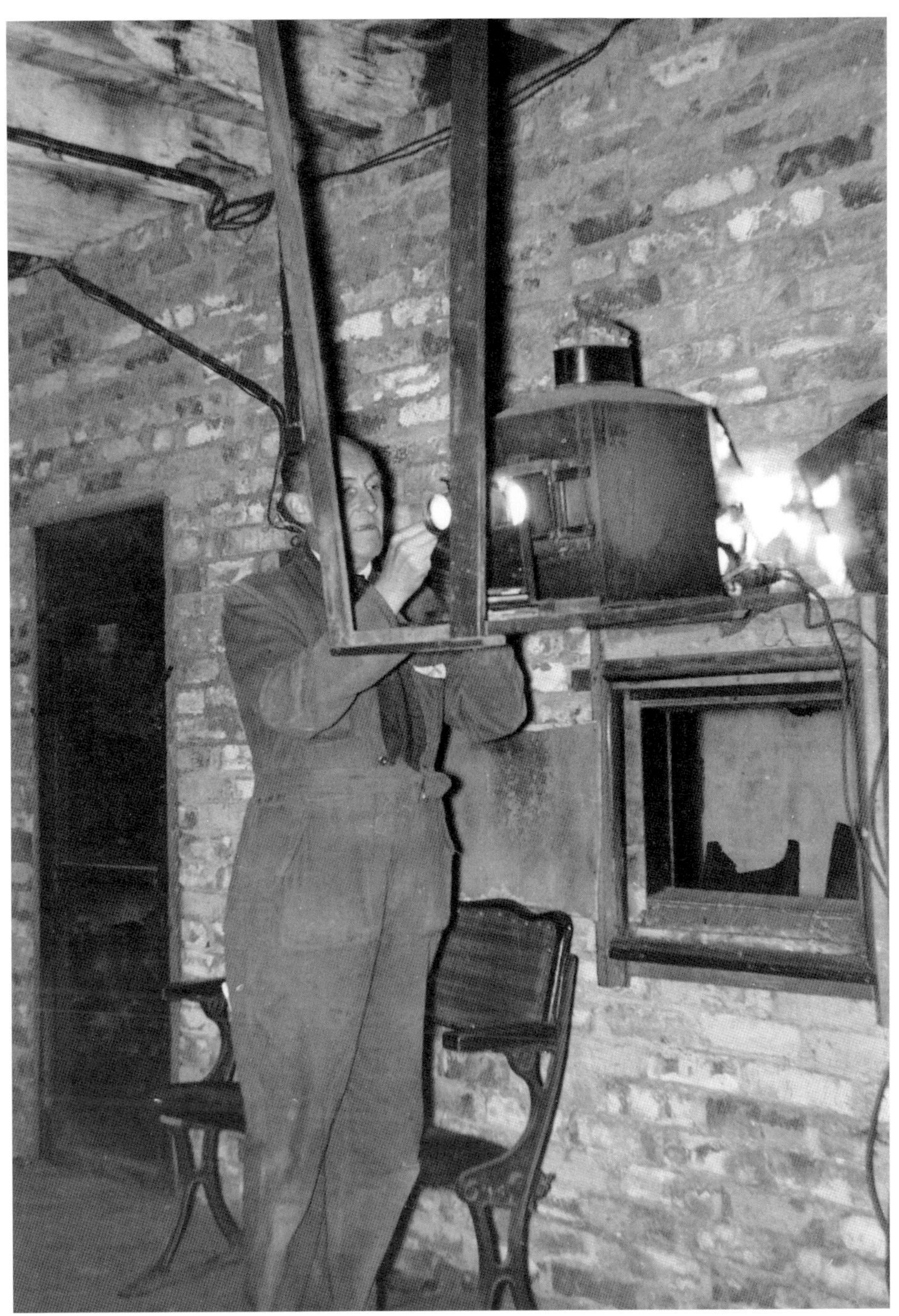

Lighting the Magic Lantern projector for the show.
While this projector is an electrical one, the older lanterns
were illuminated by fire, powered by paraffin.

The captured images were 'burned' onto glass slides that were approximately 8cm squared. Another advancement in the 2D image was what was called 'stereo pairs'. This is when a pair of photographs of the same subject are taken from slightly different positions, which gives an almost 3D effect when properly mounted and viewed through an apparatus which is held up to the eyes. This contraption looked like an elaborate set of opera goggles. The information about each slide was printed on the back of stereo pair cards and could be read out to the audience or viewer as the corresponding image was being viewed.

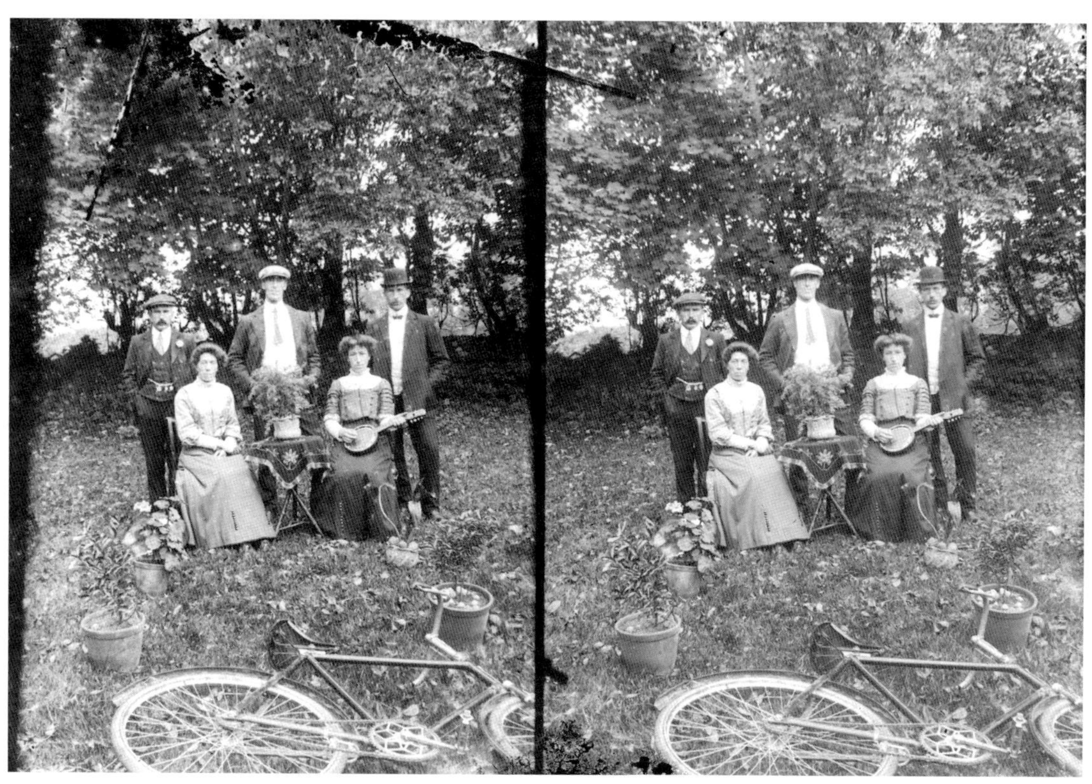

An example of a stereo pair photograph.

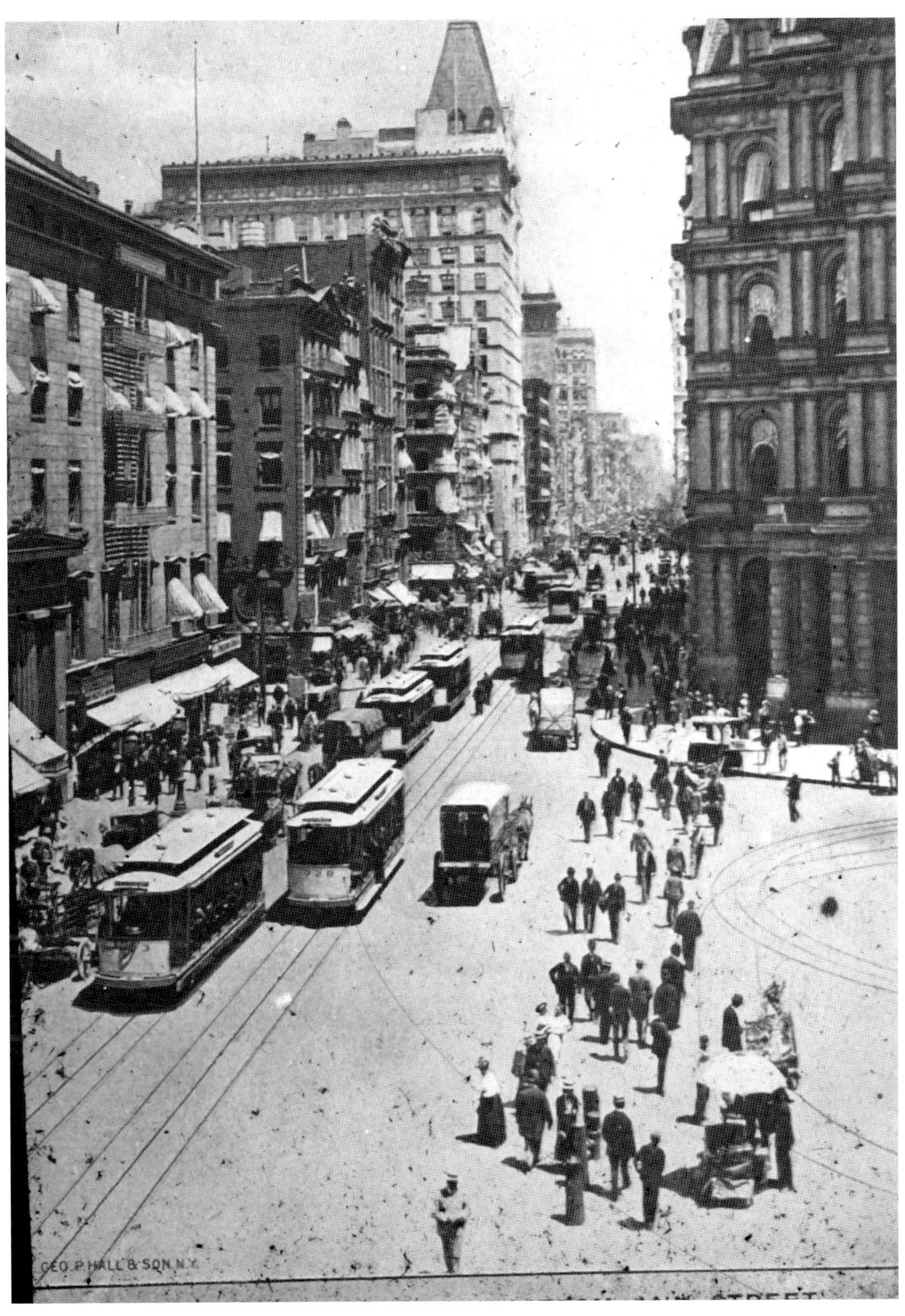

Glass Magic Lantern slide of New York.

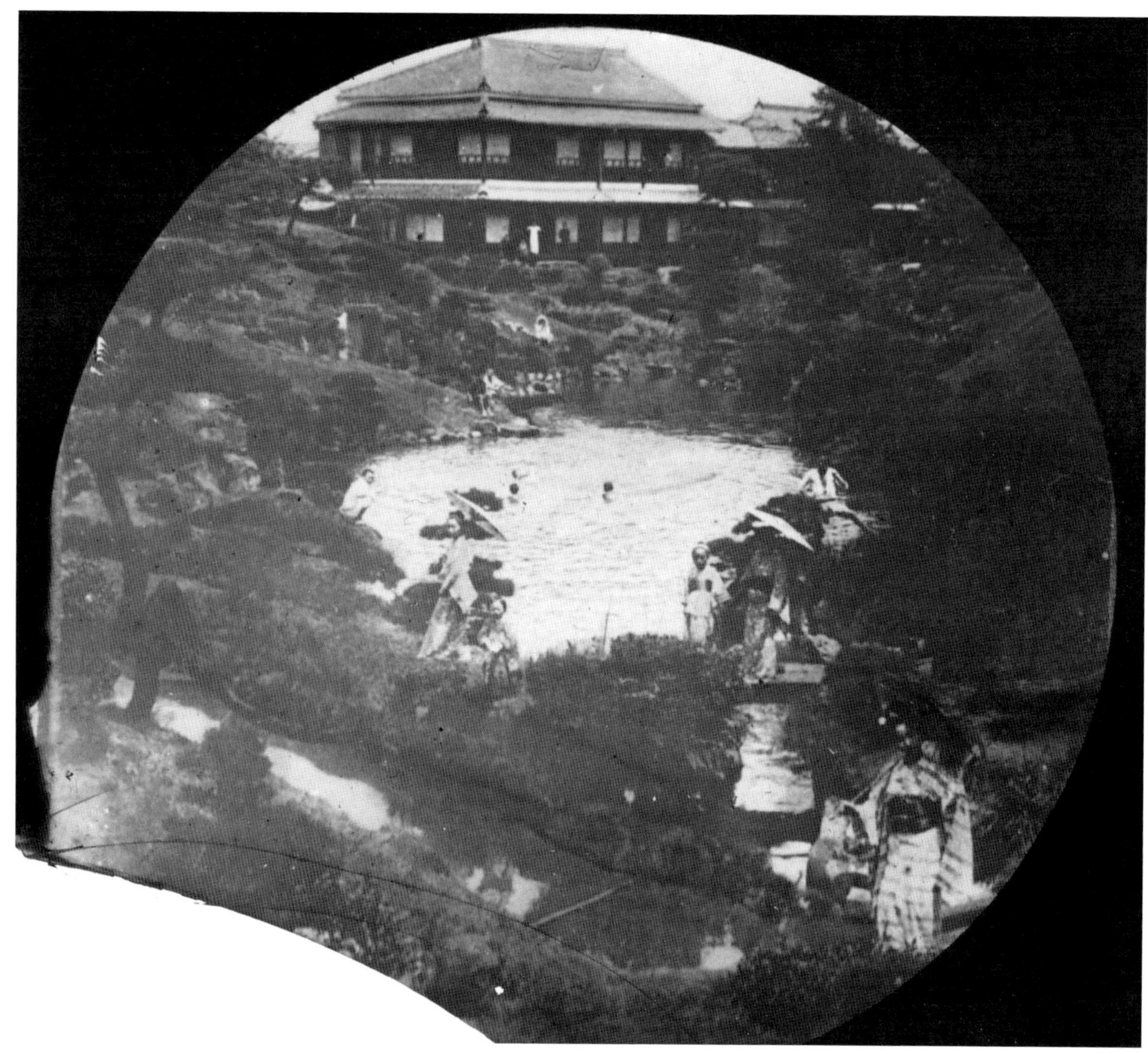

Magic Lantern slide of Chinese gardens.

The travelling magic lantern shows quickly developed into a community event and an opportunity for other acts to perform in front of a gathering of people from the local community.

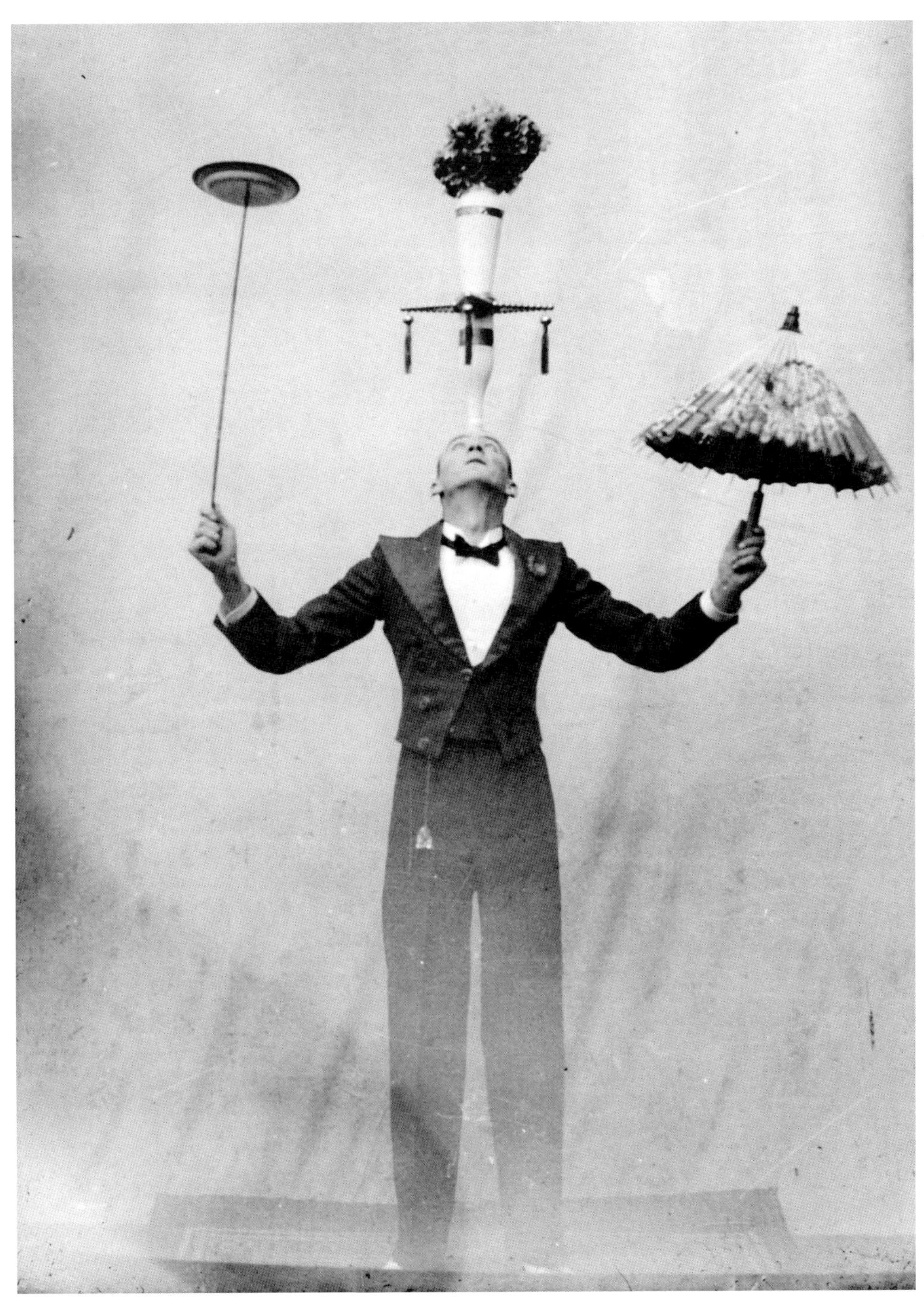

Juggler performing at a Magic Lantern Show.

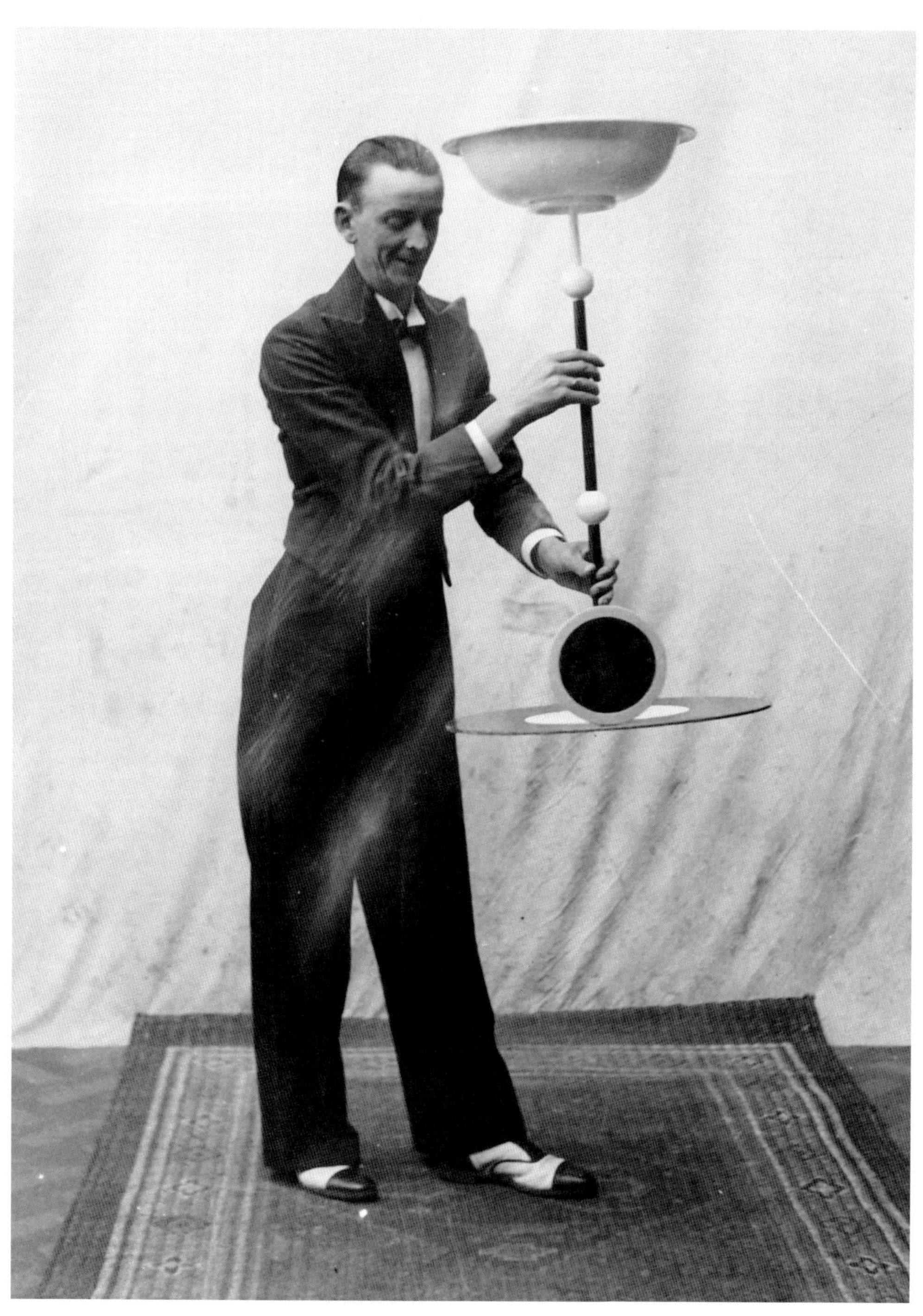

Another performance at a Magic Lantern Show.

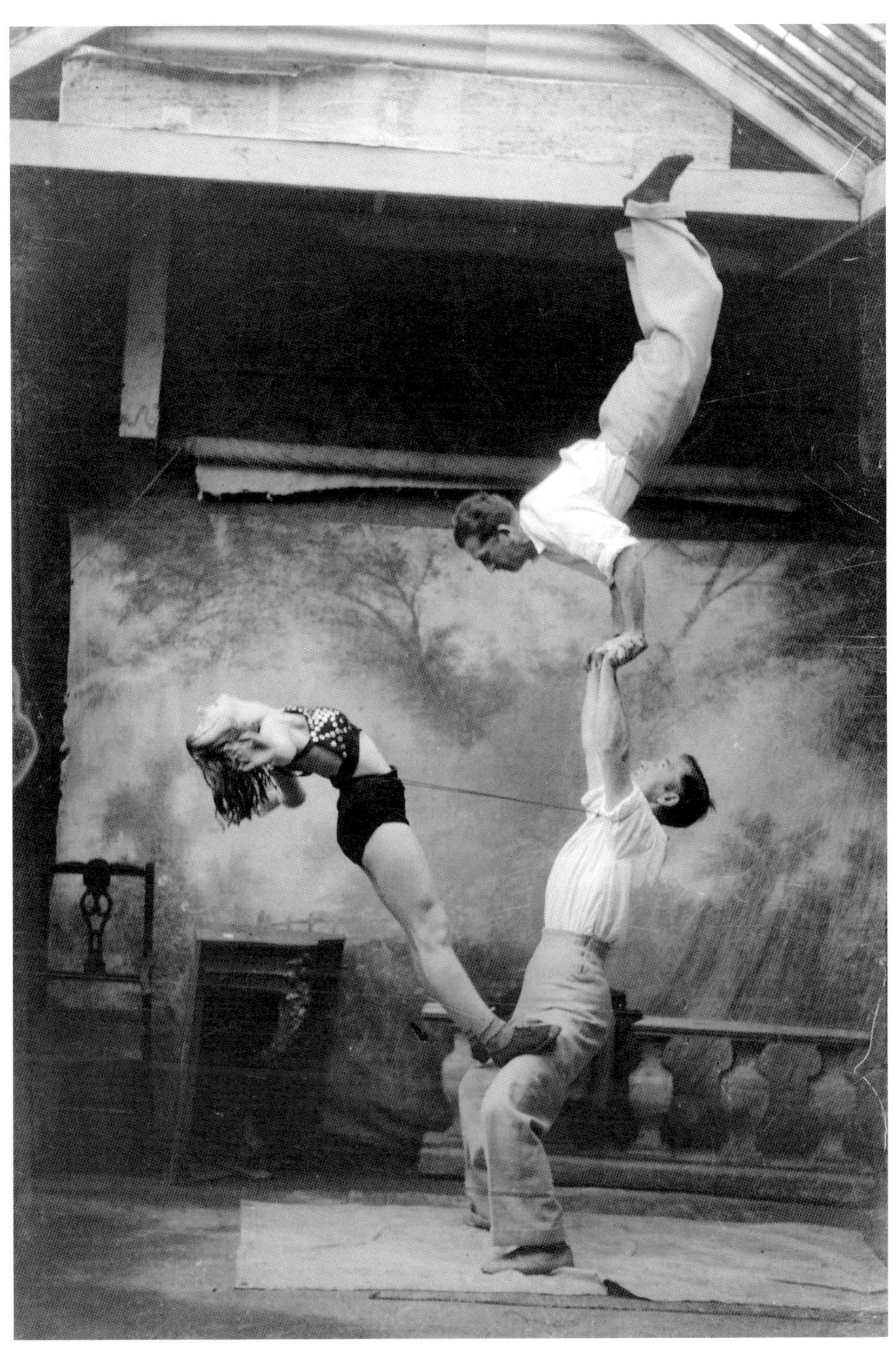

Gymnasts performing at a Magic Lantern Show.

After the educational and news items, local musicians such as the Faire brothers, gymnasts and dancers entertained the crowds. Slides were projected to enhance most items. For example, if the Faire brothers struck up a well-known tune about emigration, a slide showing a family with bags on their backs or waving to an immigrant ship would be displayed on the screen. These songs and slides resonated with rural communities as emigration had taken great swathes of the population to the USA and England after the Great Famine.

Particular favourites were the slides depicting popular songs of the time. A number of glass slides still exist which were obviously meant to accompany popular songs, which the whole audience would sing as the slides were projected.

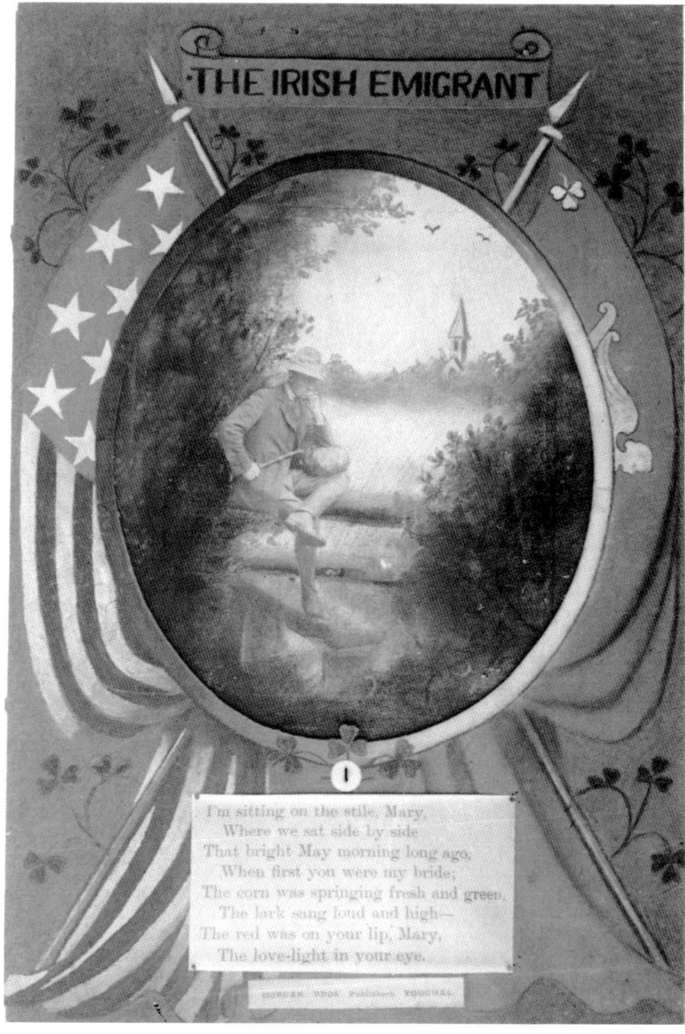

The first slide of an Irish Emigrant *with lyrics to a song that the crowd would sing.*

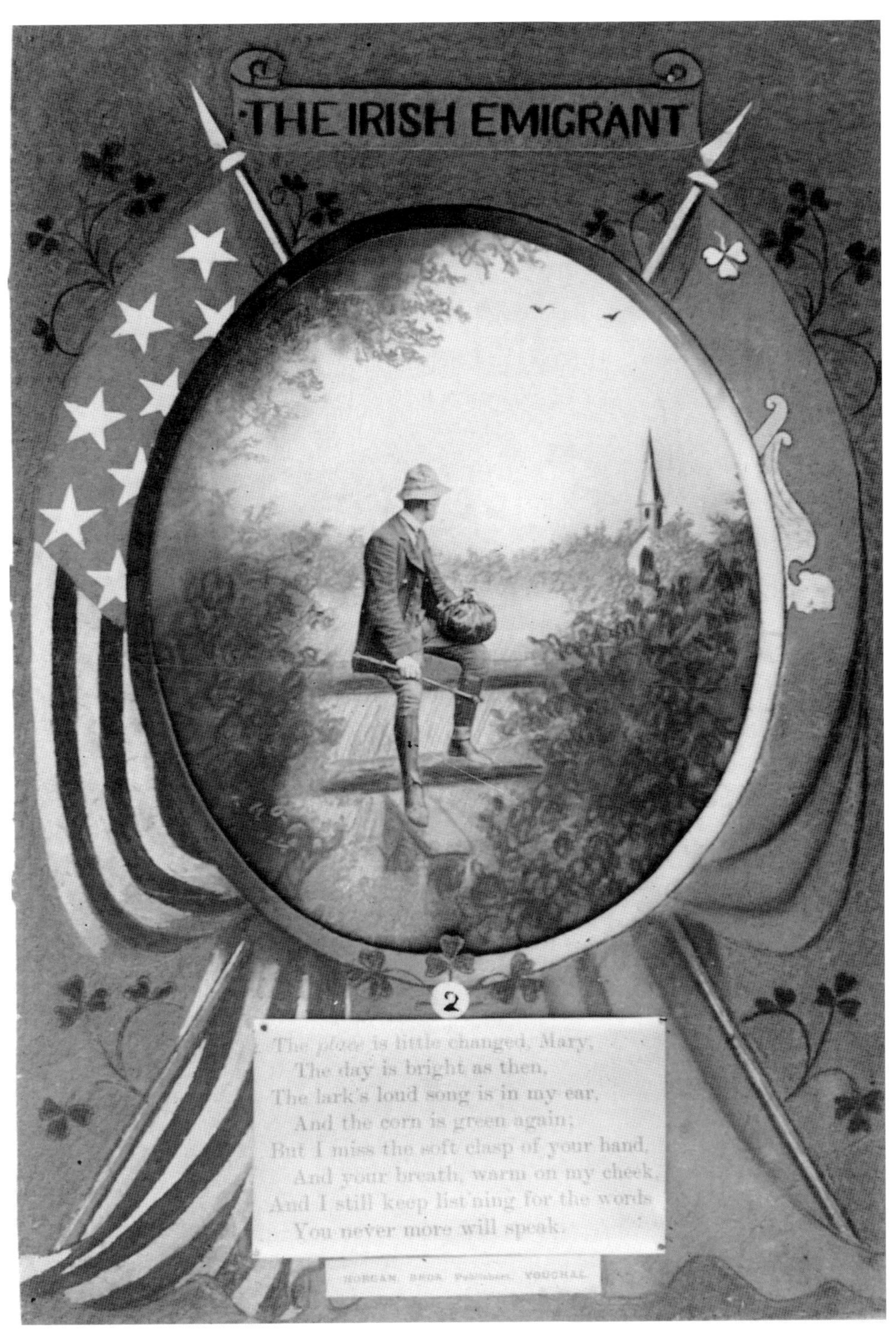

The second slide to the song of an **Irish Emigrant** *which the crowd would sing at a Magic Lantern show.*

The Lumière brothers in France had been selling photographic equipment from their factory in Lyon for years. They were the first to make the progression to capturing moving images when they developed the Cinématographe. Their public screening of a short film on 28 December 1895 in Paris is generally regarded as the birth of cinema. The Lumière brothers sold their films throughout Europe to travelling shows as well as a device that was attached to a magic lantern projector which made showing the films possible.

These films for the people in rural Irish villages were magical and drew big crowds.

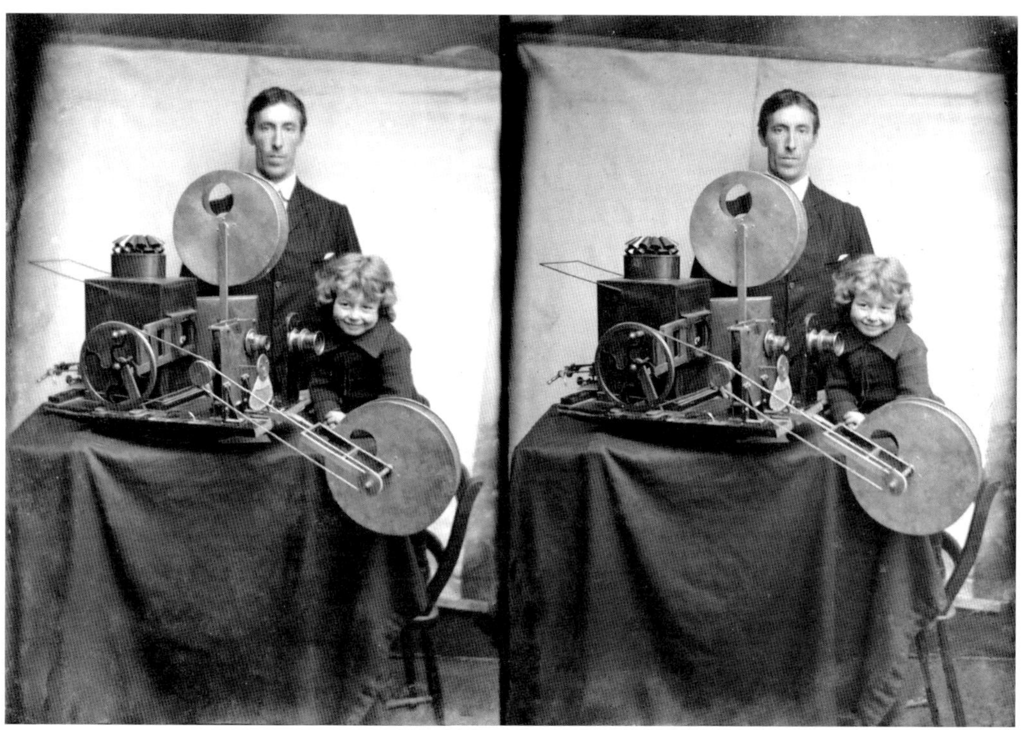

James Horgan with his niece Nelly and the adapted projector.

The Horgan Brothers adapted their own camera using the Lumière projection device and successfully began creating their own films, so they began the first ever newsreel series, 'The Youghal Gazette'. The brothers filmed all the major local events: Corpus Christi processions, May processions, hunger strikers returning from Wormwood Scrubs prison, the mass of the soldiers and sailors returning from the First World War, and 'Féile Déaglán Naofa' in Ardmore and the first record of horse-racing in Ireland at Frogmore in Youghal. When these films were screened at the magic lantern shows, the locals were especially raucous when they saw themselves on the screen. Some were even known to shout, 'Look, it's me!' or 'There's Paddy!'

The success of their business allowed the brothers to invest in a motor car. This allowed them to travel even further afield, taking more photographs on their journeys and capturing villages, towns, and rural life in Ireland.

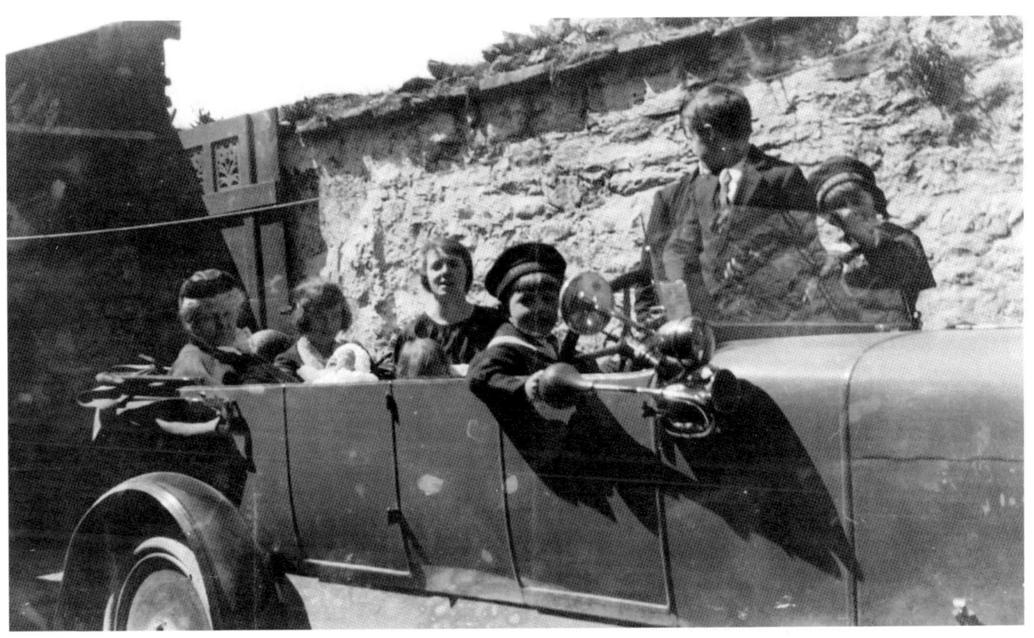

The Horgan family car on Strand Street.

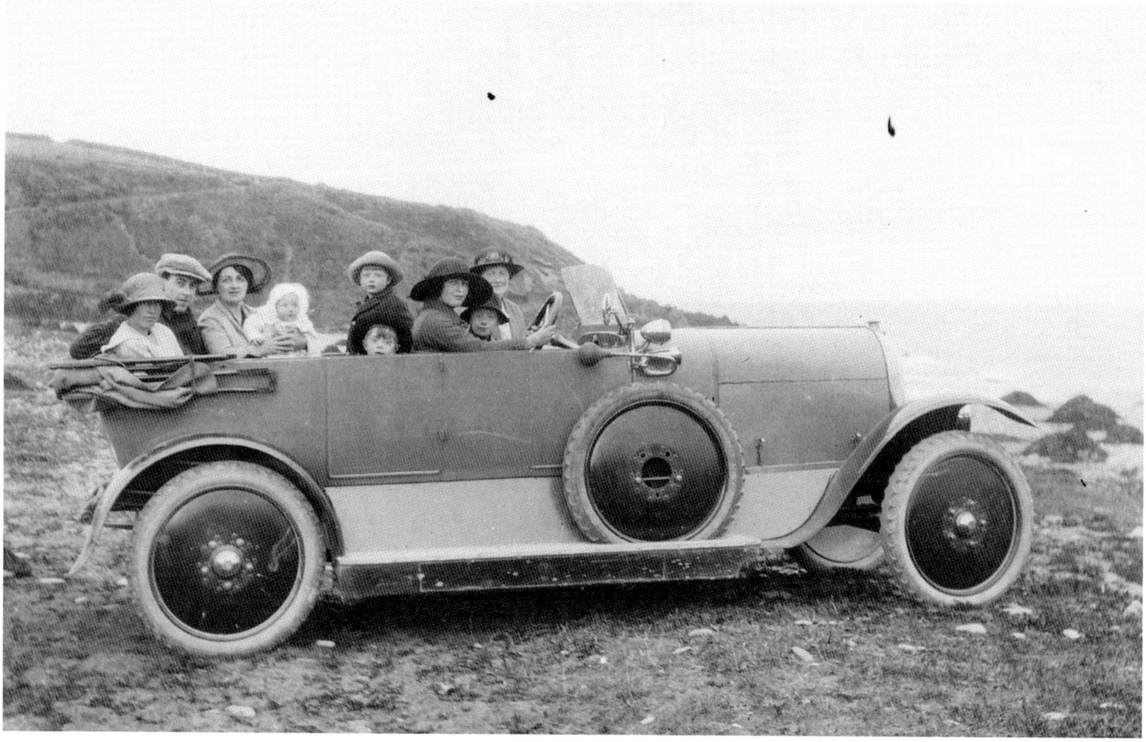

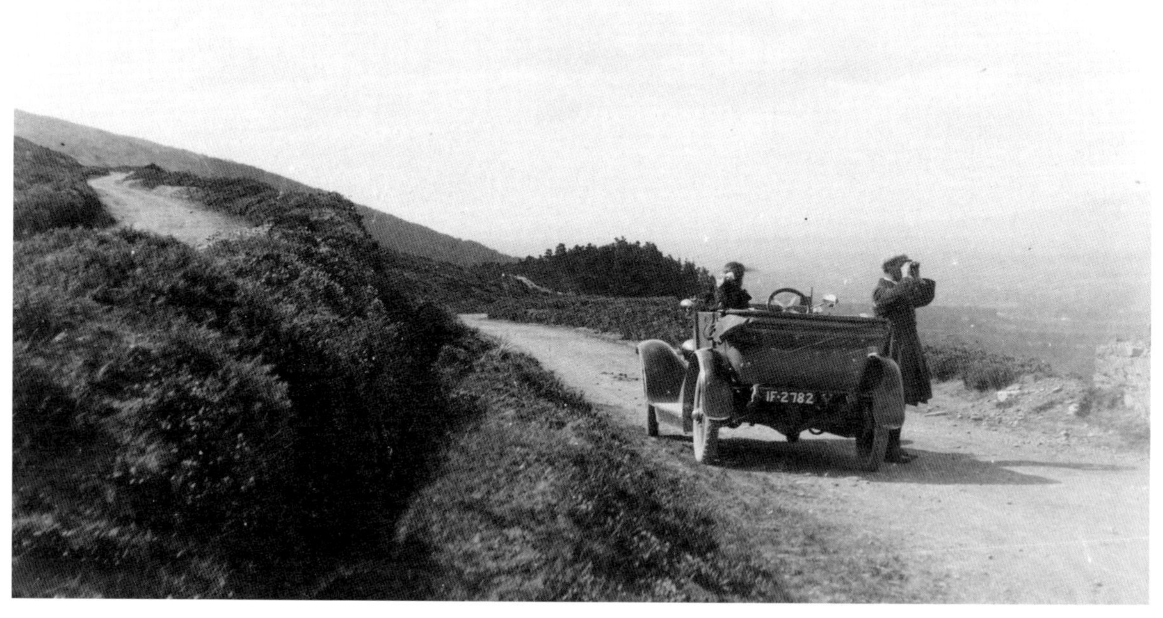

Horgan family car by the coast and below in the mountains.

Óglaig na h-Éireann.

SOUTHERN AREA.
HEADQUARTERS, CORK.

NOT TRANSFERABLE.

No. A 000 1905

Owner's Permit for Motor Vehicle.

Name

Address

Date

Make of Car

Regd. No.

This Permit is issued subject to the following Regulations, a breach of which will result in the withdrawal of Permit, and Confiscation of Vehicle, also proceedings will be taken against the Holder of Permit.

(1.) That the holder of this Permit does not engage in any activities prejudicial to the ELECTED GOVERNMENT of the people.

(2.) That the vehicle in respect of which this Permit is granted will not be used for any purpose prejudicial to the ELECTED GOVERNMENT of the people.

(3.) The motor vehicle in respect of which this Permit is issued must be kept at address specified above.

(4.) This Permit must be kept on the vehicle in respect of which it is granted.

(5.) In case of change of Ownership this Permit must be returned to the Issuing Officer.

DESCRIPTION.

Age

Height

Build Medium

Hair Black

Thomas Horgan   Owner's Signature.

J. C. Dalton

or General

GENERAL OFFICER COMMANDING

Competent Military Authority.

Thomas Horgan's car permit.

The following photographs represent just some of the villages the Horgan brothers visited with their Travelling Magic Lantern Shows.

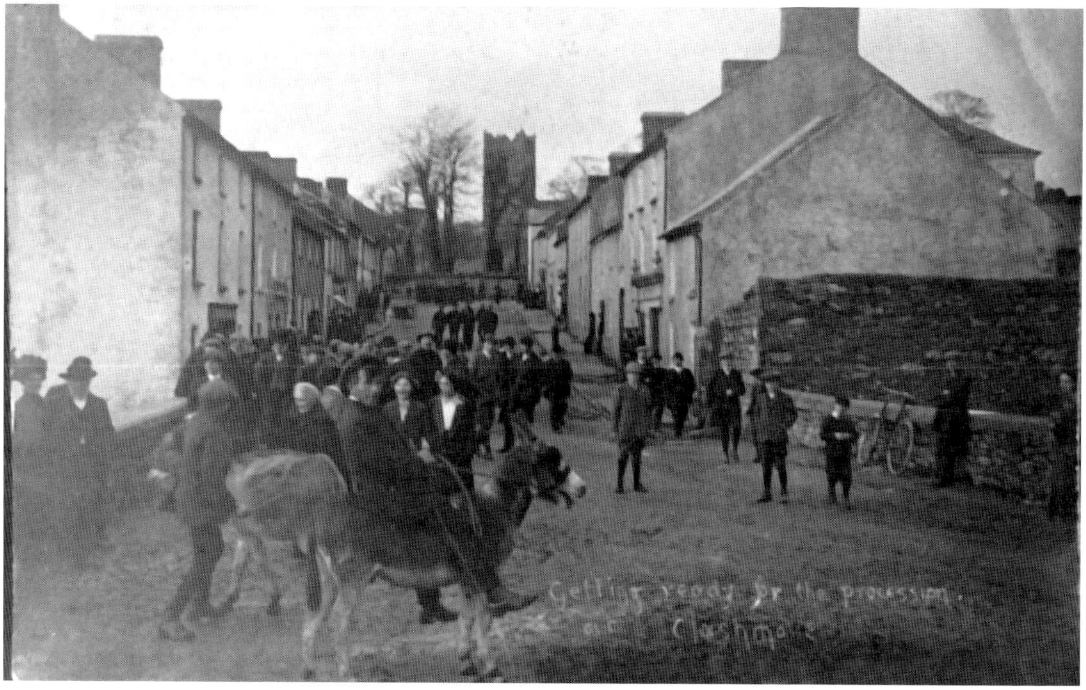

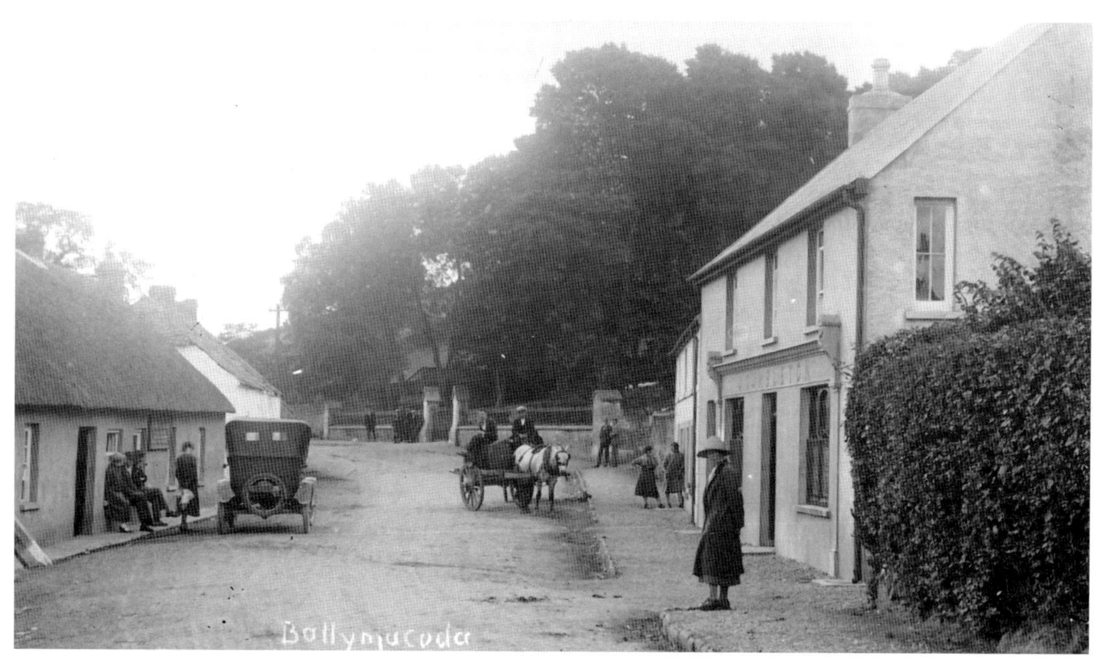

Getting ready for the procession in Clashmore.

Ballymacoda village.

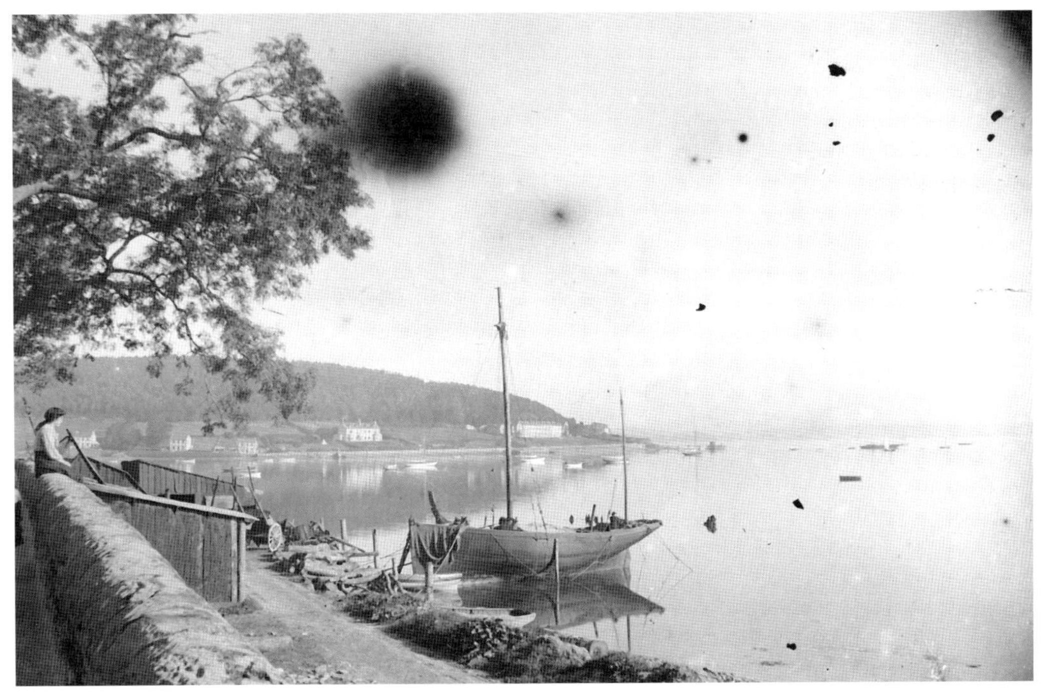

Crosshaven.

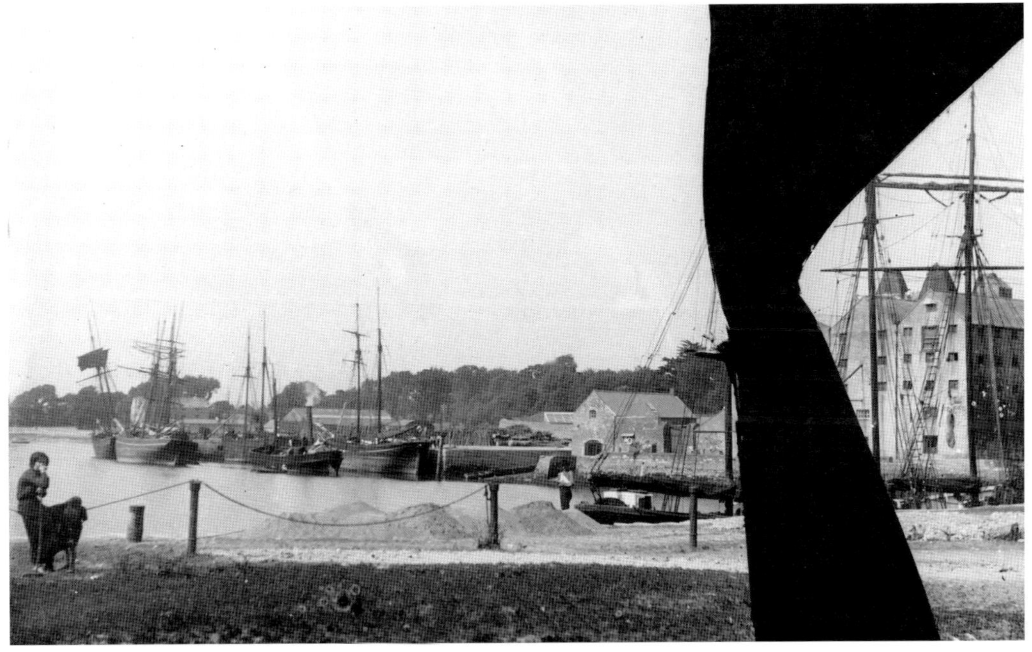

Ballinacurra.

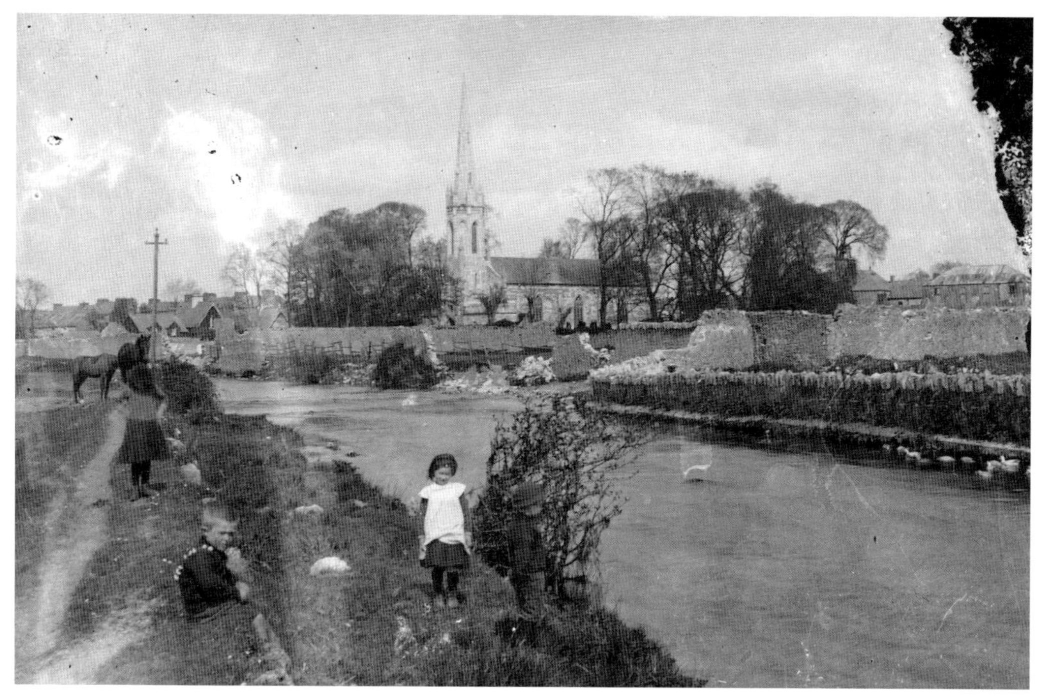

Midleton.

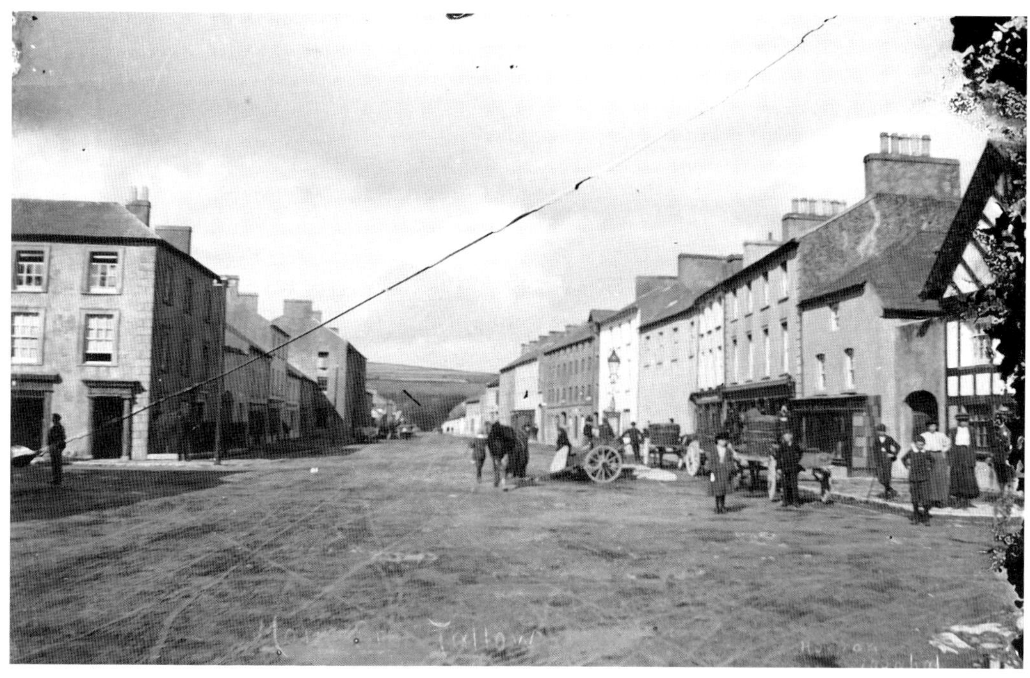

Main Street, Tallow, County Waterford.

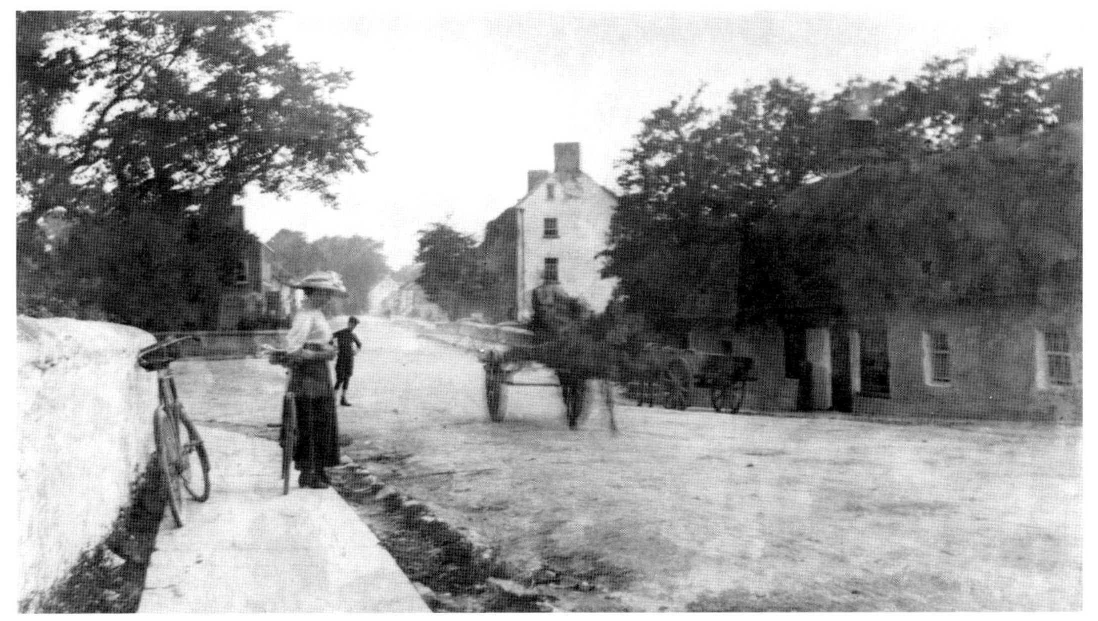

Killeagh, The Thatch on the right.

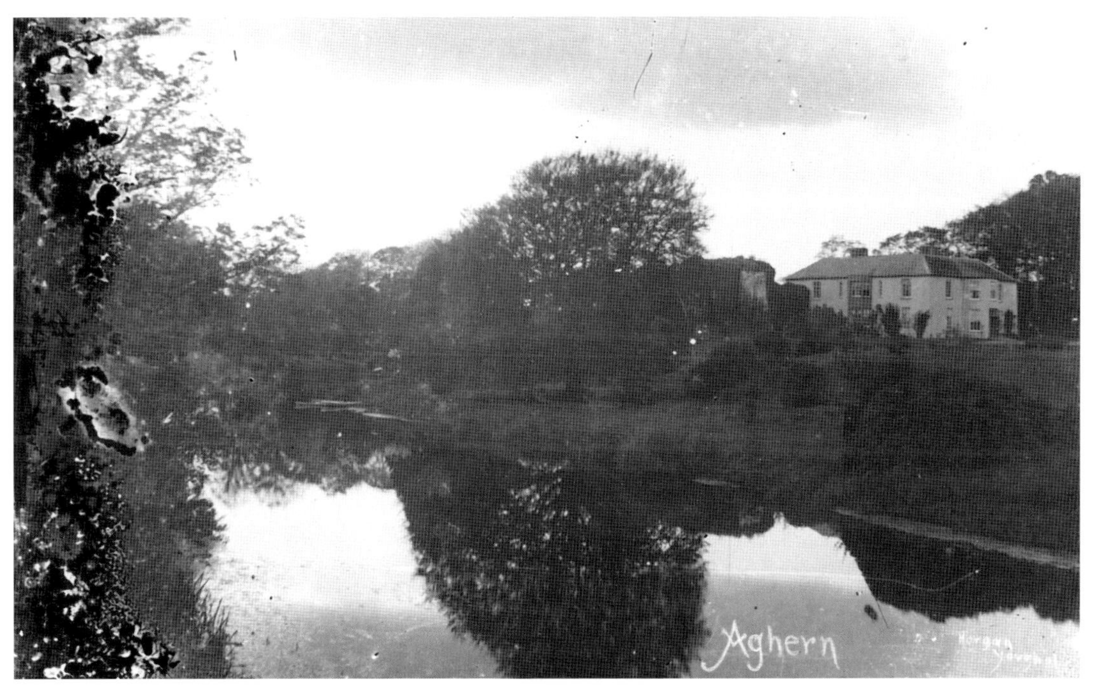

Aghern.

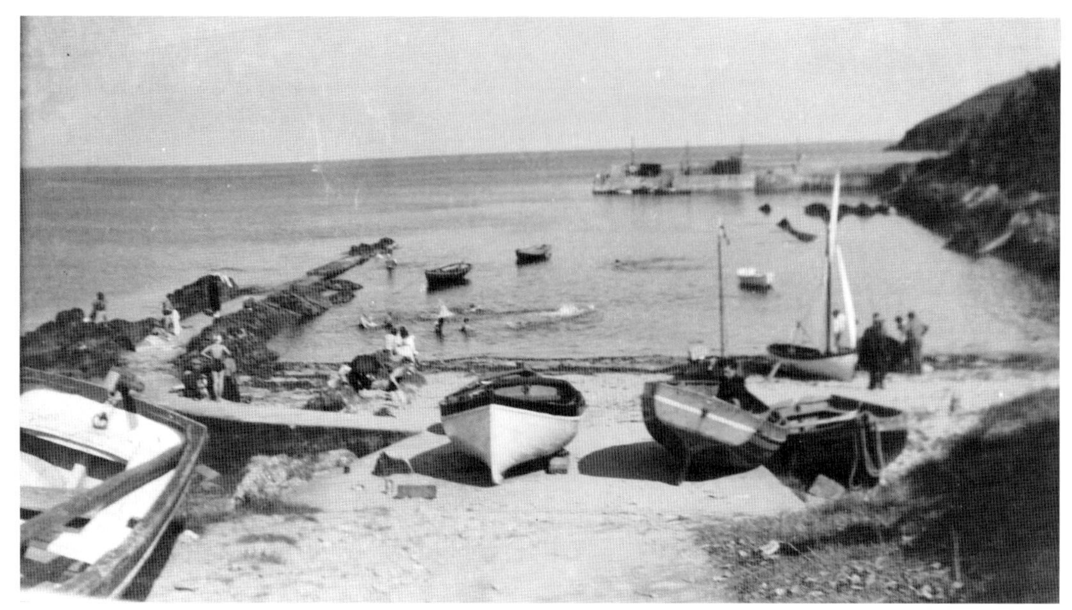

Ardmore, County Waterford.

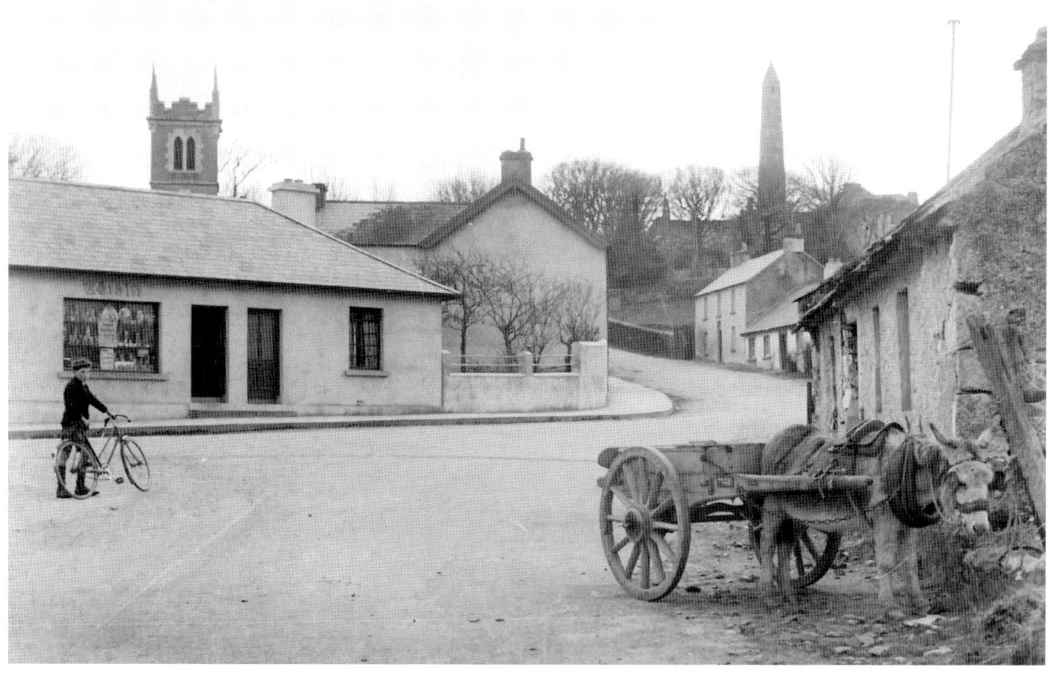

Ardmore village.

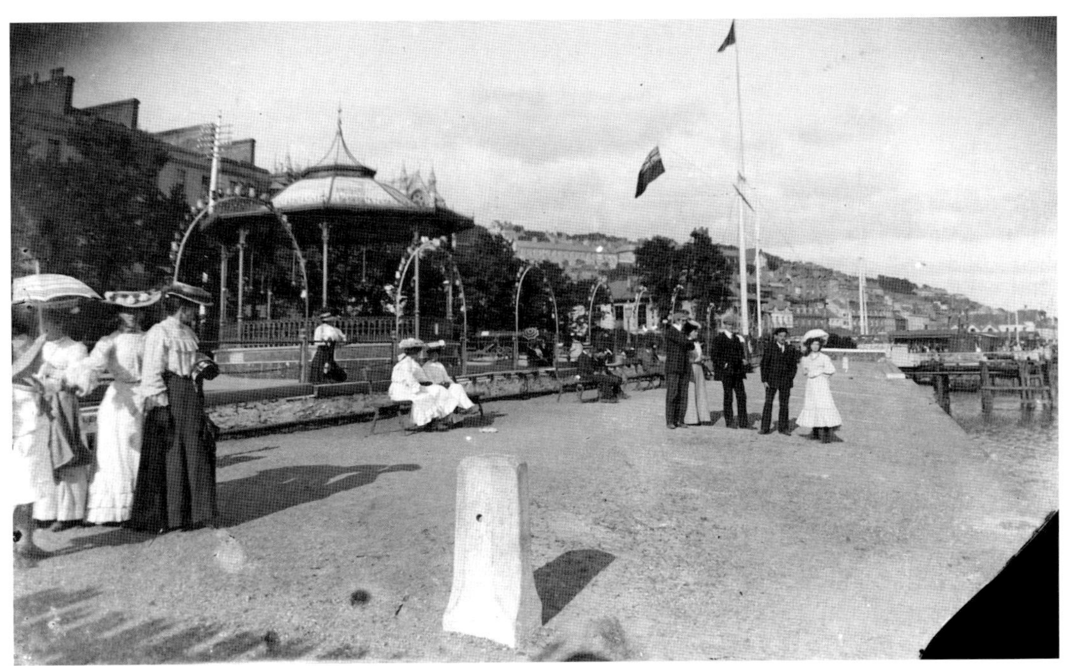

The bandstand in Cobh.

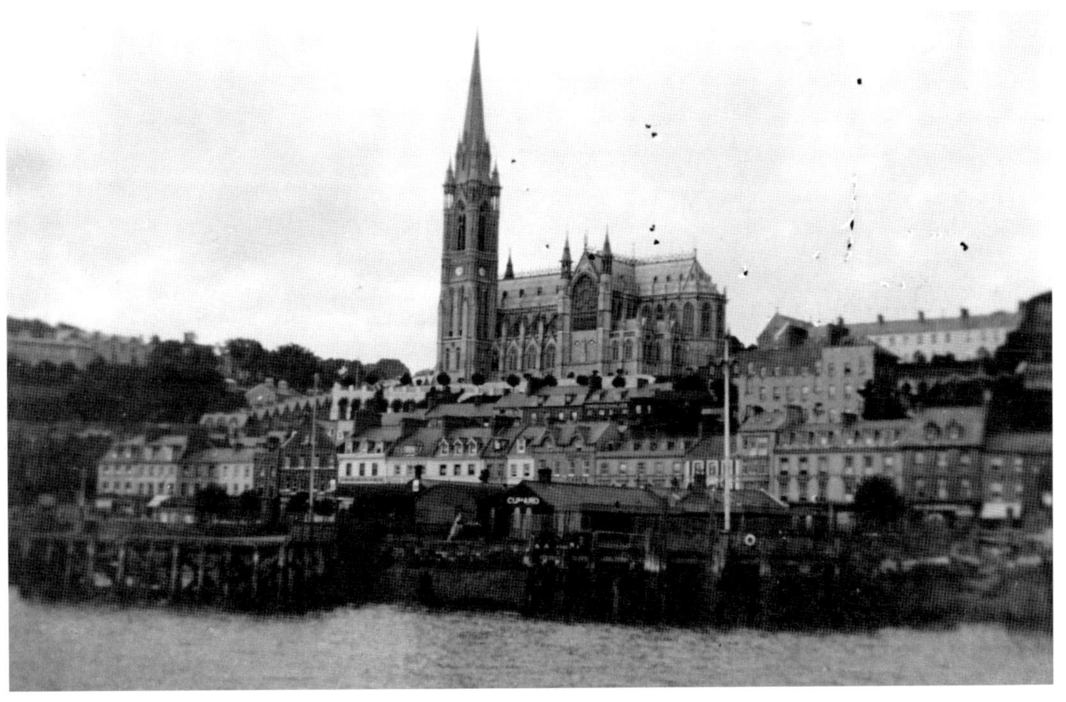

St Coleman's cathedral in Cobh.

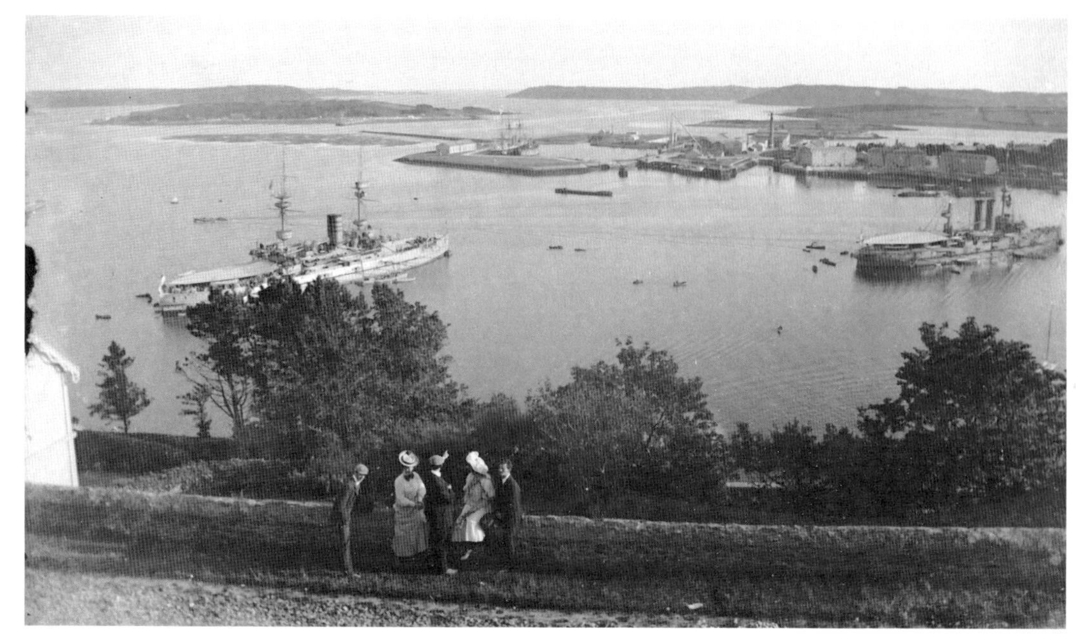

Naval vessels in Cobh.

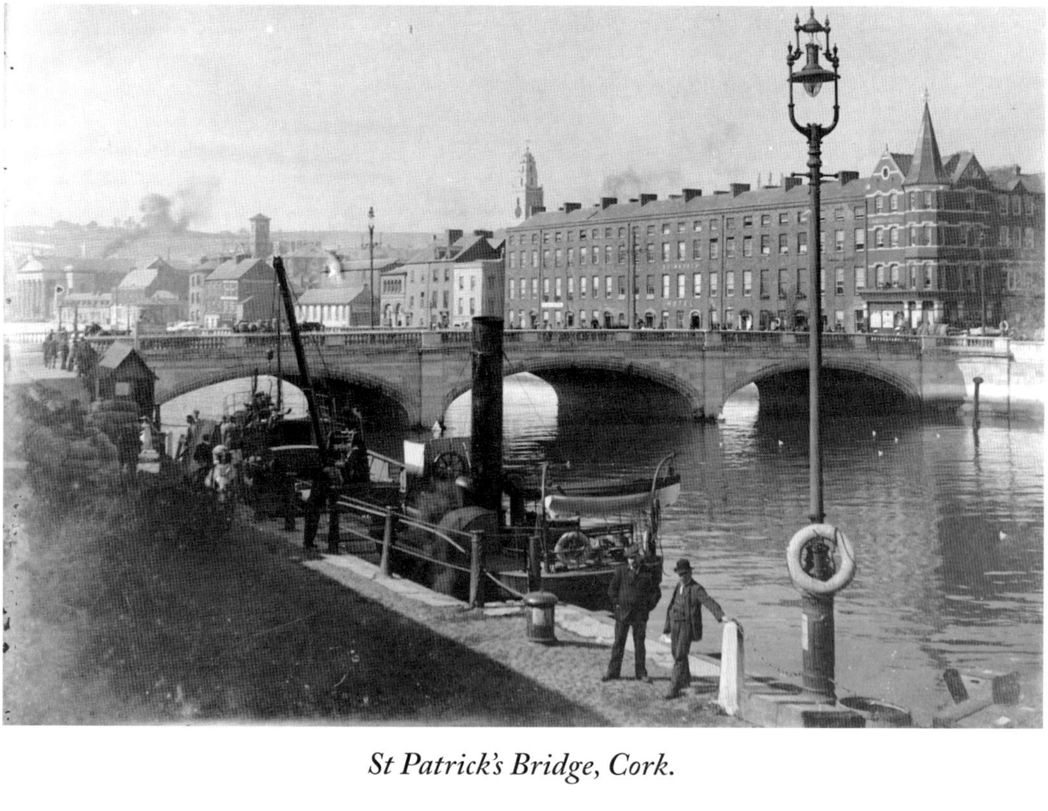

St Patrick's Bridge, Cork.

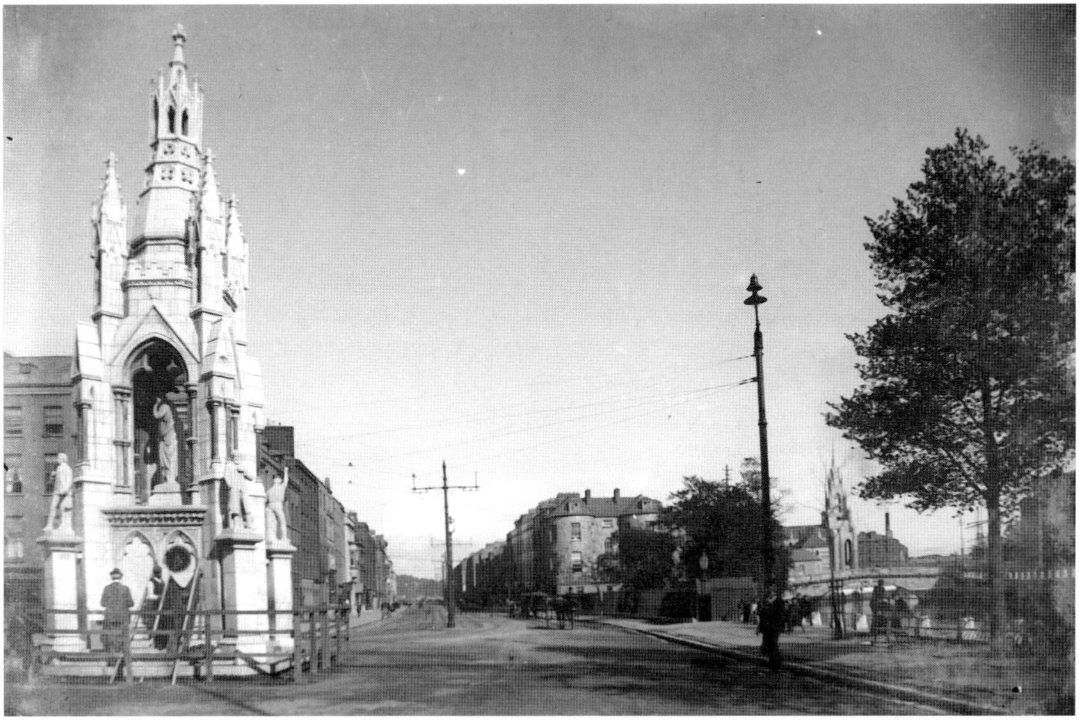

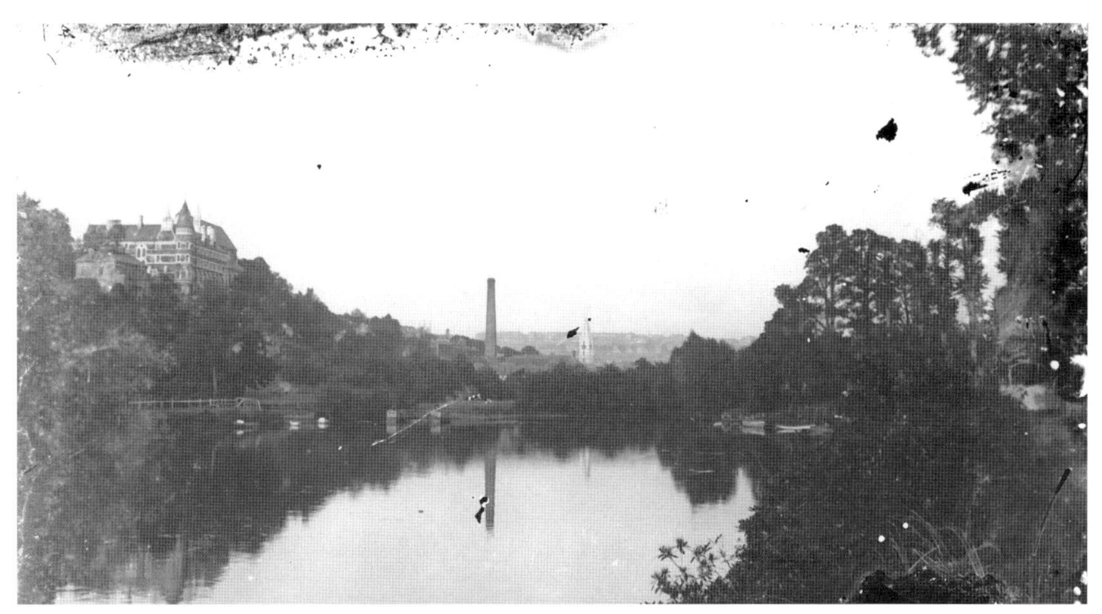

Looking down the South Mall from the Grand Parade, Cork.

River Lee, Cork.

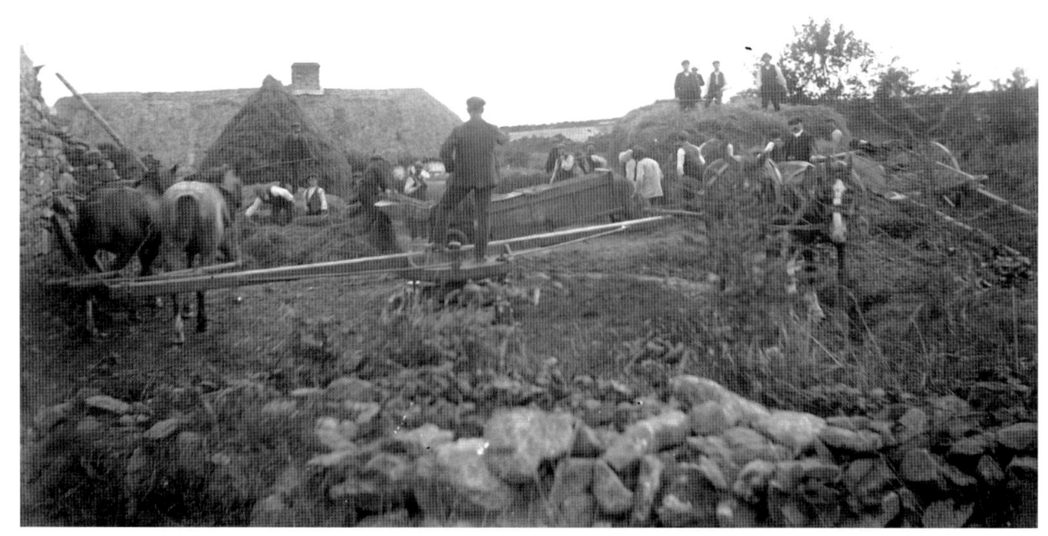

Farming by a thatch cottage with horses.

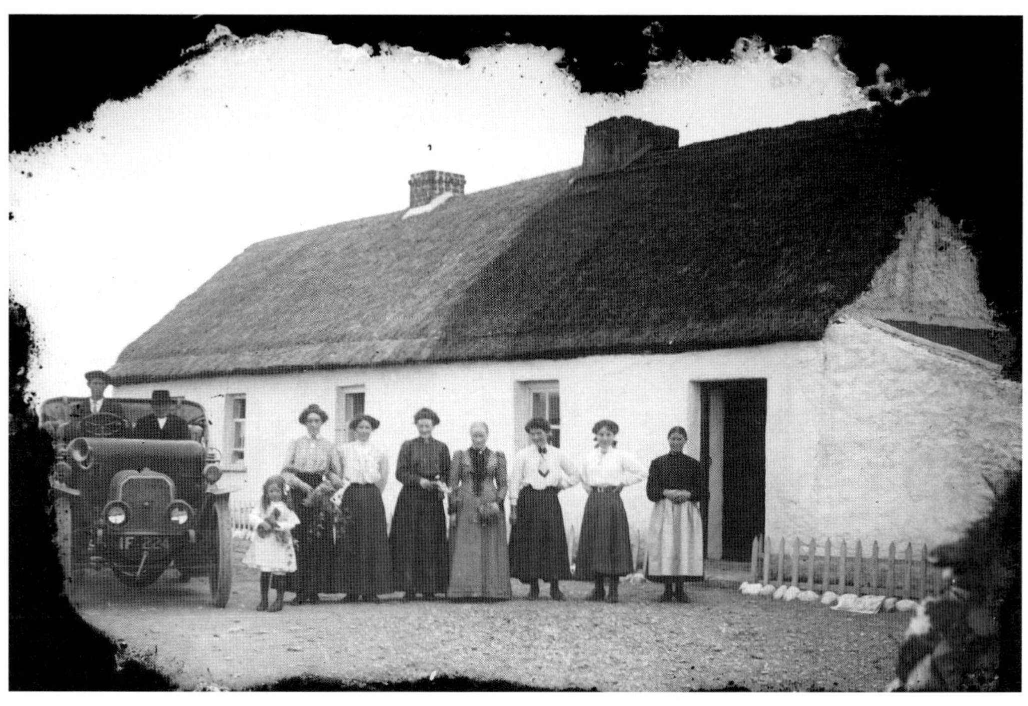

*The family of Thomas Horgan's wife Hanora, née Kelly,
at Caliso Bay. They were married in February 1903.*

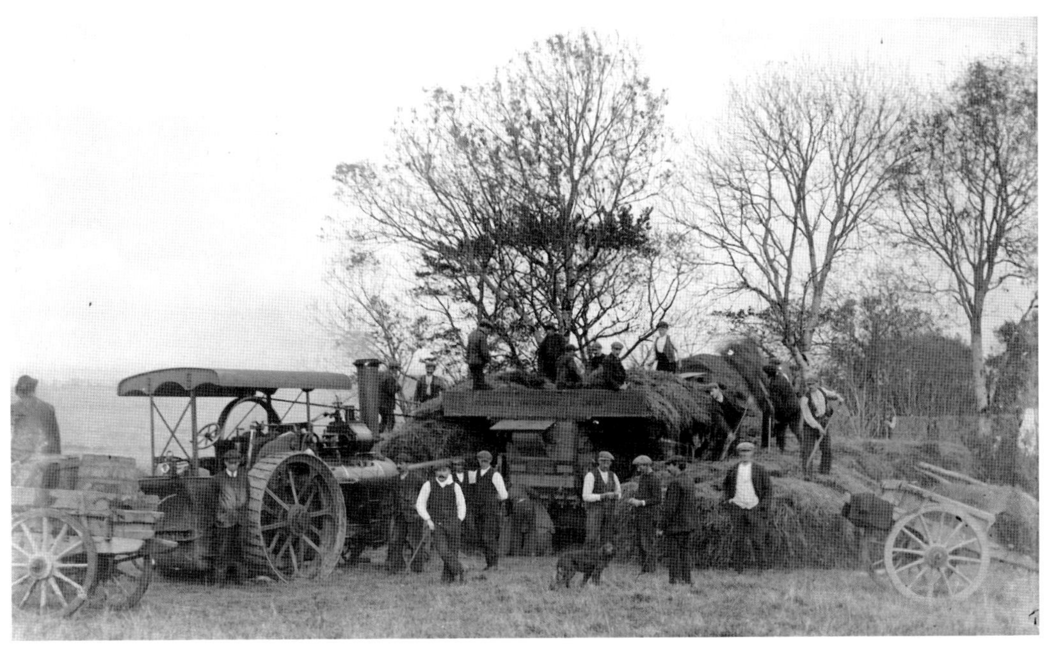

A group of farmers.

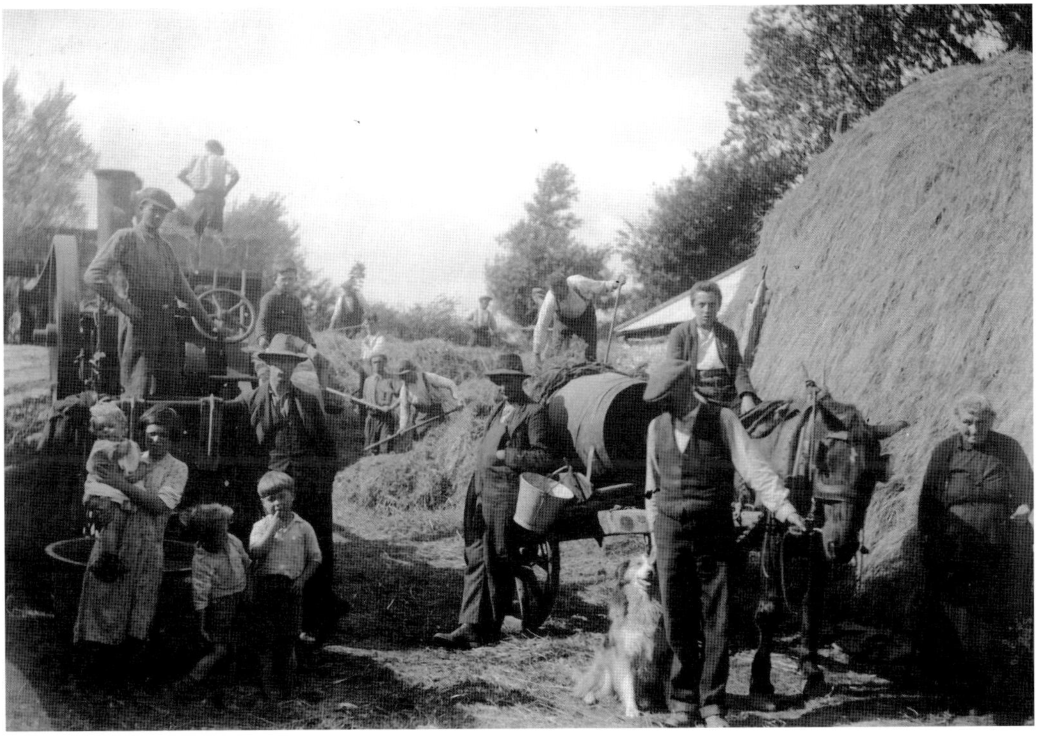

Farmers bringing in the hay.

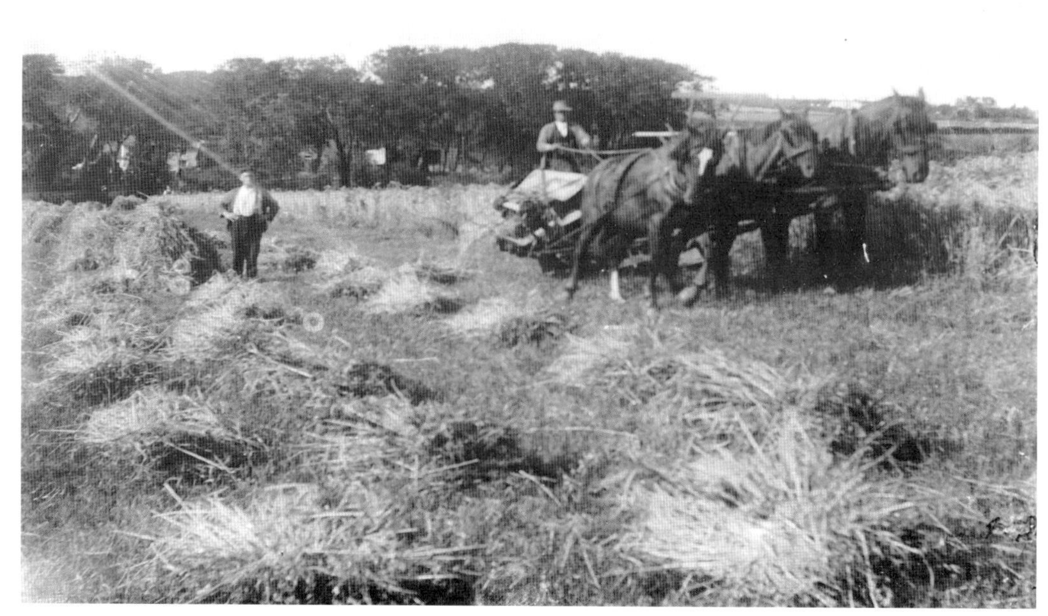

Farming in rural Ireland.

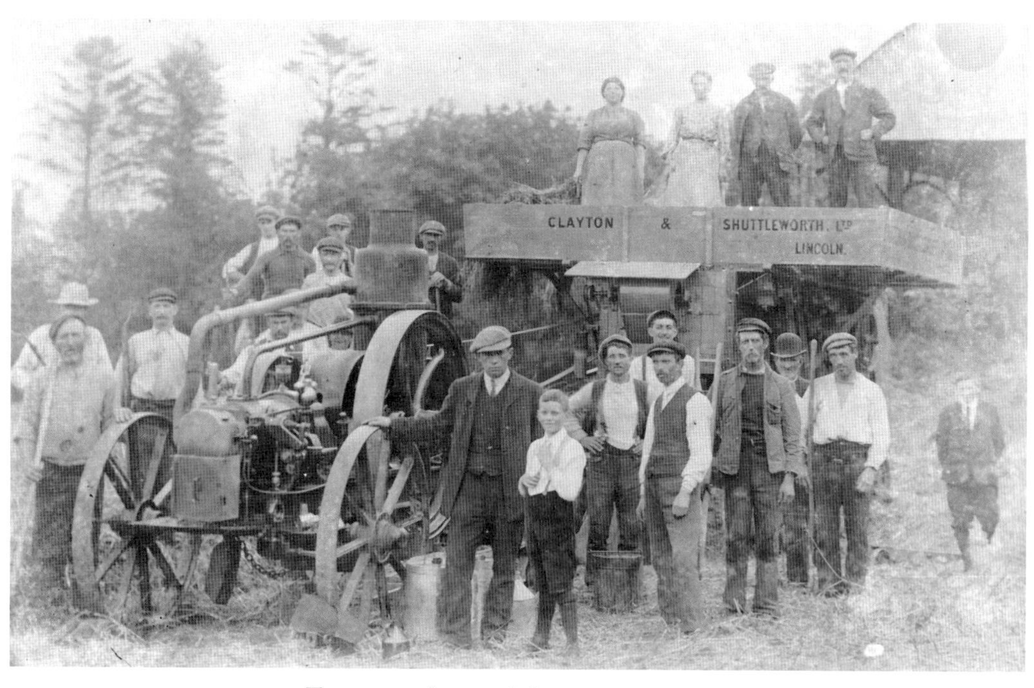

Farm workers with a steam tractor.

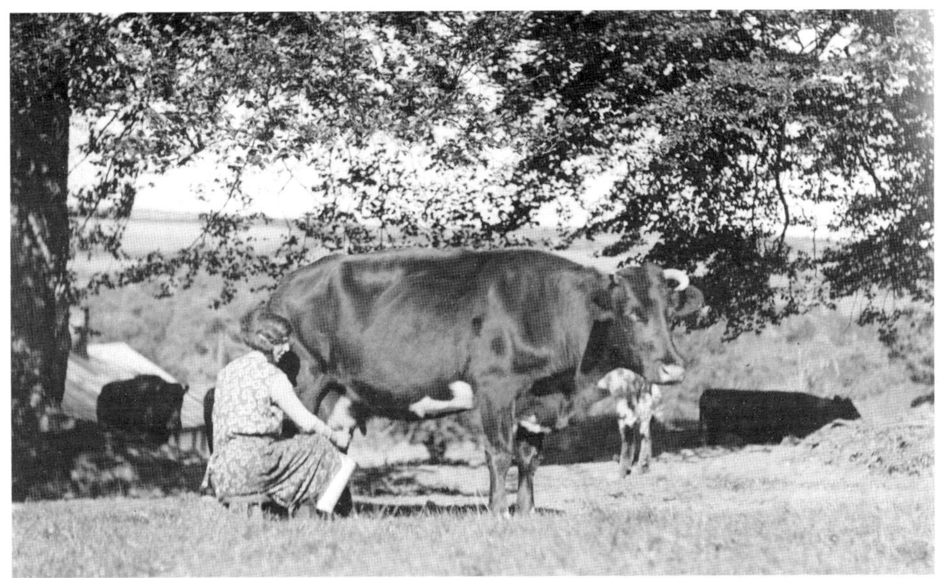

A woman milking a cow.

The Horgan Brothers captured the tapestry of the many community events and activities that took place throughout their career, from sports teams and parades to evolving political parties reflecting the strong cultural influences of the time.

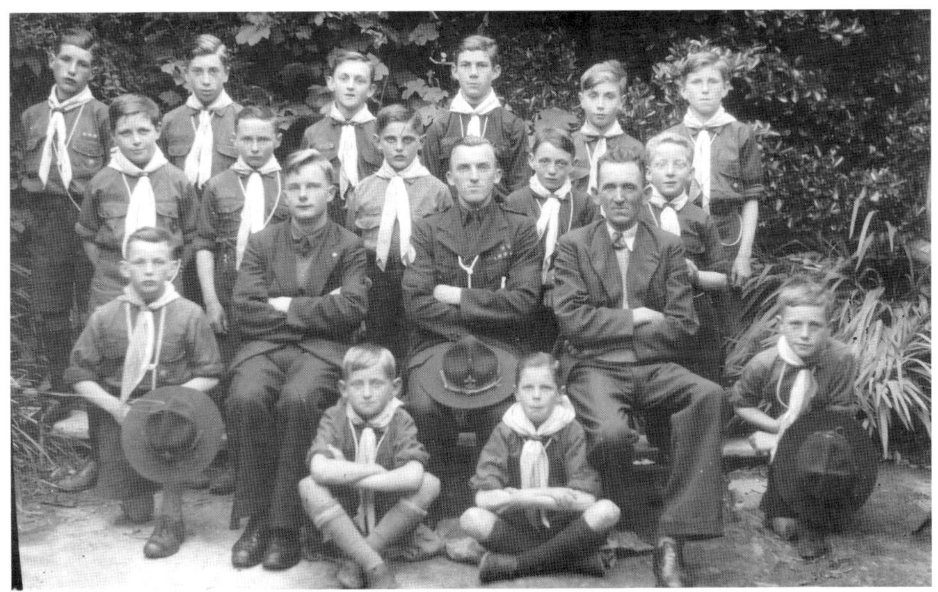

Group of scouts.

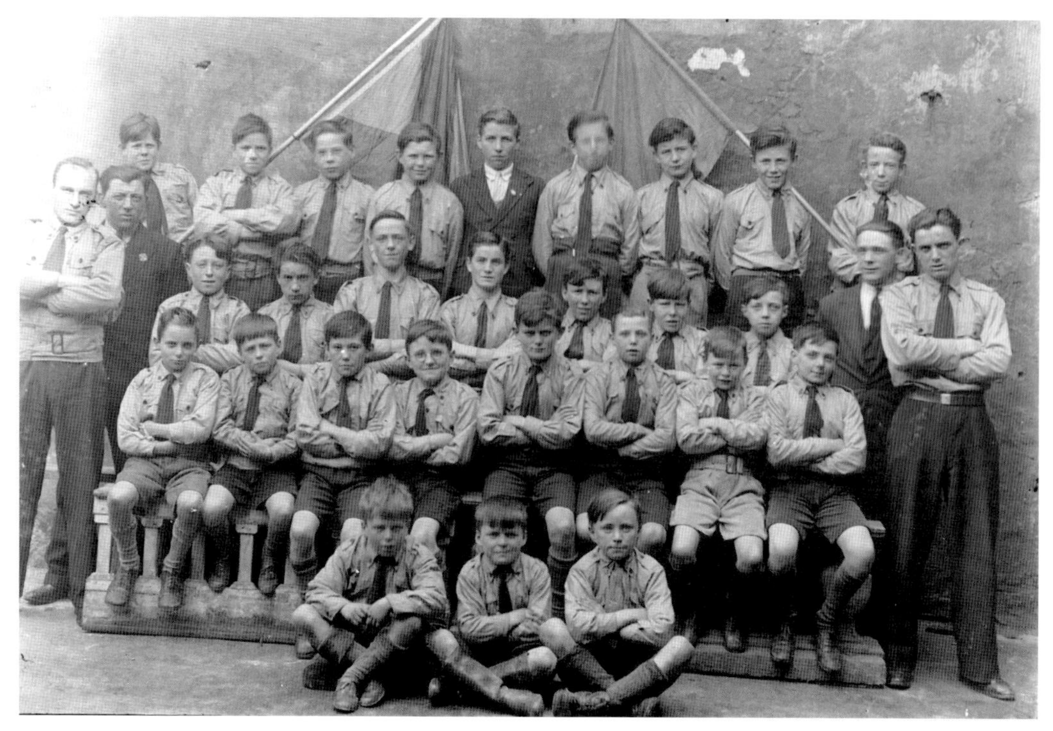

Larger scout group.

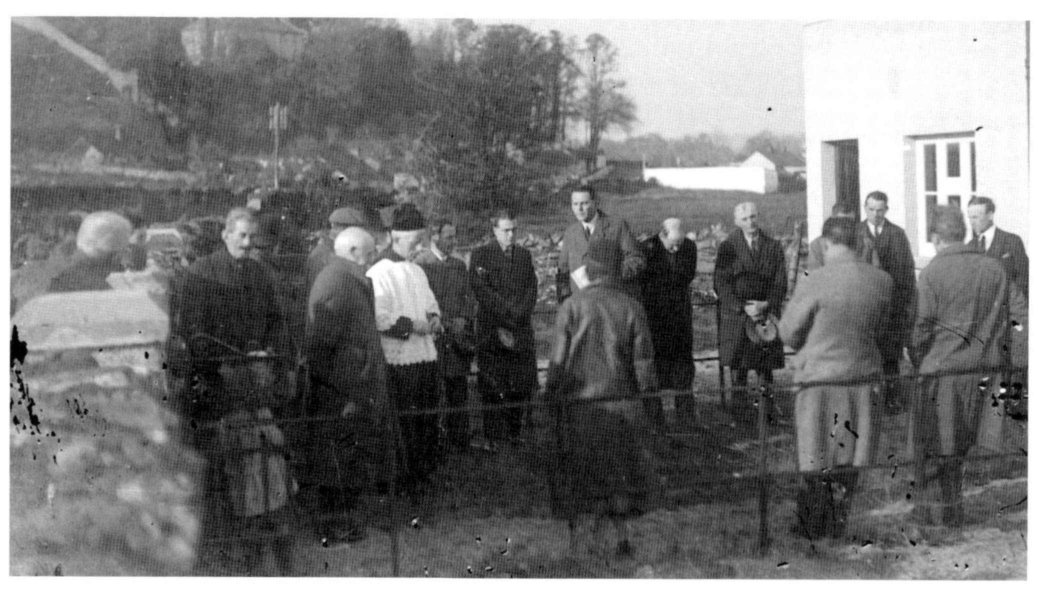

Priest praying with men outside a house.

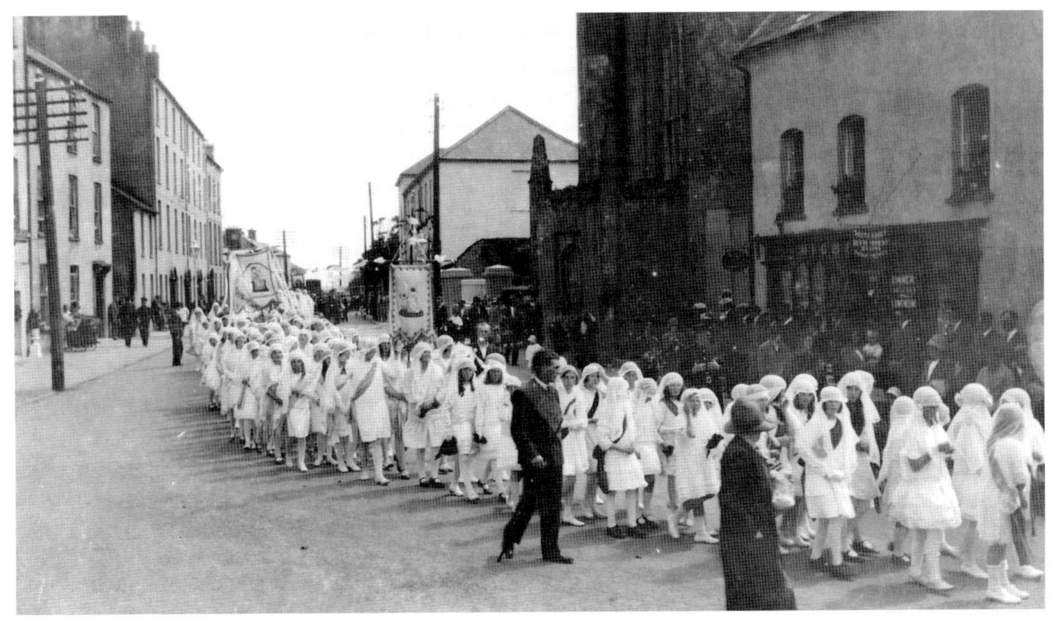

Corpus Christi procession at South Abbey, Youghal.

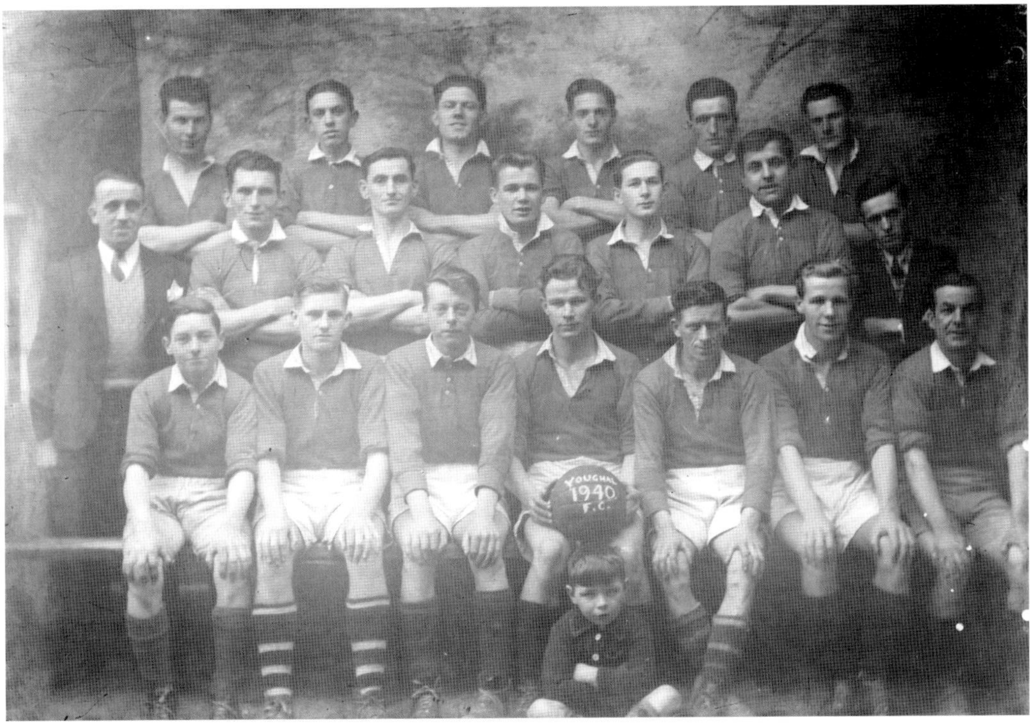

Gaelic football team 1940.

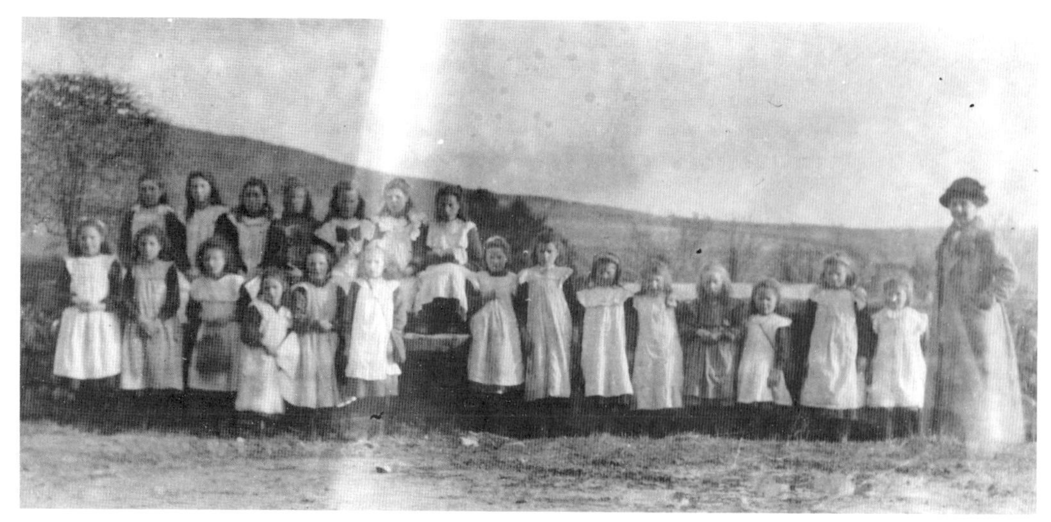

School children at Ballycurrane.

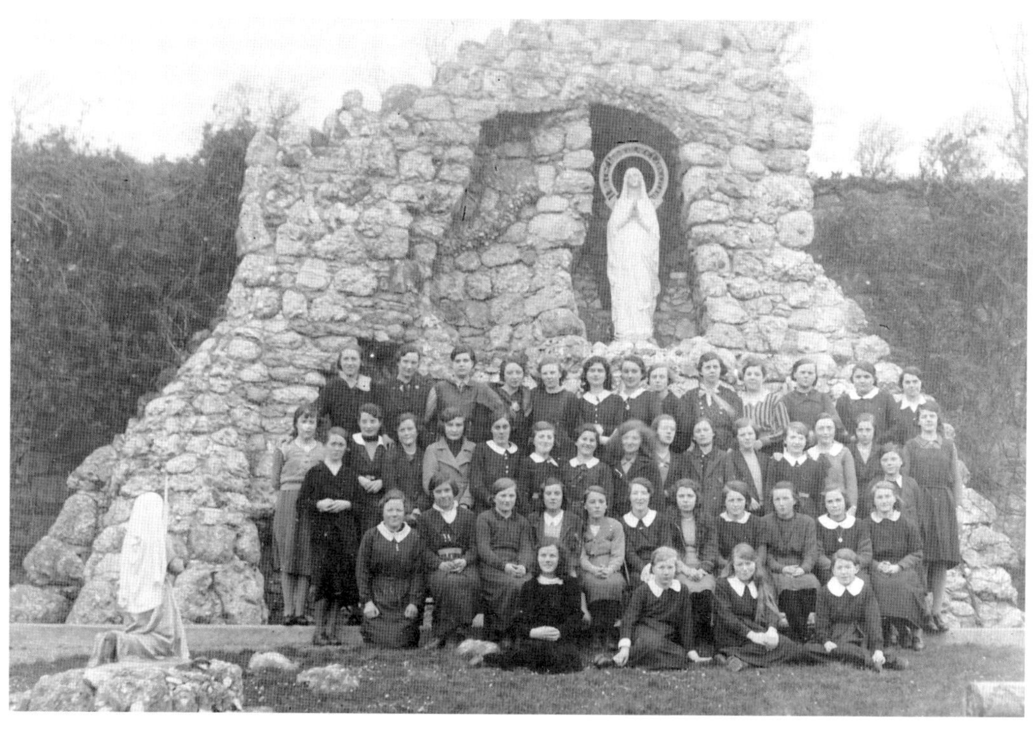

Presentation school grotto.

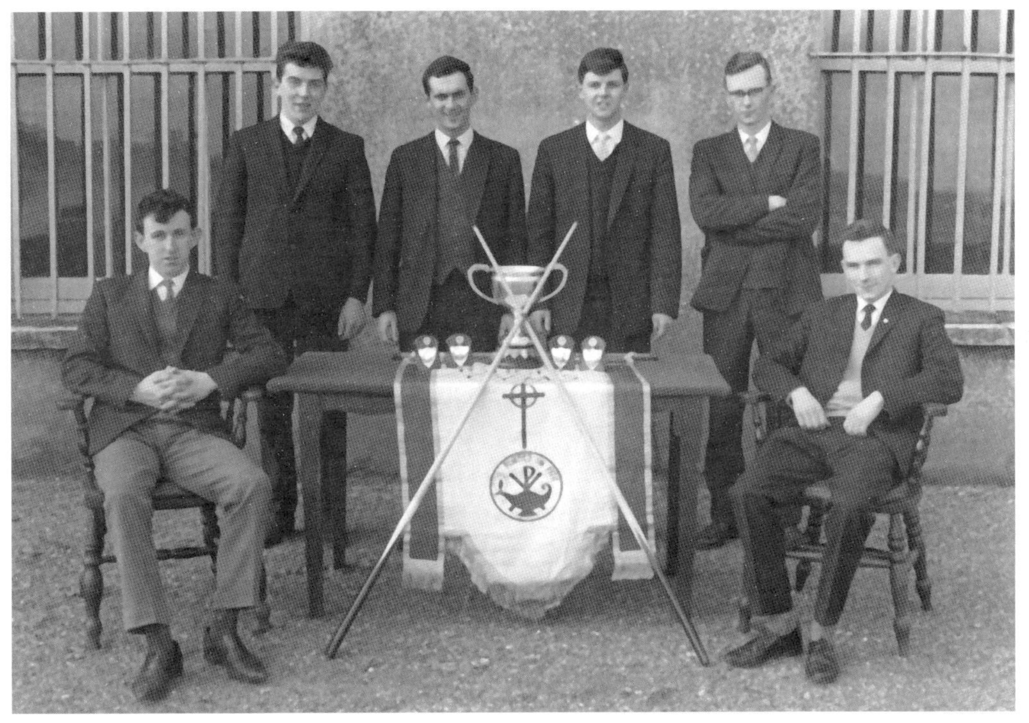

Youghal CYMS snooker prize.

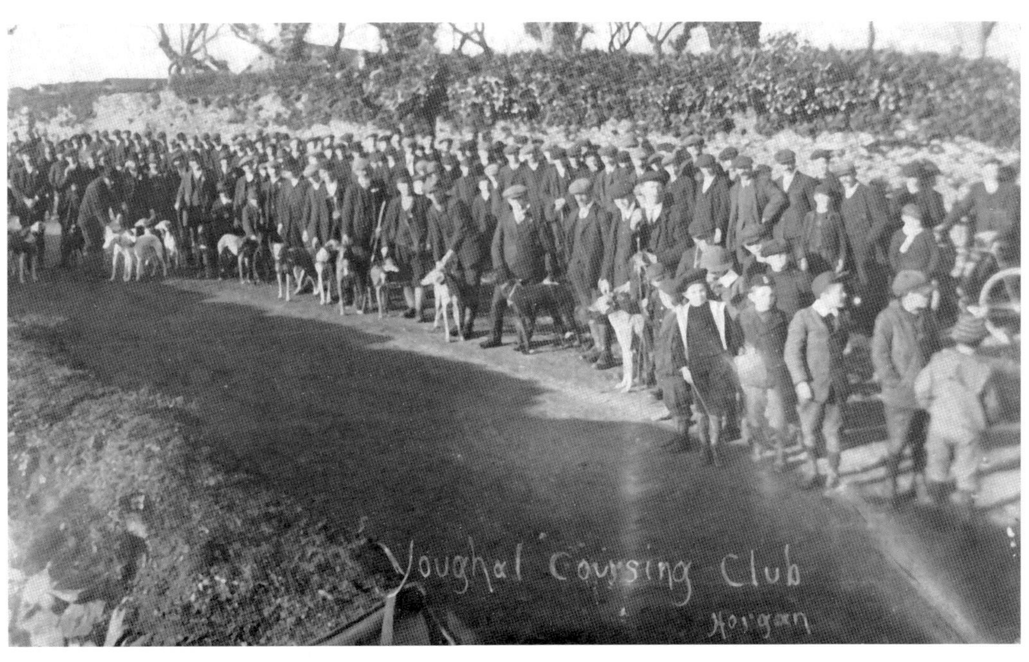

Coursing club, Youghal.

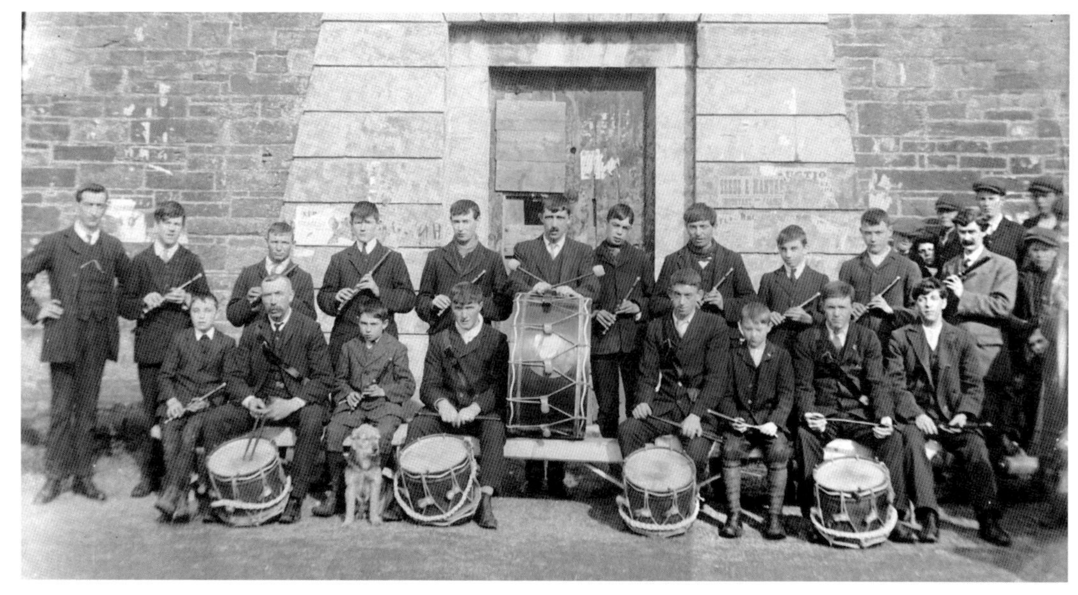

Youghal Fife and Drum Band at the old jail, Youghal.

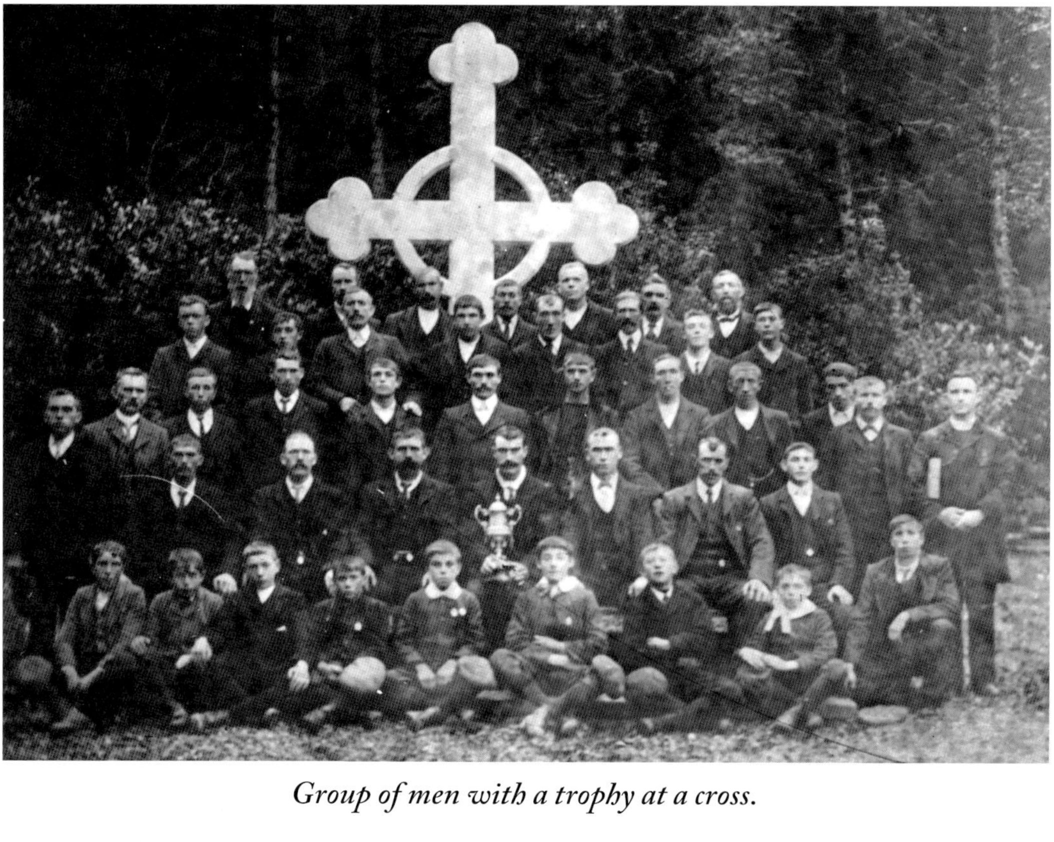

Group of men with a trophy at a cross.

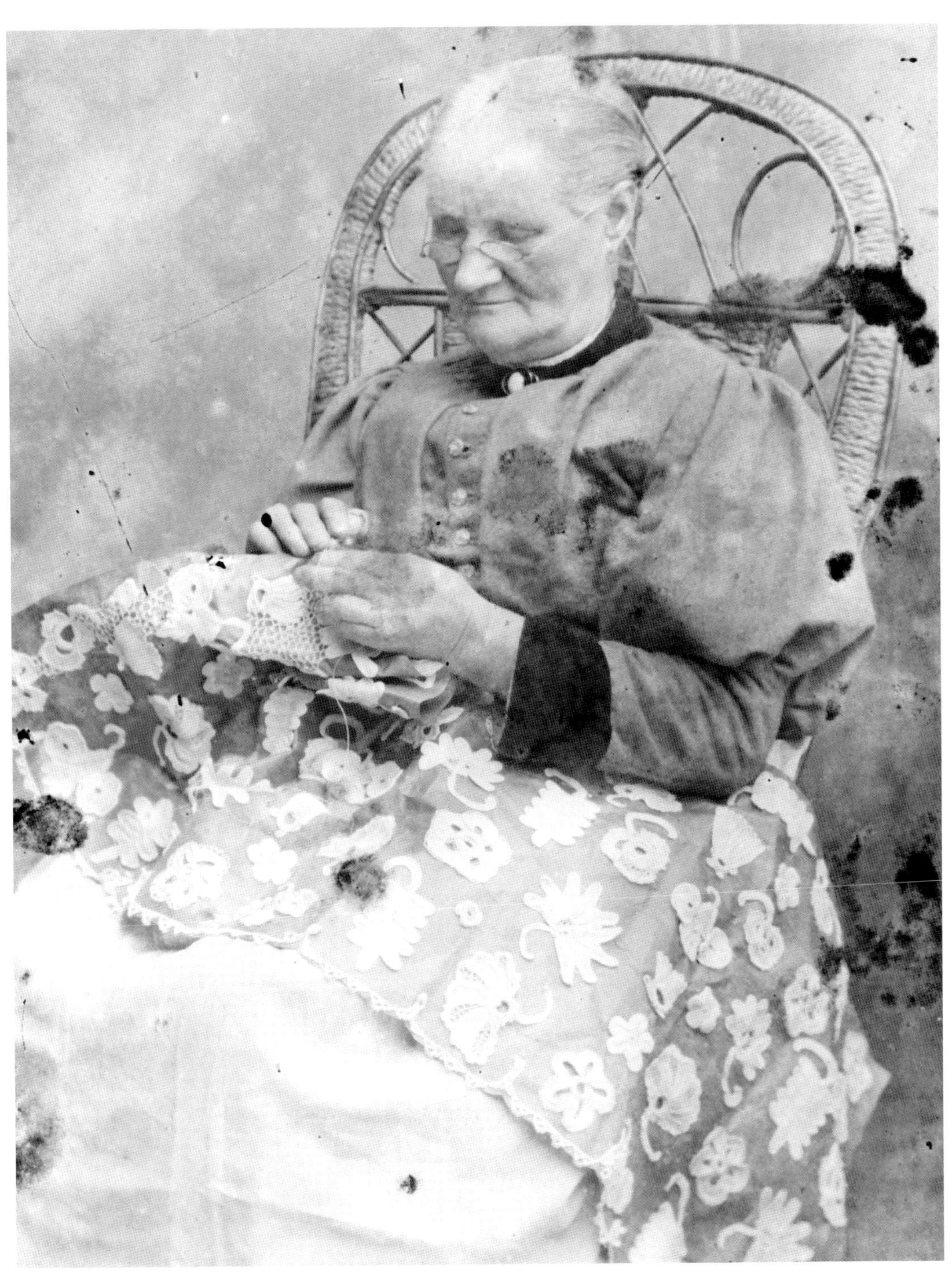

Elizabeth Horgan working on a piece of Youghal lace.

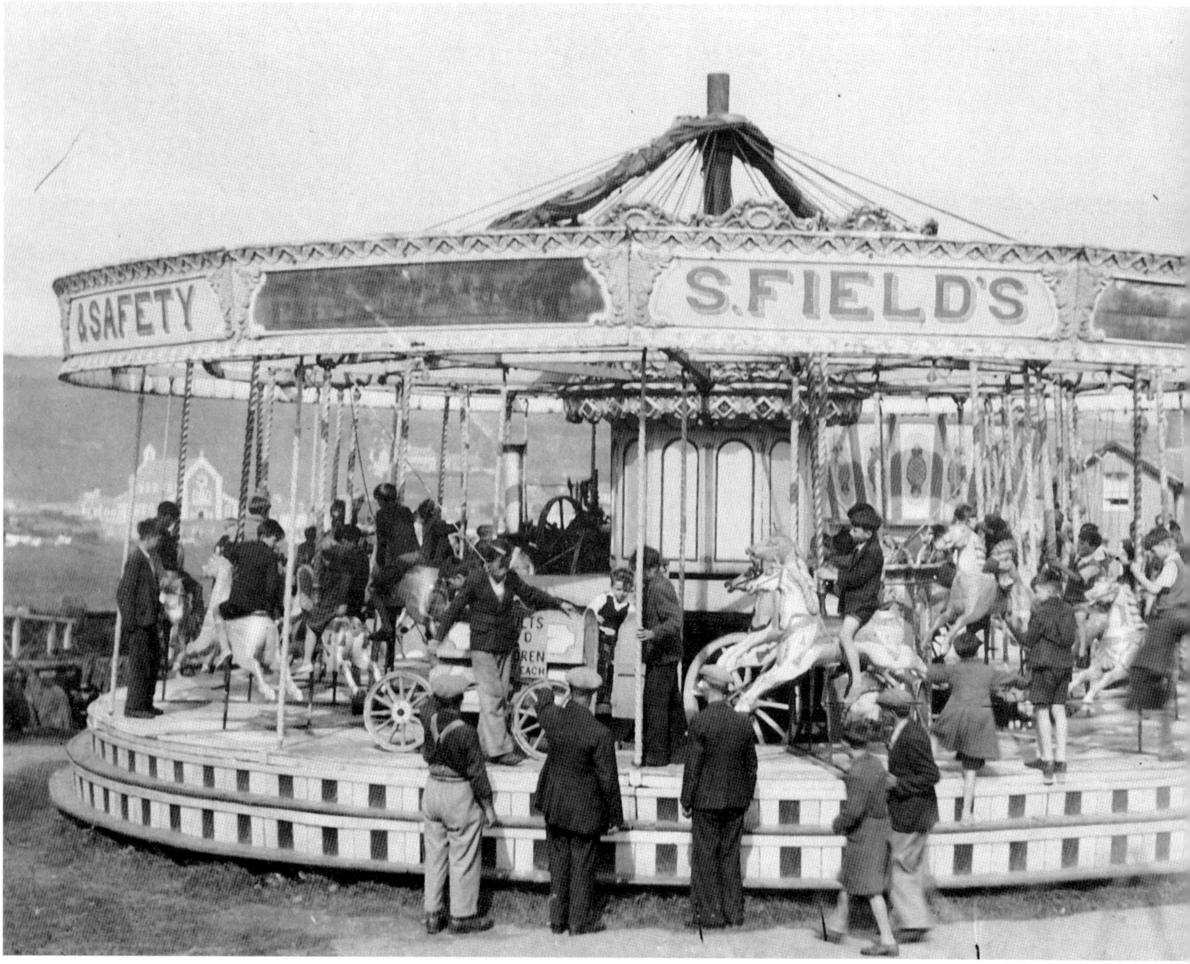

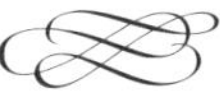

Merry-go-round at Claycastle, Youghal.

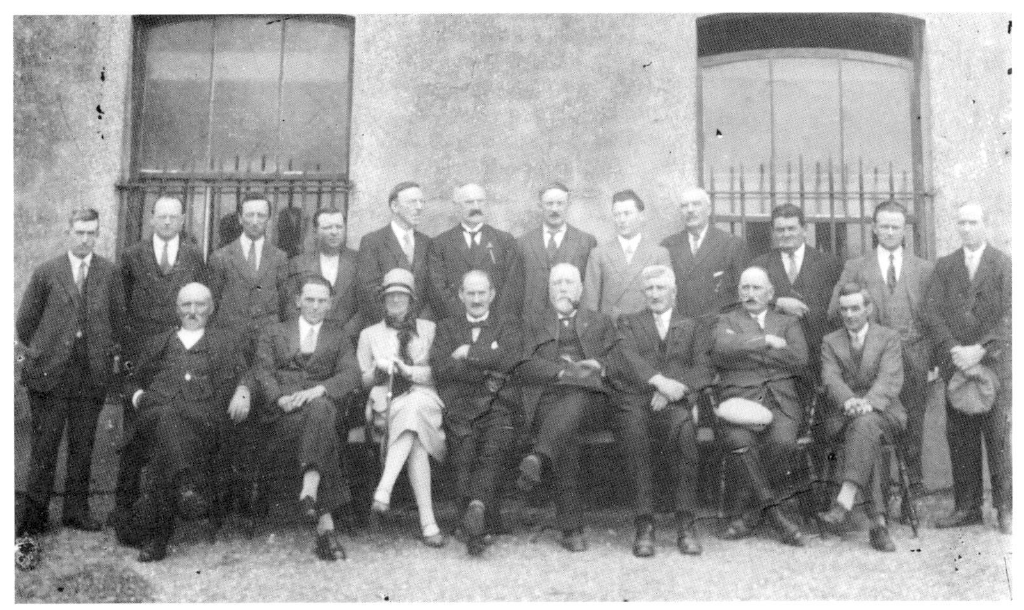

Youghal Urban District Council, 1929.

L. to R. (standing) John Kennedy, J. Fowkes, E. P. Lynch, Tom Beausang, D. J. Genihan, W. J. Broderick, M. D. Broderick, Joe Power, D. Dennehy, P. J. McMahon, E. Clancy, T. Murphy. L. to R. (Sitting) Capt. P. Dunne, P. J. O'Gorman, Mrs Susan Hurley, J. R. Smyth, MI. Whelan, P. Kenneally, John Hennessy, T. Harrington.

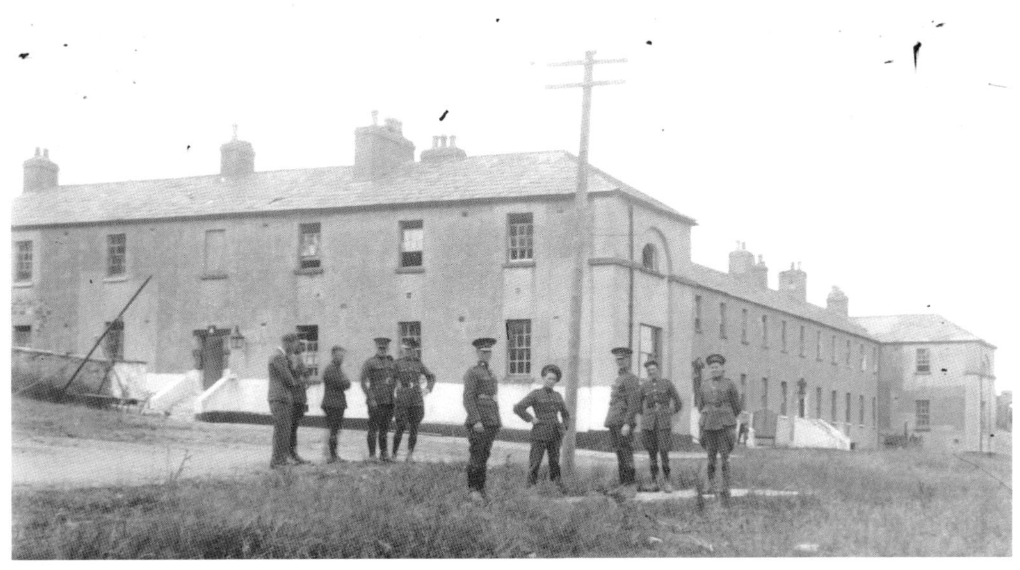

Irish army barracks after the handover to the Irish Free State.

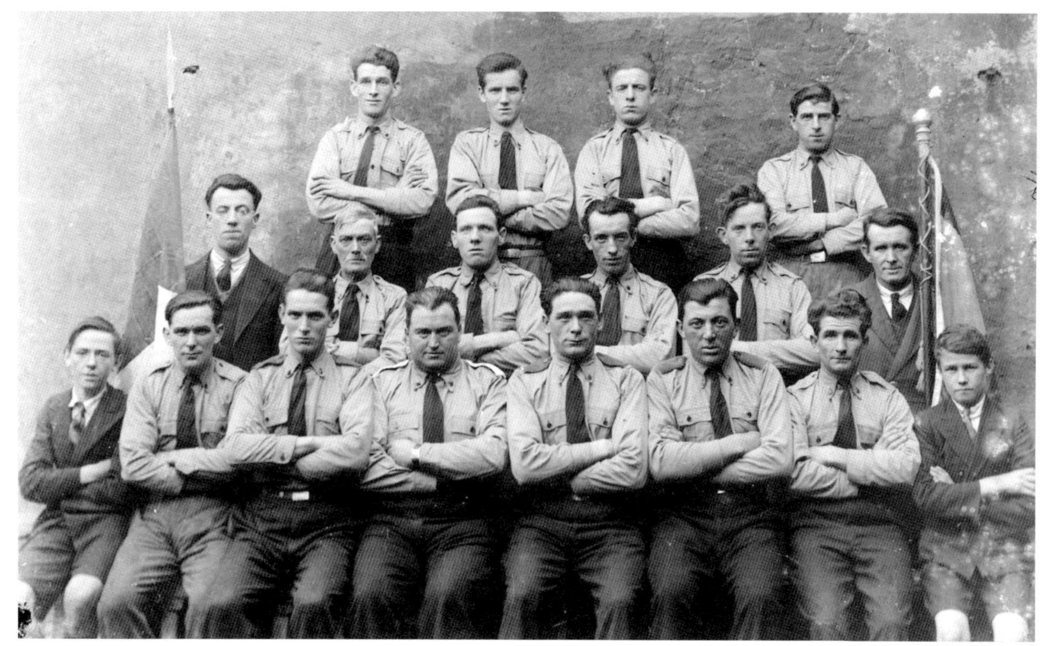

Blue Shirts from Youghal.

*The Army Comrades Association, ACA, which ultimately became the League of Youth,
but was most commonly known by their nickname, the Blue Shirts,
was a paramilitary organisation in the Irish Free State.*

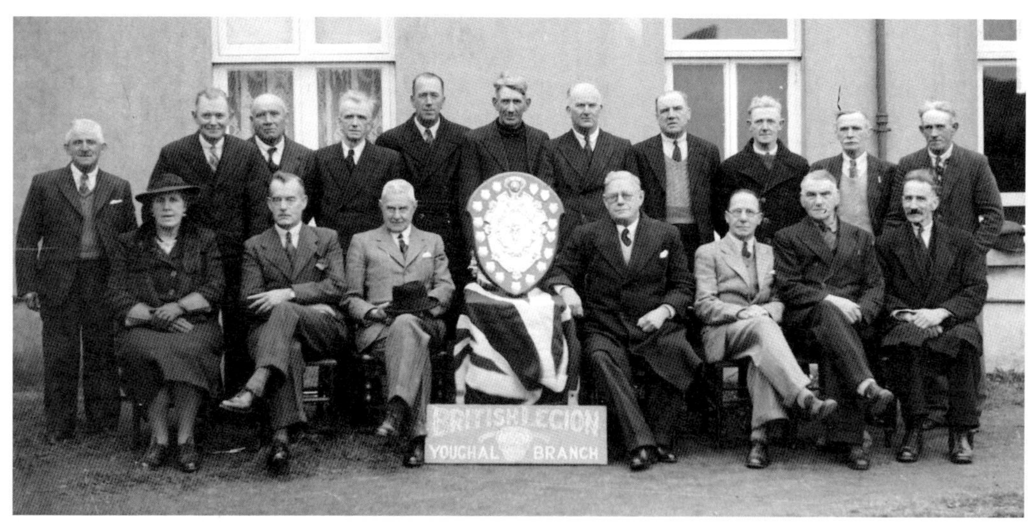

British legion, Youghal.

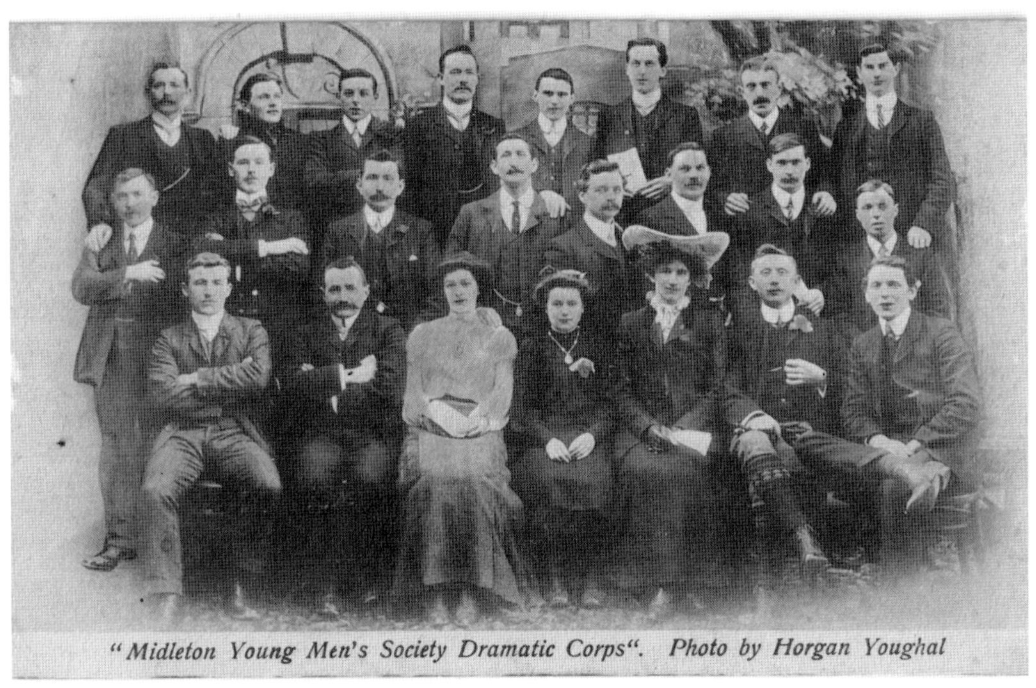

Midleton Young Men's Society dramatic corps.

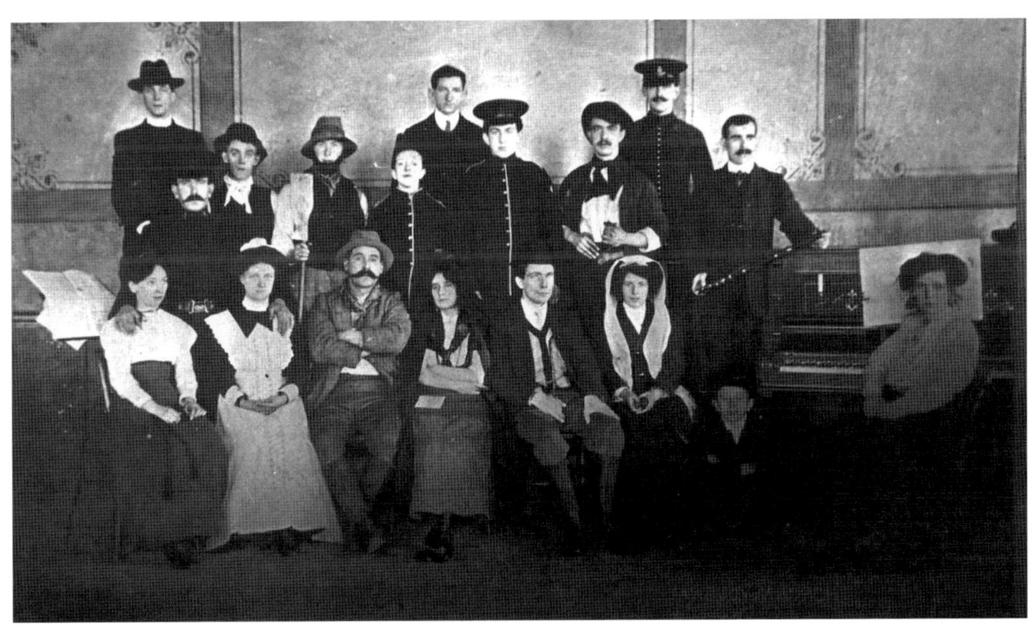

Youghal dramatic club.

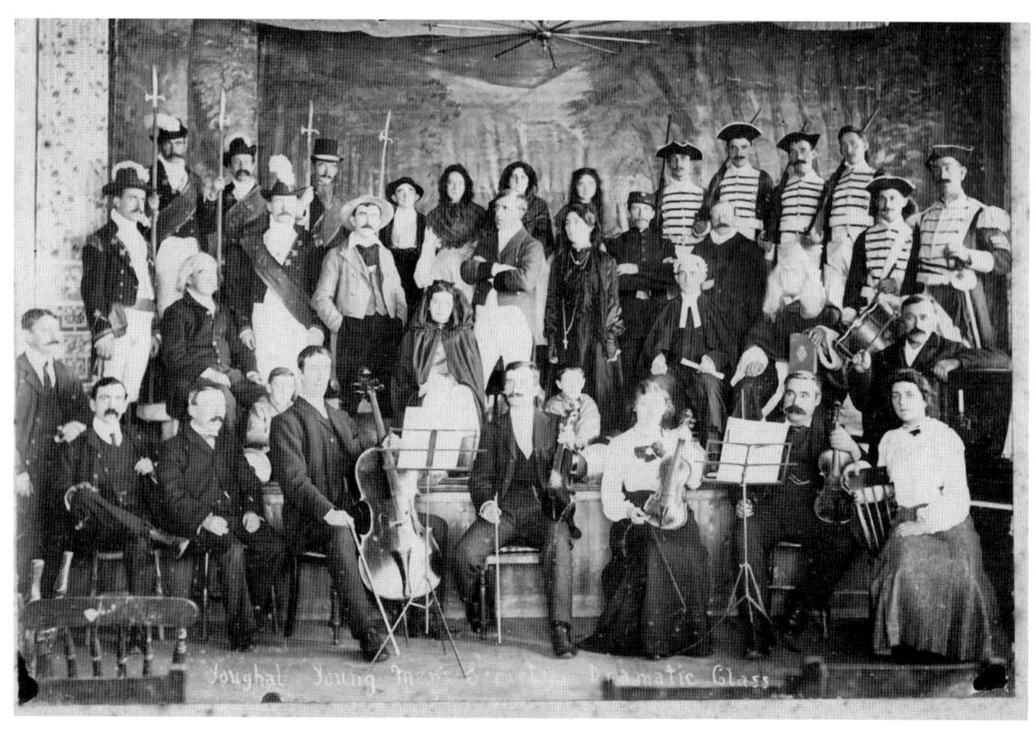

*Youghal Dramatic Society with James Horgan at the front
holding a cello that he made himself.*

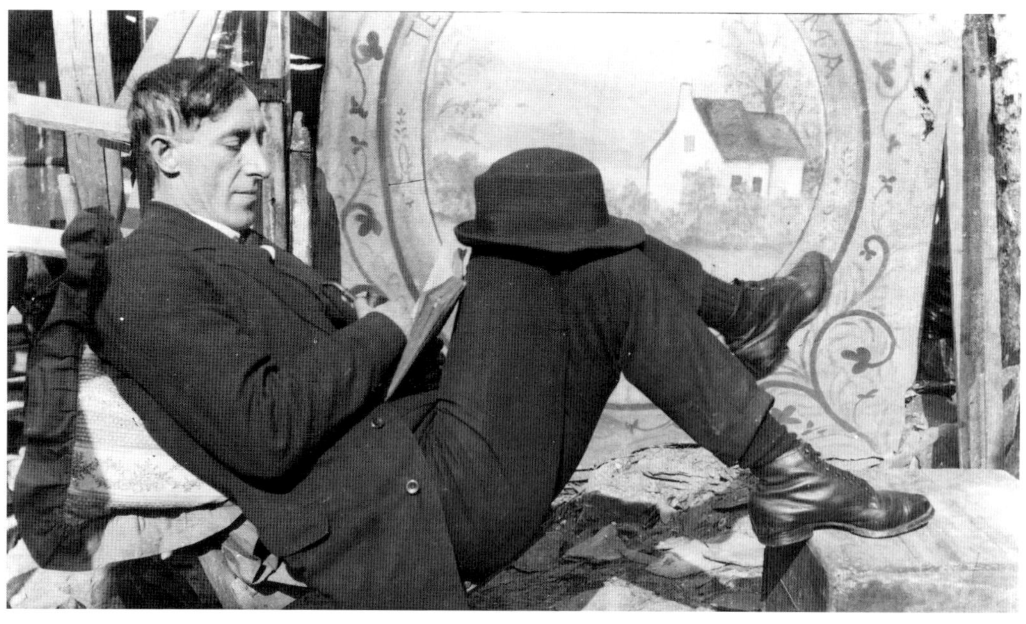

James Horgan sitting by a Horgan set or backdrop.

CAPTURING THE DRAMA OF HISTORY

THE RISING OF THE MOON

James Horgan was significantly involved in the local drama group. Apart from his musical talents, he was often appointed as set designer and painter of the scenery on stage, a talent he used in his photography and later creative endeavours. *The Rising of the Moon* by Lady Gregory was one of the plays produced by the Youghal Dramatic Society.

He painted a dark landscape with a colourful sky and a circle that was to be the moon. He dyed the circle to give it a yellowish lunar glow. He then borrowed a headlamp and battery from his motorcar. He positioned the lamp so that it shone through the coloured moon and made a moonbeam right through the hall.

The electrics were simple. As the positive wire was already connected, all you had to do was connect the negative wire to the battery with a 'crocodile clip'. Unfortunately, it would cause a spark, and exaggerated by the darkness backstage, it was startling to an audience who were unfamiliar with electricity at the time. A stagehand was appointed to make the connection to send a moonbeam down the hall on cue: '… behold the rising of the moon'.

As the dramatic moment drew nearer for the stage hand, the fear of the spark grew to panic. In the end, they couldn't do it and instead, they set fire to a newspaper and stuck it behind the moon.

The audience could see the hand and the burning paper and laughed, spoiling the flow of the drama. The stagehand tried to put out the fire by shaking the newspaper but this only spread the fire backstage and the actors joined in the efforts to extinguish the flames by stomping on the stage. The audience roared with laughter and were cheering enjoying the impromptu action.

The following night the play was performed without a hitch to the delight of the actors. However, the audience was disappointed. One of the actors asked a member of the audience why, and his response was 'the play was fine, but it lacked the excitement of the night before'.

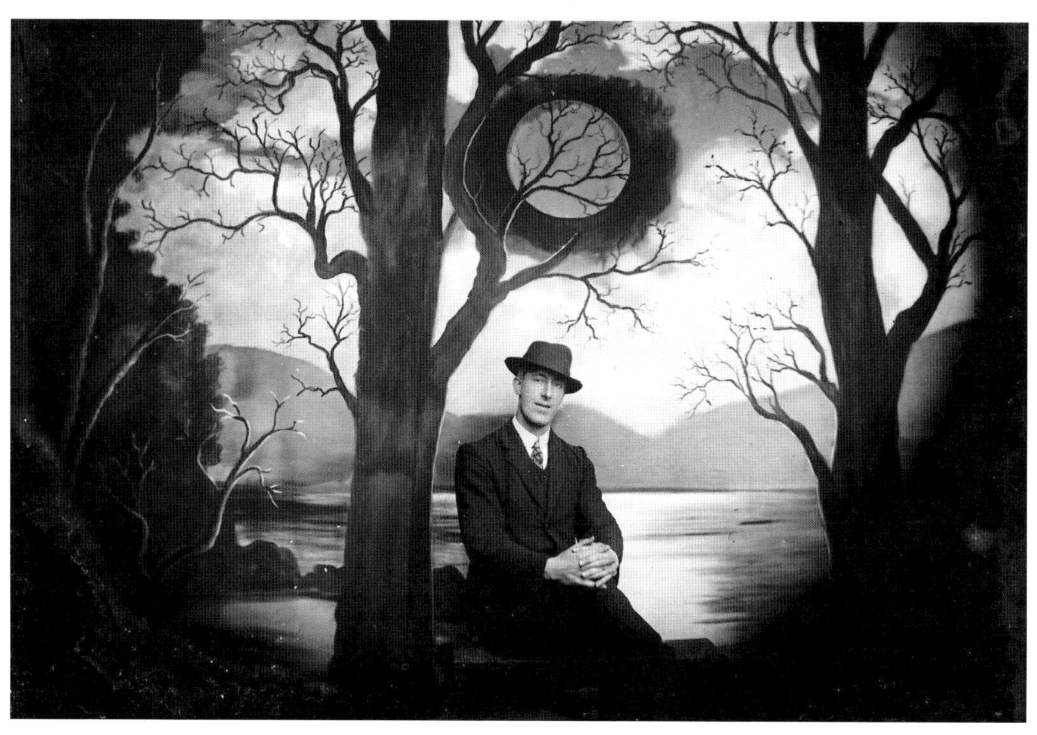

James in front of **The Rising of the Moon** *set.*

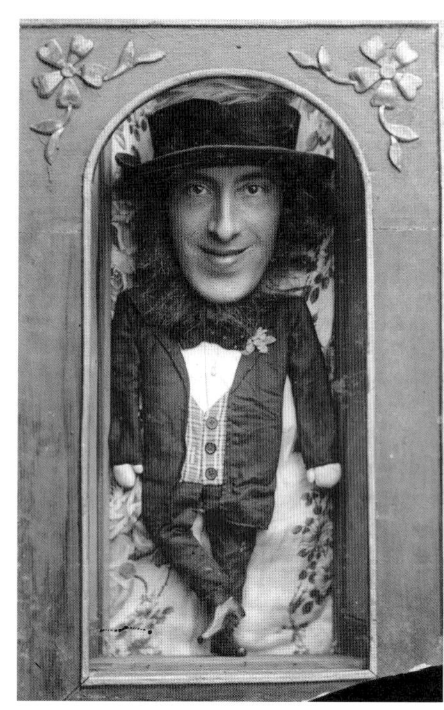

*James photographed in
a leprechaun stand in board.*

The brothers continued to capture events at a local level, as news reporters or social historians. These events often had national or international relevance.

MYRTLE GROVE WAS HOME to Sir Walter Raleigh when he was mayor of Youghal, but in this photograph, it is home to Sir Henry Arthur Blake, who retired here after his time as a governor to the Bahamas, Jamacia and Hong Kong. Both he and his wife, Lady Edith Blake, are buried on the grounds of Myrtle Grove.

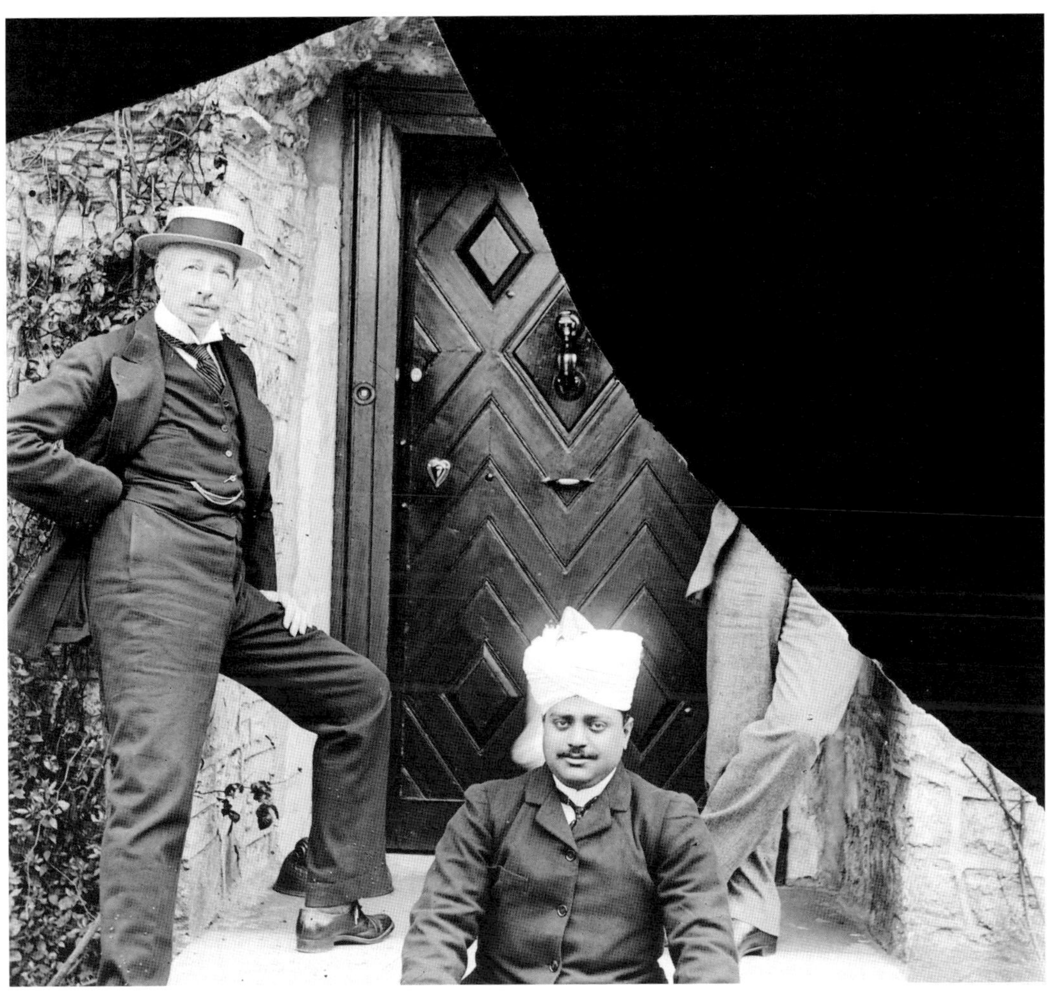

*The Maharaja of Sarawak photographed at Myrtle Grove in Youghal
with a member of the Blake family to the left.
This is what remains of the glass plate negative.*

Kam Tin is a region in China that is made up of several villages. It lies in what the British called the New Territories and formed part of Hong Kong while leased to Britain. When the British began the occupation of the New Territories in 1899, the residents of Kam Tin had the most organised resistance movement. The ancient walls of the village were blasted on each side of the gates to reprimand their resistance. In an act of submission, the villagers carried the gates to Flag Staff Hill (Tai Po).

Sir Henry Arthur Blake was the British colonial administrator and governor of Hong Kong from 1898 to 1903. He admired the gates and acquired them for himself. When Blake retired to Myrtle Grove in Youghal with his wife, Lady Edith Blake, the gates of Kam Tin were transported there where they hung until the Tang Clan petitioned for their return in 1924.

Once again the Horgans photographed this momentous and progressive example of repatriation of colonial artefacts. The photograph depicts a representative from Hong Kong who travelled to Youghal to oversee the removal of the gates and their safe return to Kam Tin where they hang to this day.

On 26 May 1925, there was a huge ceremony for the return of the revered gates which was deemed a successful public relations exercise by the Hong Kong government. The *Hong Kong Telegraph* noted that 'there has perhaps been no incident in the whole history of Hong Kong and of the New Territories which has more eloquently and genuinely revealed the Government's friendly feeling and sympathy towards the Chinese of the New Territories'.

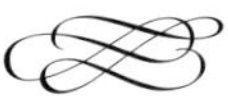

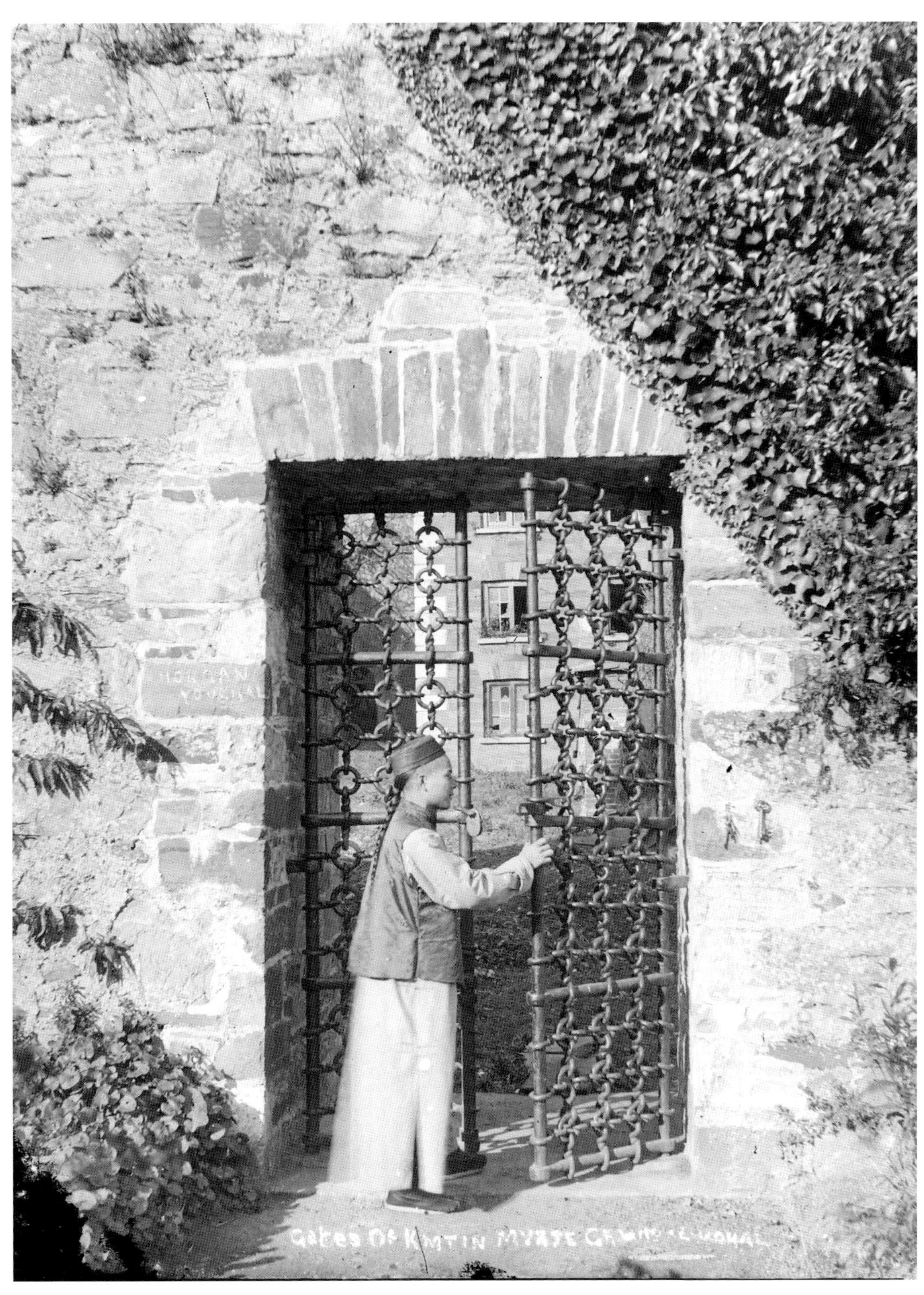

Gates of Kam Tin hanging at Myrtle Grove in Youghal.

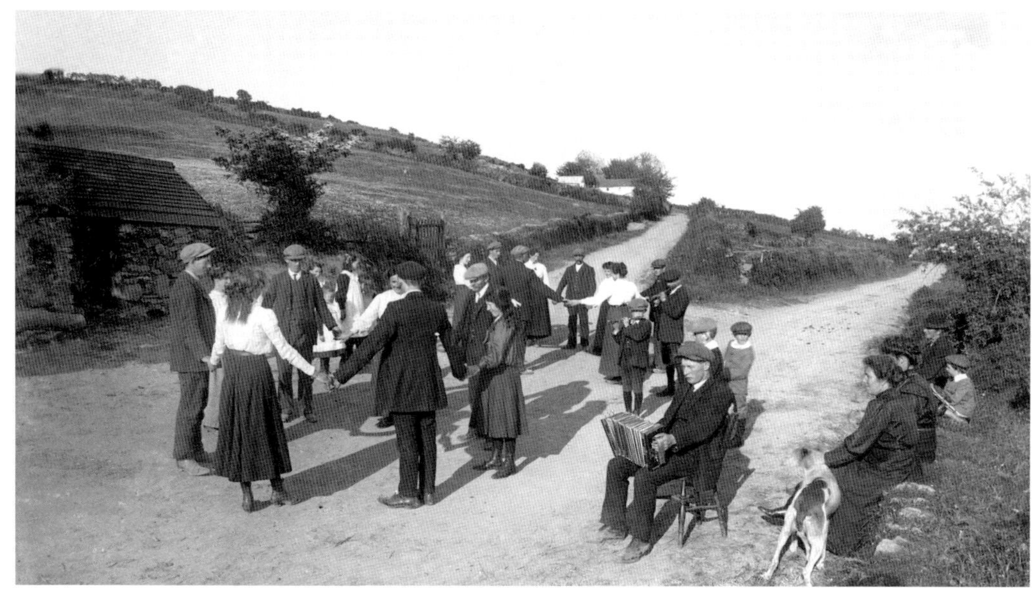

The photograph above was taken in Knockmonlea between Youghal and Killeagh. Several of the dancers, including the Foley family, were affiliated with nationalist organisations and had active roles in the Easter Rising of 1916. The Foleys deeply resented British occupation, possibly having been evicted from the Ponsonby Estate in 1889 during the Land Wars. Various family members were active in the Republican Brotherhood, the Irish Volunteers and Cumann na mBan.

The family ran the Foley Typewriting Trading Company in Dublin and the offices were used as a pre-Rising meeting place by the rebels. Two of the dancers Bríd and her sister Maggie played for Craobh an Chéitinnigh against Cúchulainns in the first official camogie match, in Navan on 17 July 1904.

The people in the photograph were identified by Manus O'Brien:

*R. to L.: Michael Foley, Abina 'Gobnait' Foley (Later O'Brien),
possibly John Foley, Maggie Mountaine, Timothy 'Tadhg' Foley, Jack Smith,
Willie Foley, Cáit/Kate Foley, Maurice Hennessy, Ellie Long, Pad Murphy,
Maggie Foley, Brigid Foley, Margaret 'Peg' Foley, Jerry Curtain.*

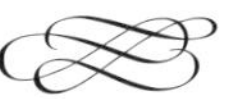

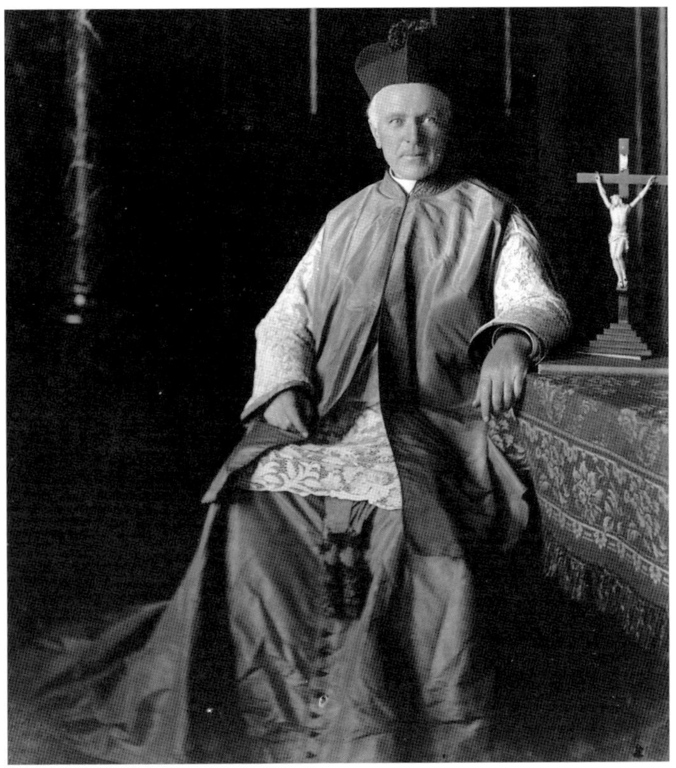

CANON DANIEL KELLER

In 1885 Daniel Keller was parish priest of Youghal and became embroiled in the land war in Ireland quite quickly. The tenants of the Ponsonby Estate just outside Youghal were the first in the country to take on the 'Plan of Campaign' and sought a rent reduction. When the reduction was refused, the Plan incorporated a trustee who was believed to be Fr Keller. He was summoned to a court hearing in Dublin and when he failed to arrive, a warrant was issued for his arrest which caused a protest in Youghal, during which a fisherman was killed. Keller was imprisoned in Kilmainham jail, with no legal grounds, and never betrayed the tenants of the Ponsonby estate. While still in jail, he was appointed a canon of St Colman's cathedral in protest against his imprisonment. He was released after two months. He was a man of strong principles and his motivation for supporting the Plan had been sympathy for the tenants. He remained in Youghal until his death in 1922.

As the First World War raged, the Horgan Brothers photographed many young Youghal men who went to fight under the banner of the British army as well as the volunteer camps in Youghal. Of the 154 local men who served, many never came home. A memorial to all who fought and died can be found in the Chapel of Remembrance in St Mary's collegiate church in Youghal.

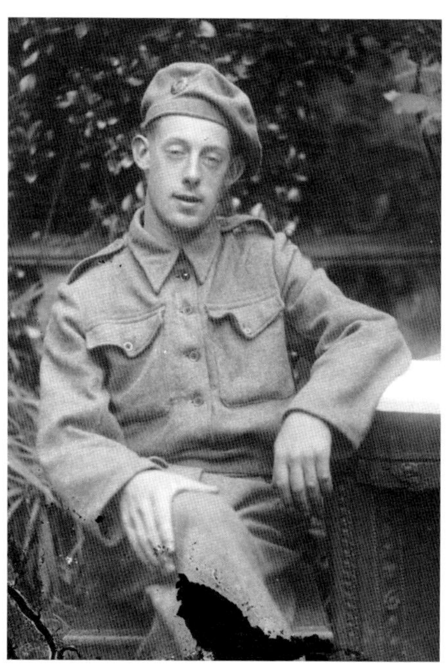

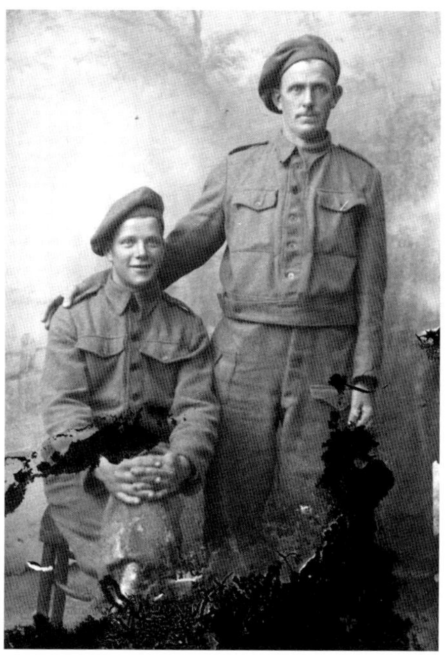

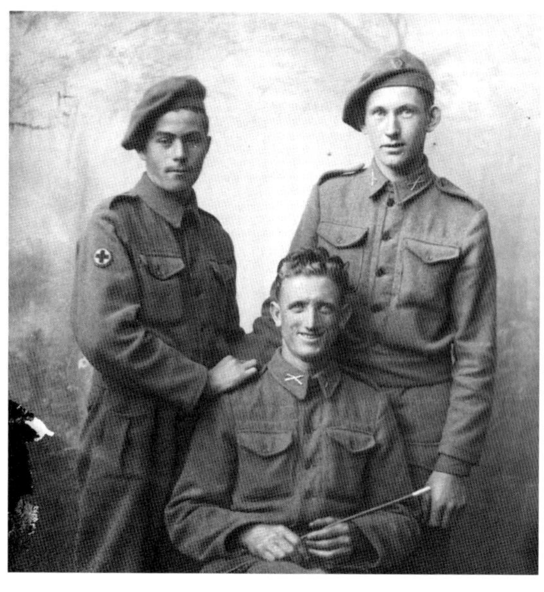

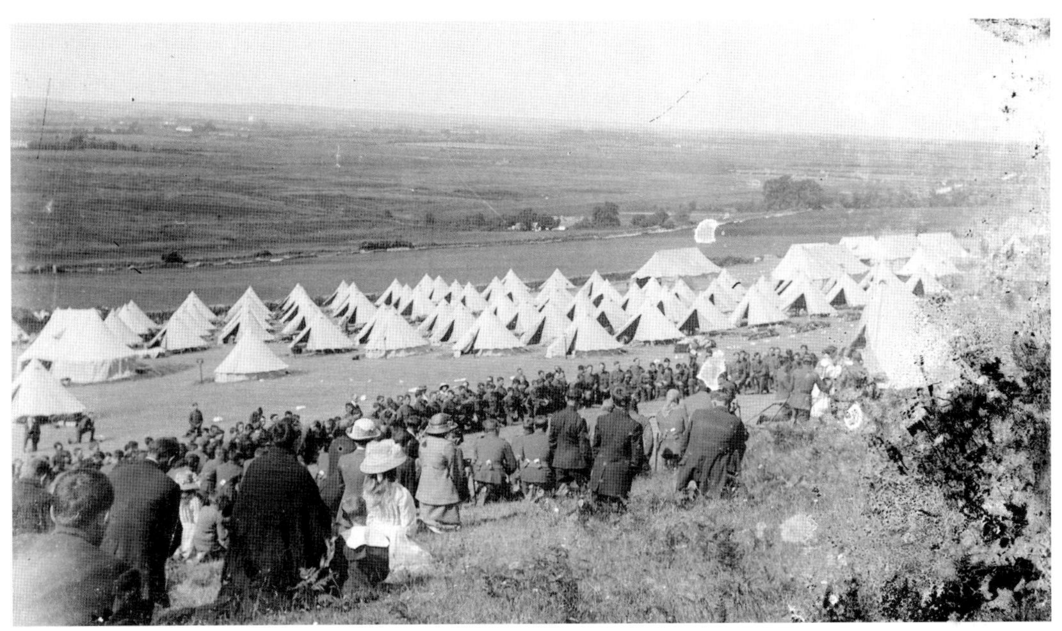

First World War Volunteer camp at Summerfield in Youghal.

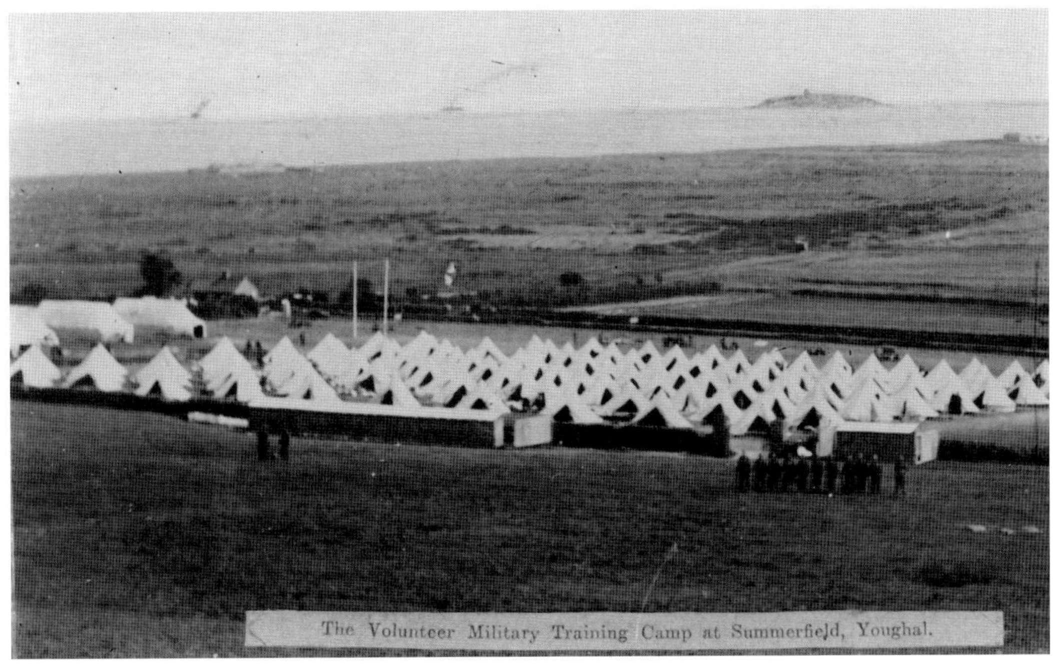

First World War Volunteer camp with Capel Island in the background.

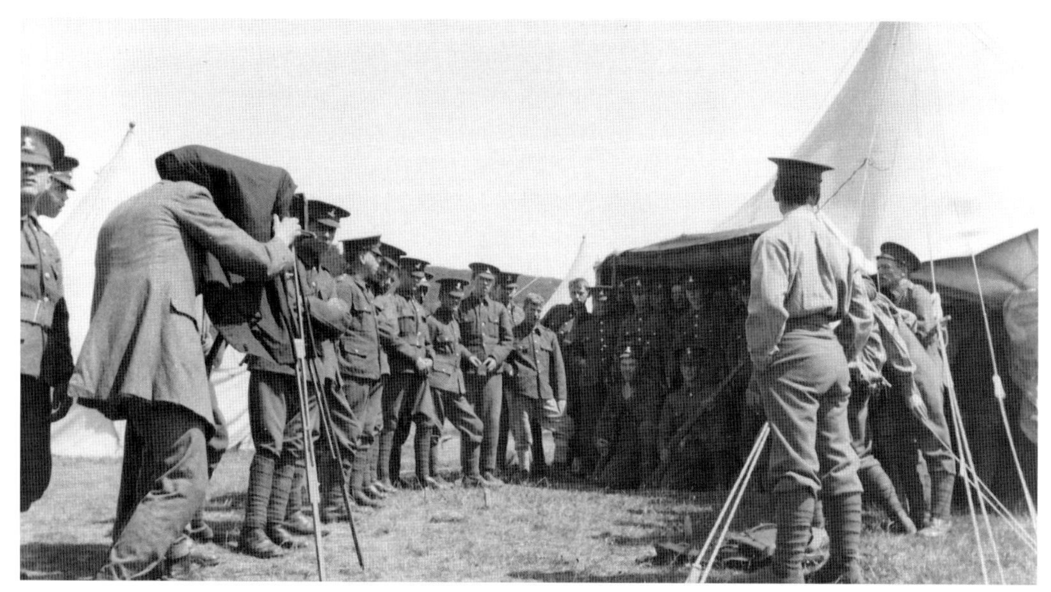

A rare photograph of the photographer taking a picture at the Royal Dublin Fusiliers camp in Youghal.

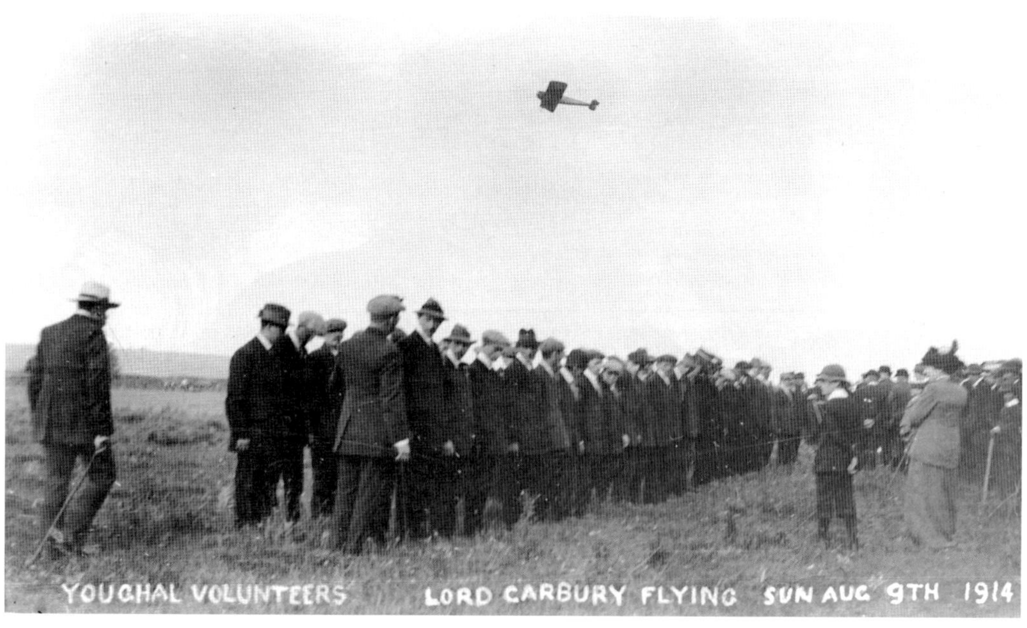

John Freke Evans, 10th Lord Carbery, a keen aviator, flew over a group of Youghal First World War Volunteers on Sunday, 9 August 1914.

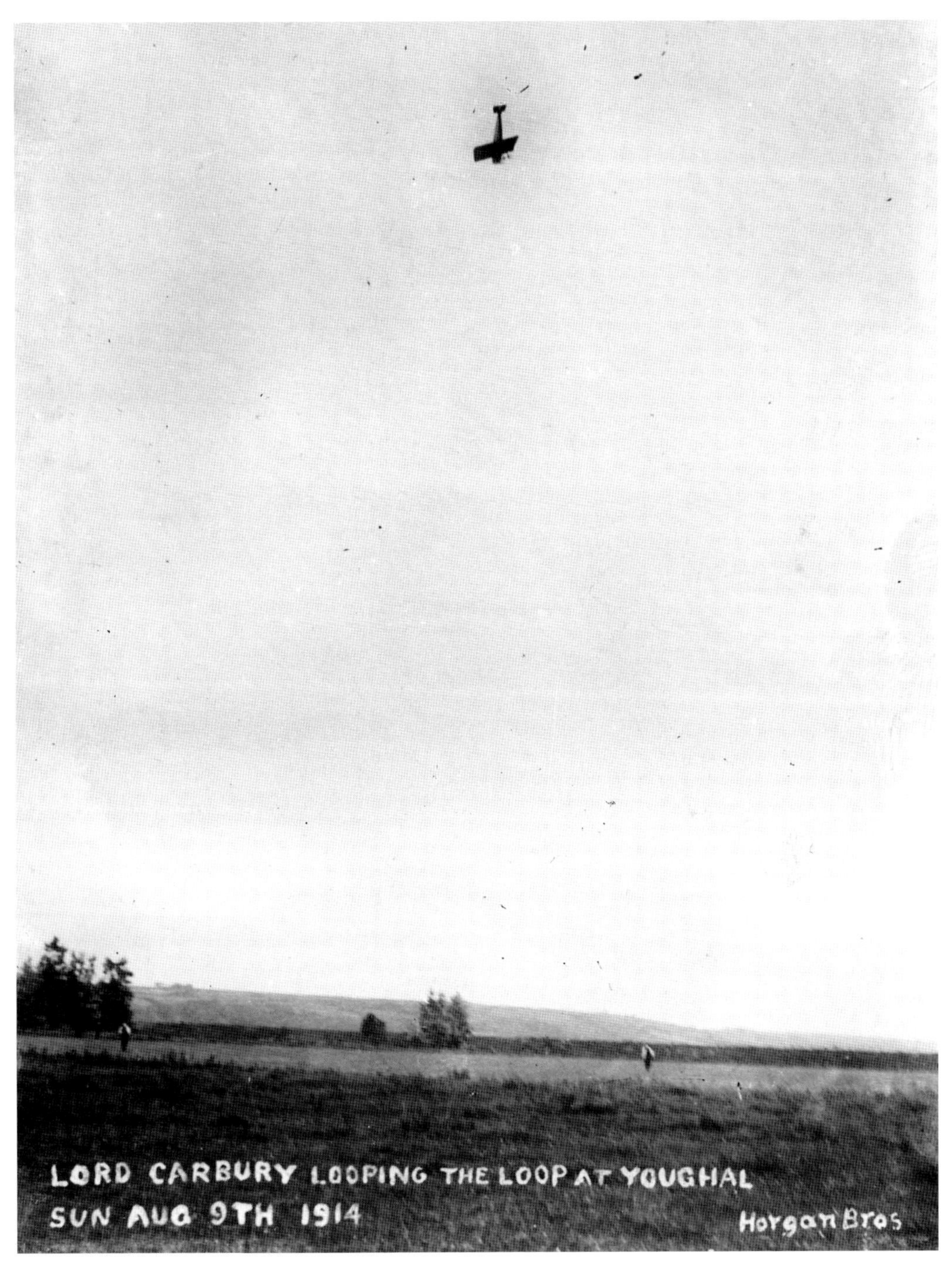

Lord Carbery looping the loop at Youghal.

*B*OMBING THE *Y*OUGHAL *QUAYS BY THE* **IRA** *IN 1922* *DURING THE* *C*IVIL *W*AR

The Civil War in Ireland erupted between those who accepted the 1921 Treaty and those who opposed it. The barracks in Youghal was taken over by anti-Treaty forces who then bombed the quays in the town to prevent the landing of troops.

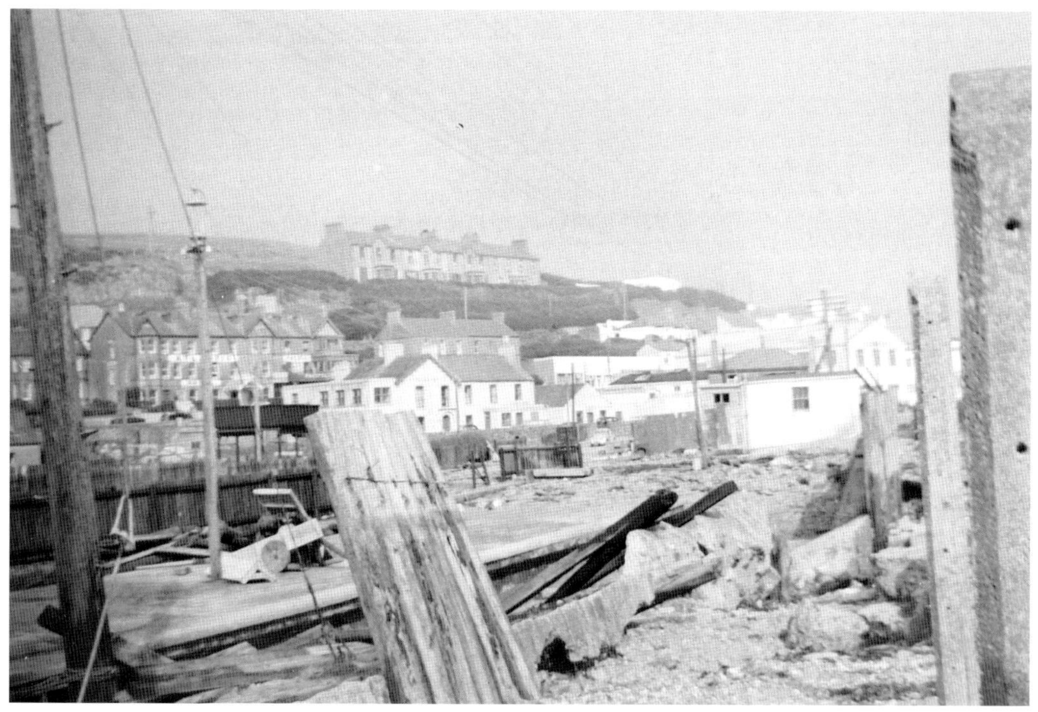

Across top: *The double slips at Youghal reduced to rubble when bombed during the Civil War.*

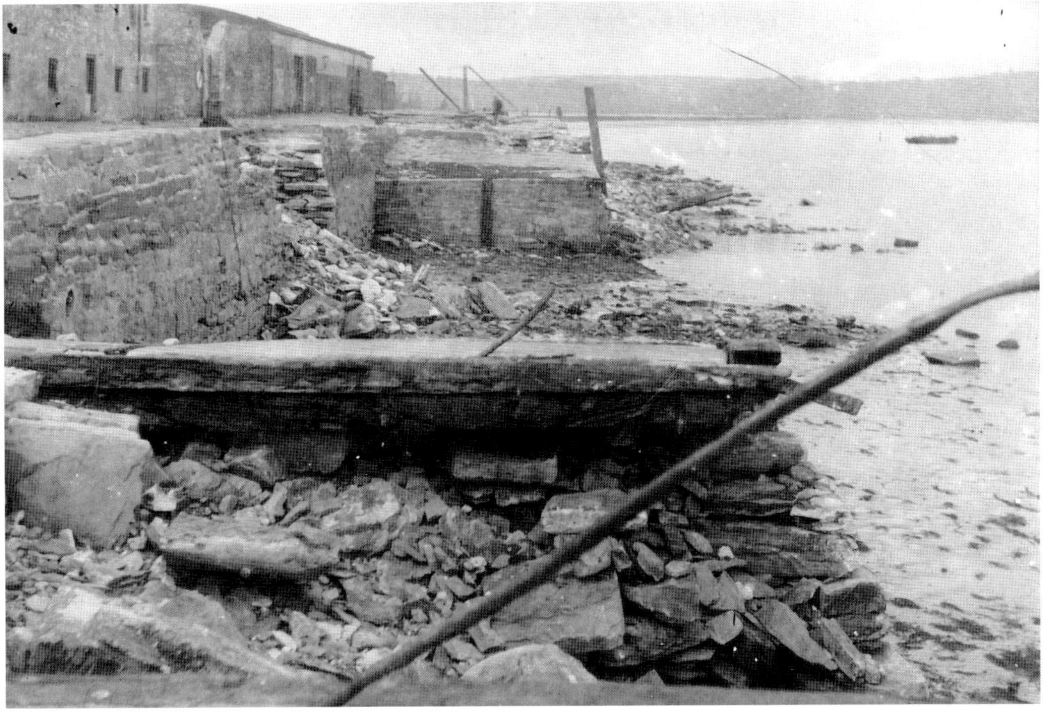

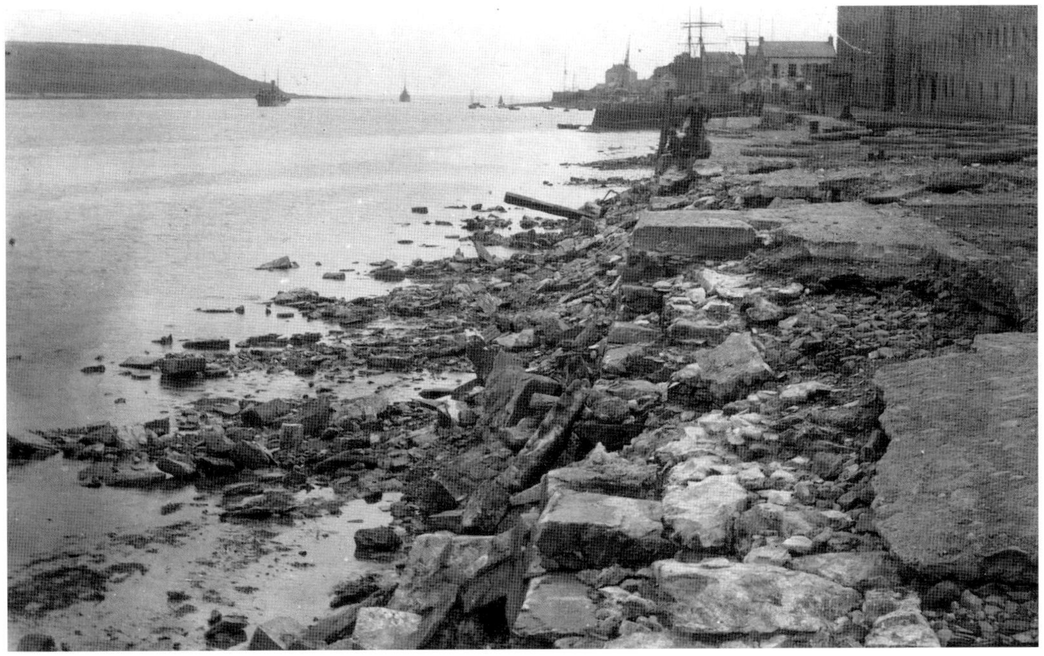

The quays bombed, with tall ships in the distance.

Philip Horgan

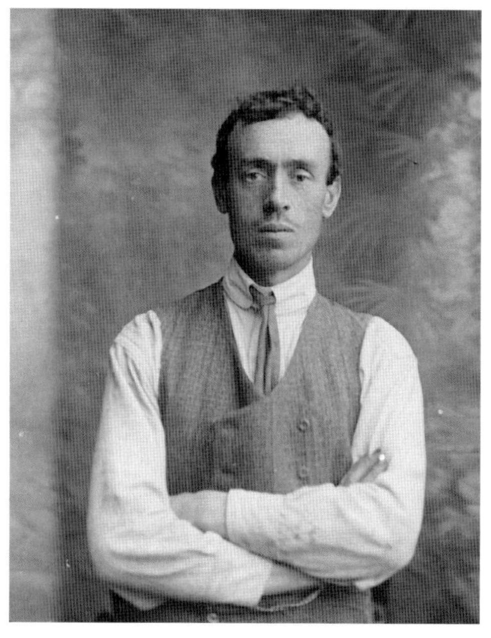

Philip was the youngest of the Horgan Brothers. Despite being an accomplished photographer with a lucrative business, photography was not generally recognised as a stable source of income. Echoes of the famine resonated loudly from the previous generation, and land was seen as the best form of financial security. The land was permanent.

When Philip fell in love with a Waterford lady, her family, it is thought, would not permit them to marry as his job as a photographer was not a stable enough income. Philip decided to join the British army, which would have a guaranteed income for life, and even if the worst were to happen, a pension would be provided to a spouse.

Phil and his friend were sent on training manoeuvres to Scotland. On the first day, Phil witnessed his friend being accidentally shot in the head and he passed out on the spot. Worse was to follow, the next morning he passed out again.

The army knew Phil had to go, so the authorities devised a plan. They sent Phil with a 'message' to Cardiff in the hope that he would desert. He took the hint and travelled on a coal boat back to Youghal, throwing his uniform overboard into the Irish Sea during the night.

His desertion was reported in the *Dungarvan News*. Philip remained a bachelor for the rest of his life.

MARITIME INTERESTS

The Horgan brothers were surrounded by water. The immense Blackwater River flows from County Waterford into Youghal as it joins the Atlantic. The last of the tributaries is the Tourig River, which divides County Cork and Waterford on the outskirts of Youghal. As a result, the town was full of working and touring boats. Their homes were just across from the RNLI lifeboat station on The Mall.

The Urban District Council ferry ran from Ferrypoint at the tip of the sand bar in County Waterford, to the quayside in Youghal. Schooners like the *Kathleen* and *May* & the *De Wadden* would bring their cargo up and down river, as well as paddle steamers, such as *Dartmouth Castle*, and pleasure boats as far as Cappoquin. The *De Wadden* was the last of the large steamers to make the journey up the Blackwater before the construction of the new bridge in 1958.

The brothers documented the activities of these vessels and those who travelled aboard them. However, mother nature often intervened, and vessels were often shipwrecked. The brothers captured these tragedies also, along with the triumph of human endeavour at the worst of times.

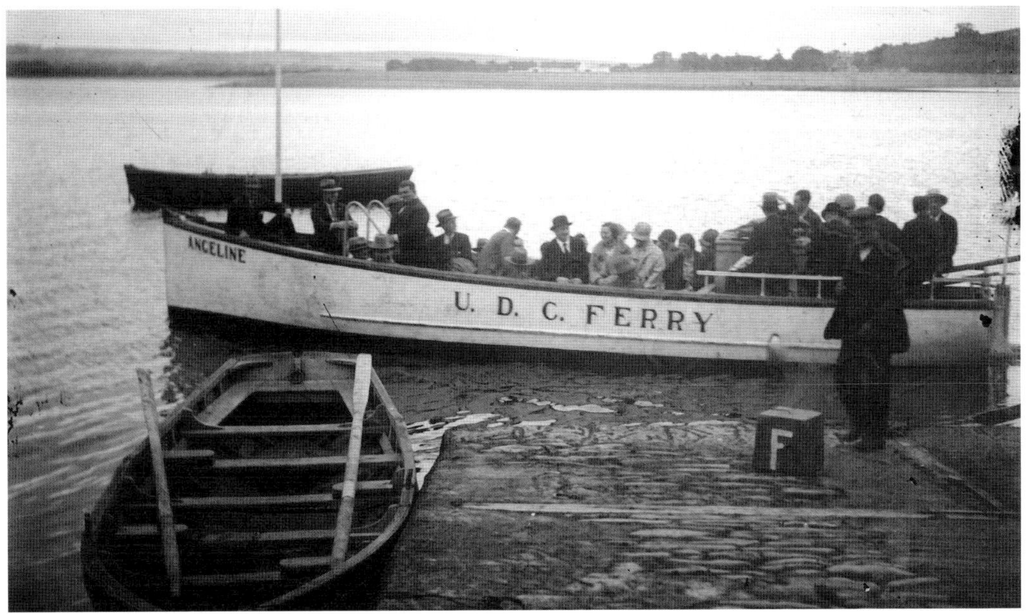

Youghal Urban District Council ferry at the slip in Youghal.

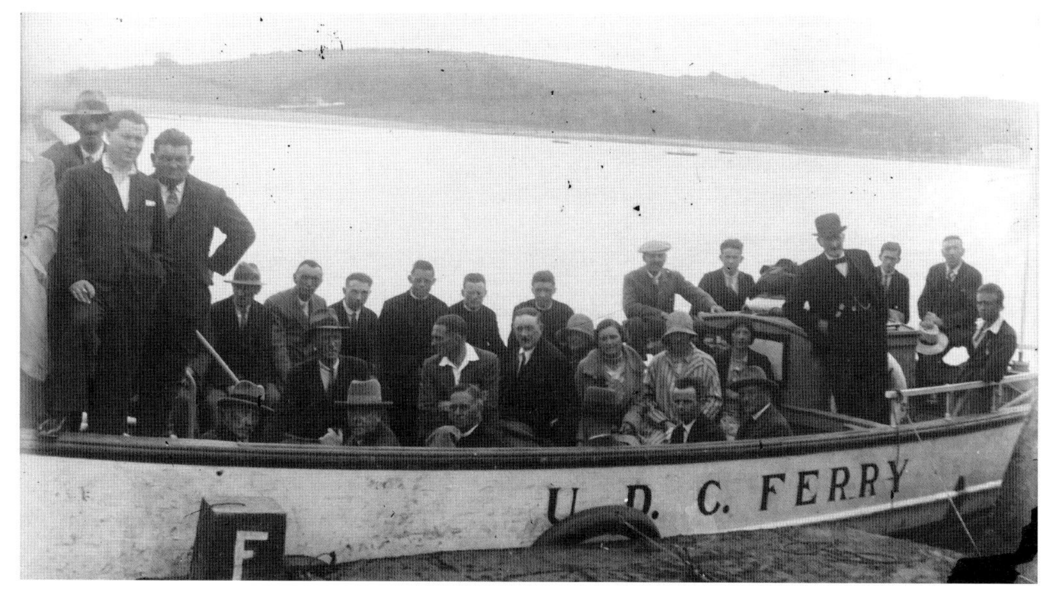

A group of people travelling on the Youghal to Ferry Point ferry.

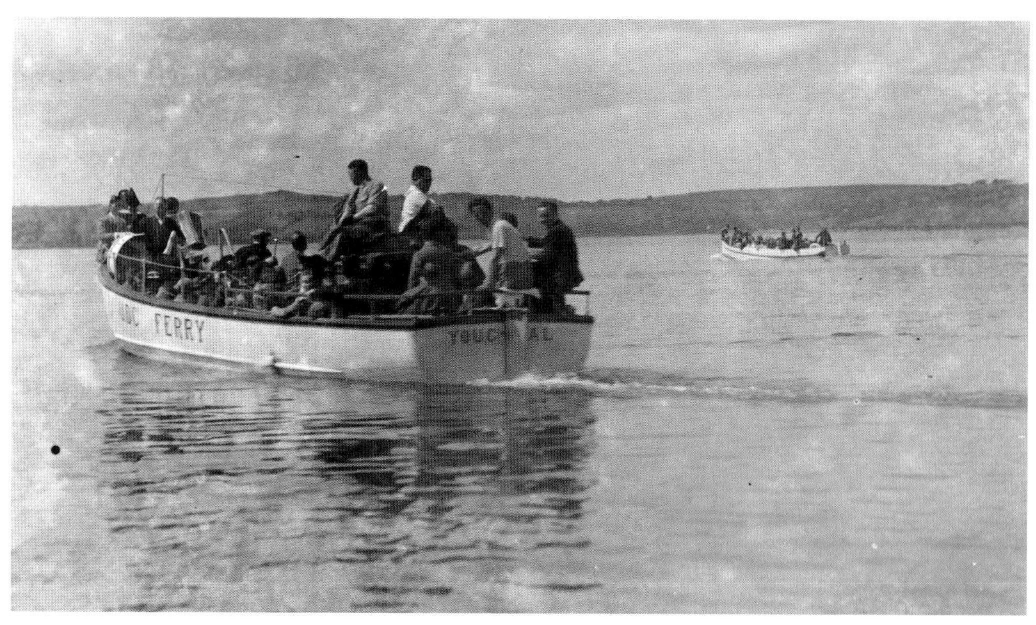

Youghal UDC Ferry on the Blackwater.

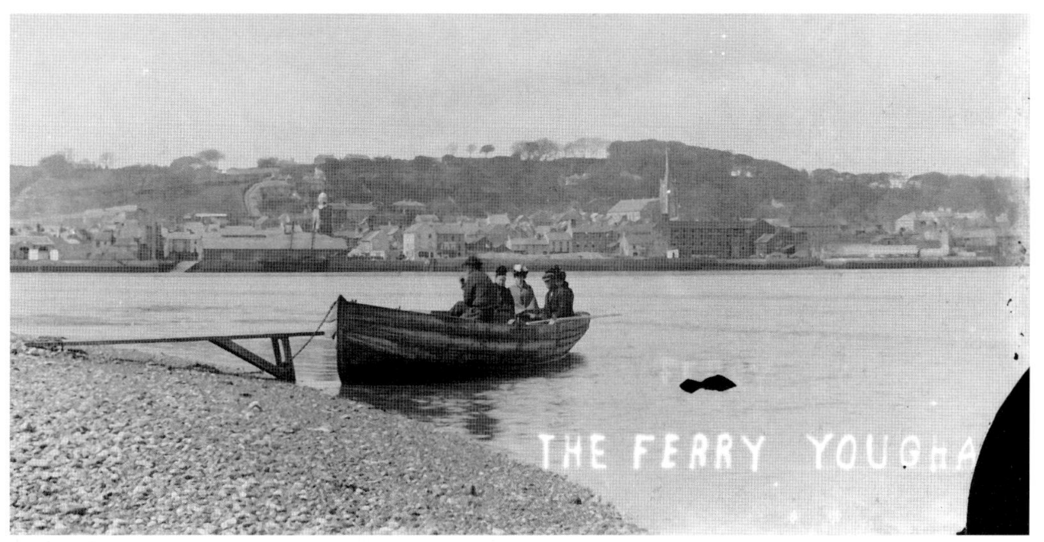

The ferry at Ferry Point near Monatray.

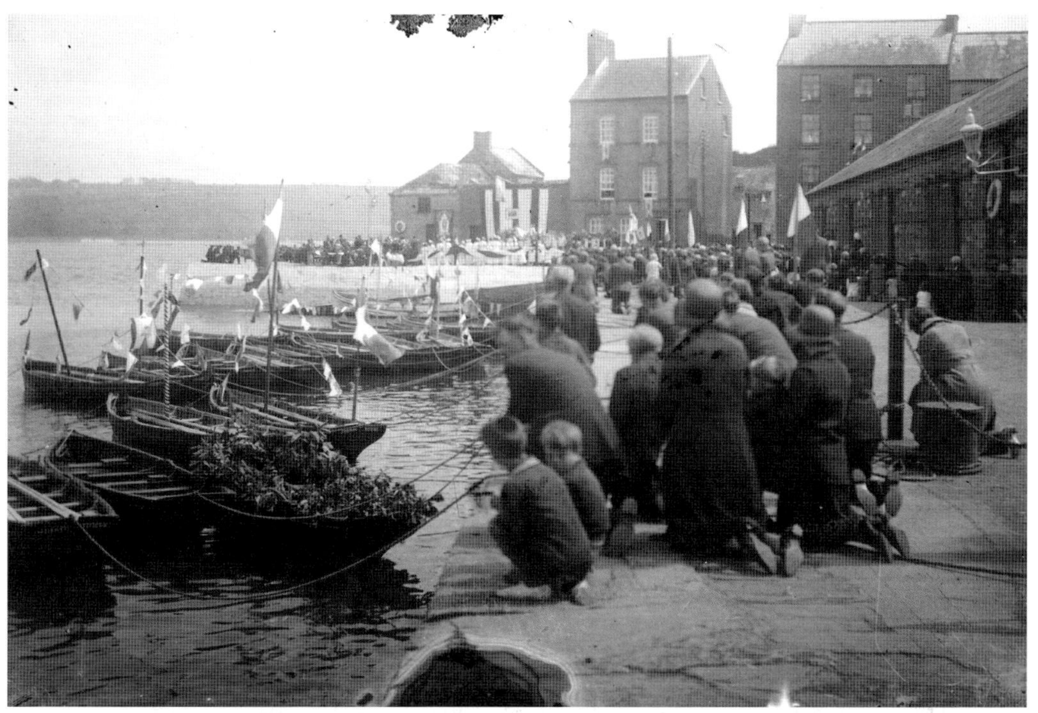

The blessing of the boats in Youghal was an important annual event.

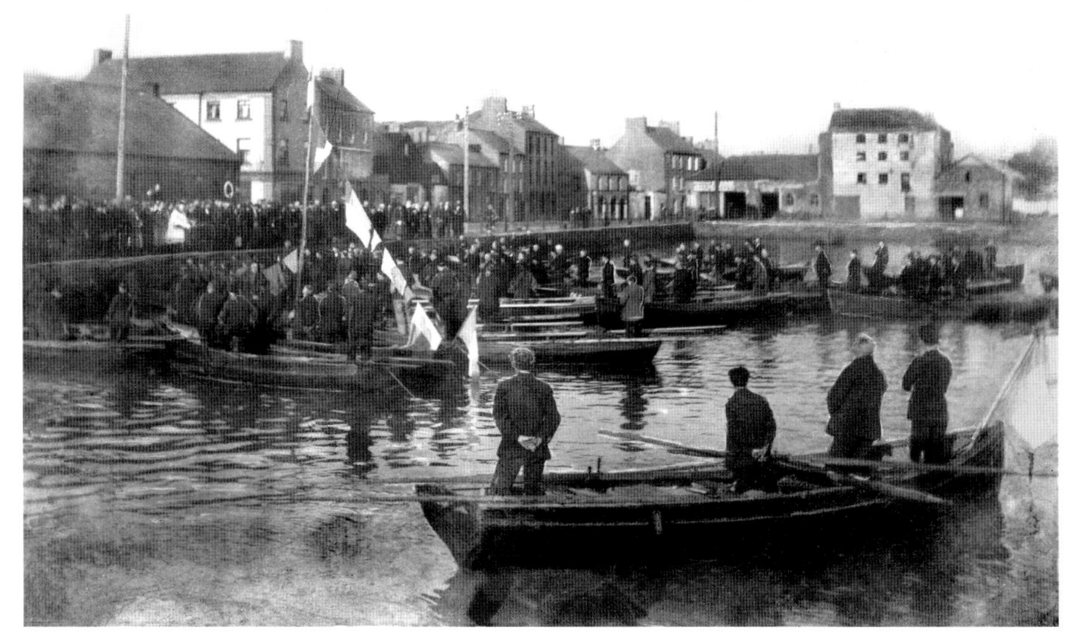

Blessing of the boats.

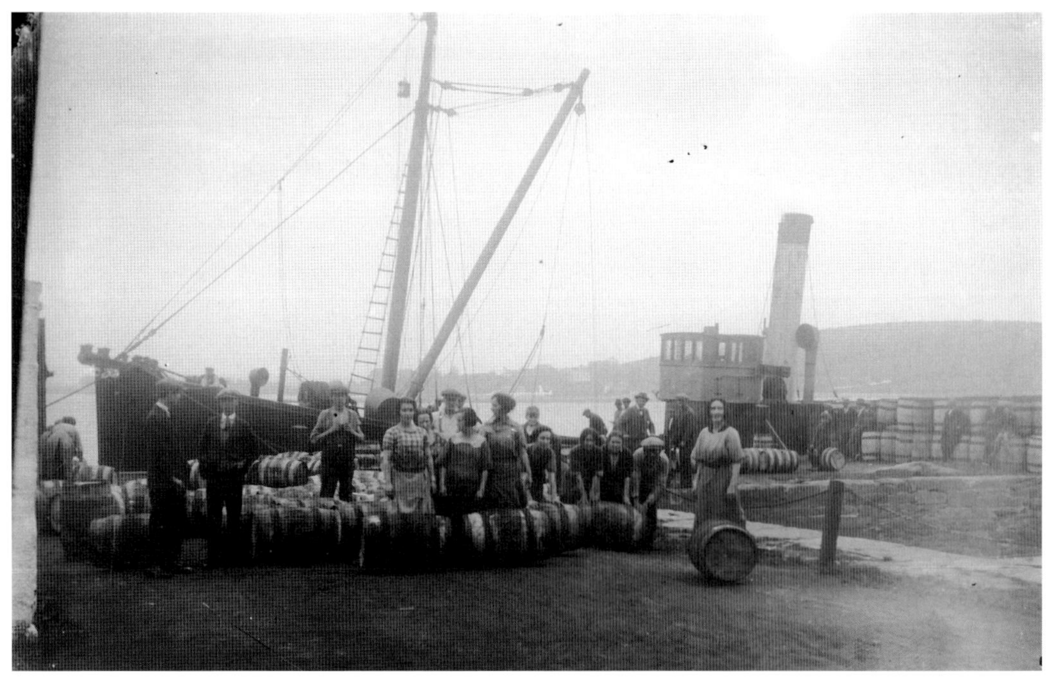

Working boats on the quays with cargo.

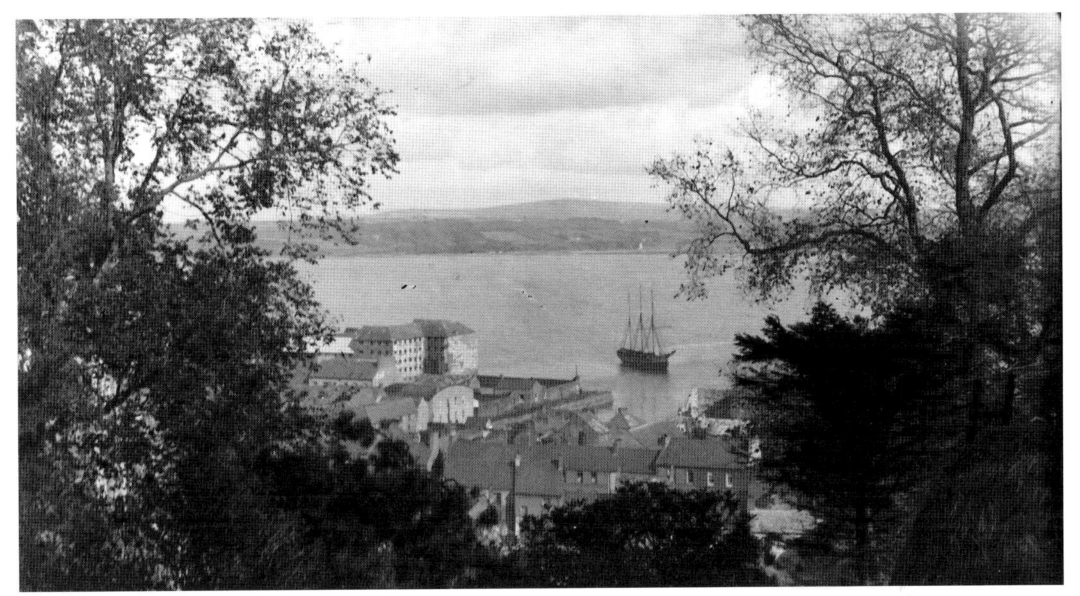

A tall ship in Youghal harbour.

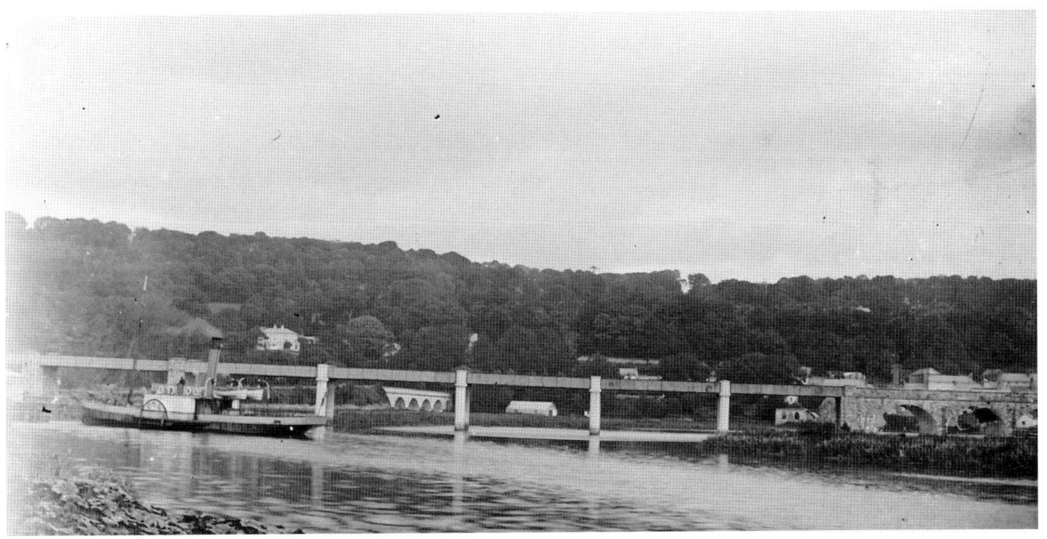

A paddle steamer near Cappoquin Bridge.

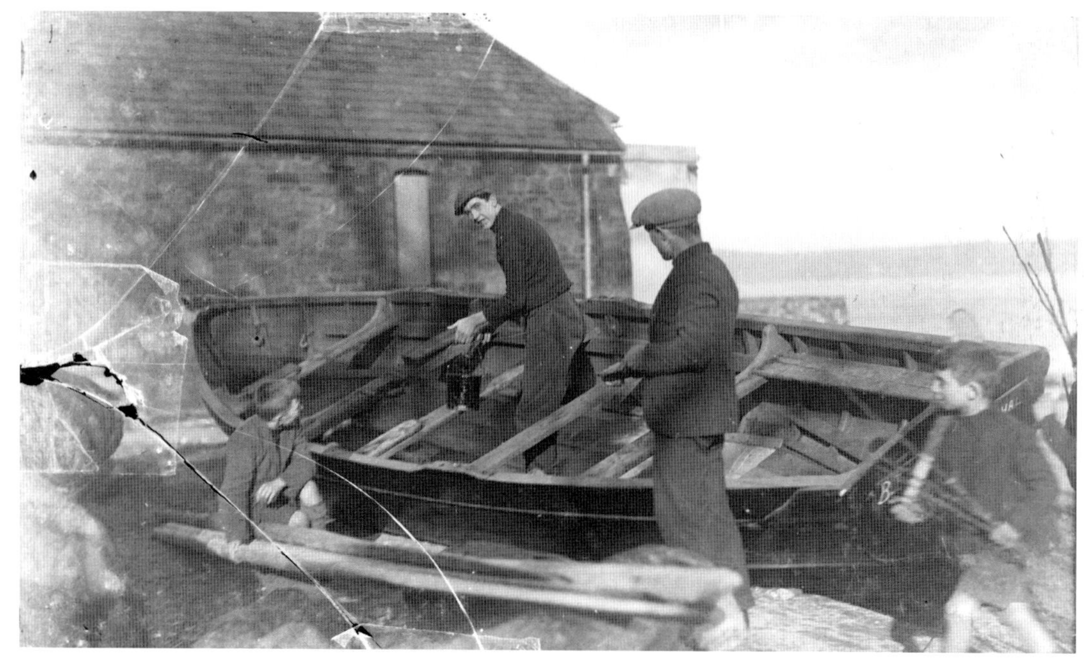

Fishermen on Youghal quayside.

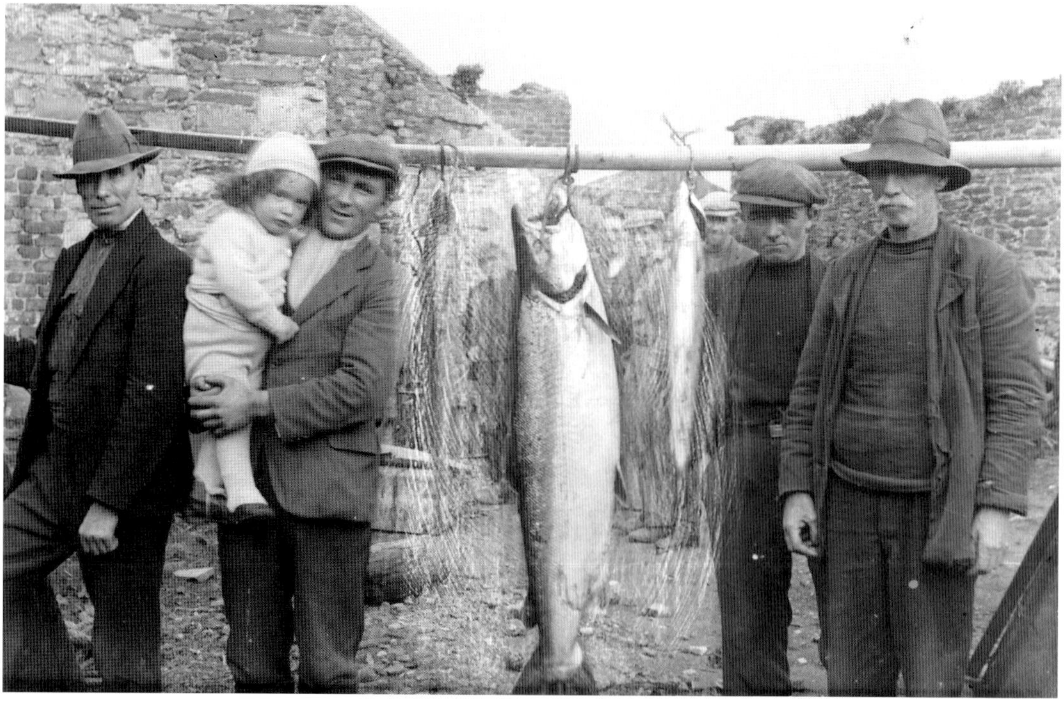

Fishermen with their catch and a child.

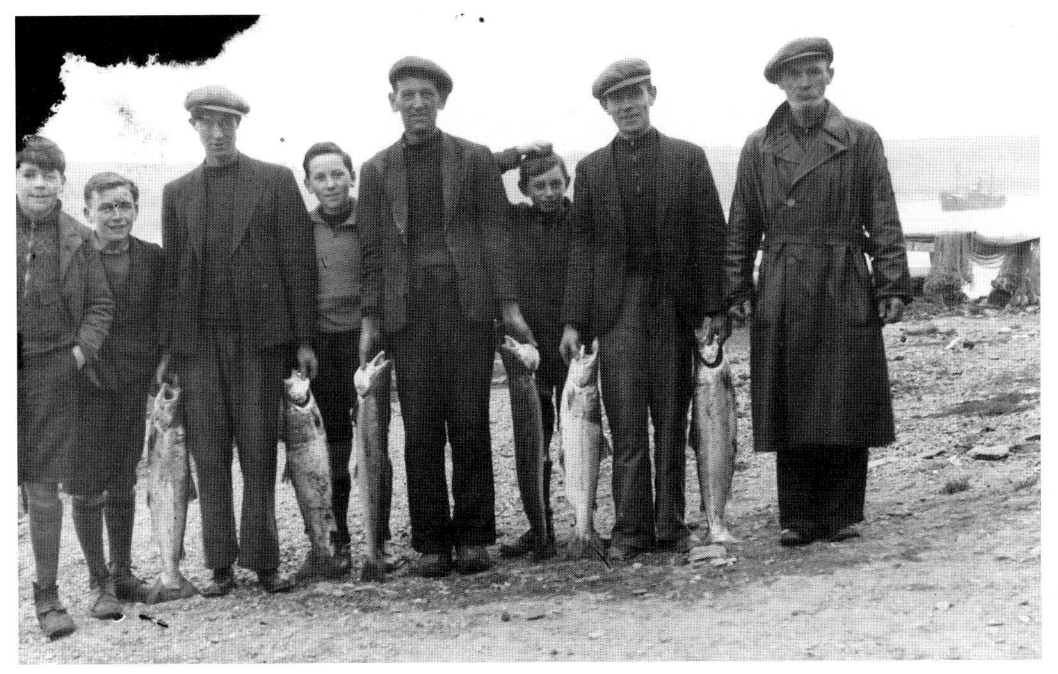

Salmon fishermen with their sons and their catch.

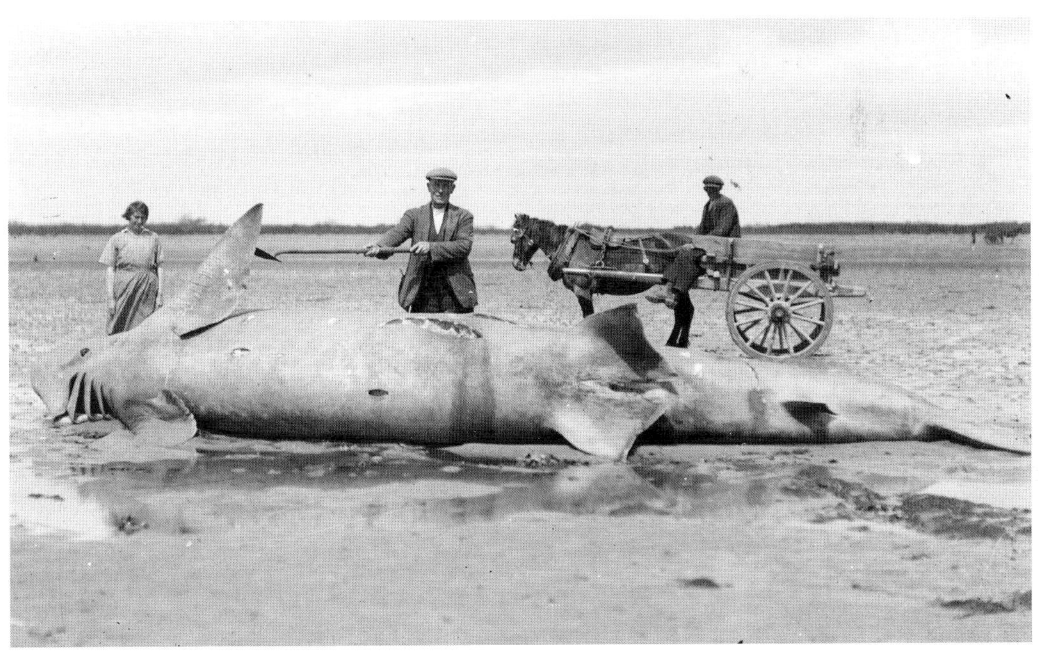

Basking shark on Youghal Strand.

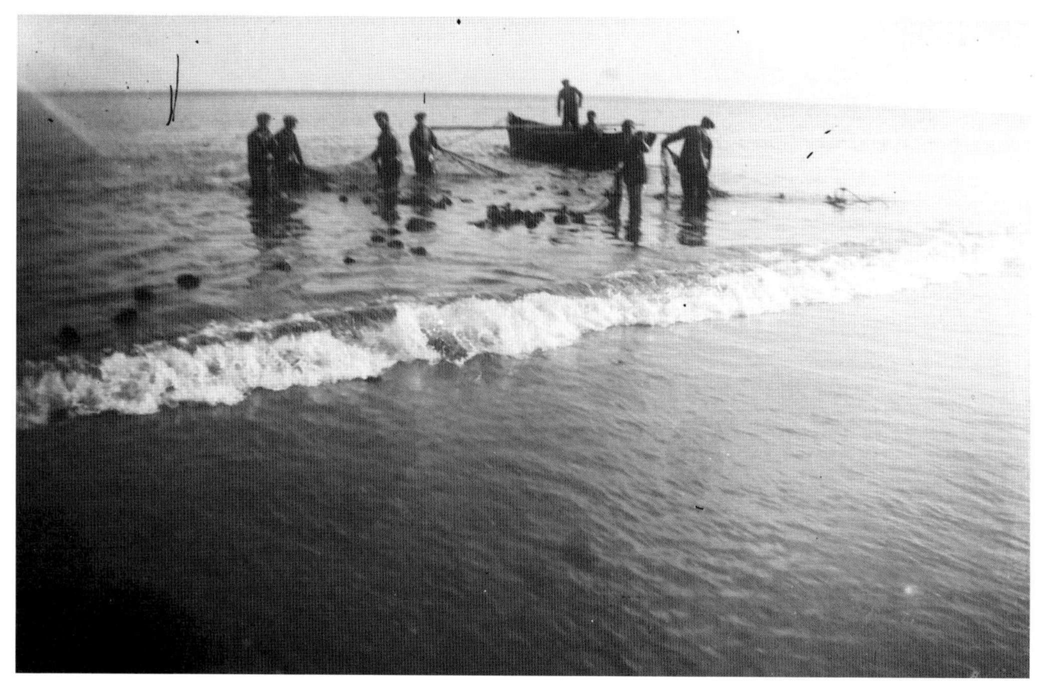

Fishermen catching mackerel near the shore in Youghal.

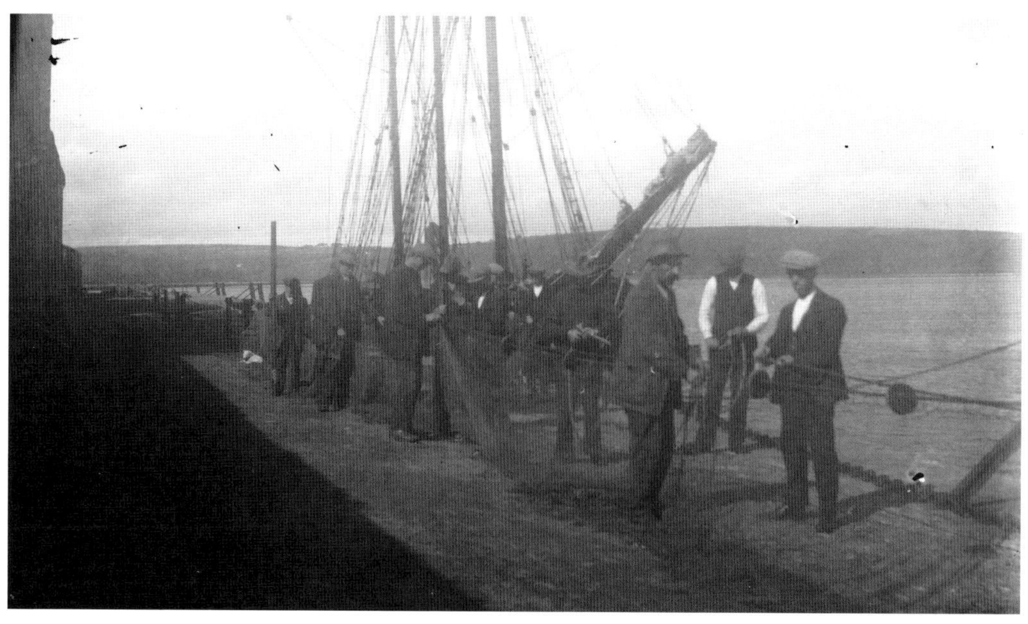

Men mending salmon nets beside the schooner Nellie Fleming.

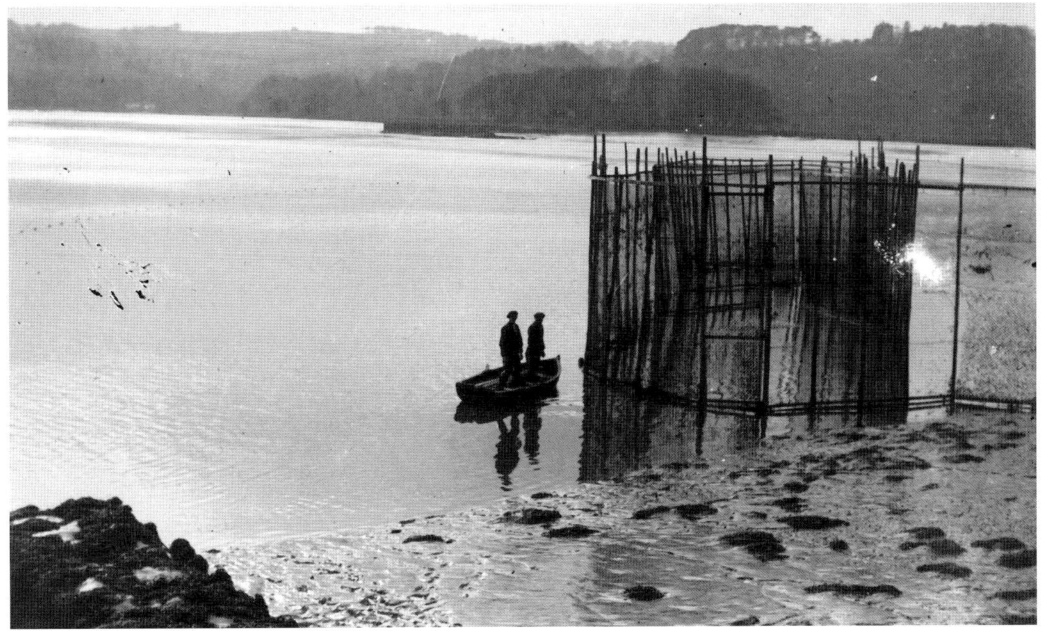

Fishermen at the salmon weir at Molana Abbey on the Blackwater.

The Wreck of The Annetta

On Sunday 17 December 1905, *The Annetta* from Dungarvan was washed onto the rocks by Moll Goggin's corner during a storm. Once again, in spite of the valiant efforts of the RNLI lifeboat and the coastguard rocket crews, two of the five souls on board were lost. An account of this wreck can be found handwritten by Jack Finn of Water Lane Youghal, on Dúchas, whose grandfather found the captain among the rocks.

The rescue was particularly dramatic, as the remaining crew held on to the rigging. Coxswain Michael Hannagan took the lifeboat to the wreck, with the seas breaking over the ship, and brought the three other men to safety. That night, the rocket flares over-exposed his attempts to capture the sight of the lifeboat and wreck battling the waves on camera. He took what remained of the image on the glass plate and created this drawing from the outline with charcoal pencils.

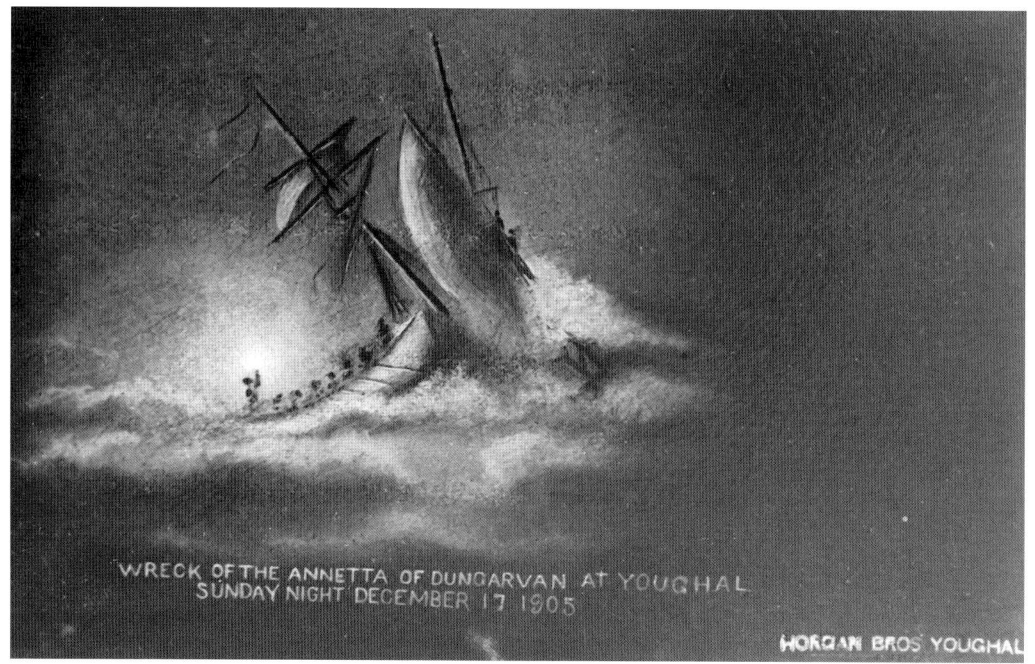

The wreck of The Annetta, *17 December 1905.*

THE TEASER

On 18 March 1911, *The Teaser*, a two-masted schooner, ran aground on the rocks of Ardmore Bay at Curragh. The coastguard rocket crew immediately went to the rescue. They fired several rockets at the ship, but the crew was exhausted. Valiant efforts to reach the crew were foiled by the waves.

Rev. John O'Shea, the curate from Ardmore, realised that the only hope of rescue had to be carried out by boat. Accompanied by a crowd of willing hands, Fr O'Shea secured a boat a mile from the wreck and rowed out against huge waves and surf in an effort to save the crew, who had tied themselves to the rigging. Unfortunately, the heroic efforts of the volunteers were unsuccessful, and the three crew of *The Teaser* died.

The Ardmore men were decorated by, the king of England at Buckingham Palace on 2 May 1911. Fr O'Shea received the George Cross. They also received medals from the Royal National Lifeboat Institution.

The Horgan brothers commemorated the Ardmore men and the crew with this series of photographs designed onto one card.

The Maréchal de Noailles

On 12 December 1912, the *Maréchal de Noailles* of Nantes left Glasgow en route through the Celtic Sea to a French colony in the South Pacific. A fierce storm raged during its voyage and eventually near Mine Head in County Waterford, the ship's French crew made a last attempt to survive and dropped both anchors. Both chains broke and she was driven ashore alongside a cliff near Old Parish, where Mine Head Lighthouse stands. The Helvick RNLI Lifeboat could not reach the ship, so the Ardmore Coastguard rocket crew carried the rocket equipment manually to the cliff edge.

The rocket men managed to fire the rocket over the top mast of the ship, and the crew secured the line. Overcoming the language barrier and extreme conditions, the crew was instructed on how to work the breeches buoy – a rope pully system from ship to shore, with a sort of trousers into which a person would sit and be pulled. Despite the cliff being eighty-seven meters high, all the crew safely came ashore.

In the aftermath of the wreck, the Horgan brothers took a series of photographs of it, one of which is below.

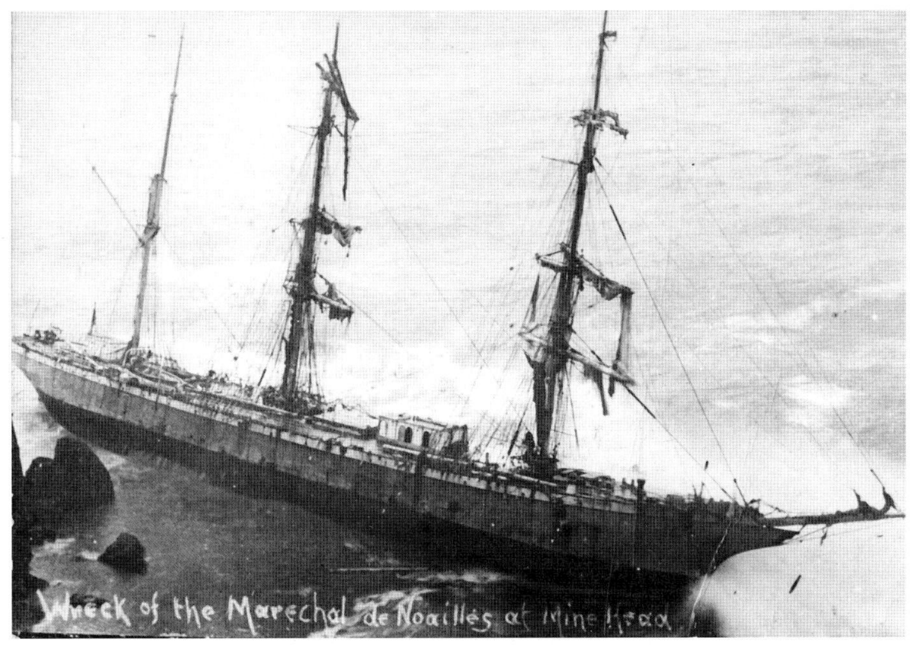

The wreck of the Maréchal de Noailles *at Mine head.*

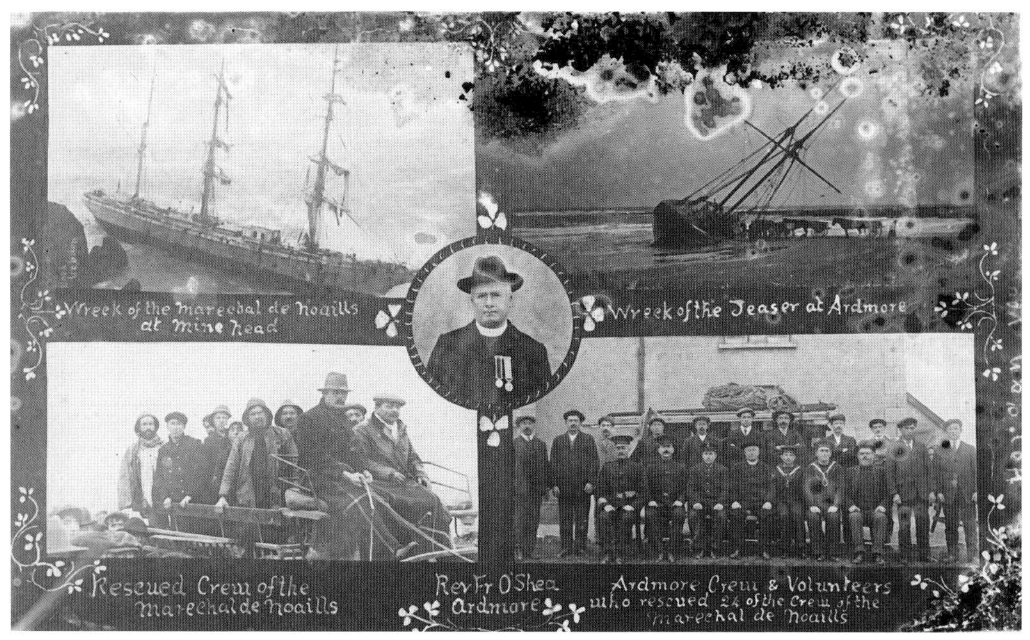

Horgan postcard showing the crew of the Maréchal de Noailles *and the people from Ardmore who saved them.*

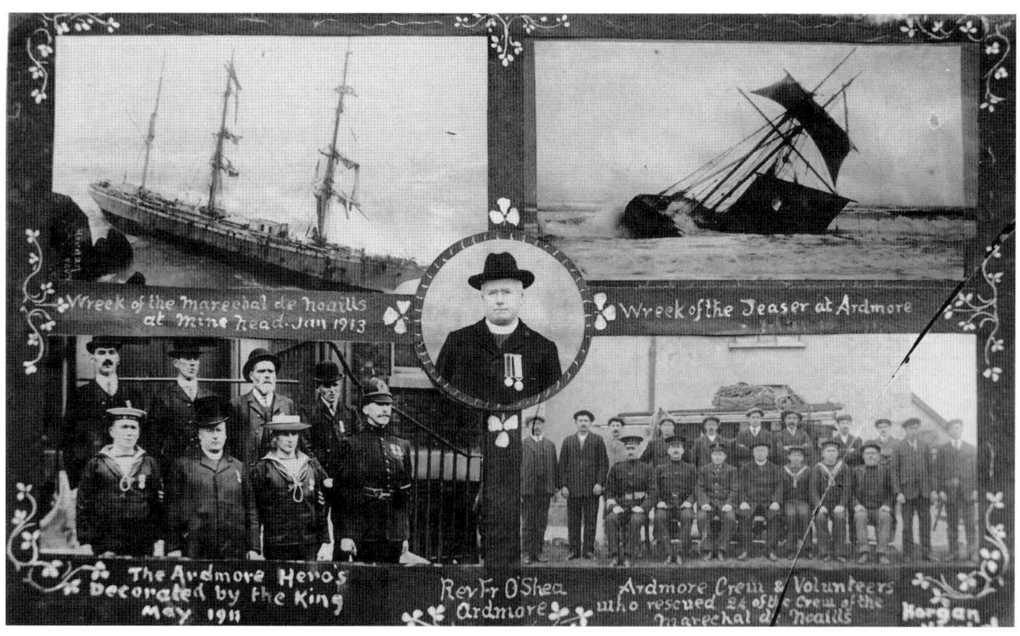

Horgan postcard showing the Ardmore heroes honoured by King George V. Both postcards include a photo of The Teaser.

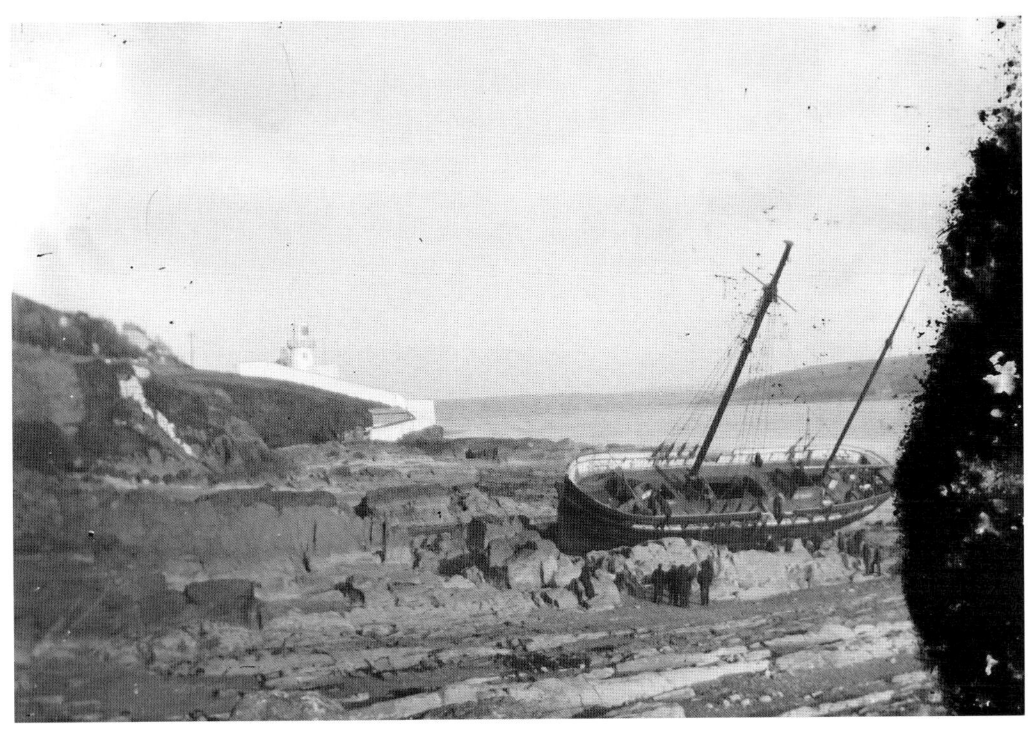

Wreck of the Queen of Gloucester *at Youghal, 1911.*

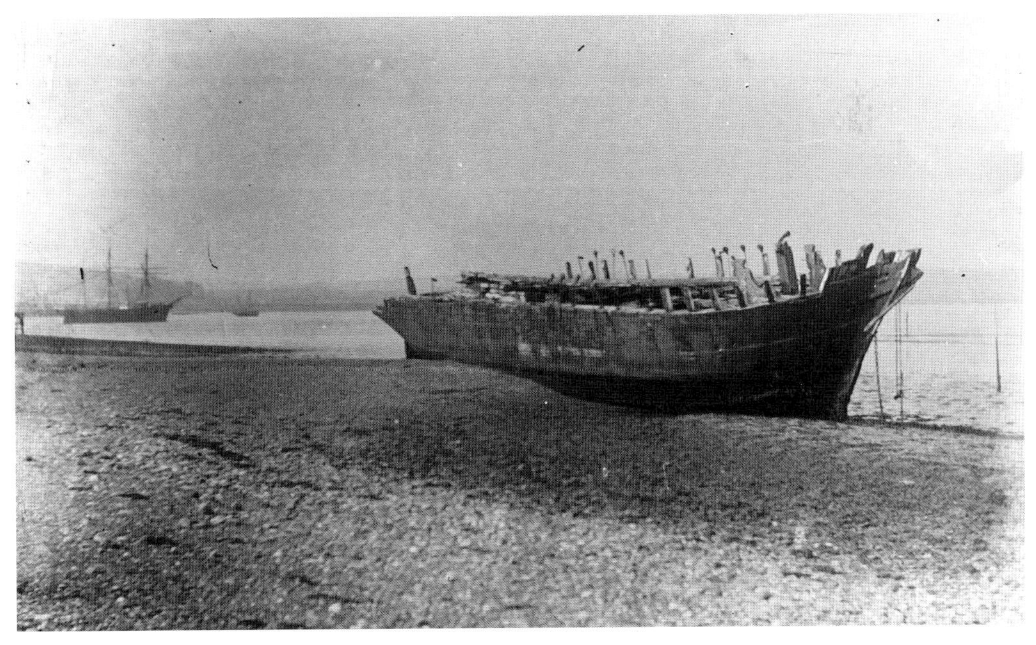

Ship graveyard at Youghal.

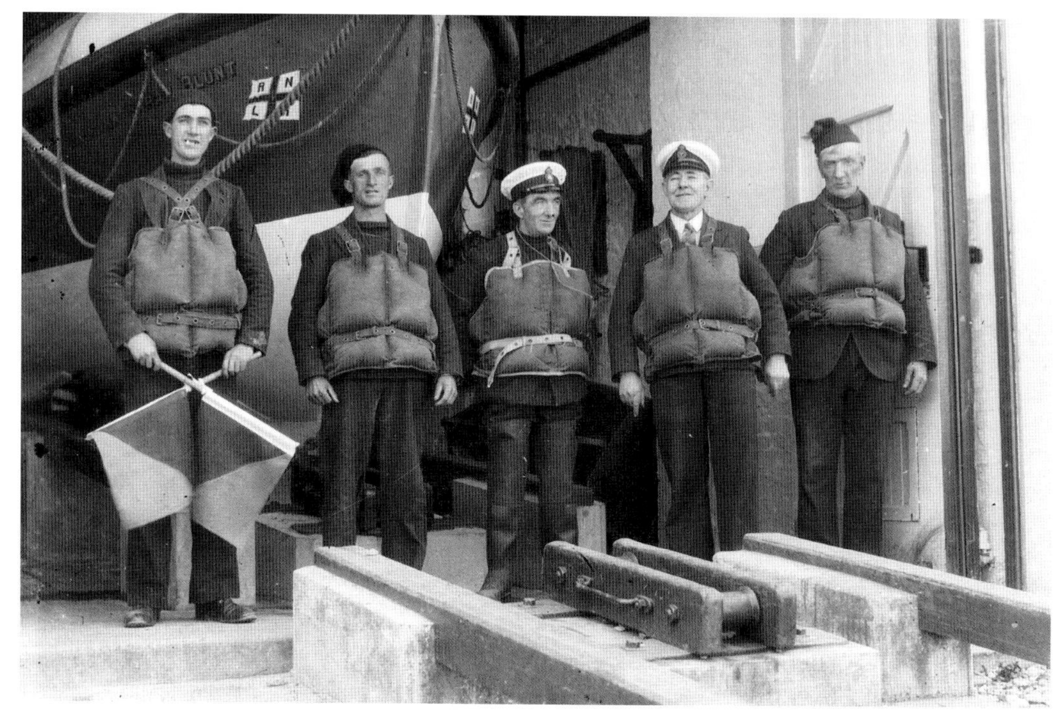

An RNLI crew at Youghal lifeboat station.

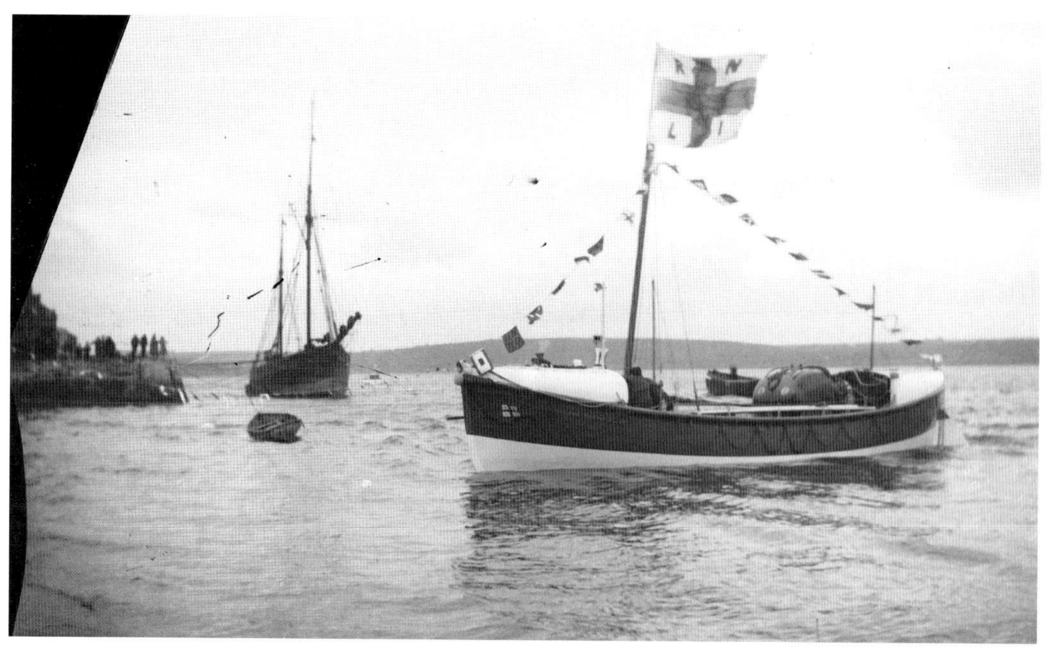

RNLI boat by Youghal Quay.

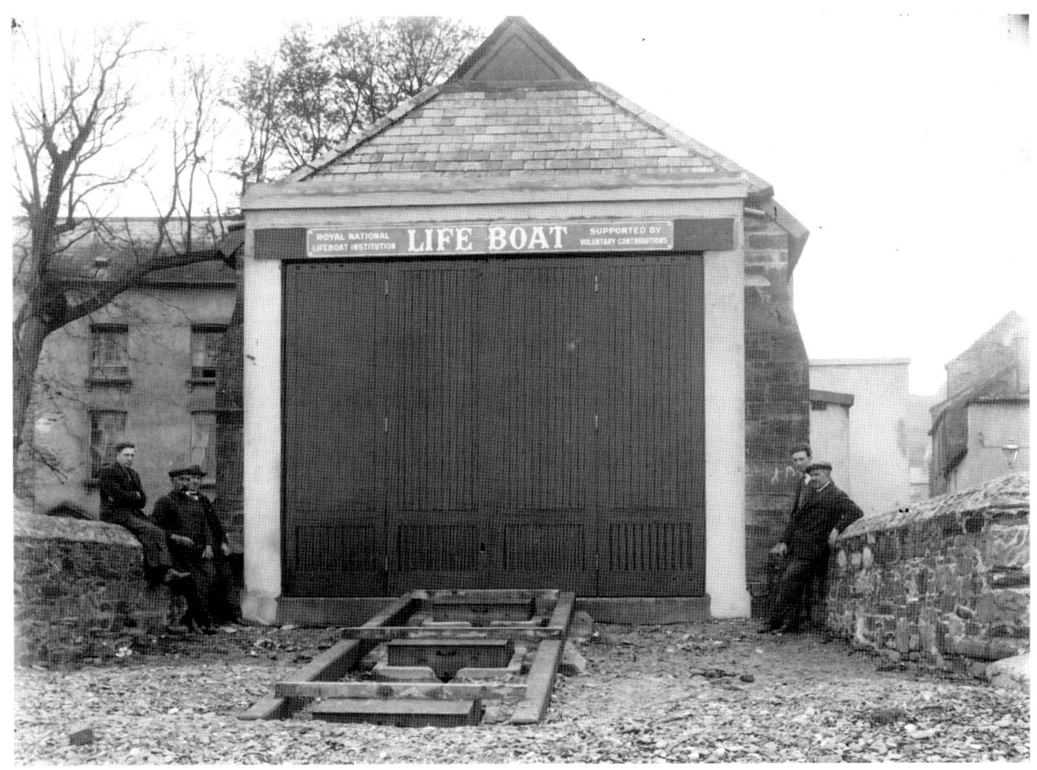

Youghal RNLI lifeboat station.

SWIMMING OR BATHING

This photo of the Horgan family would have been risqué at the time. It wasn't really acceptable to be seen in your swimming attire, let alone be photographed in it. The brothers frequently displayed their work of local scenes in the window of their photographic studio on Friar Street. The parish priest once asked them to remove photos of the beach from the window as they were considered to be indecent. Philip refused to take the photos down and told the parish priest he need only go for a walk out the beach and he'd see the same thing any day of the week. The photos stayed up.

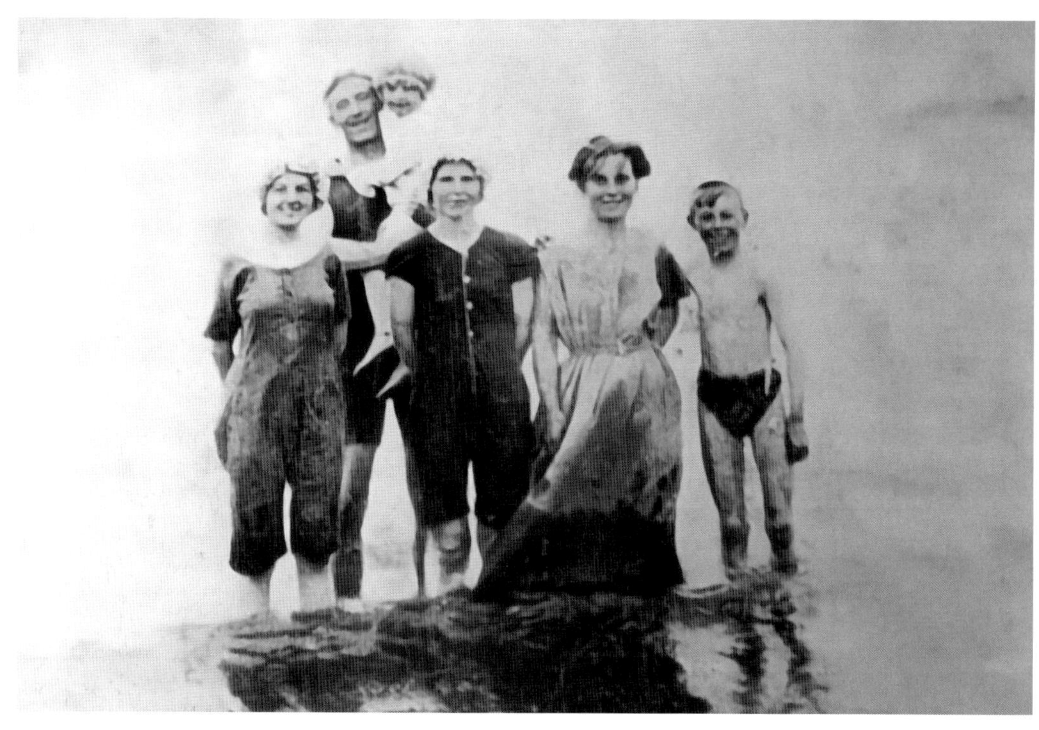

James and his family in bathing costumes, swimming in Youghal.

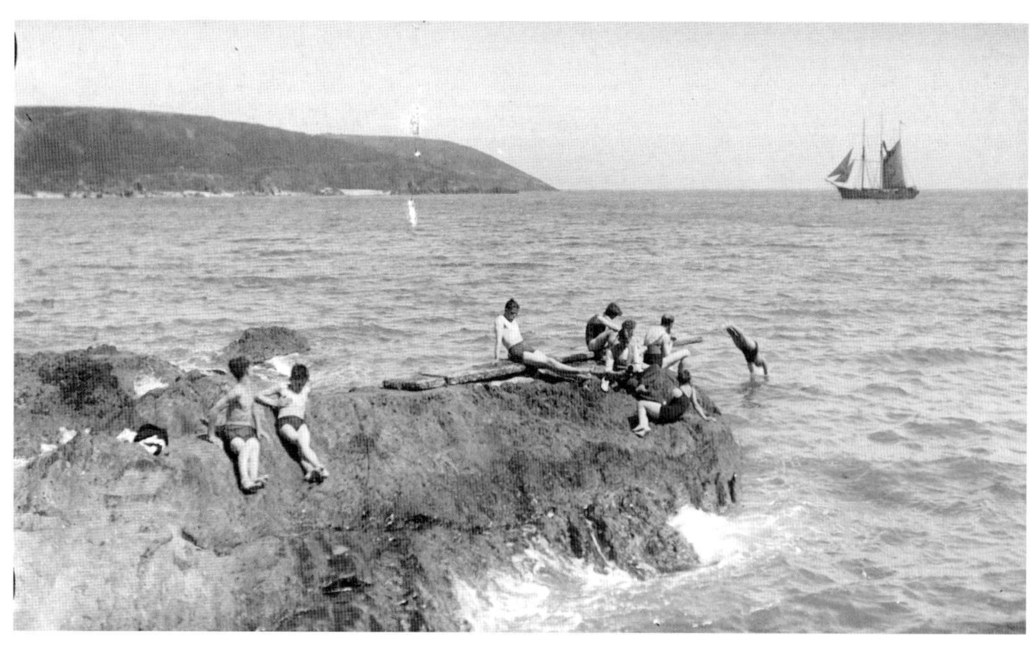

Swimmers at the diving rocks by Youghal Lighthouse.

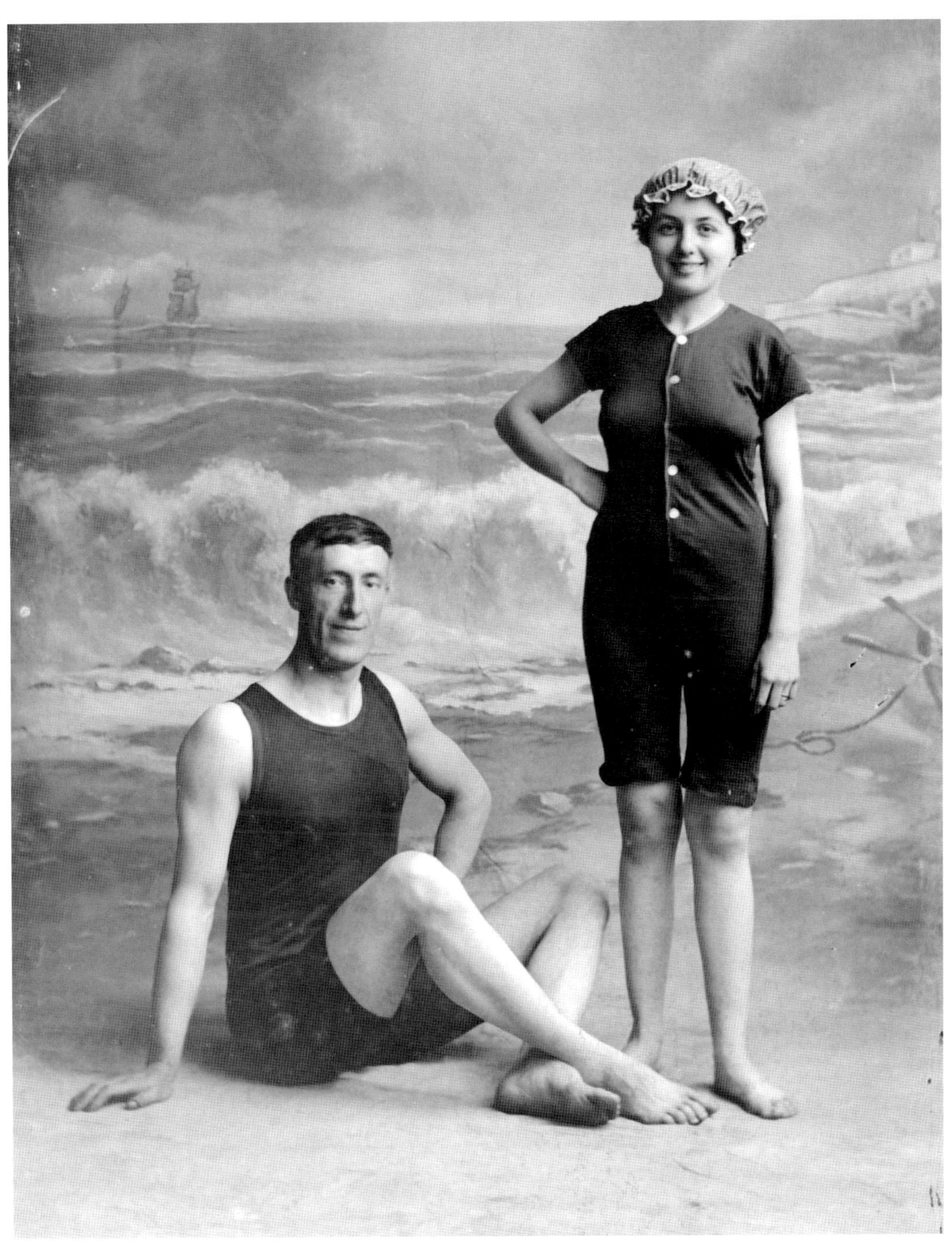

James and Marietta in bathing costumes.

The phrase a picture paints a thousand words is certainly evoked in this picture.

Thomas Lipton was a world-renowned entrepreneur, yachtsman and tea merchant. In 1898, he purchased one of the ten most powerful steam yachts in the world, weighing 1,240 tons. He registered the vessel *Aegusa* under the name *ERIN* to honour his Irish heritage. During the First World War, the ship was briefly transformed into a hospital. The Horgan brothers captured several photographs of the ship during a visit to Youghal.

Each of the children pictured here went on to play important roles in the Second World War. Paddy McGrath who became a member of the merchant navy was torpedoed three times during the war and eventually died at the age of twenty-four. Nancy and Eileen McGrath nursed in London during the blitz.

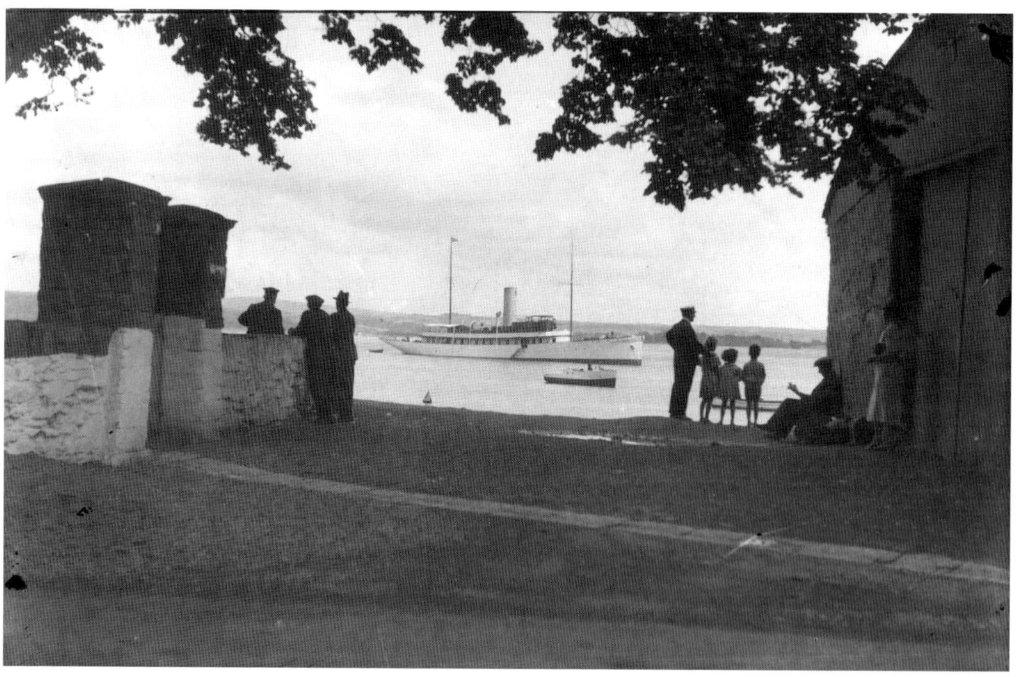

Lipton's yacht.

ROPE WALK

An essential element of every vessel at sea is rope. In Youghal, rope was made locally by the O'Sullivan family, running alongside the town walls, which was known as the rope walk. Larry O'Sullivan is pictured as a young boy helping his parents in the photo below.

Later in life, Larry was on the *HMS Exeter* during the Second World War. It was sunk in a battle with the Japanese in the Java Sea. Larry and another Youghal man were left with no choice but to jump off the ship into shark-infested waters. Local lore has it that as the men jumped from the ship, they shouted, 'Moll Goggin's corner, here we come'. Larry was later picked up by the Japanese and was held as a prisoner of war. He not only endured the camp and the atomic bombing of Nagasaki but also made it home to Moll Goggin's corner.

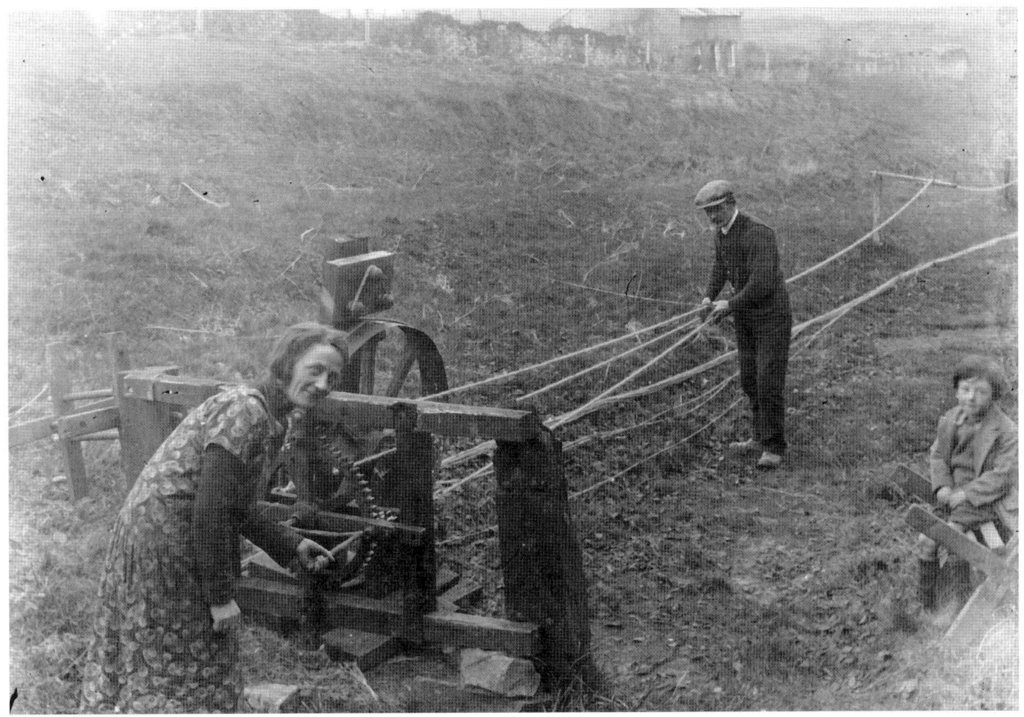

Rope making with flax along the Rope Walk near the town walls.

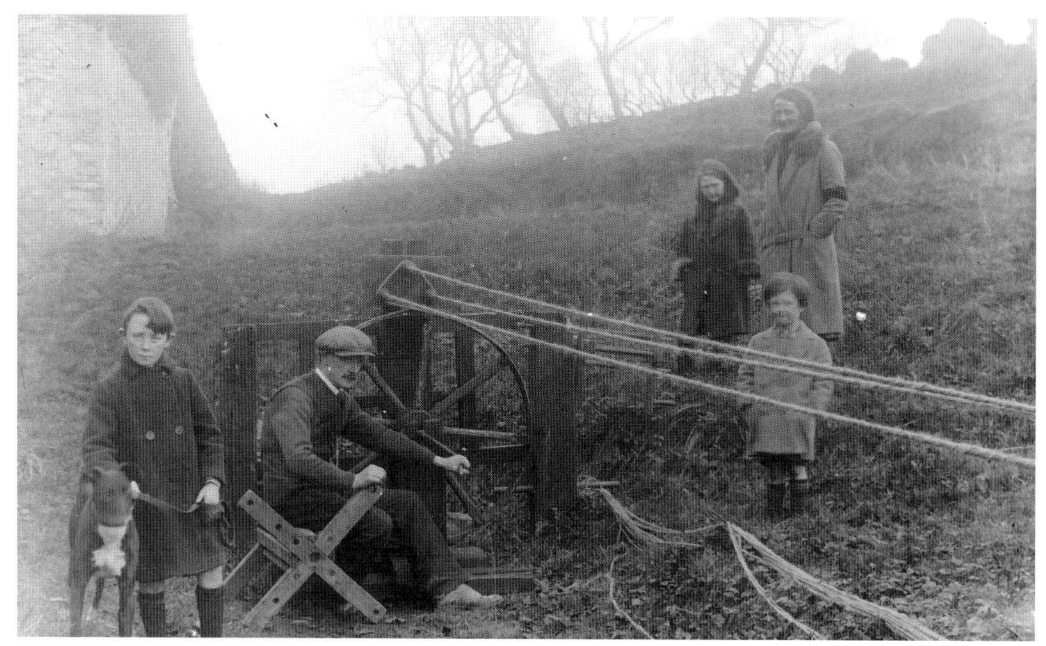

O'Sullivan family, featuring Larry as a boy, making rope along the rope walk.

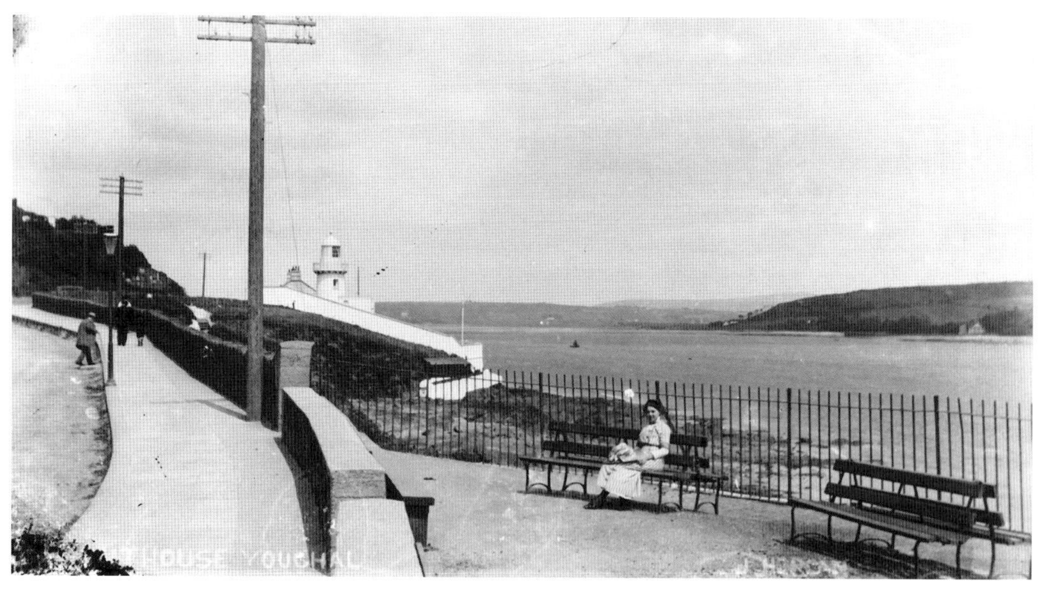

Moll Goggin's viewing platform with Youghal lighthouse.

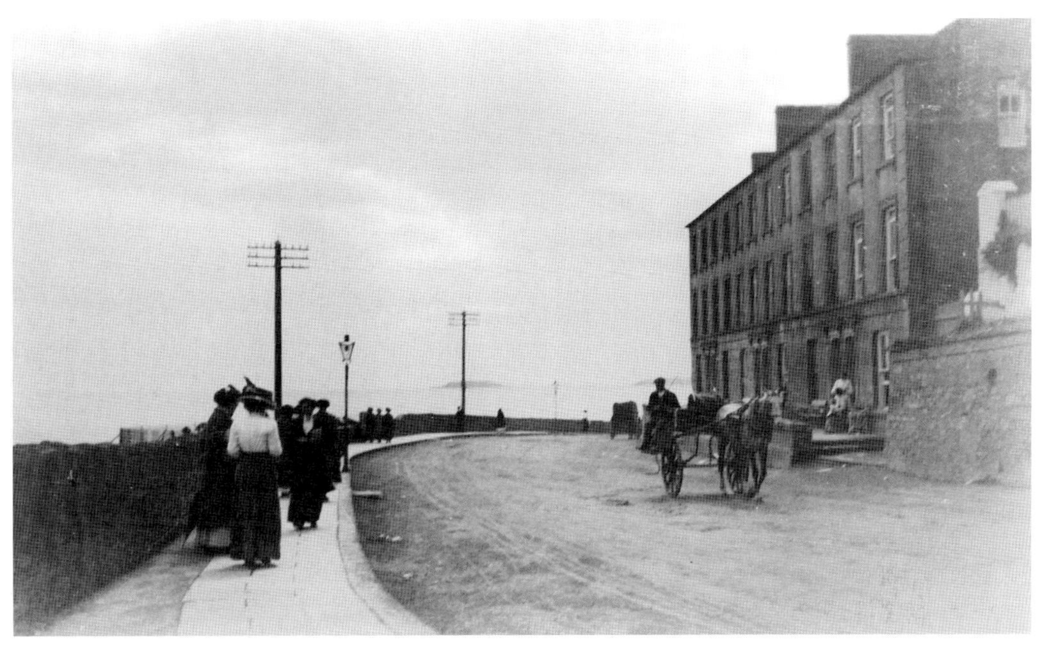

Moll Goggin's Corner towards the strand.

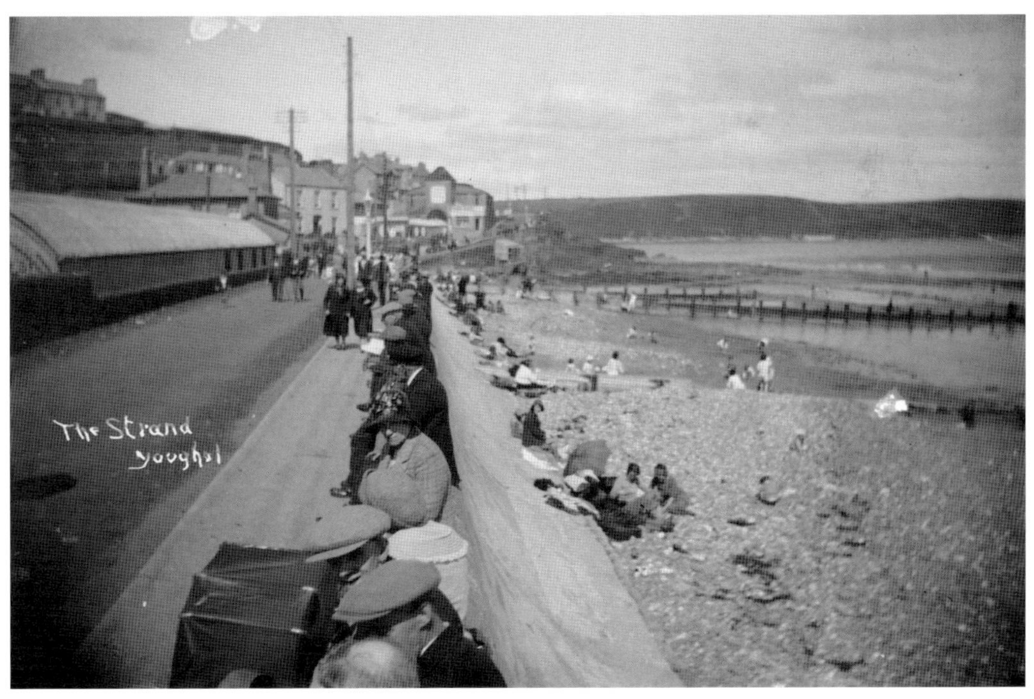

The front strand.

ADAPTING PHOTOS

The Horgan Brothers invested in the most modern photographic equipment and devised clever methods of altering photo images (the early twentieth-century equivalent of photoshopping). Their methods varied and charcoal pencils were used to re-touch or enhance any flaws in the final images. In some cases, they added creative detail to the photos, such as adding clouds to St Mary's church or a mock-up of a new bridge spanning from Youghal to Ferrypoint in Waterford. Most notably, it is their manipulated image of boats rowing down Youghal's main street that was an incredible feat of technology and captured the imagination to this day.

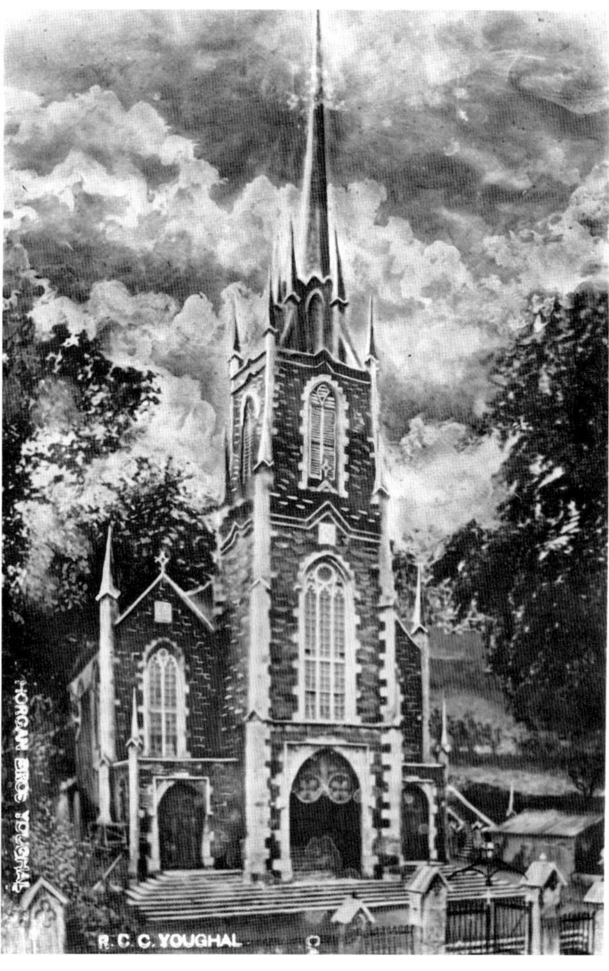

St Mary's church, Youghal,
with clouds added.

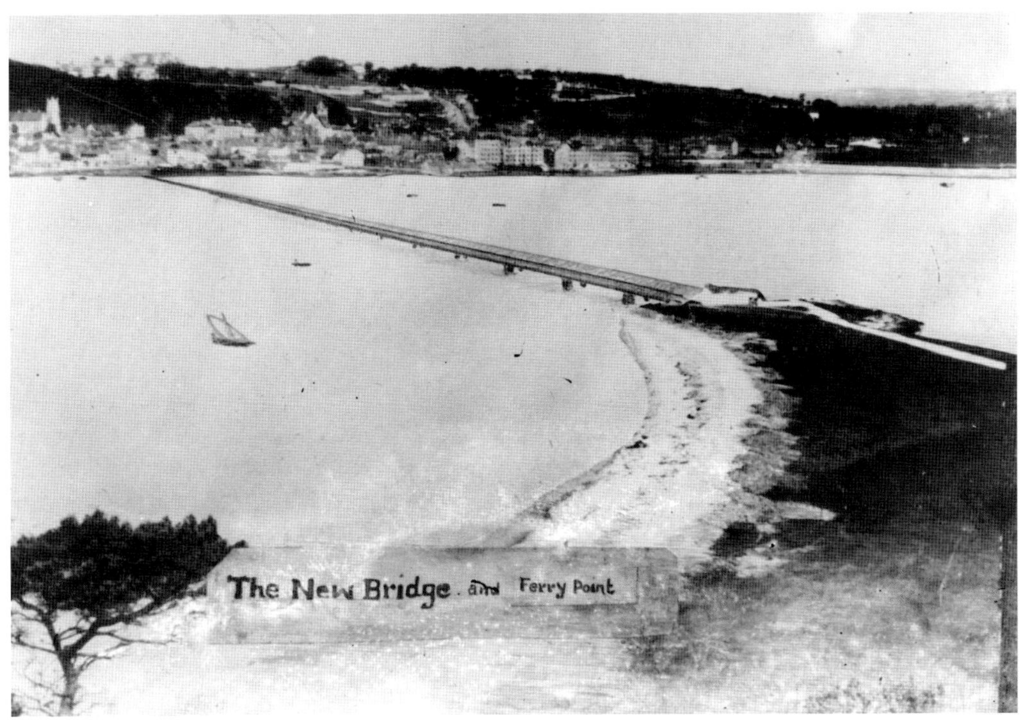

*A visual representation for the proposed new bridge spanning
the Blackwater joining counties Waterford and Cork.*

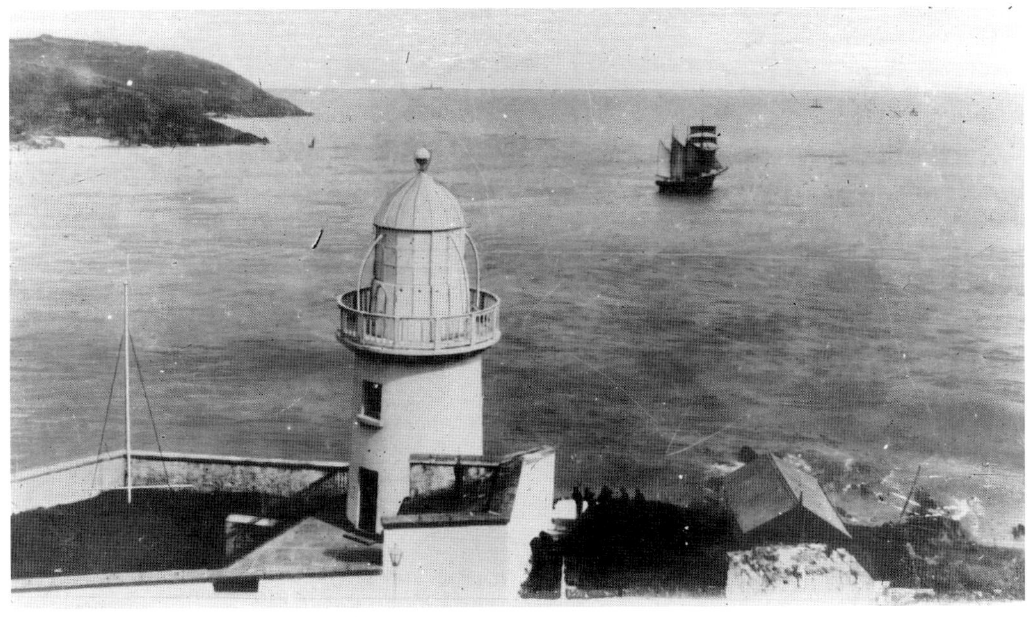

A sailboat departs from Youghal Harbour with lighthouse in foreground.

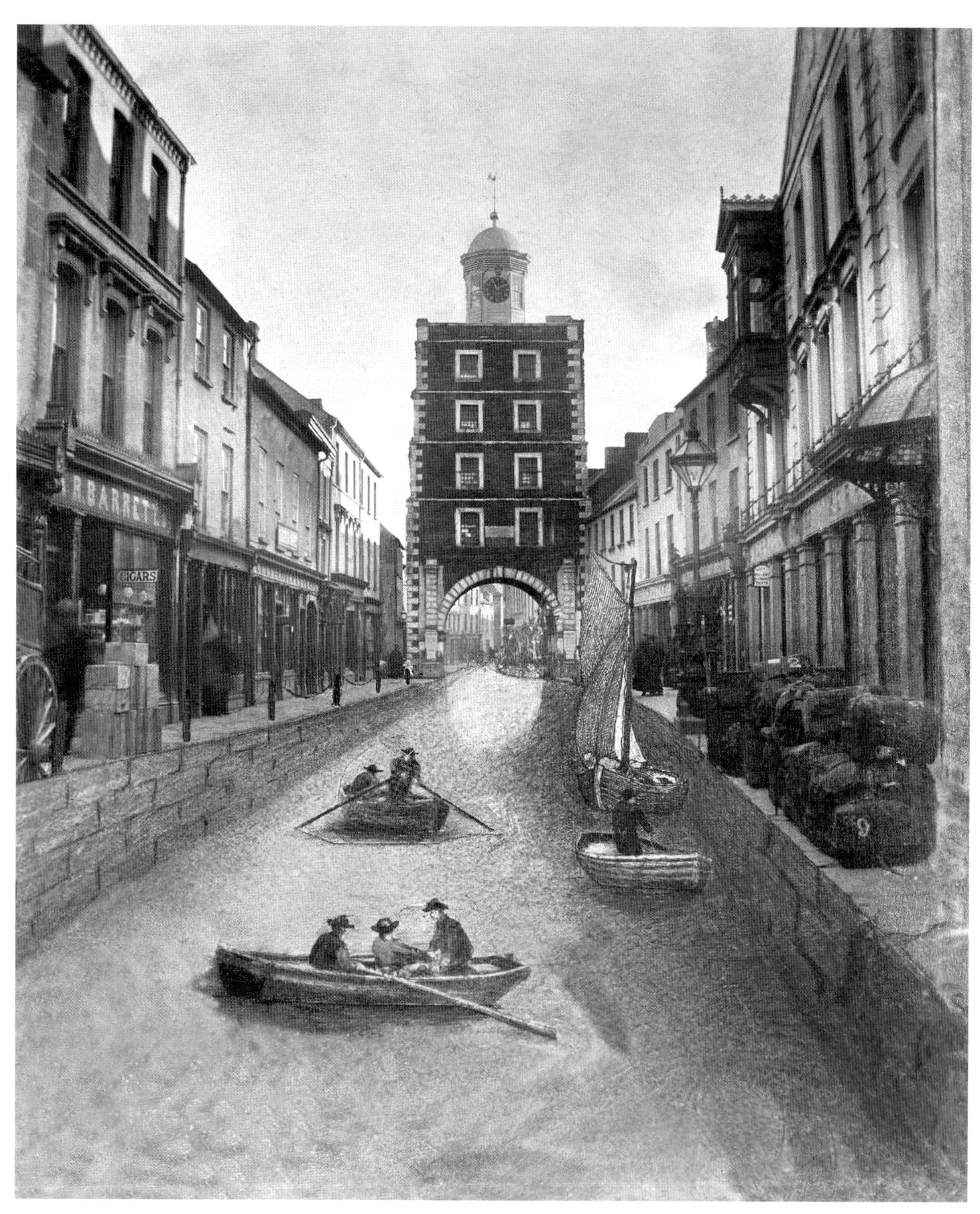

*An altered photograph featuring Youghal's Clock Gate
with water and boats floating under it like Venice.*

The iconic Clock Gate of Youghal was often photographed by the brothers. Once again, they would push the boundaries of their technical abilities and creative vision to produce what has become the oldest example of animation in Ireland, dated around 1910. The brothers created a three-dimensional model of the Clock Gate flanked with photographs of the main street to create the full 'set'. This model could easily be made to move, spin, twirl and even stand on its head by capturing the movements in stop-motion animation. It is understood from the Horgan descendants that the brothers made the structure perform a dance on the main street before it left the town and went out to sea, waving goodbye from Ardmore head as it departed.

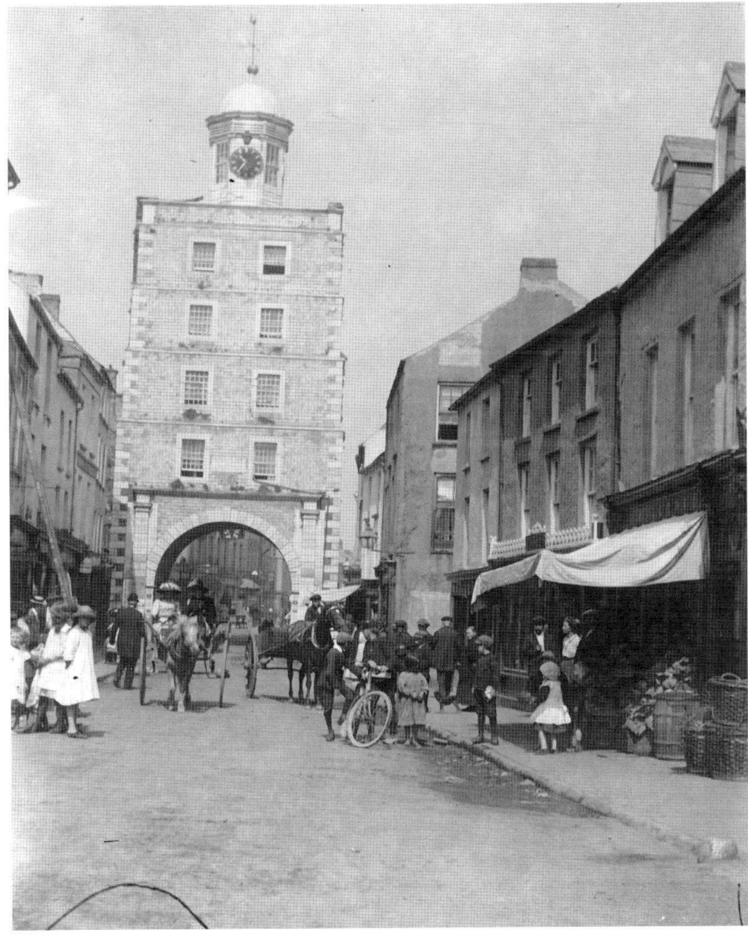

At the inaugural Galway Film Fleadh, a model of the Clock Gate was awarded to prize winners of the best animated film in honour of the Horgan Brothers.

The Clock Gate, Youghal, on South Main Street.

These are two examples of James' paintings, the same style as featured on the long walls of the Horgan Picture Theatre (original paintings are in colour).

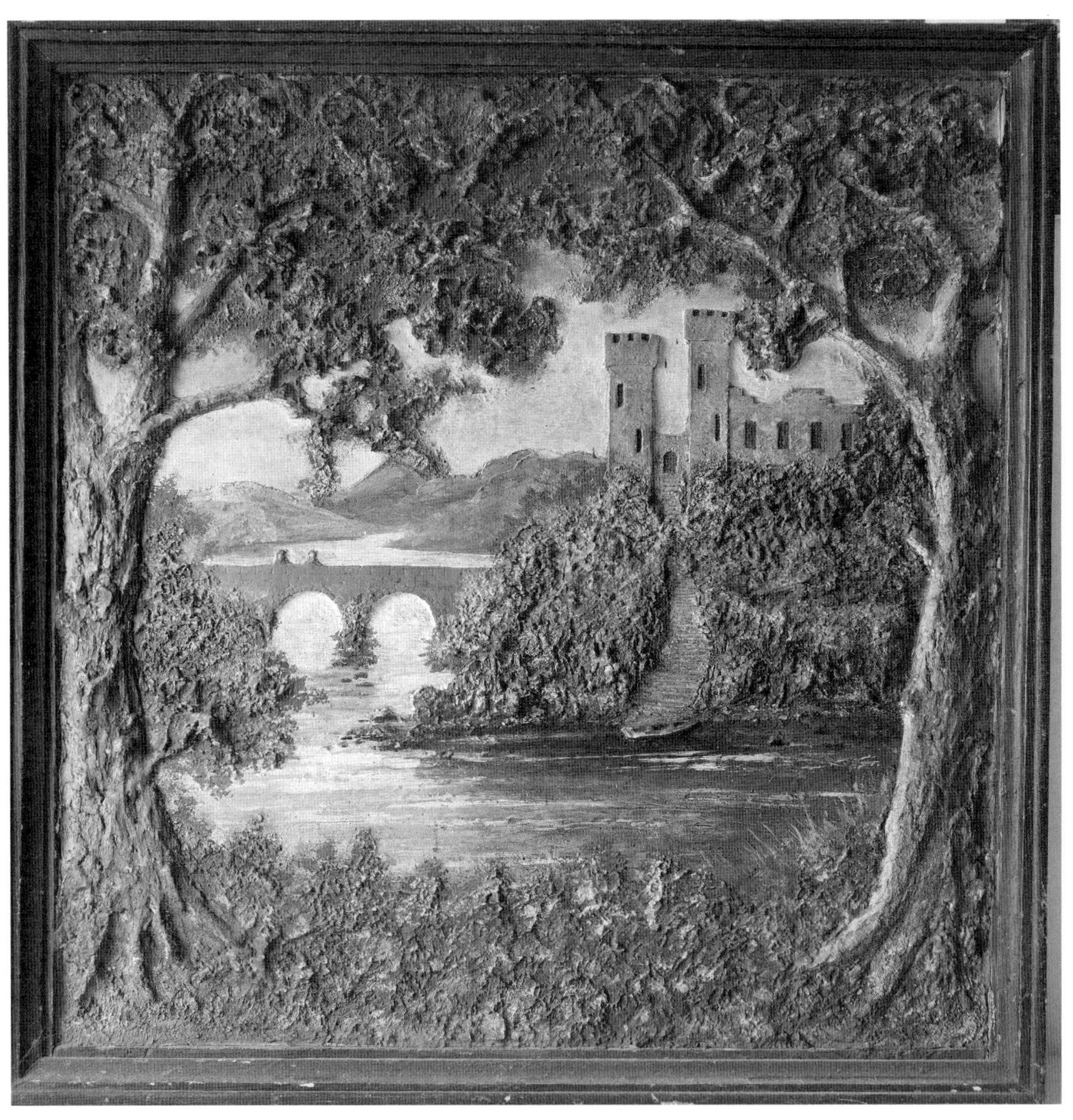

Painting of Lismore Castle and bridge by James Horgan.

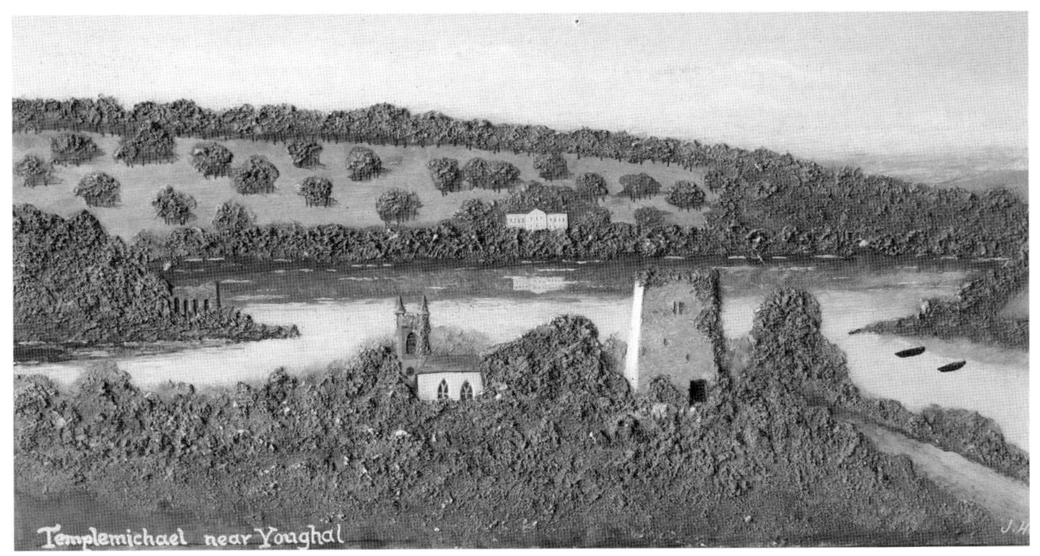

Painting of Templemichael and Ballynatray House by James Horgan.

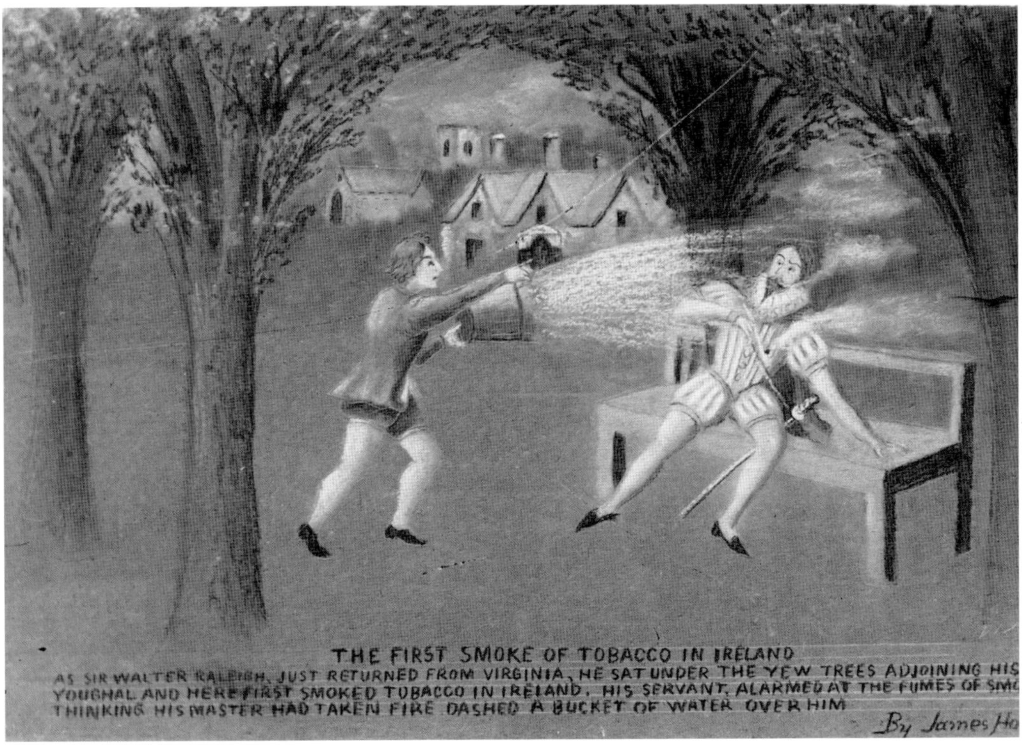

A Horgan sketch of the first cigarette smoked in Ireland by Sir Walter Raleigh.

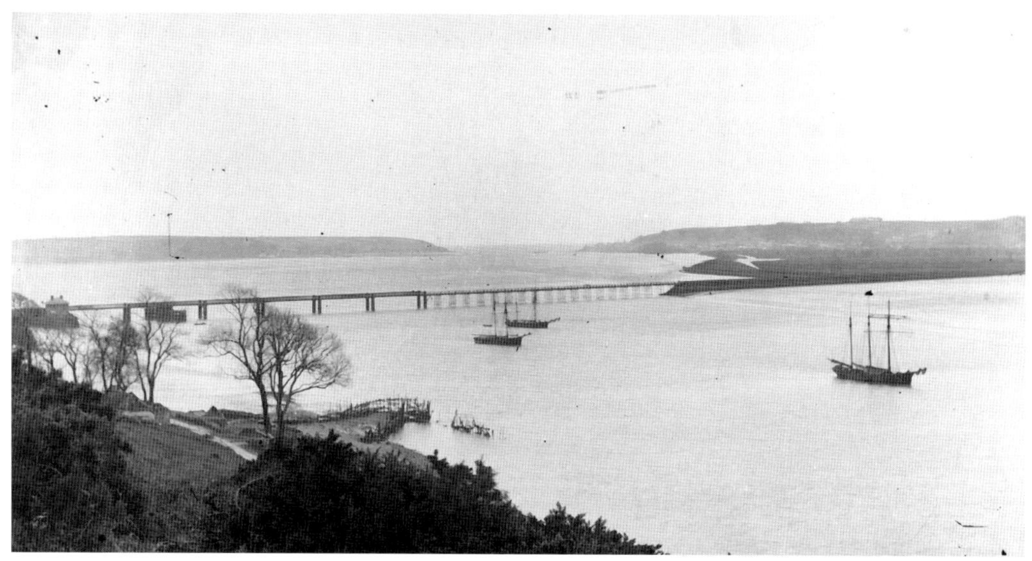

Old Youghal bridge with three ships.

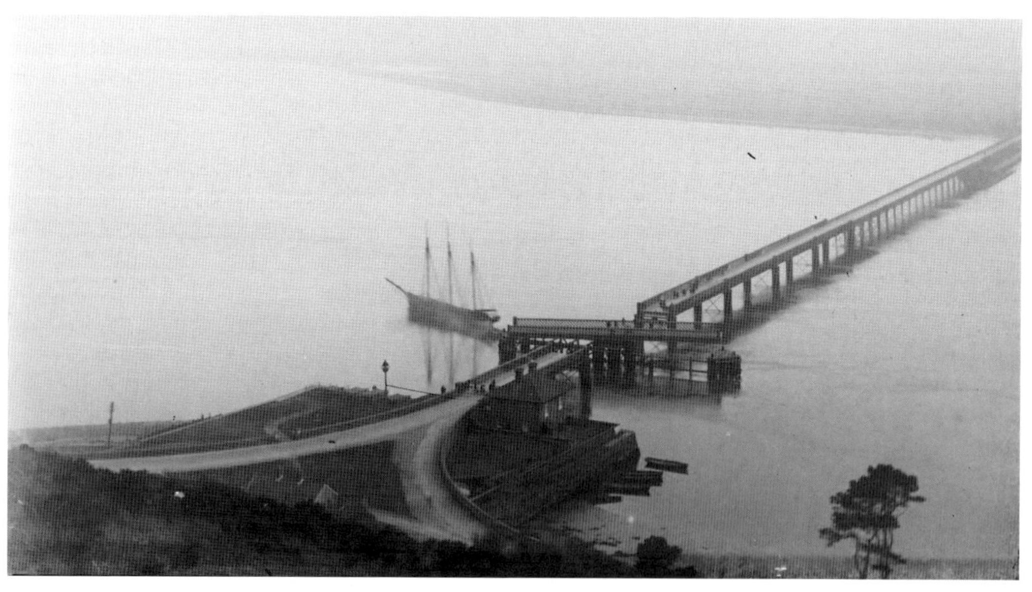

Old Youghal bridge opening to allow passage.

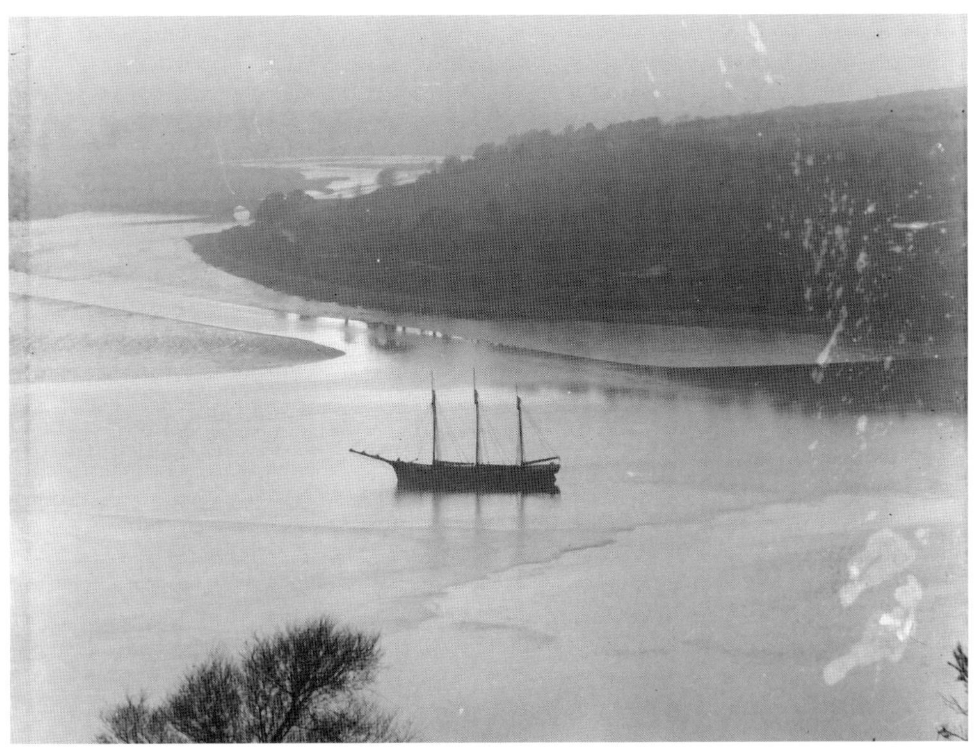

The same ship can be seen passing where the modern Youghal bridge stands.

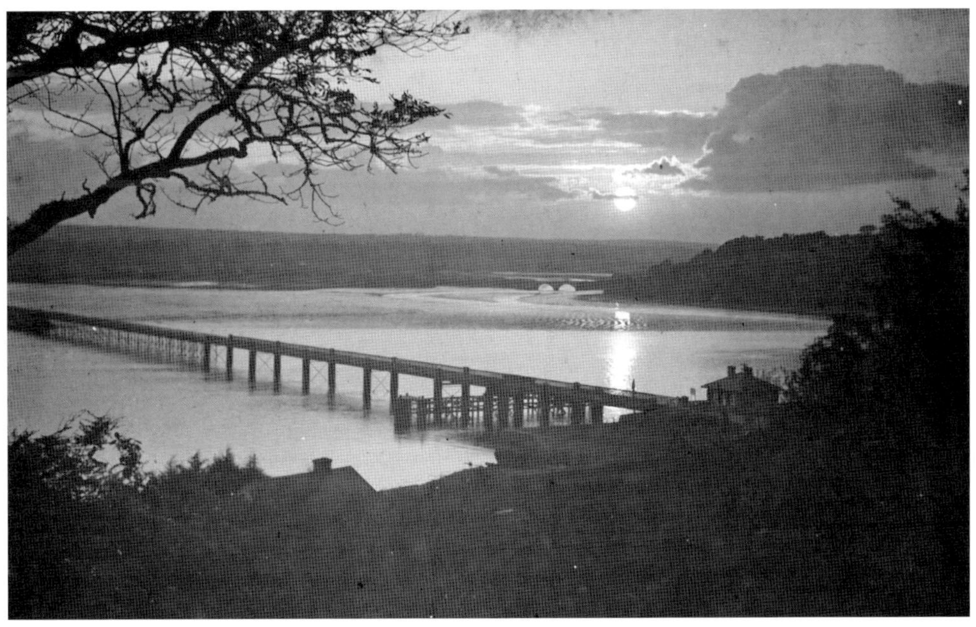

Sunset on old Youghal Bridge with bridge over the river Tourig in the background.

The Blackwater River

The Horgan Brothers love of the river Blackwater, *An Abhainn Mhór na Mumhann*, is evident from the number of photographs that remain. Its natural beauty and extensive number of houses and castles along the river were an instant attraction to young photographers. Described in 1901 as 'the Irish Rhine', the river holds a wealth of history and a beauty that captured the imagination of many before them. The Horgan brothers photographed its beauty abundantly – from the bridge stretching across from Counties Cork to Waterford to the historic monastic site of Molana Abbey, Templemichael, and many of the large houses and estates along the river, all the way through to Cappoquin and Lismore Castle. James Horgan even mounted his camera on a coal barge being towed on the Blackwater by a steam tug boat to get unique views of the river.

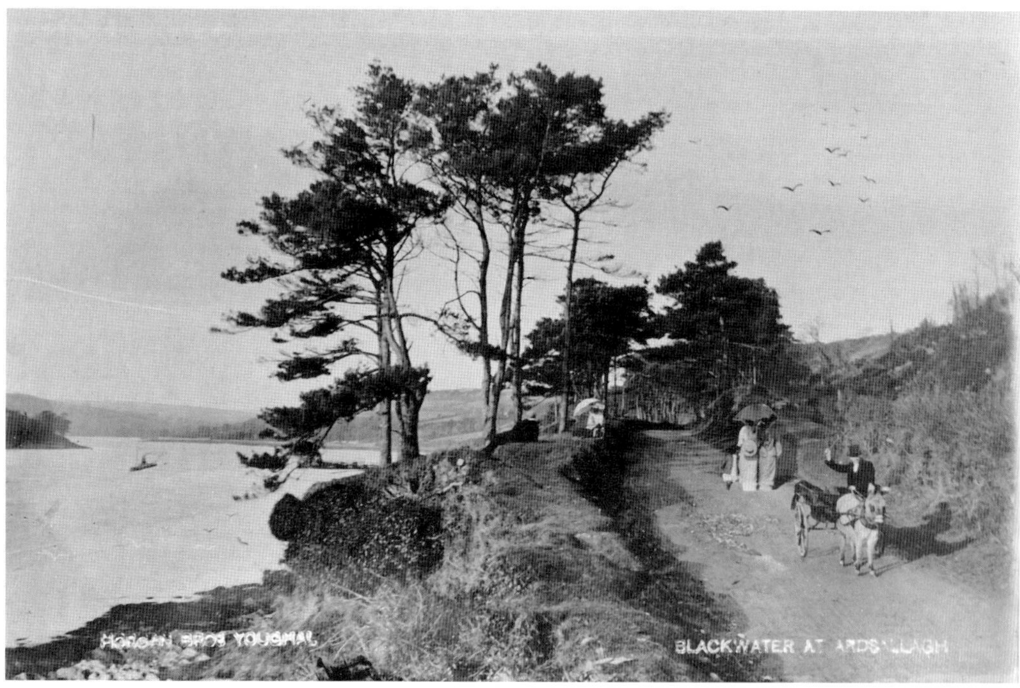

The Blackwater by Ardsallagh.

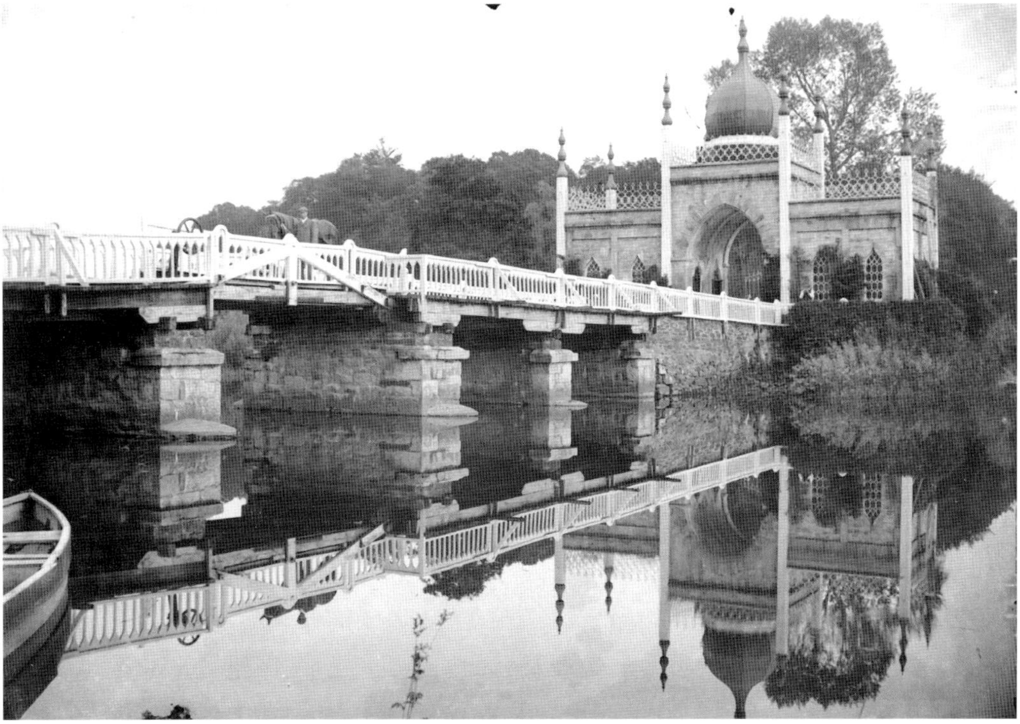

*Dromana Gate and Bridge over the Finisk River, which runs into
the Blackwater, was initially a honeymoon gift made of paper by the tenants of
Henry Villiers-Stewart in 1826, which was later reconstructed in stone.*

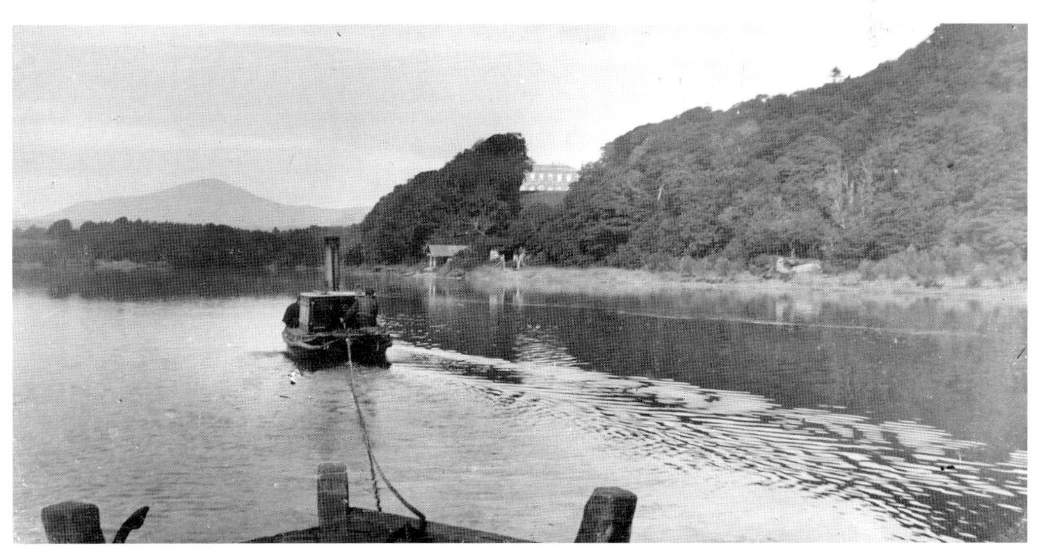

A steamer pulls a boat on the Blackwater with Dromana house on the right.

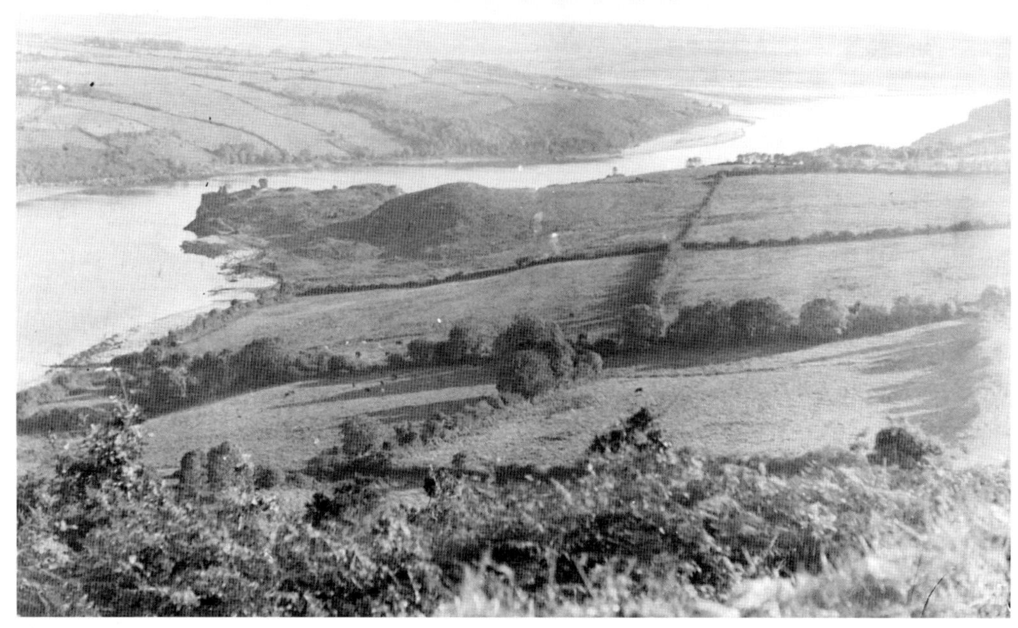

Old Strancally, or srón a cailleach, *hag's nose, as it sticks out onto the Blackwater.*

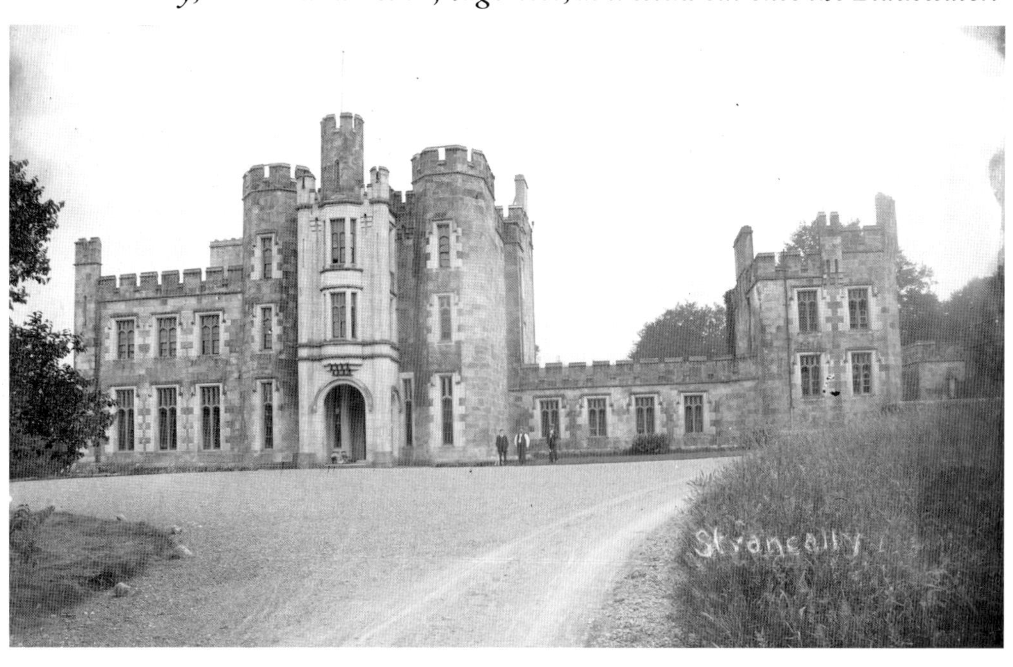

New Strancally Castle.

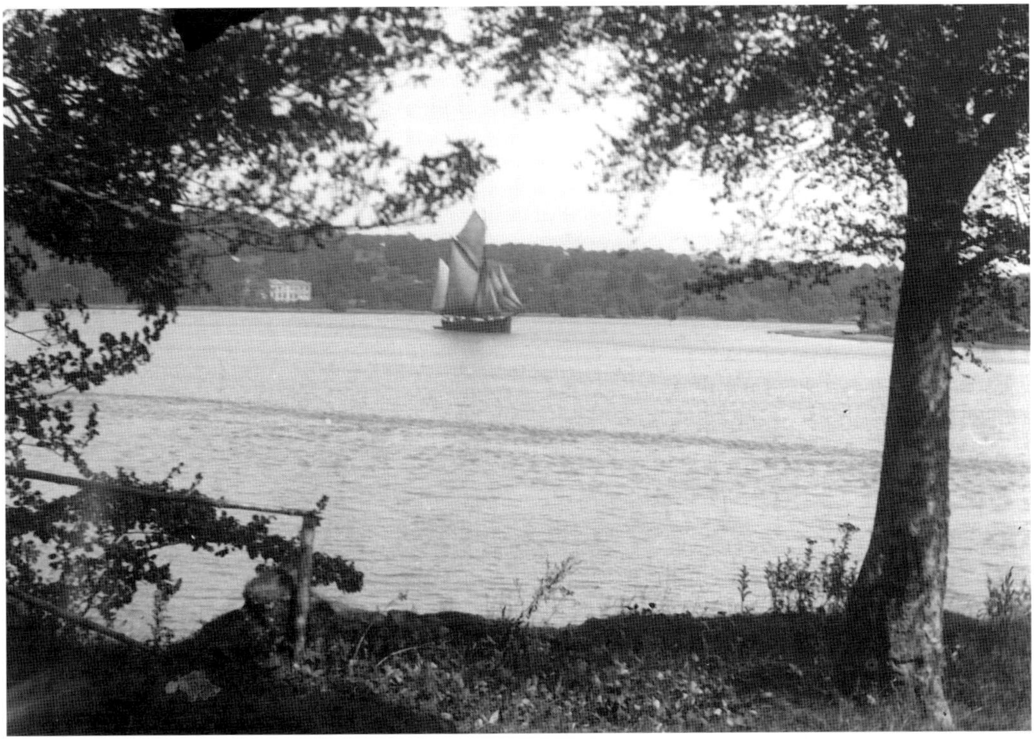

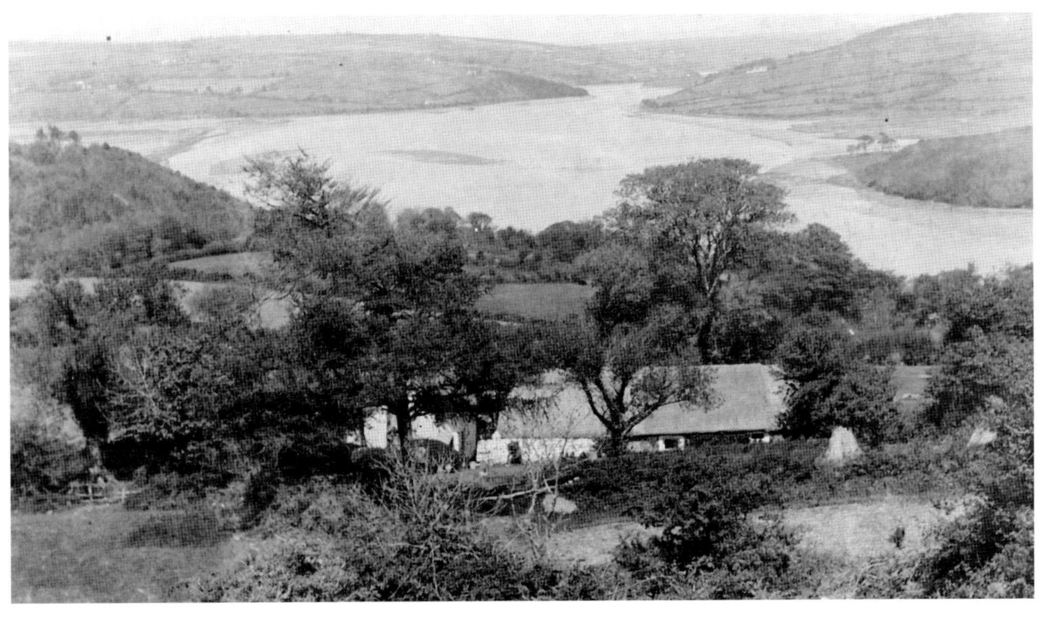

The John a Dab *on the Blackwater with Ballynatray in the background.*

The Blackwater from Ardsallagh.

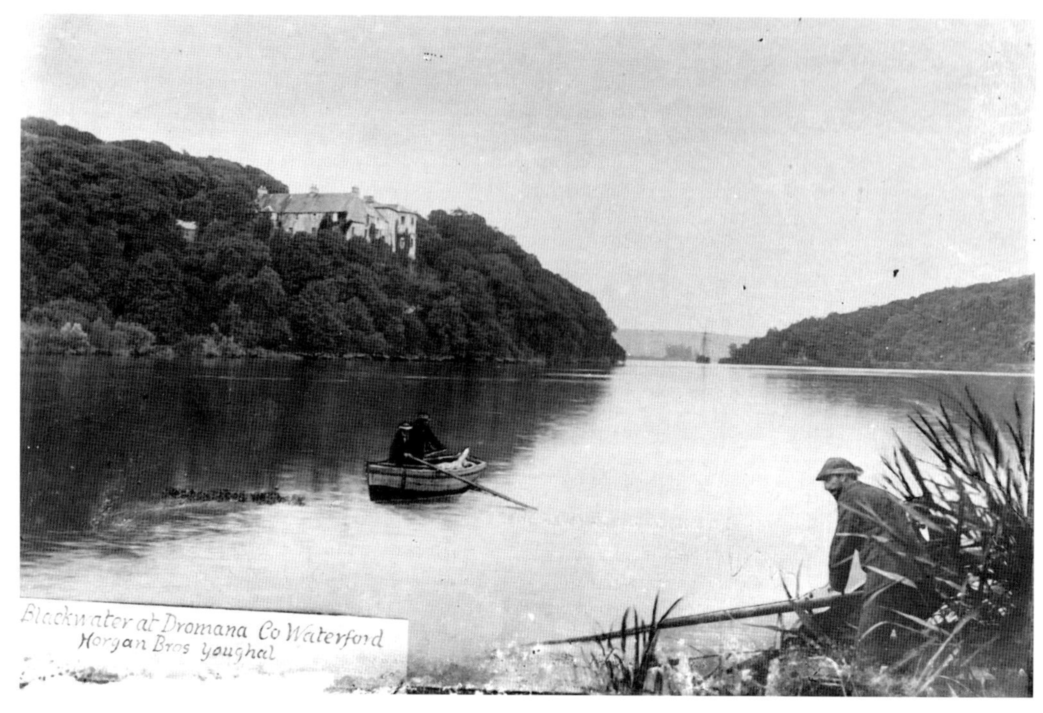

Dromana House on the Blackwater.

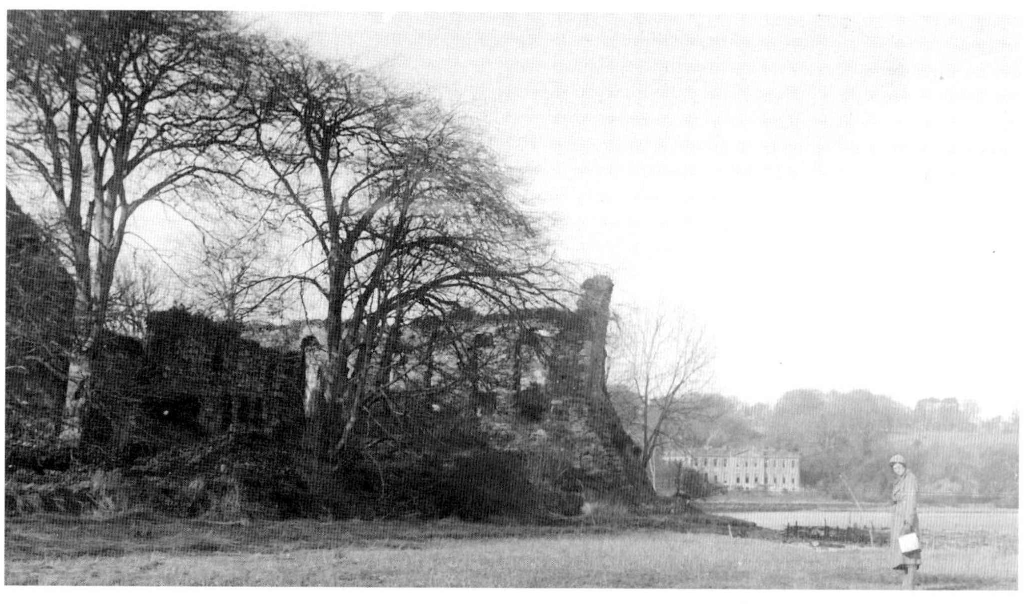

Templemichael on the Blackwater with Ballynatray House in the background.

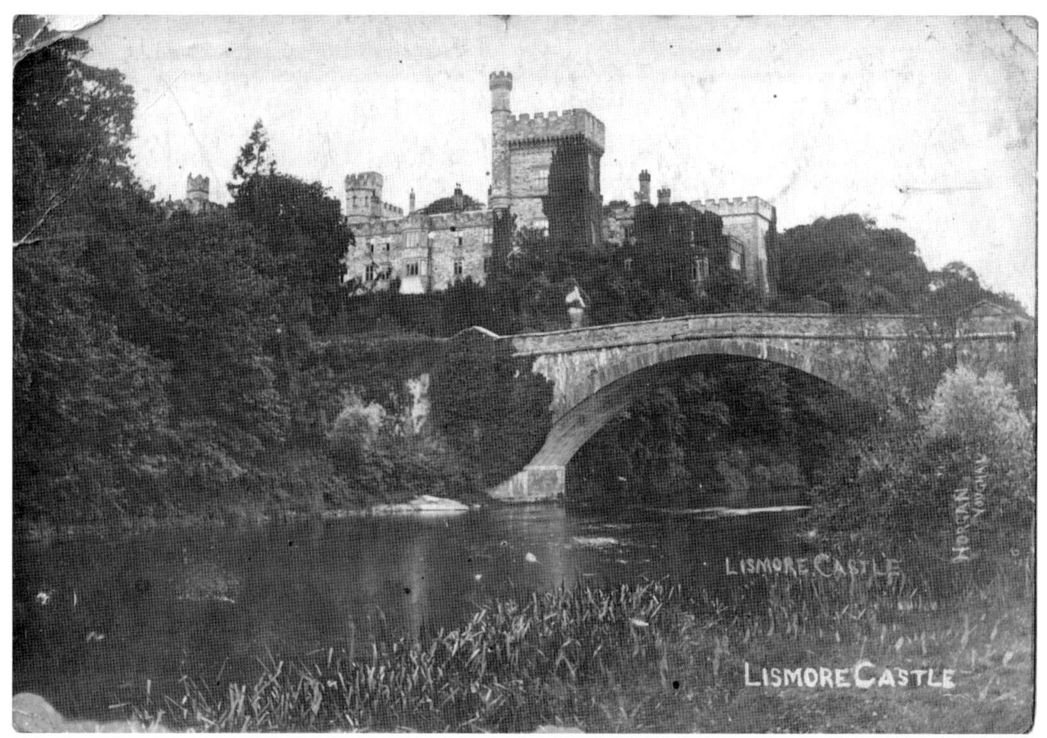

Lismore Castle.

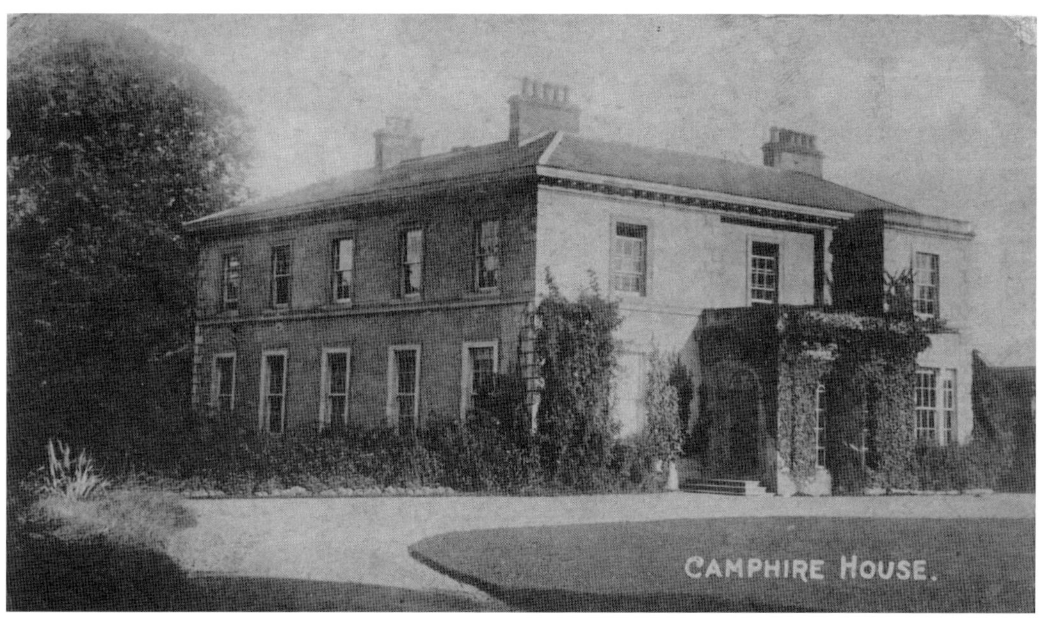

Camphire House.

Horgan Postcards

Writing letters was the primary means of communicating from a distance, and postcards became extremely popular. The brothers' extensive catalogue of photographs of the Blackwater, Youghal and surrounding areas offered them a pioneering role in the postcard business. They included Christmas cards and greeting cards for special occasions. They also formed an alliance with an English company to take as many photos of historic Youghal and the river Blackwater as they could and sold the copyright to them for one guinea each. The brothers' images were so popular they secured a regular slot with the *Evening Echo* which printed their photographs depicting life throughout the county. This venture set them on a prosperous financial road.

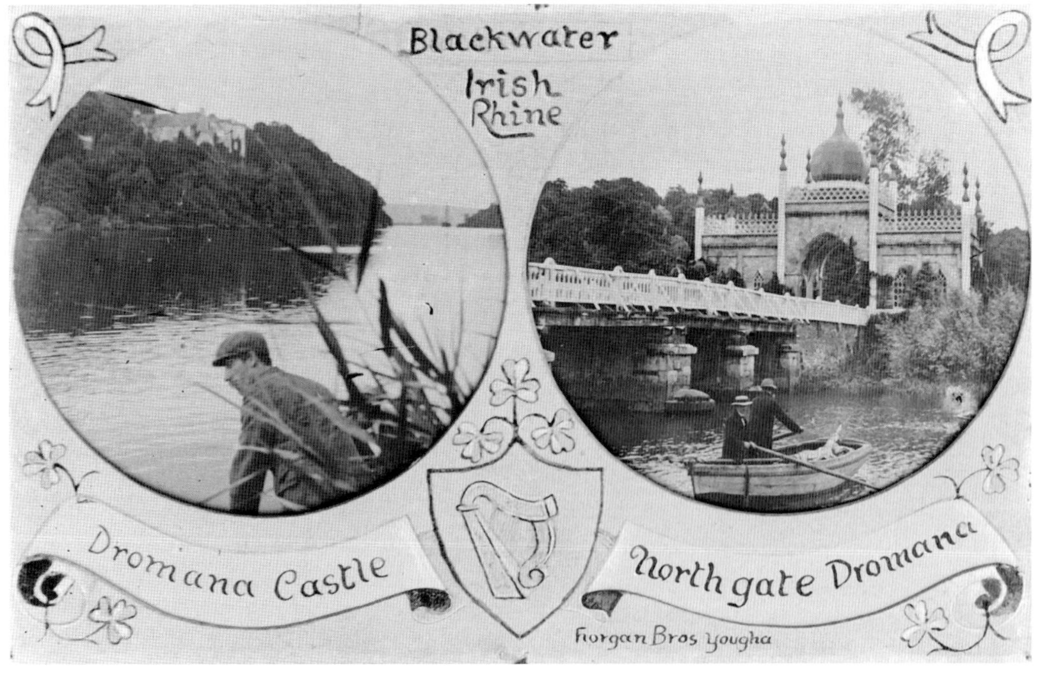

Dromana House and Gate on the Blackwater.

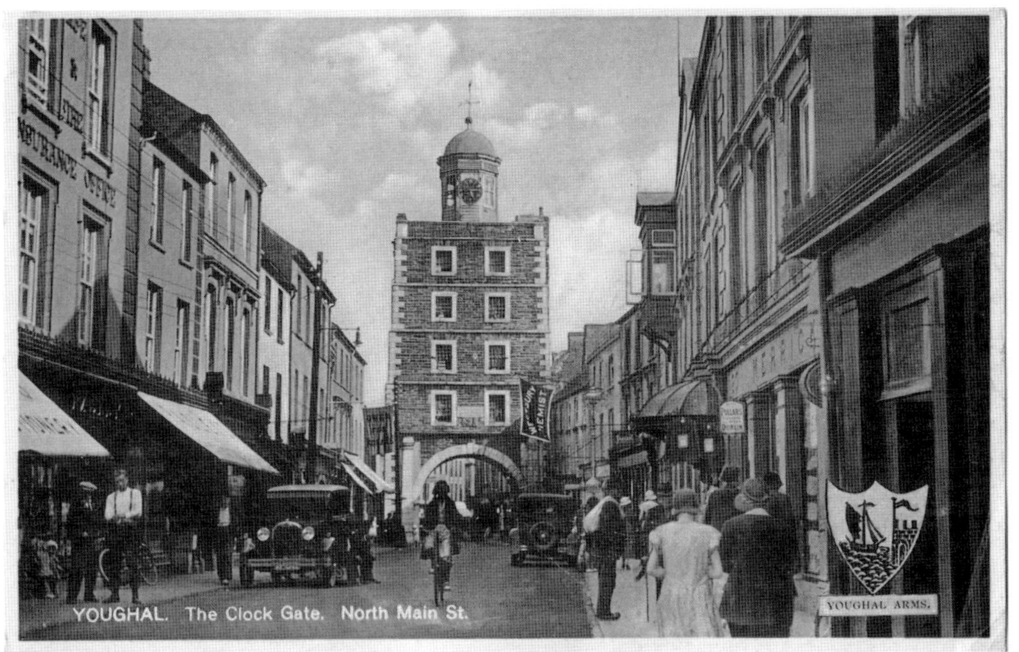

Postcard of Youghal's Clock Gate.

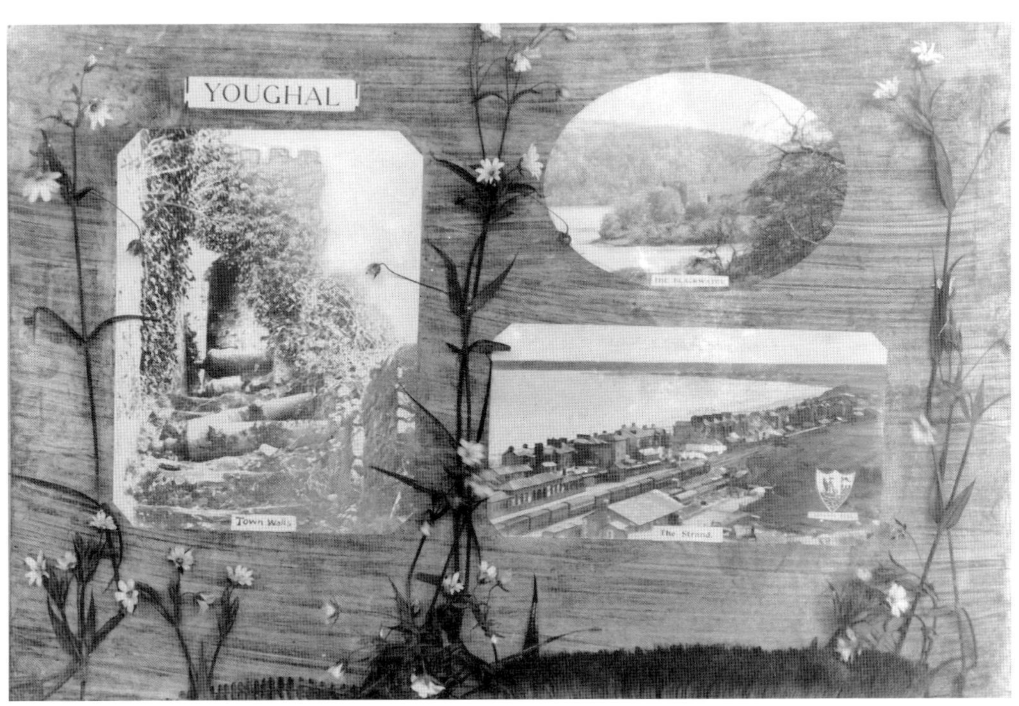

Postcard featuring multiple images and artwork.

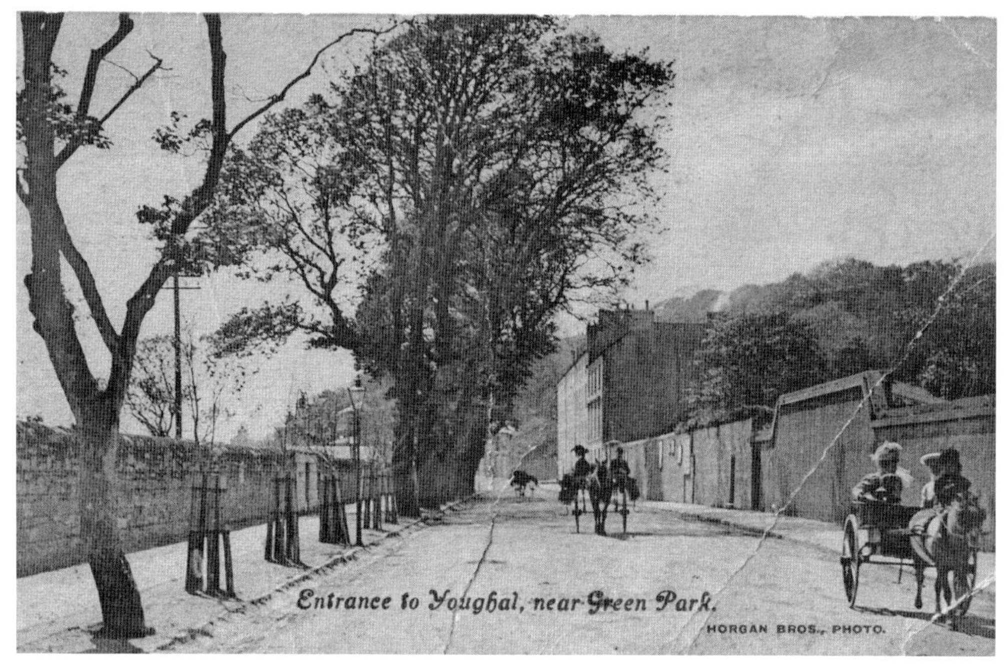

Postcard of entrance to Youghal Greenpark.

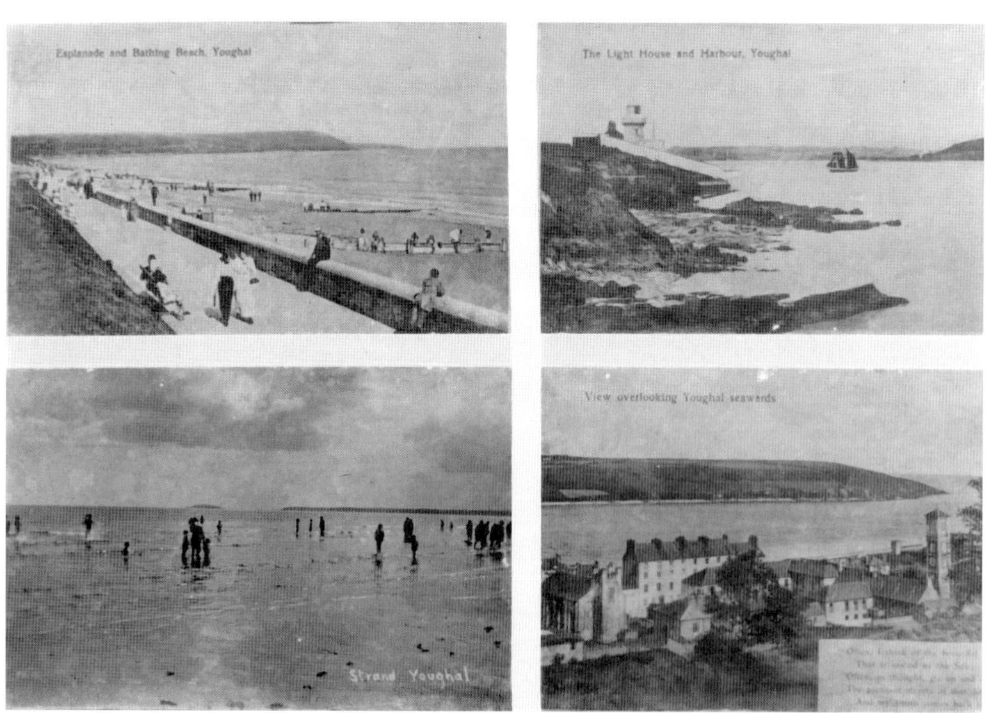

A postcard featuring a selection of photographs.

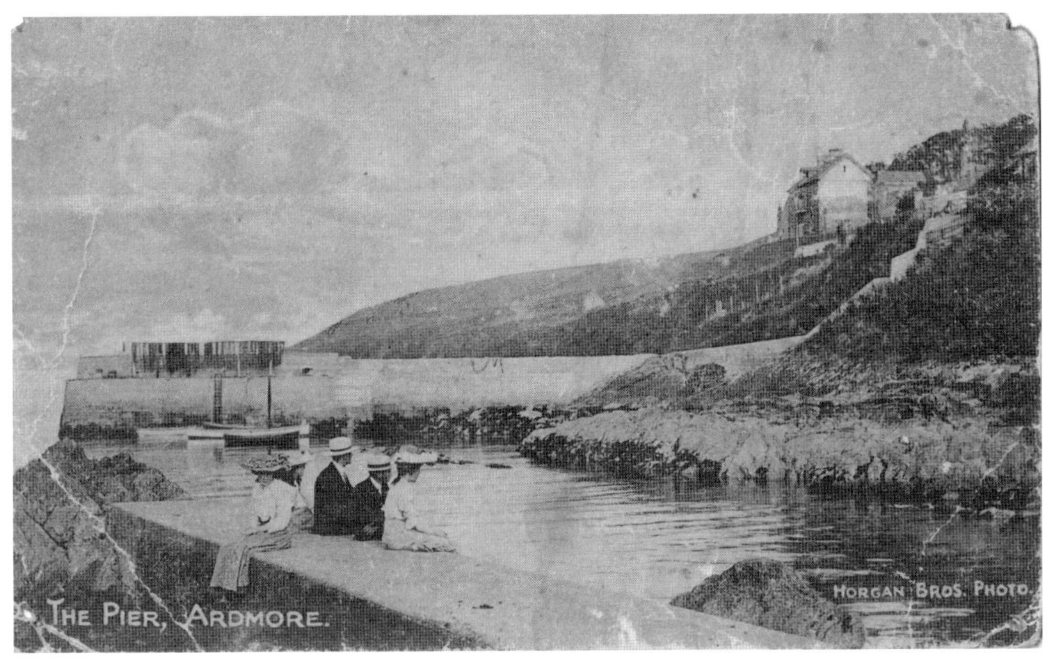

Postcard of the pier, Ardmore.

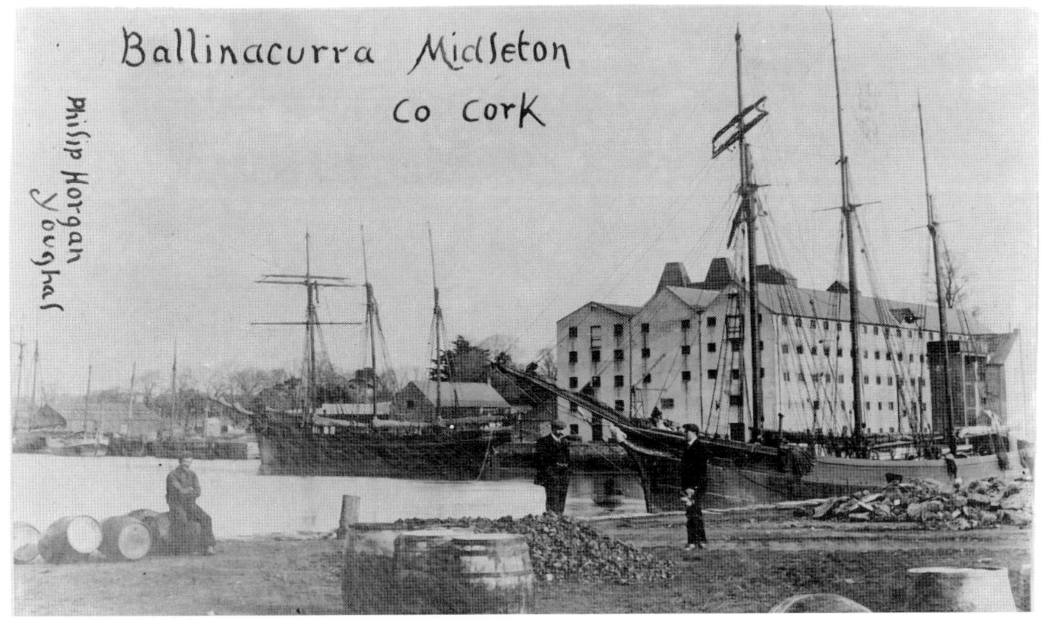

Postcard of dock workers at Ballinacurra.

The Horgan Brothers produced a series of Christmas postcards featuring Youghal as their backdrop. These greetings were sent all over the world.

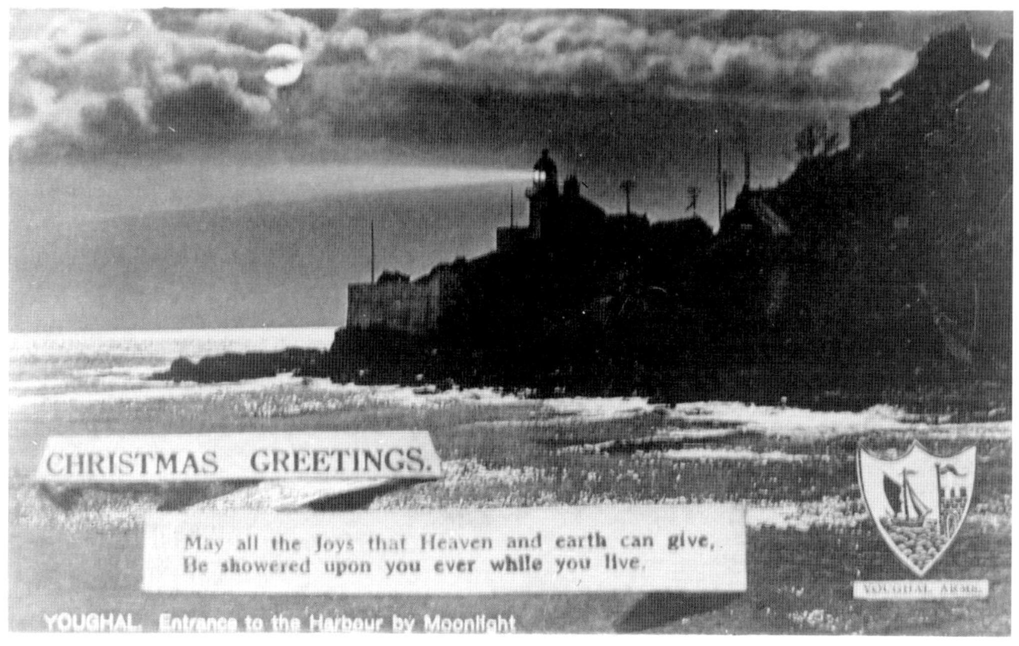

Christmas card of lighthouse at night and below *Youghal Greeting.*

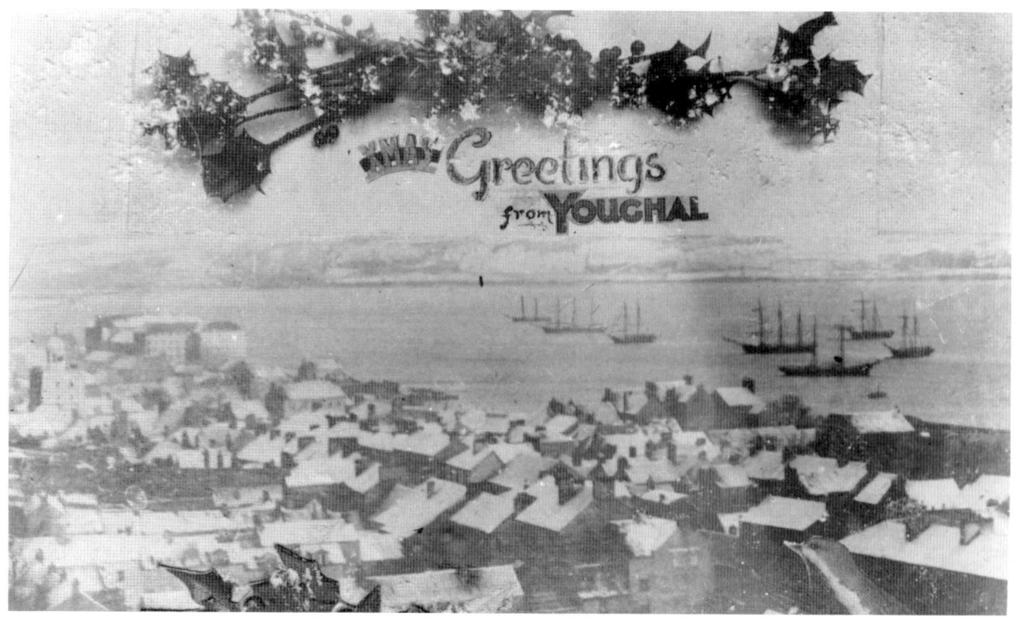

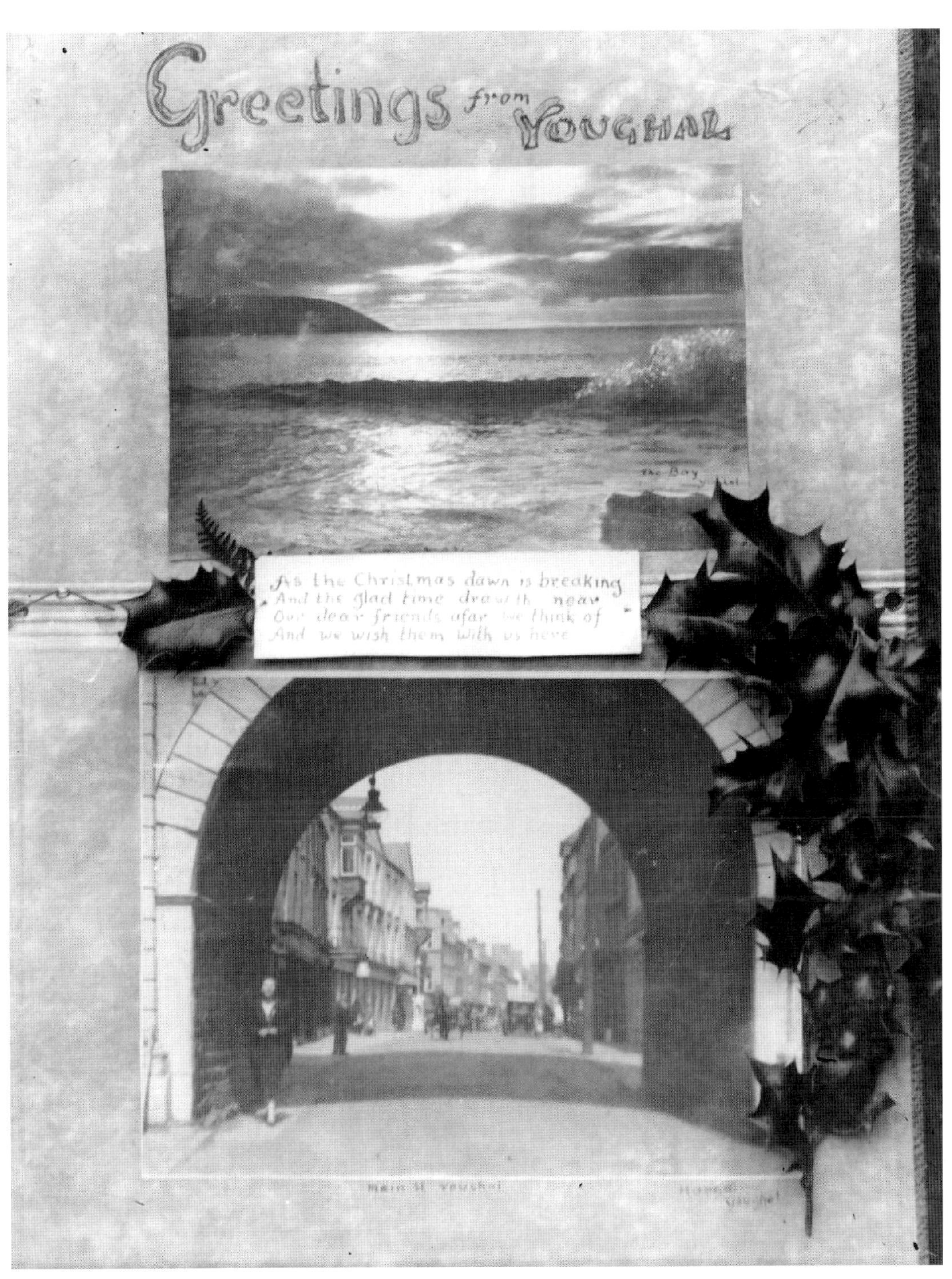

Christmas card made with collage of photo prints and holly.

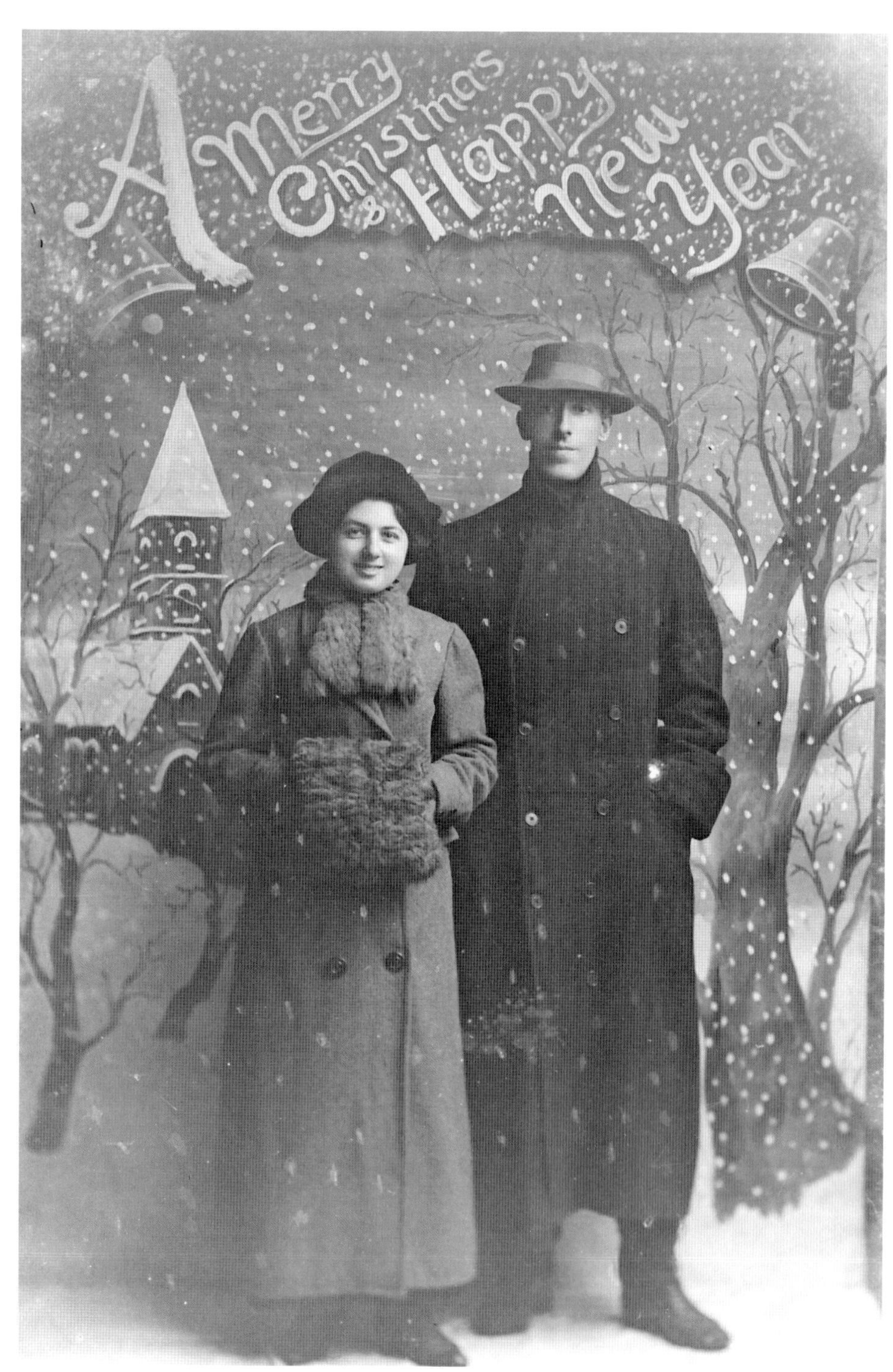

James and Marietta dressed for a Christmas card.

Their lucrative postcard business offered the brothers the opportunity to open their own photographic studio on Friar Street, Youghal.

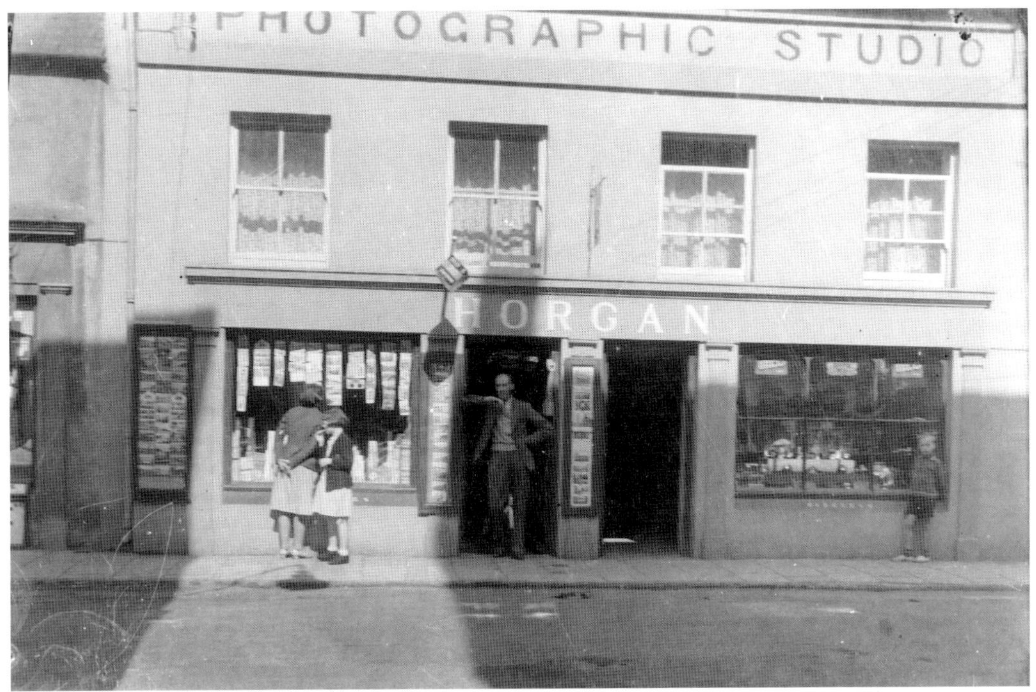

The Horgan Photographic Studio with postcards on display.

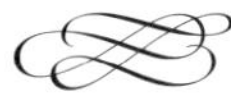

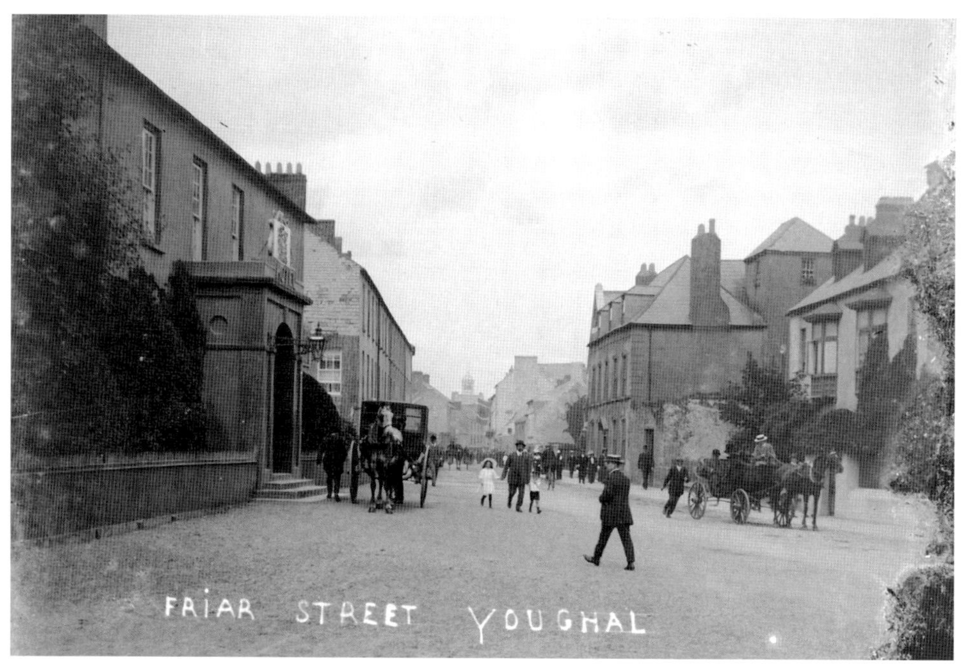

The top of Friar Street in Youghal, the location for the new Horgan photographic studio near the white gable in the mid ground on the right of the photograph.

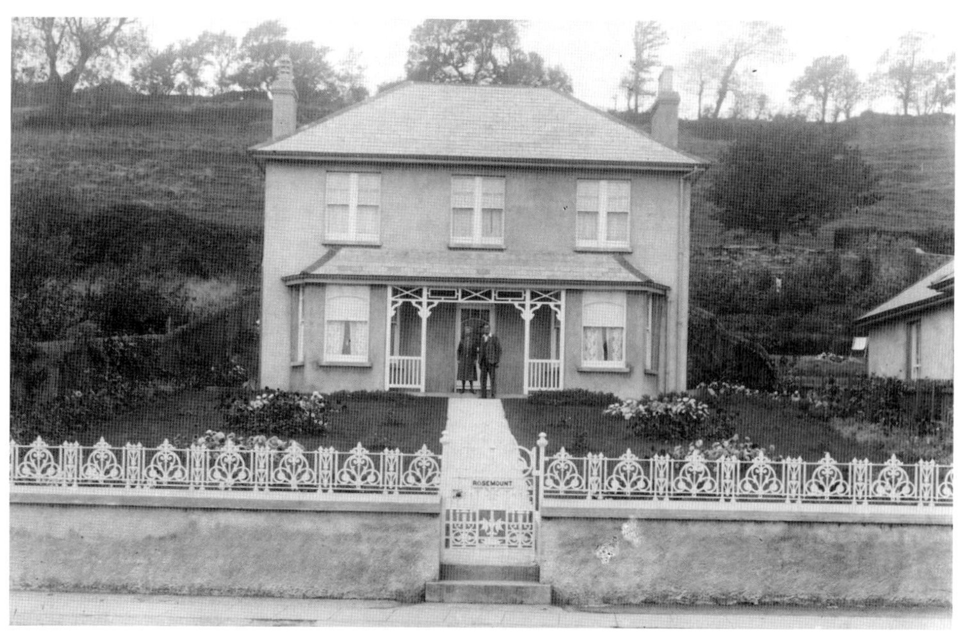

The priest's house.

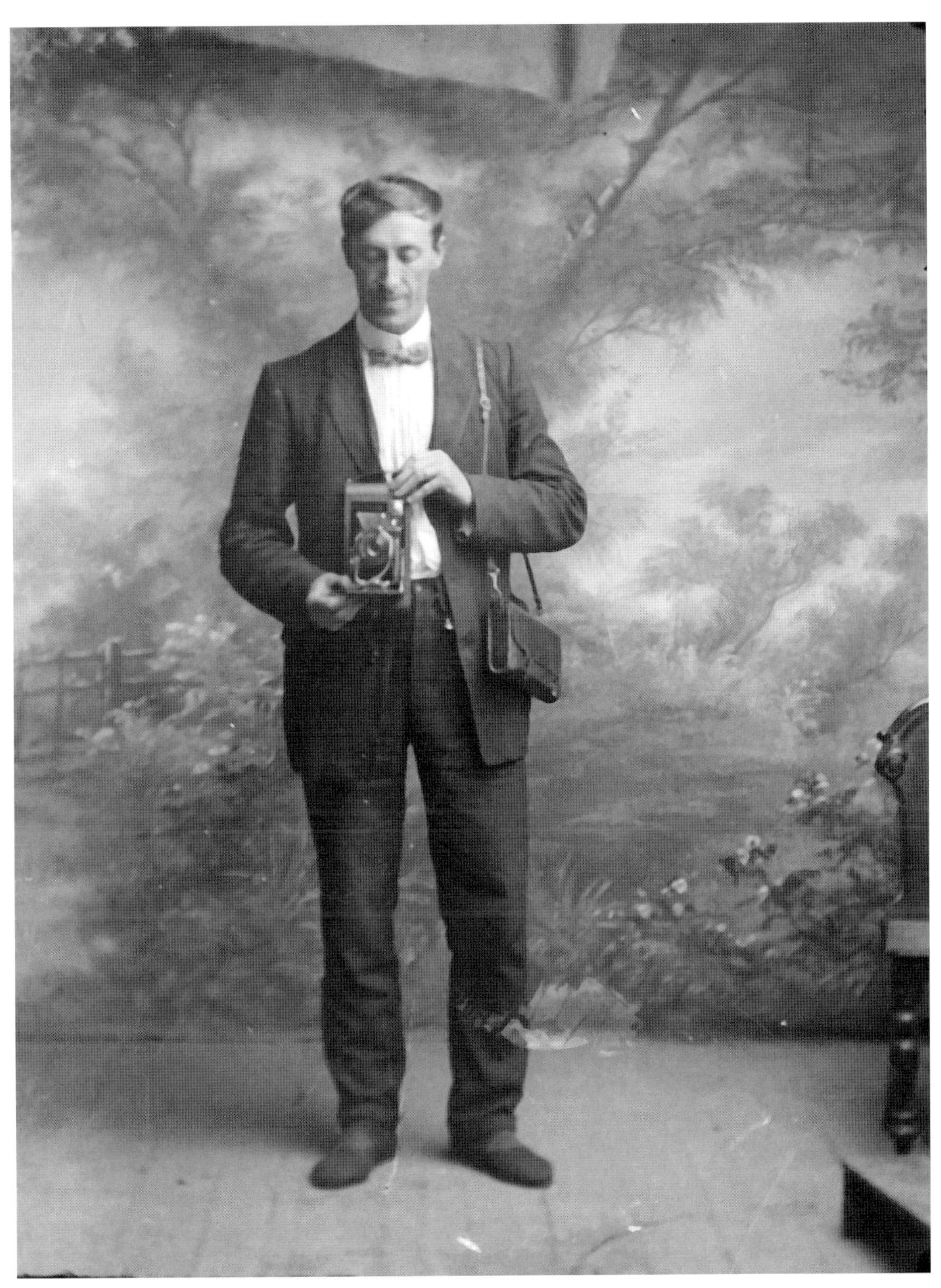

James with a camera.

The brothers developed the space to include a portrait studio, continuing to photograph key events for families in the area, such as births, weddings, communions and graduations that almost always featured the same chair.

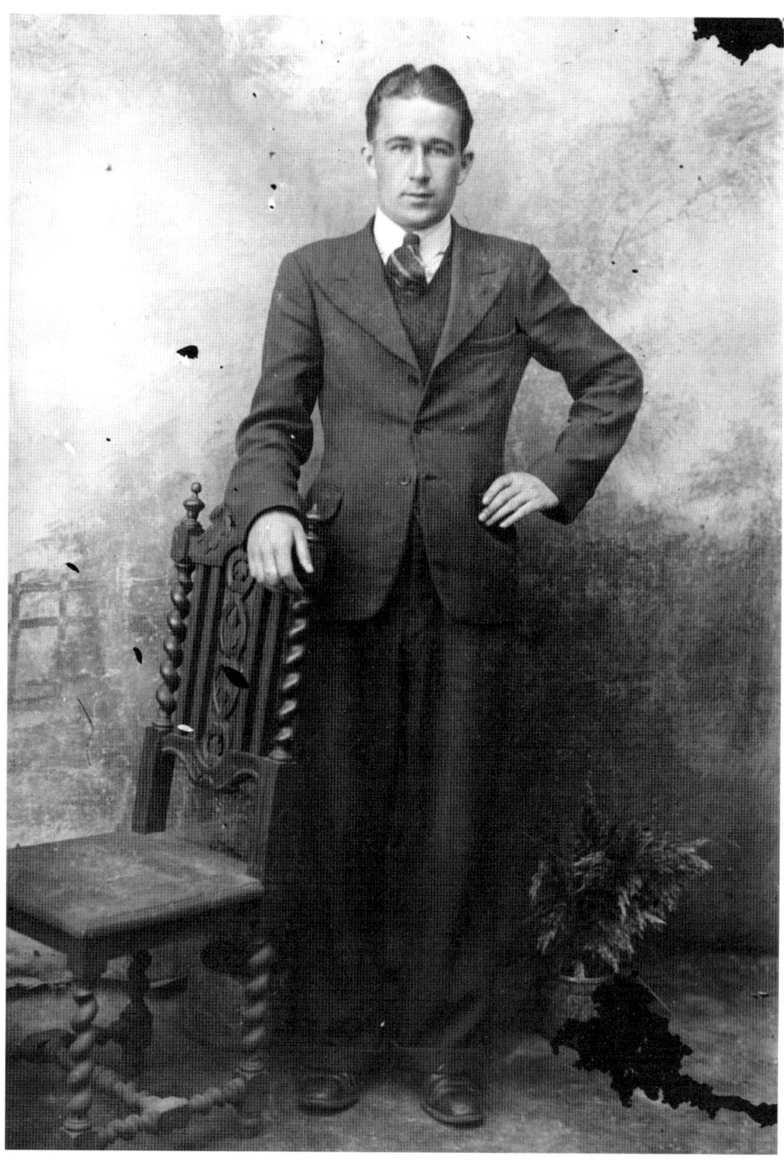

Man posing at the chair that featured in many Horgan studio portrait photographs.

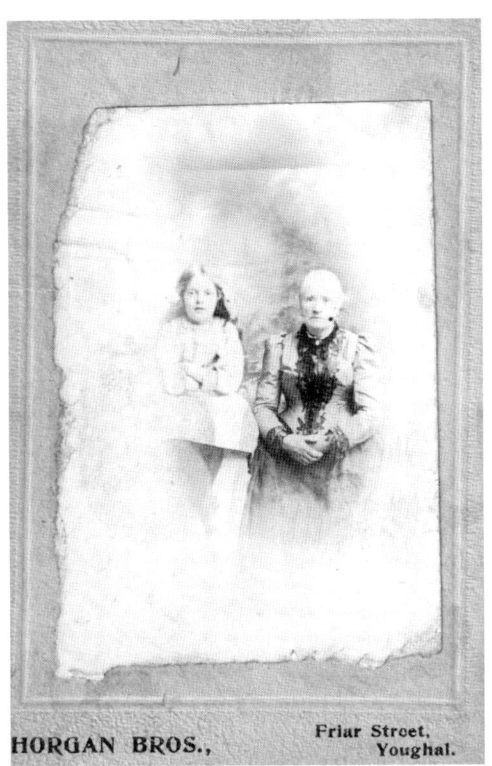

Example of a framed Horgan portrait.

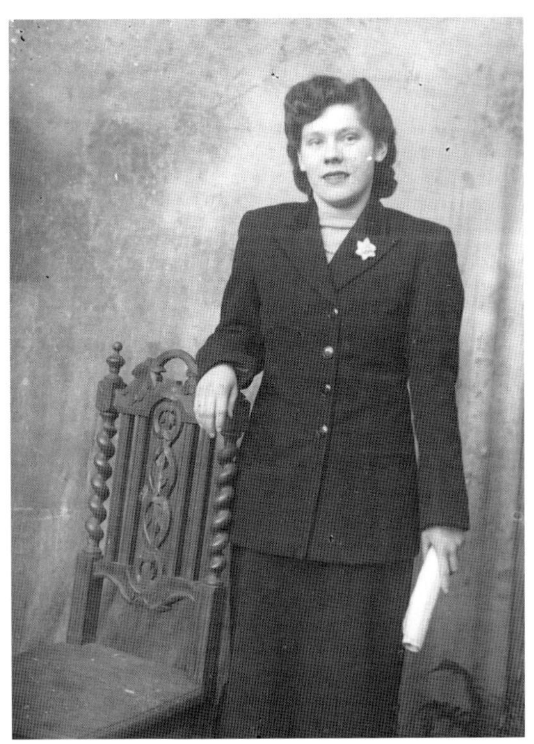

Lady with graduation scroll.

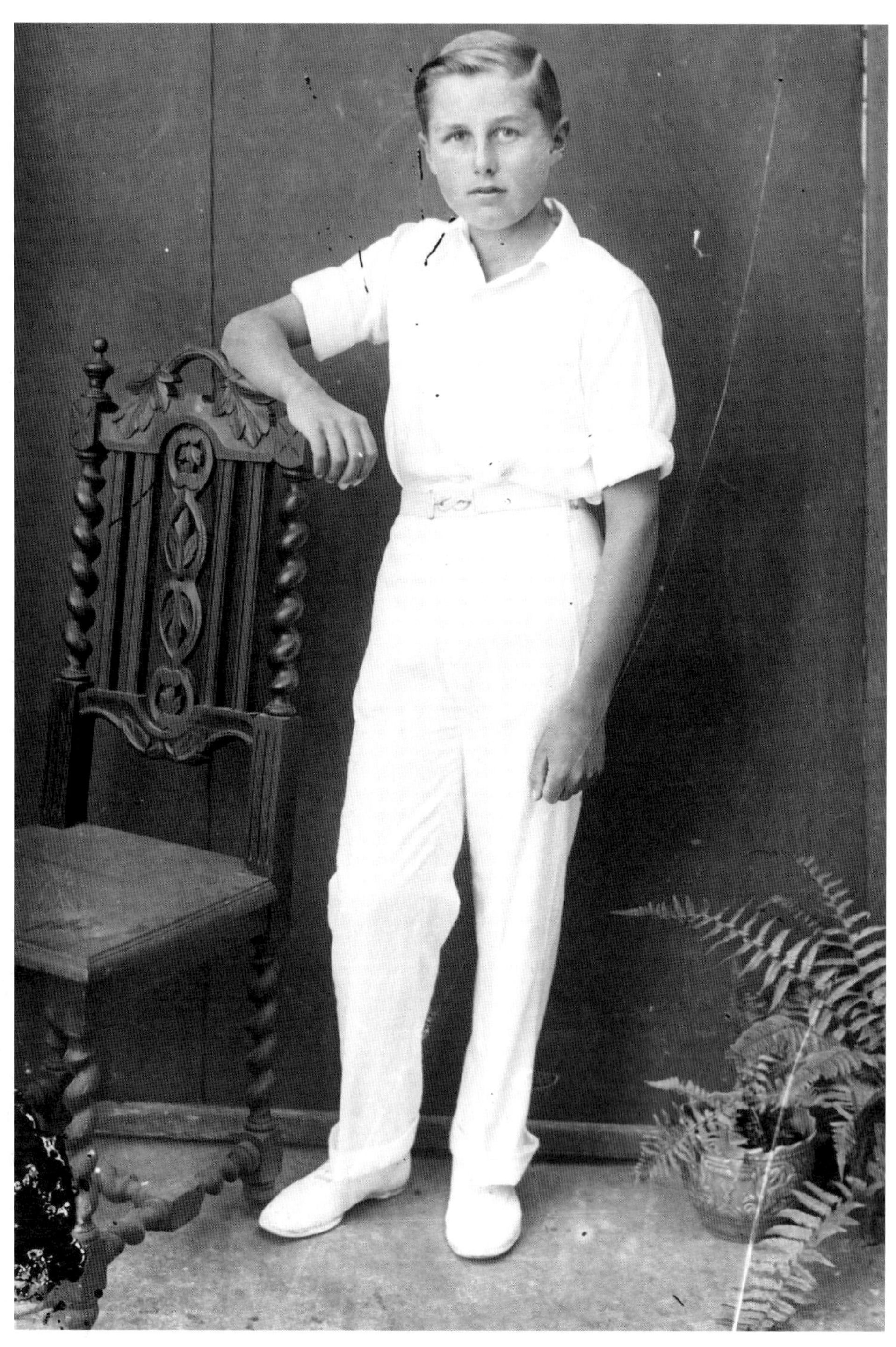

Young man at the Horgan's chair.

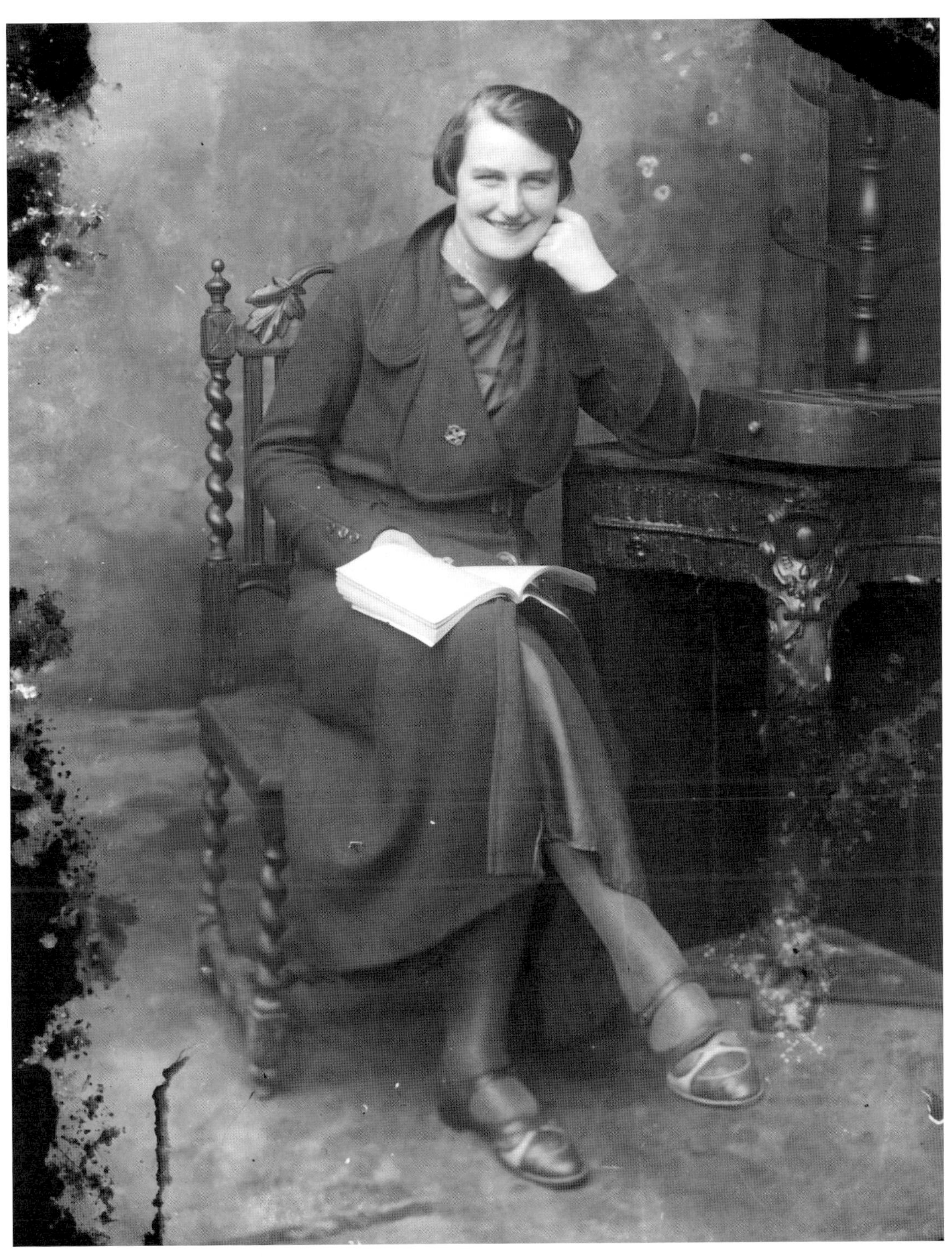

Woman posing with a book.

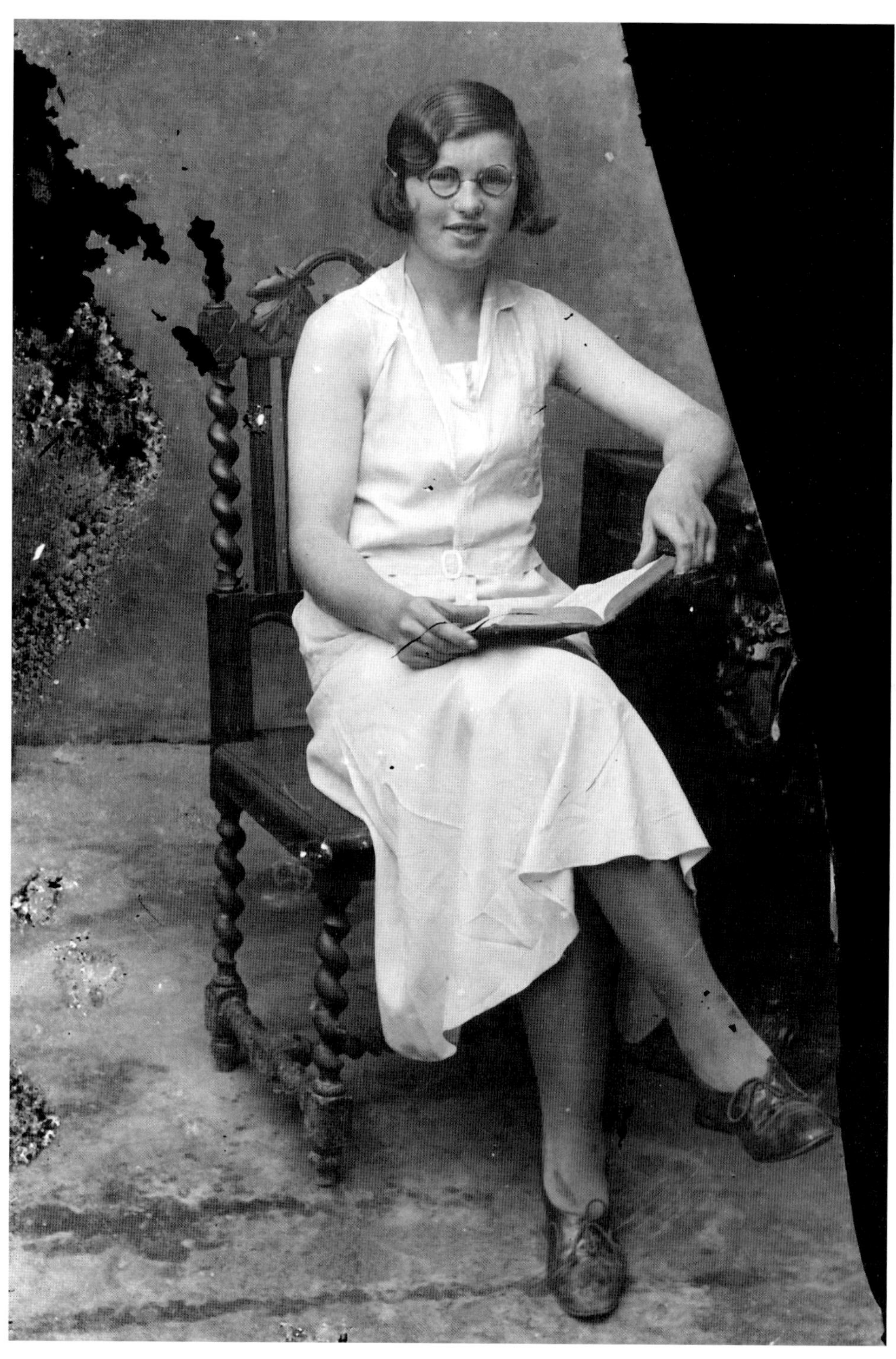

Girl posing with a book – note the broken glass negative.

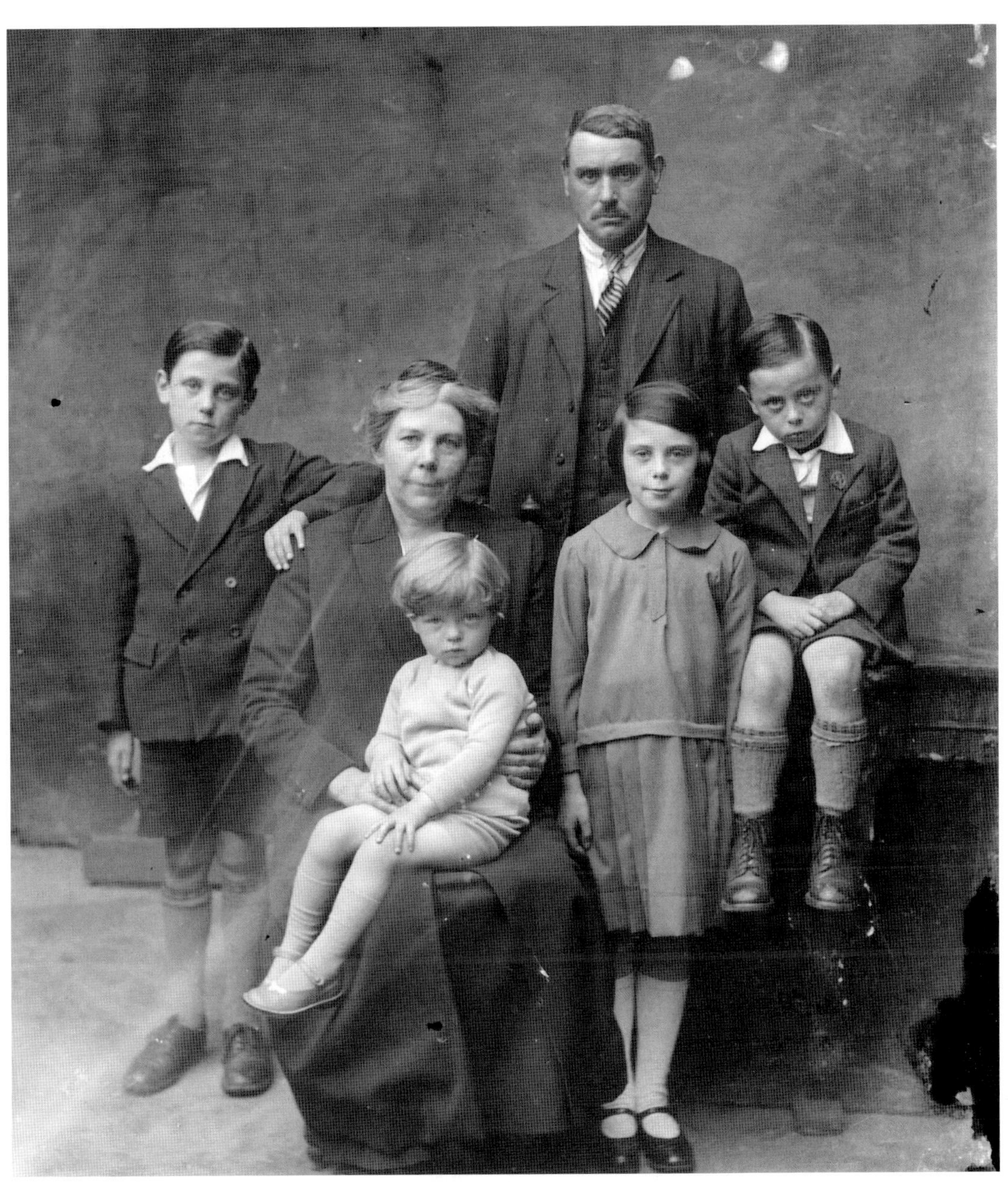

Family photograph at the Horgan Photographic Studio.

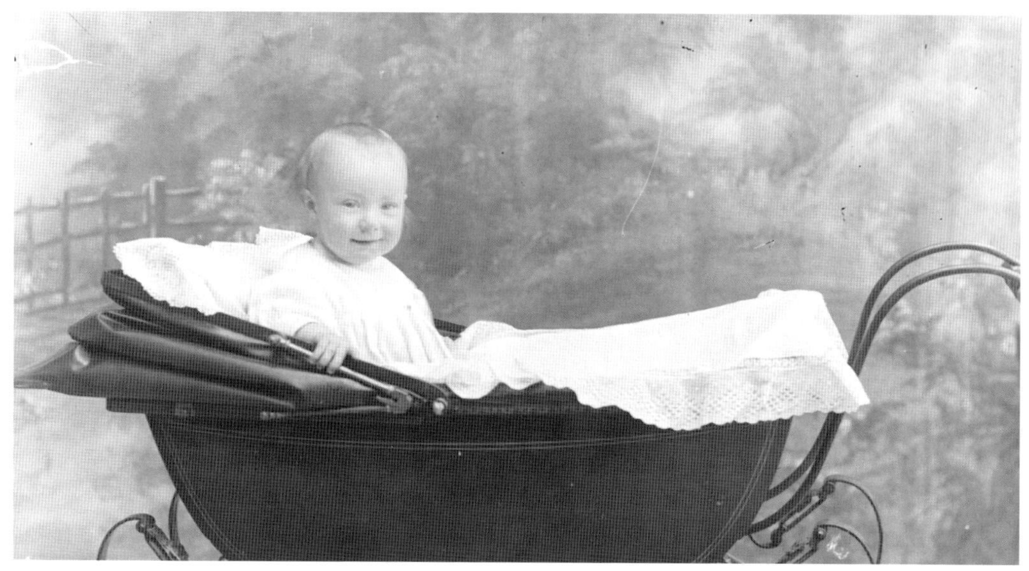

Baby in a pram with a painted backdrop.

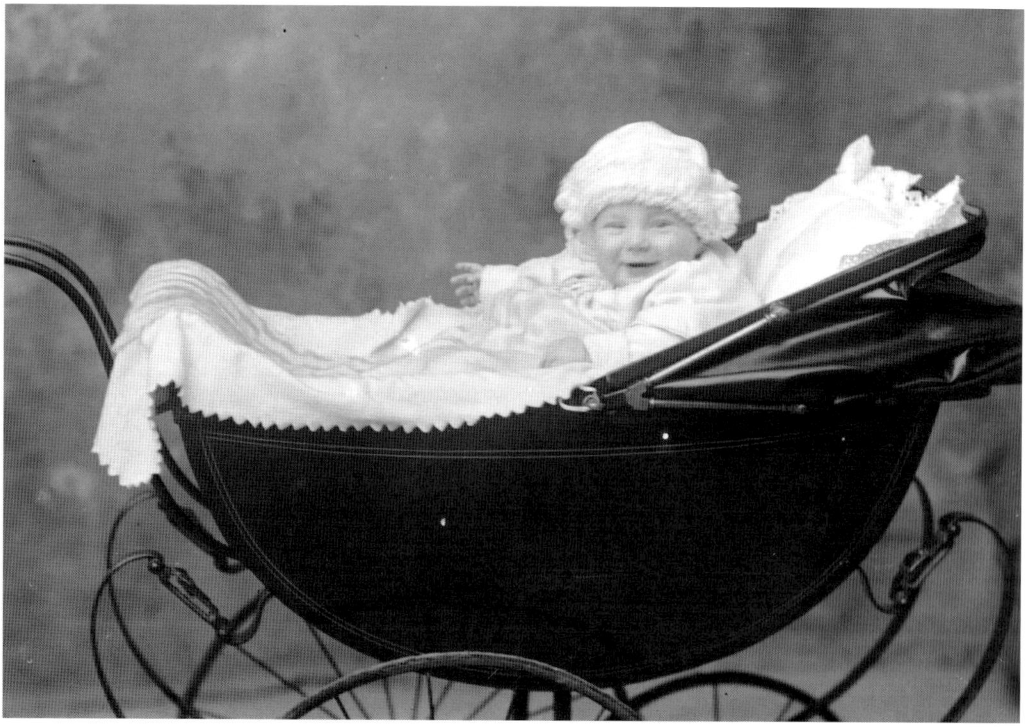

Baby with a bonnet in a pram.

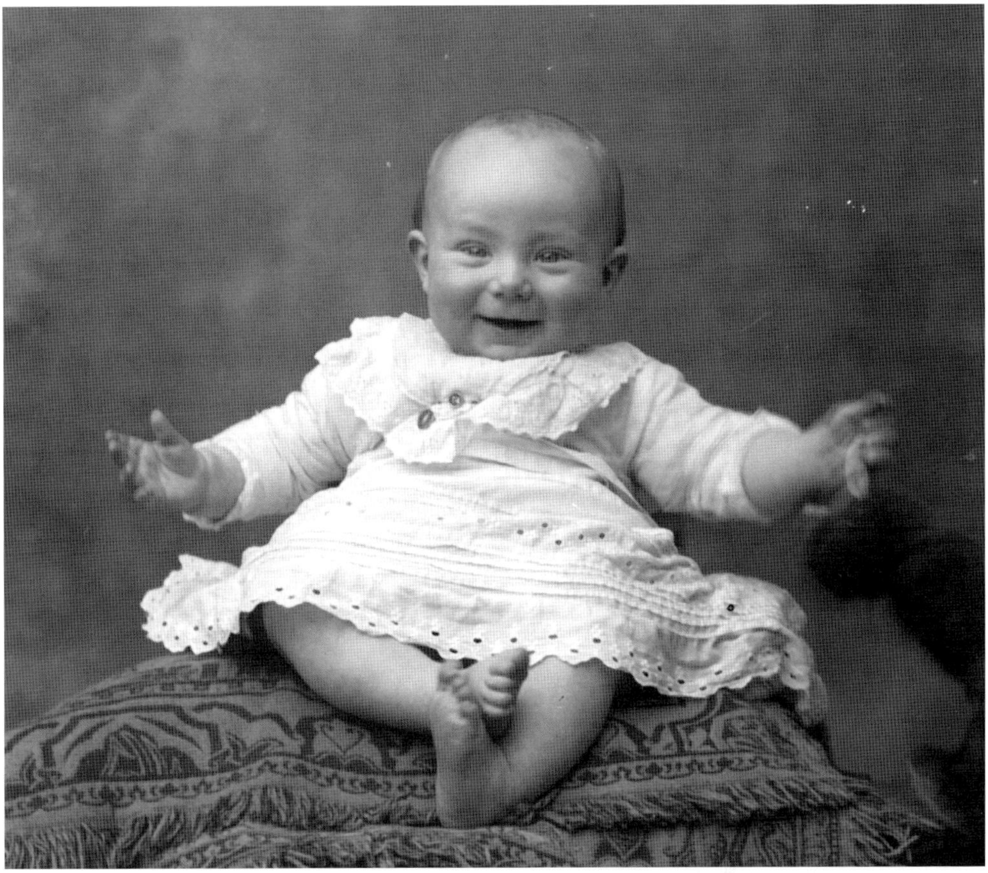

Baby in the Horgan Photographic Studio.

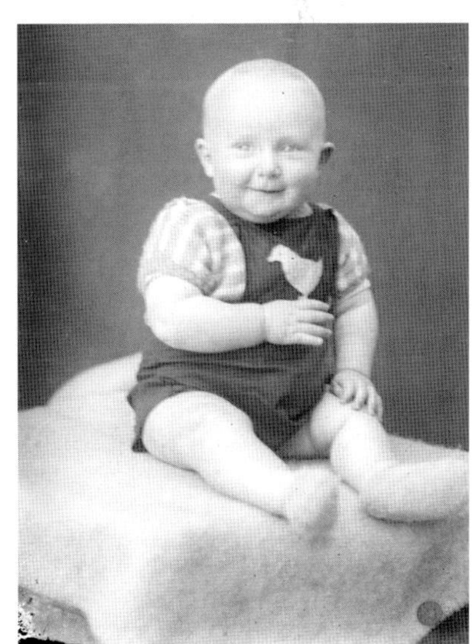

A baby portrait.

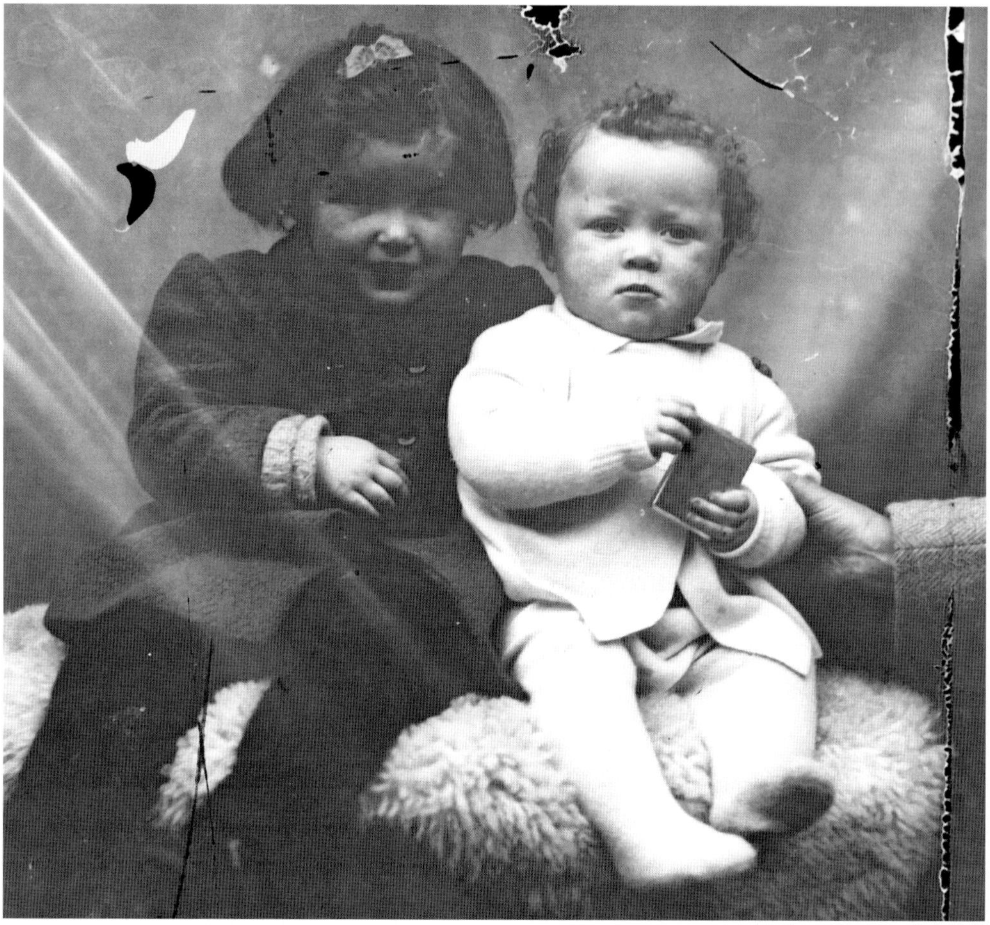

*Two toddlers with an arm of a parent,
holding the baby safely, shows how it was
a challenge to get the right shot.*

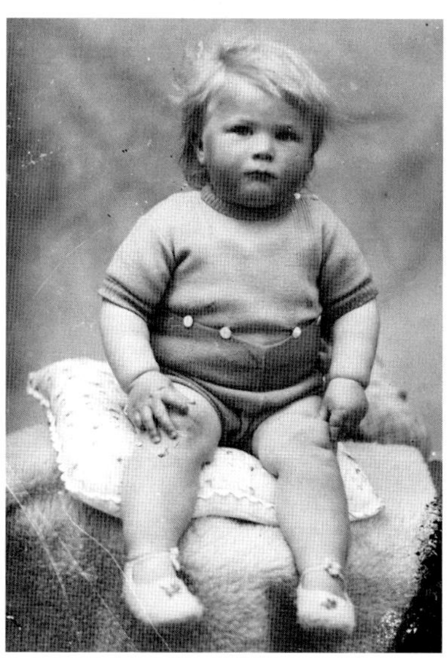

Another toddler posing for a portrait.

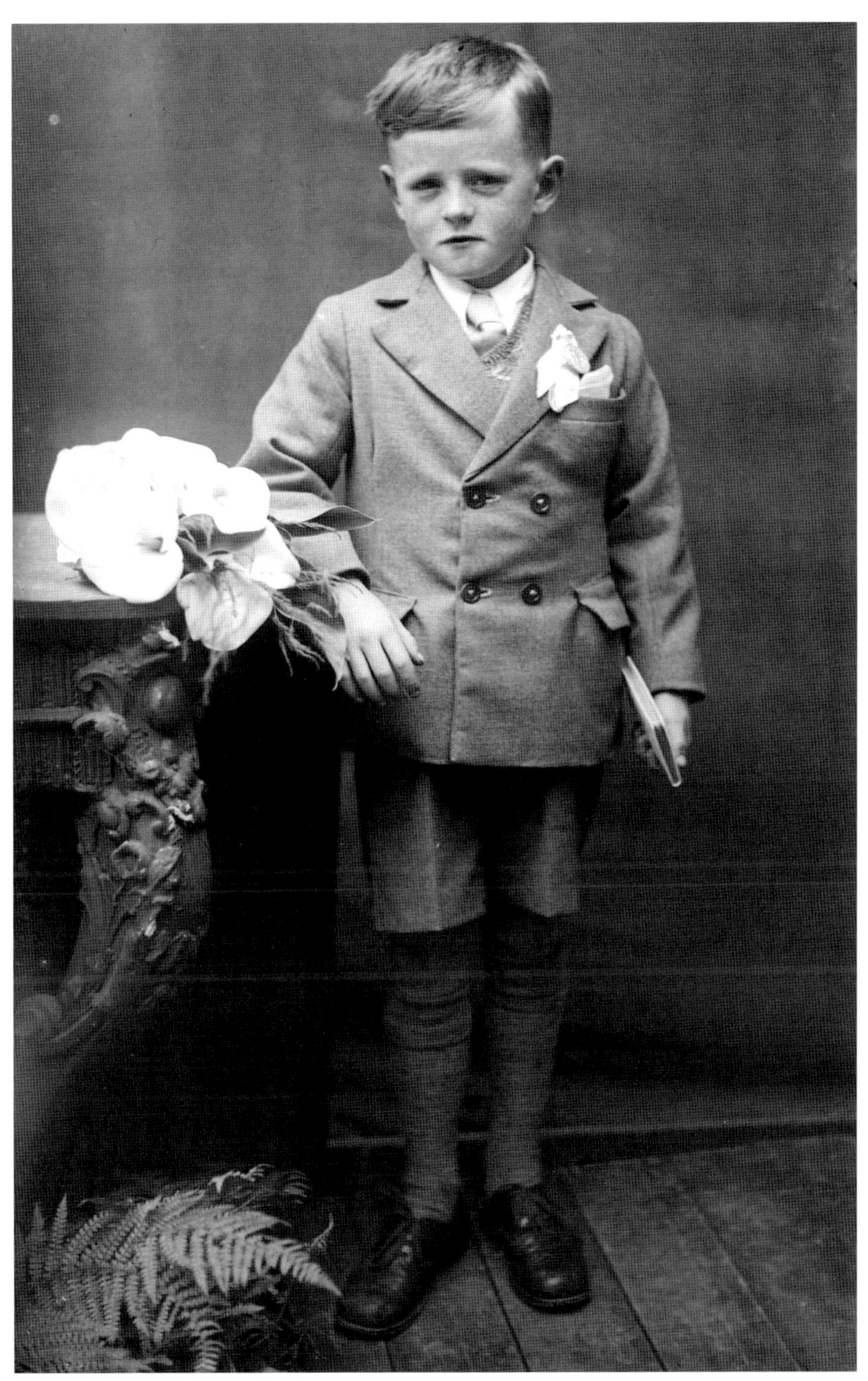

A young boy's communion portrait at the Horgan studio.

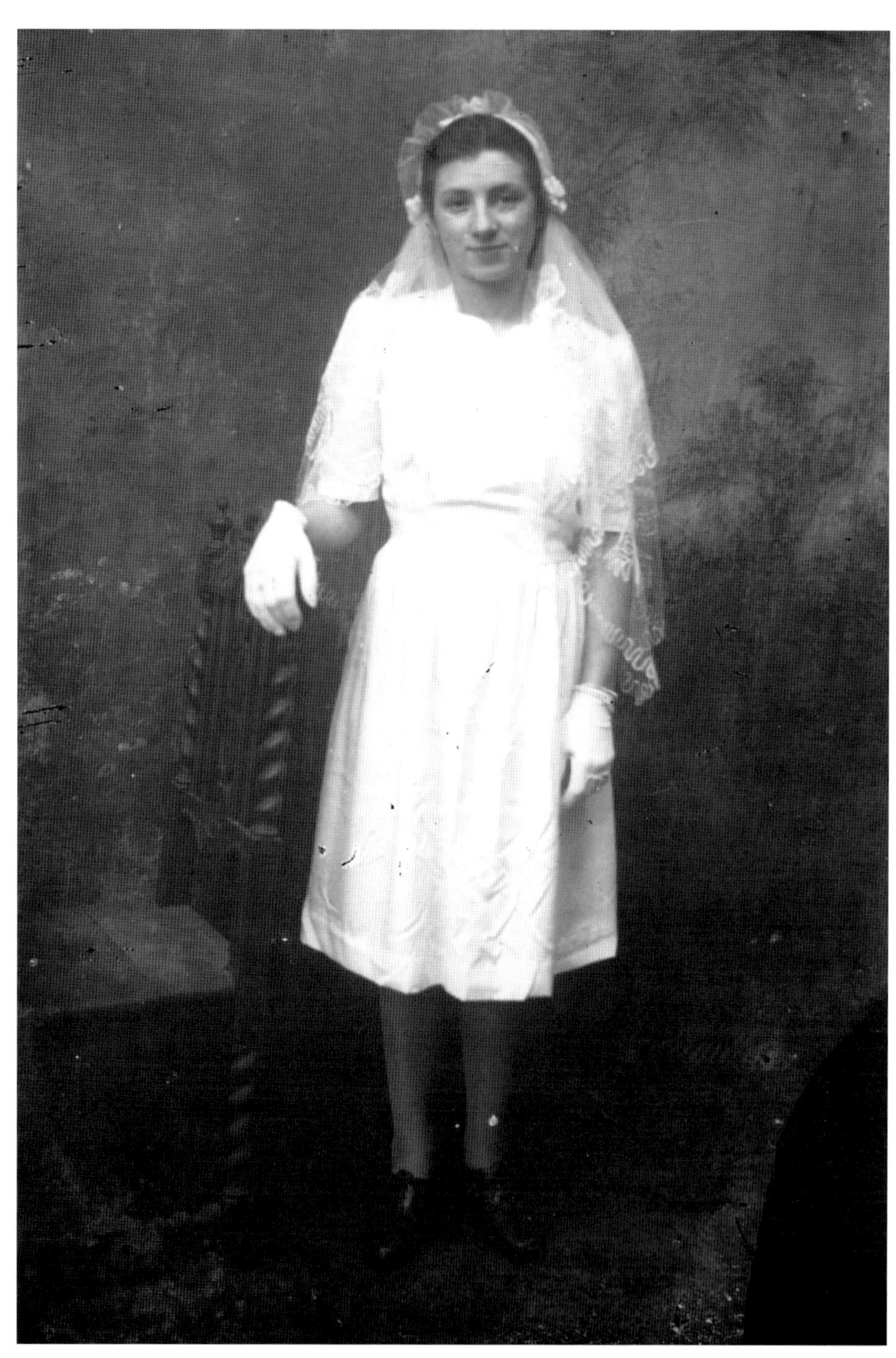

A portrait at the Horgan studio.

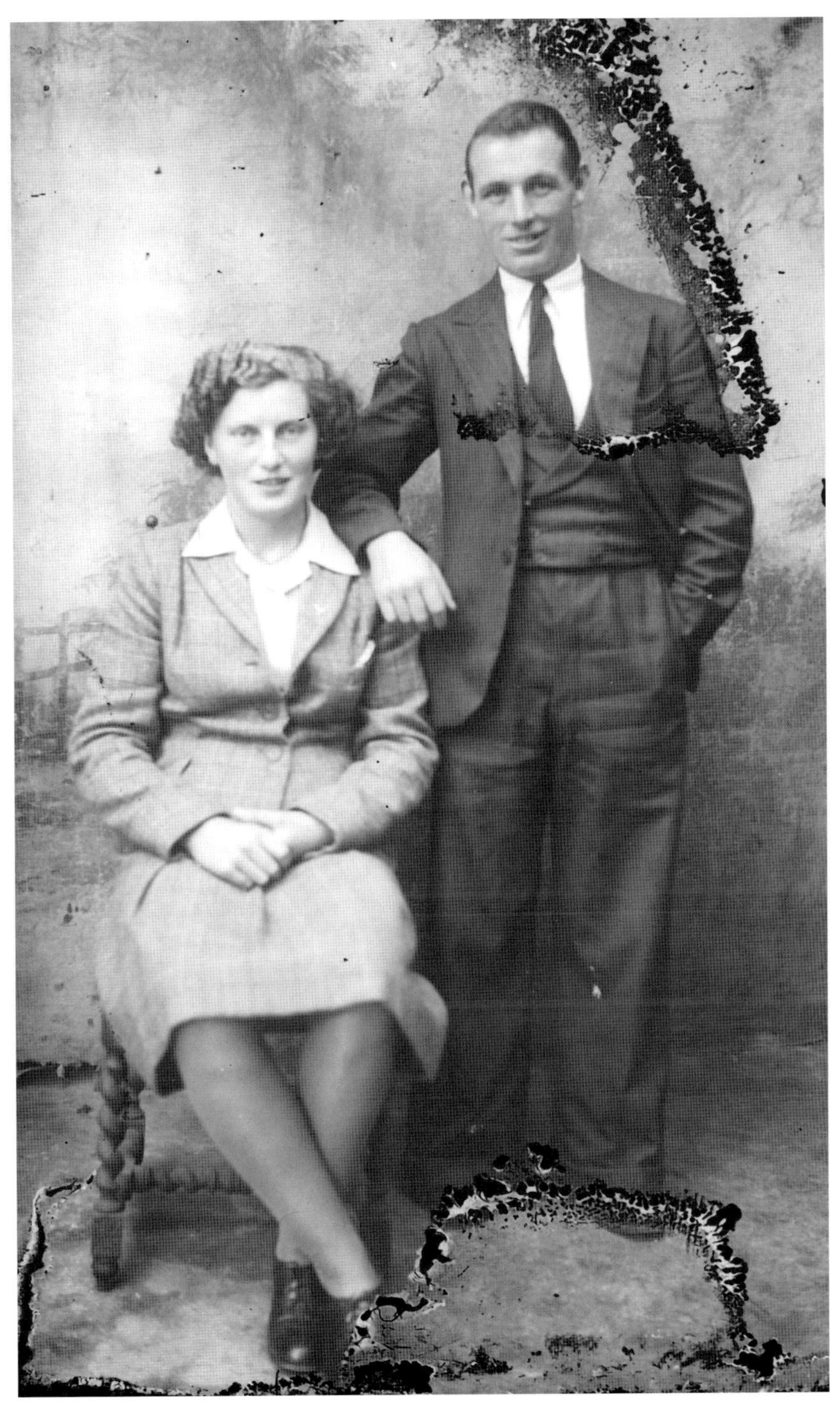

A young couple.

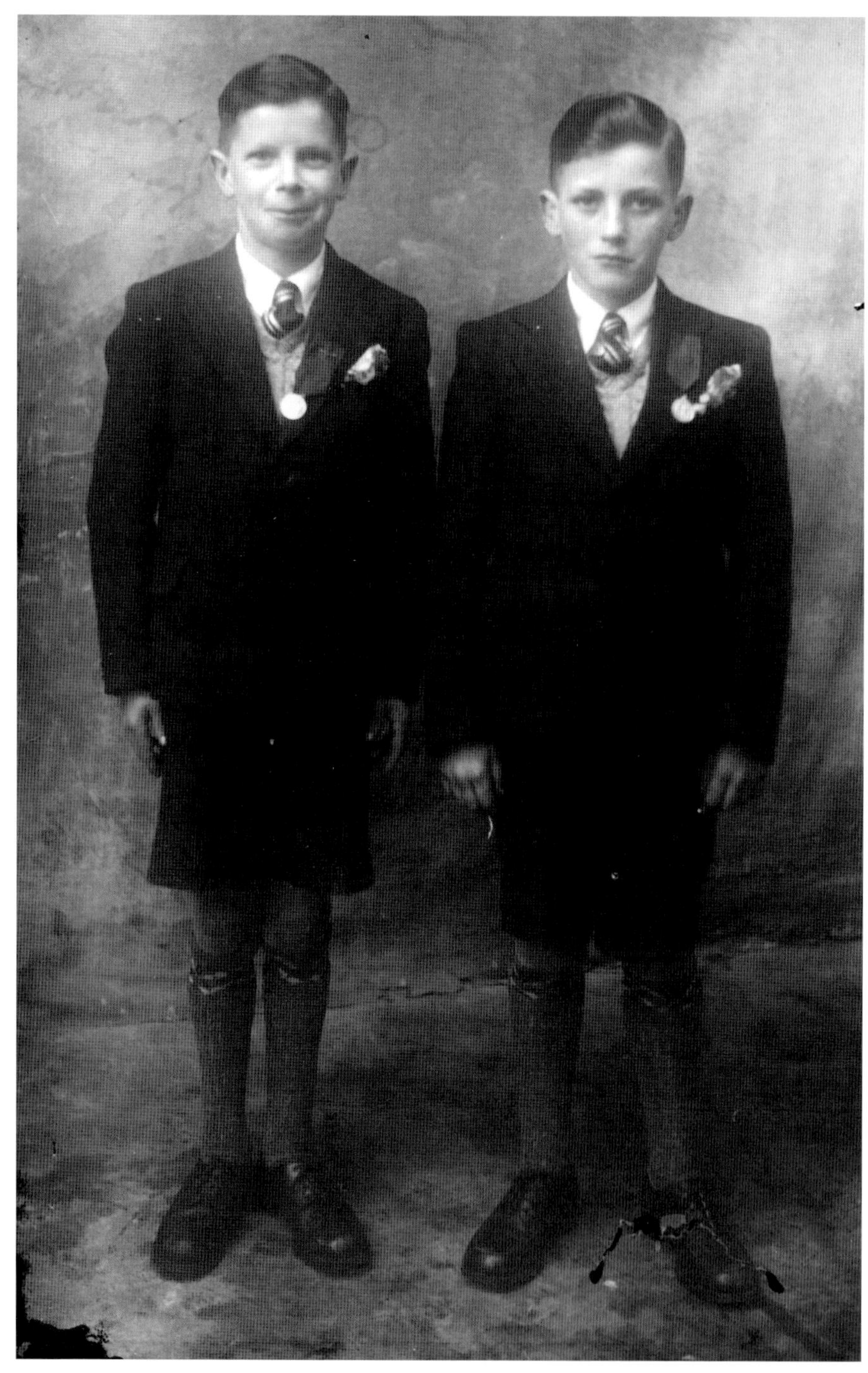

Brothers.

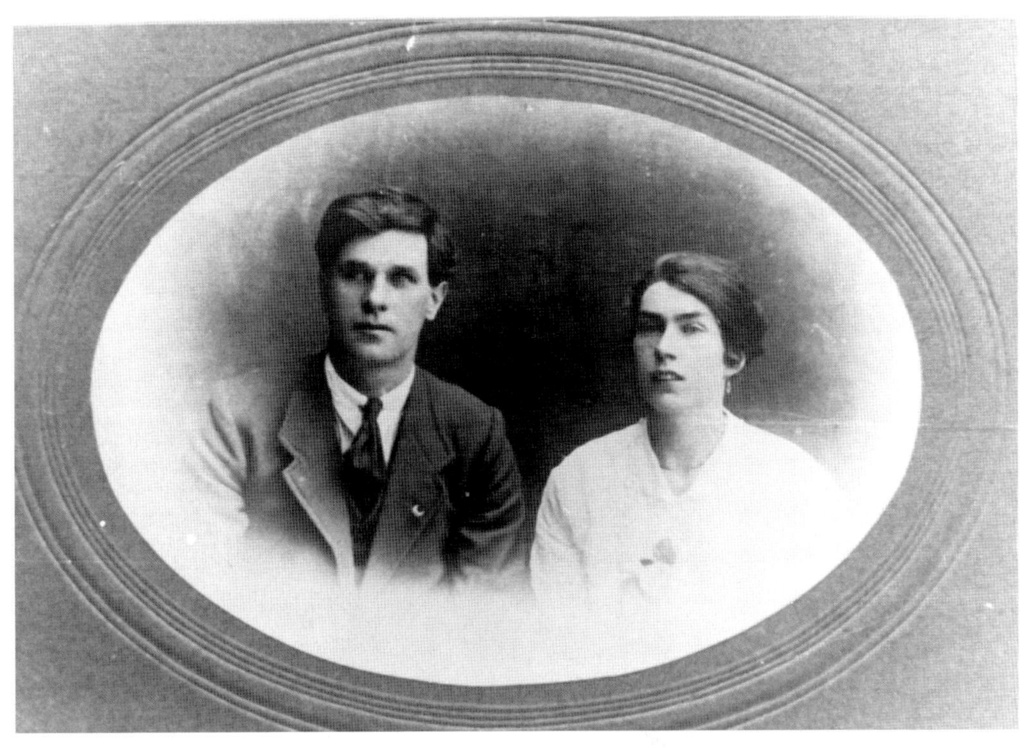

Example of an oval framed photograph.

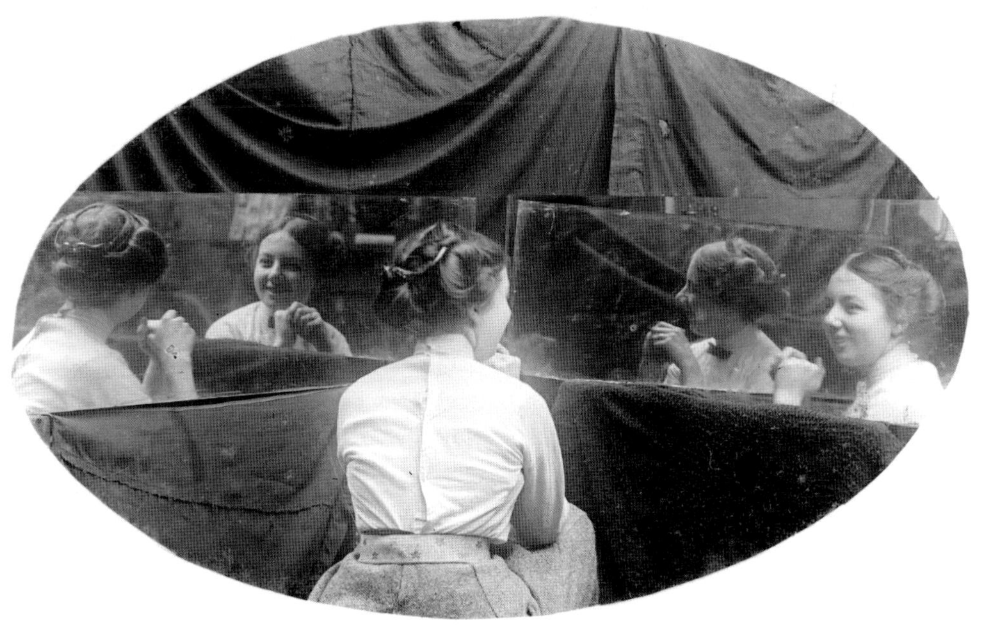

Marietta in the mirror.

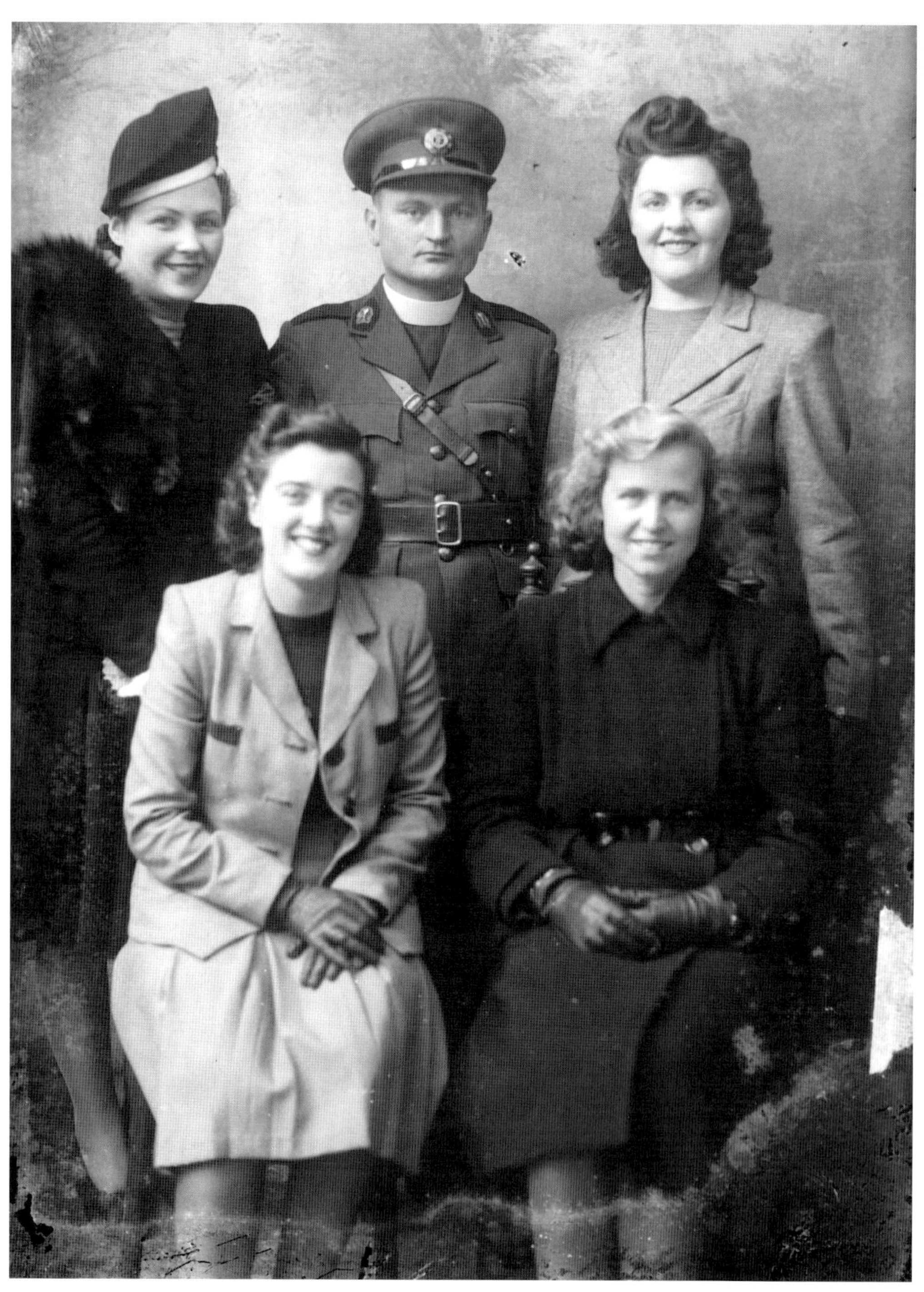

Group portrait of four women and an army chaplain.

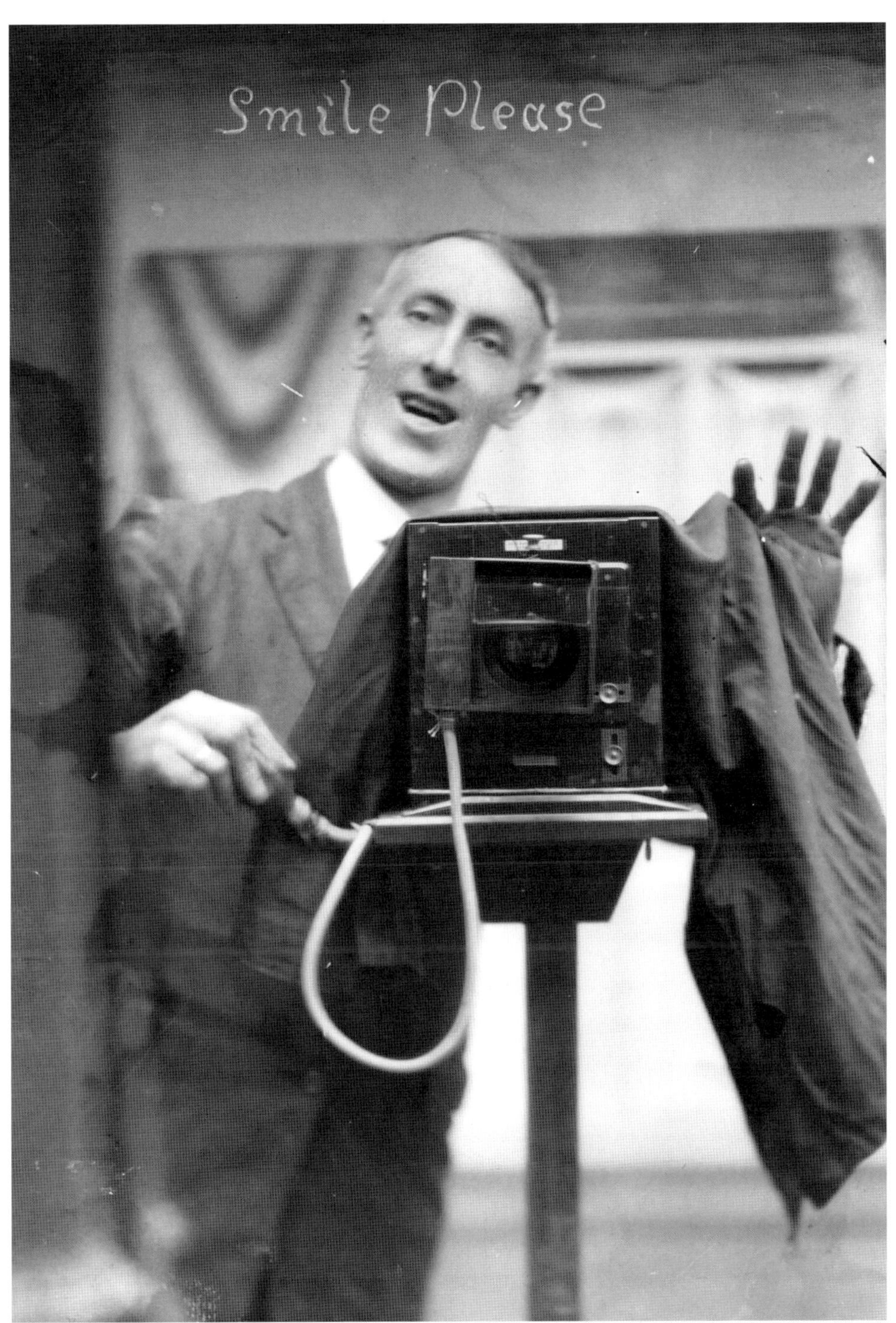

James 'Smile Please'.

The new studio offered the brothers even more scope in their photographic style. James, who had been painting sets for local dramatic productions, began to paint and create sets and backdrops for more imaginative photograph set-ups that were of their time. They always injected fun, creativity and an opportunity to experience, including driving your own motor car or flying in a hot air balloon.

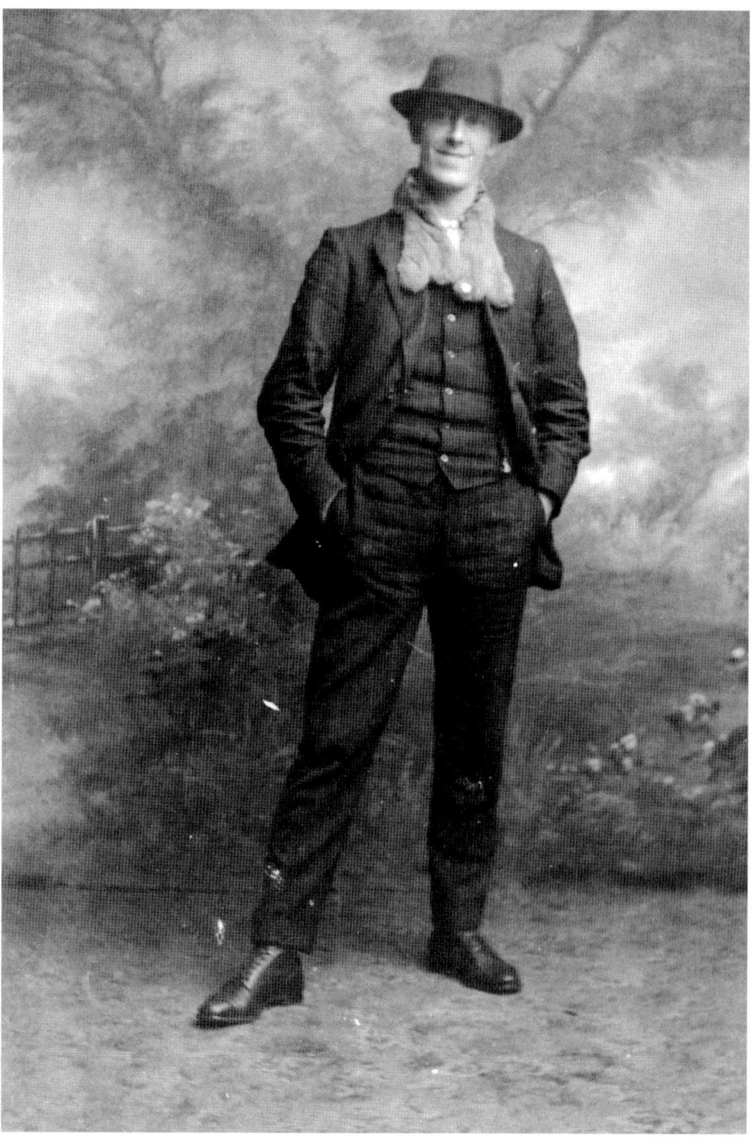

James Horgan in a workman's suit in his studio.

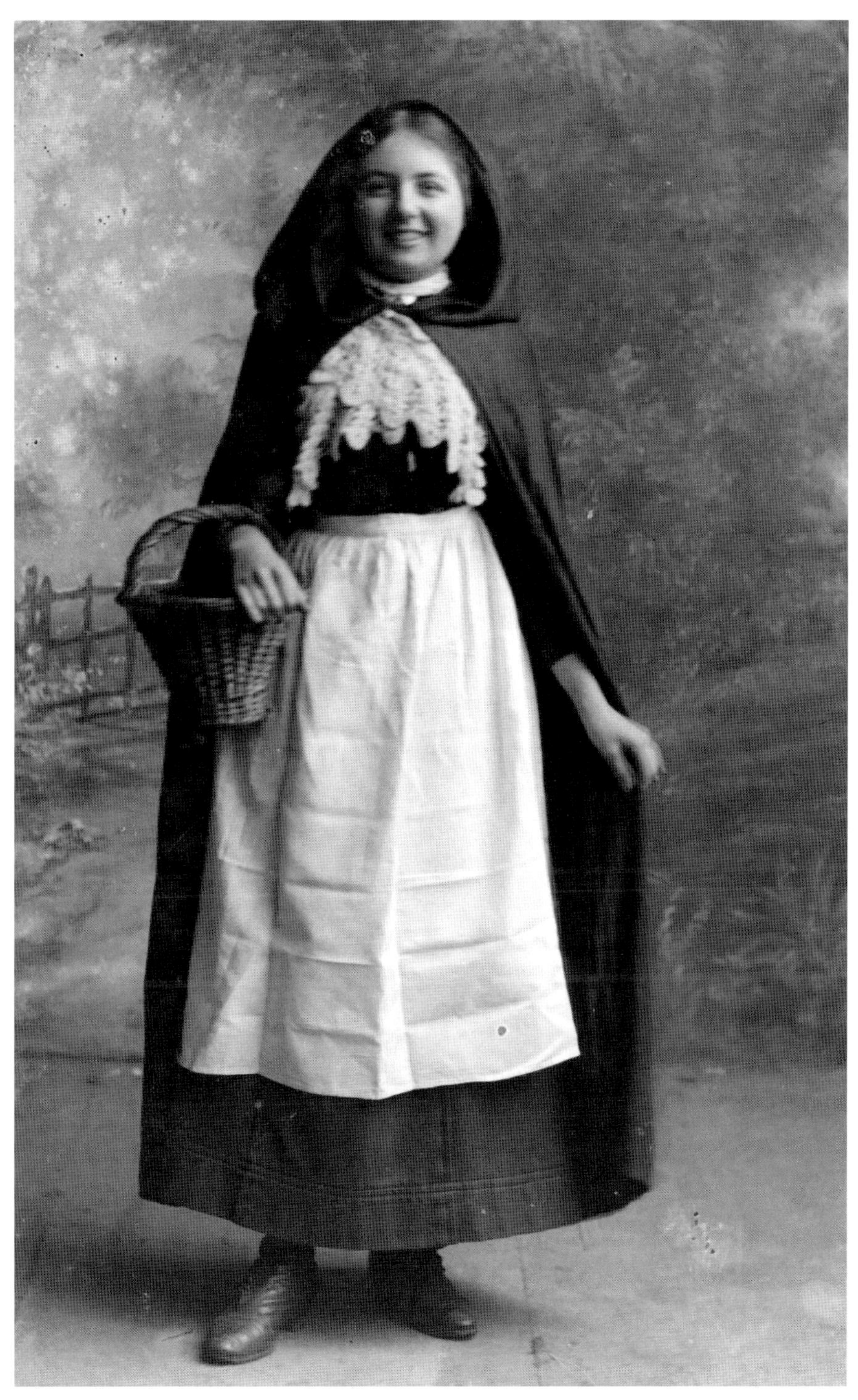

Marietta as Red Riding Hood.

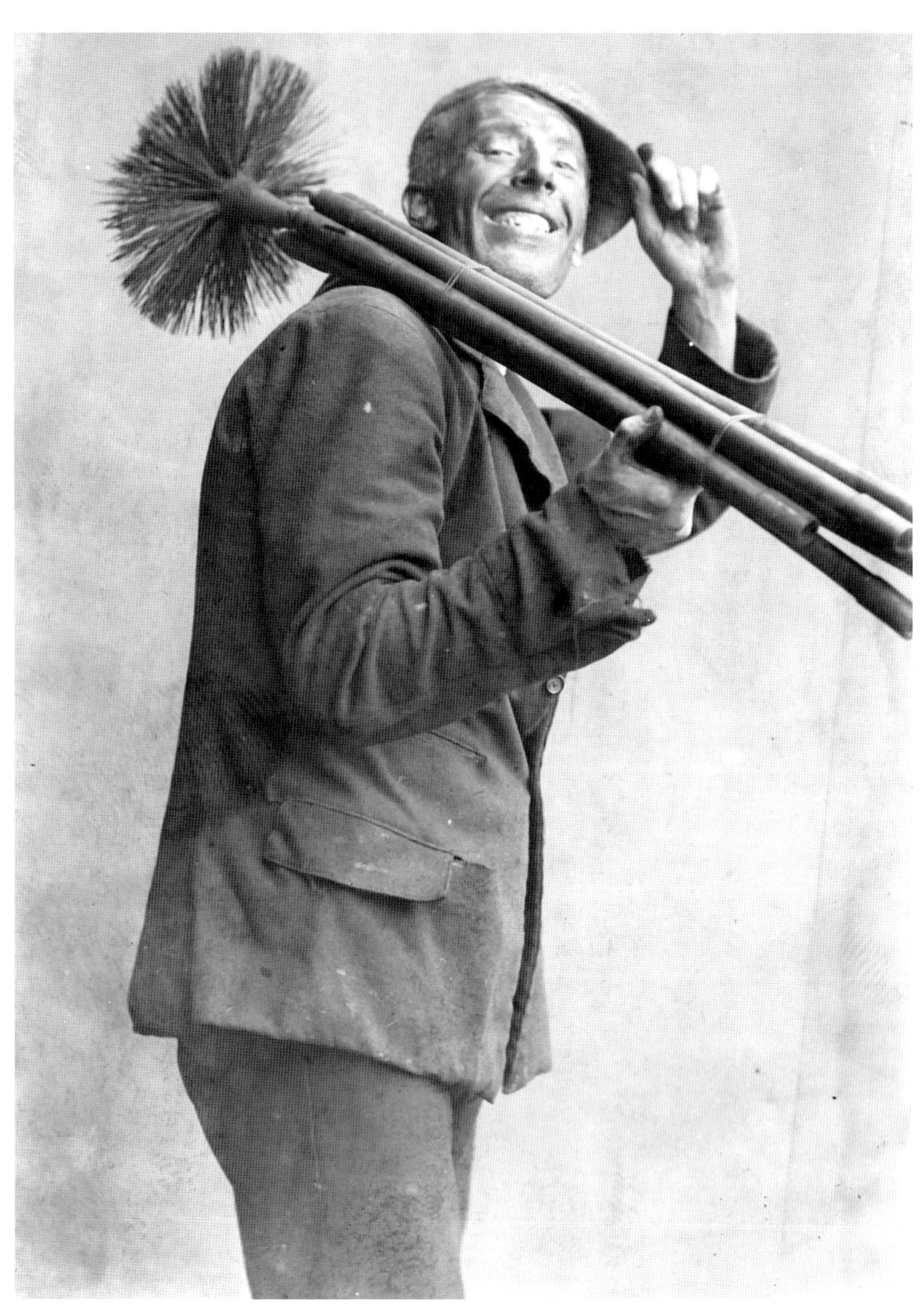

James as a chimney sweep.

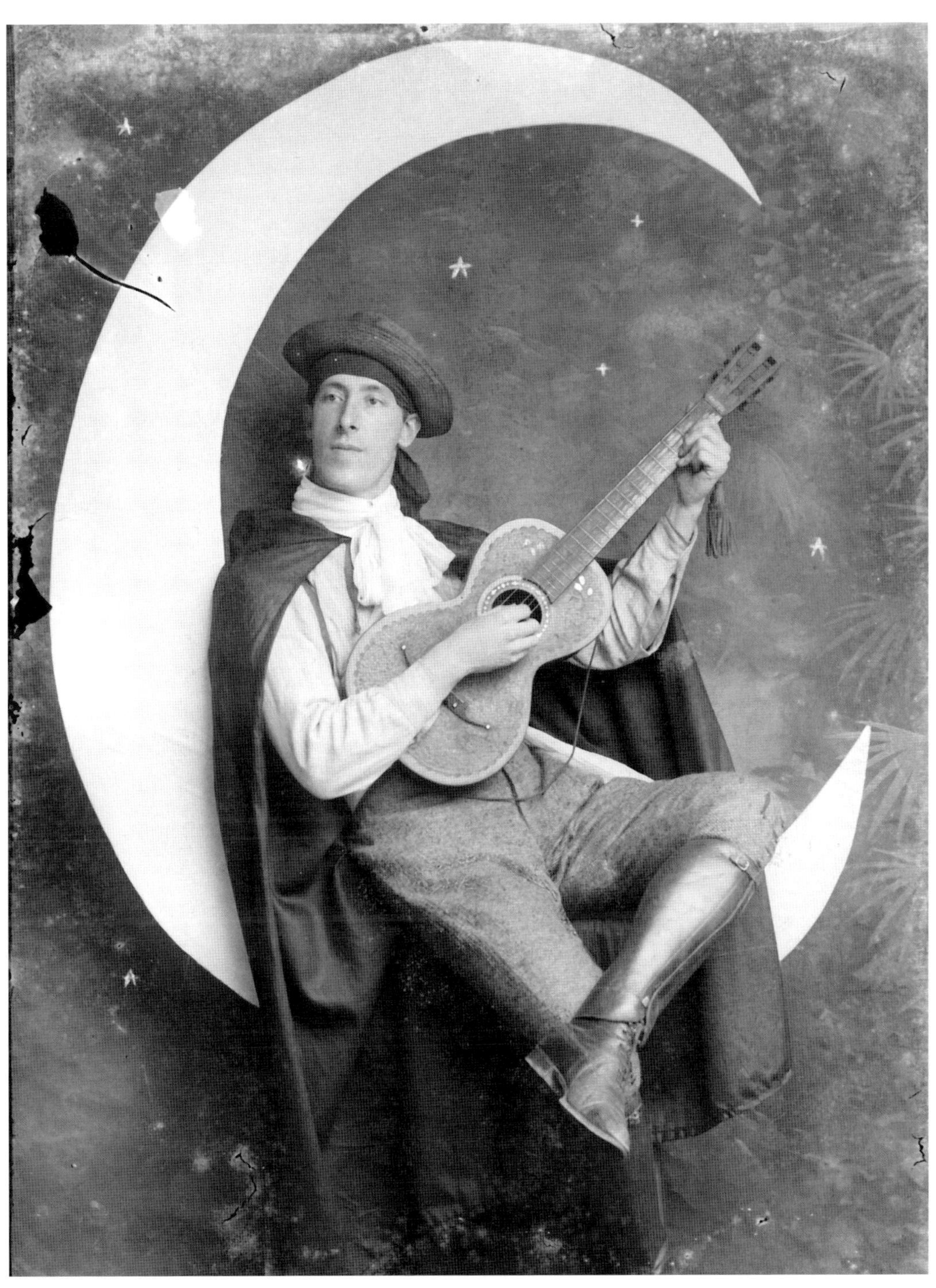

James in a half-moon set playing guitar.

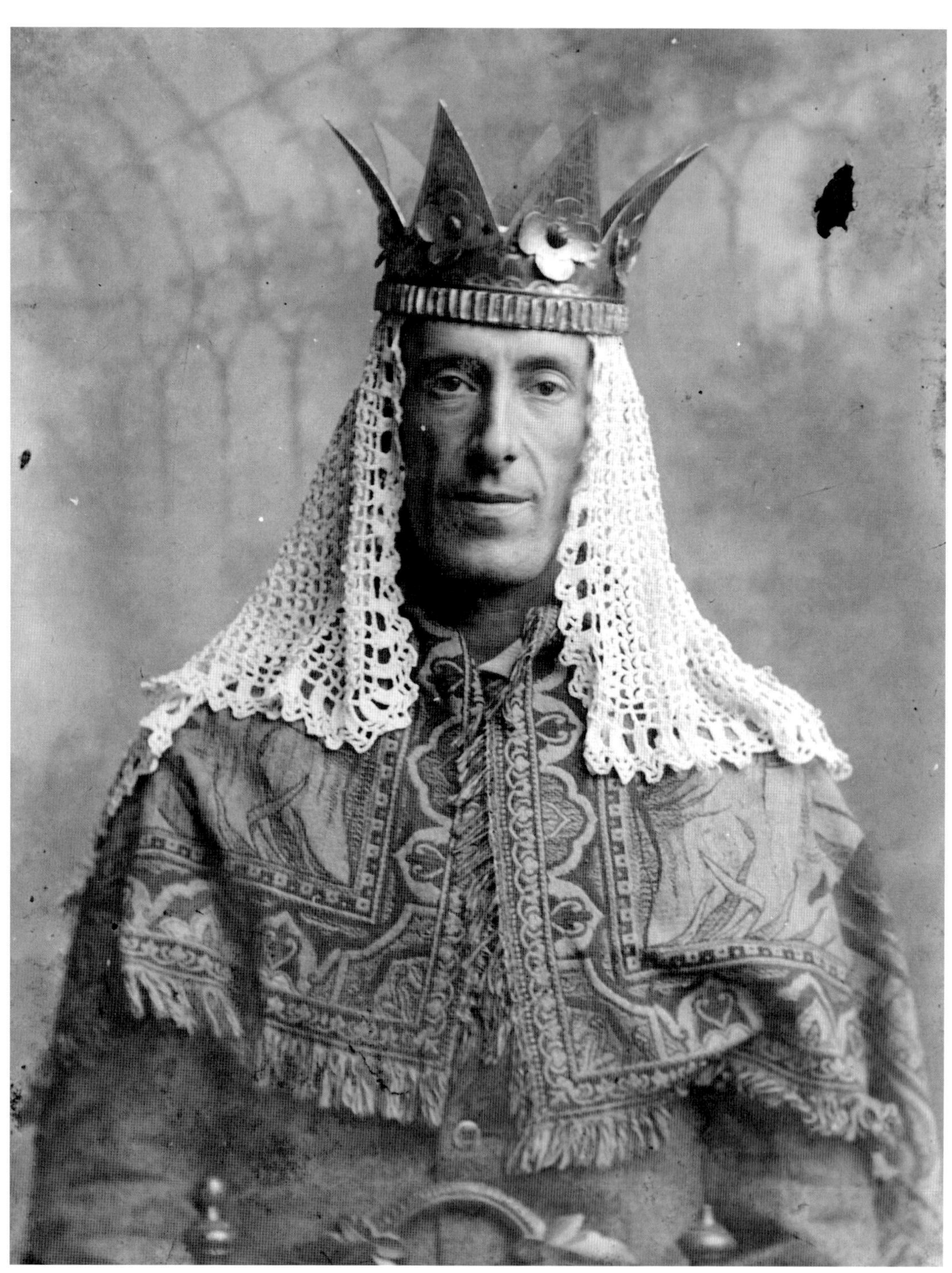

James as King Lear.

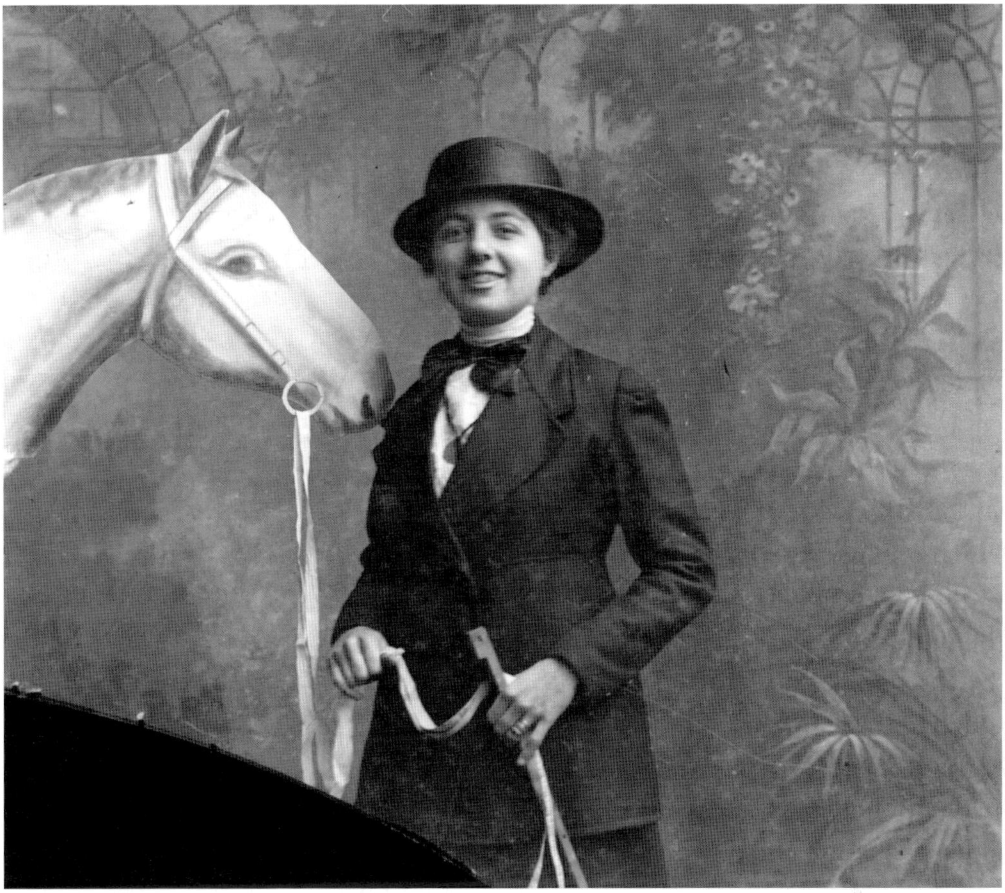

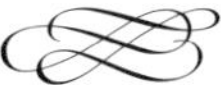

Marietta and a painted horse.

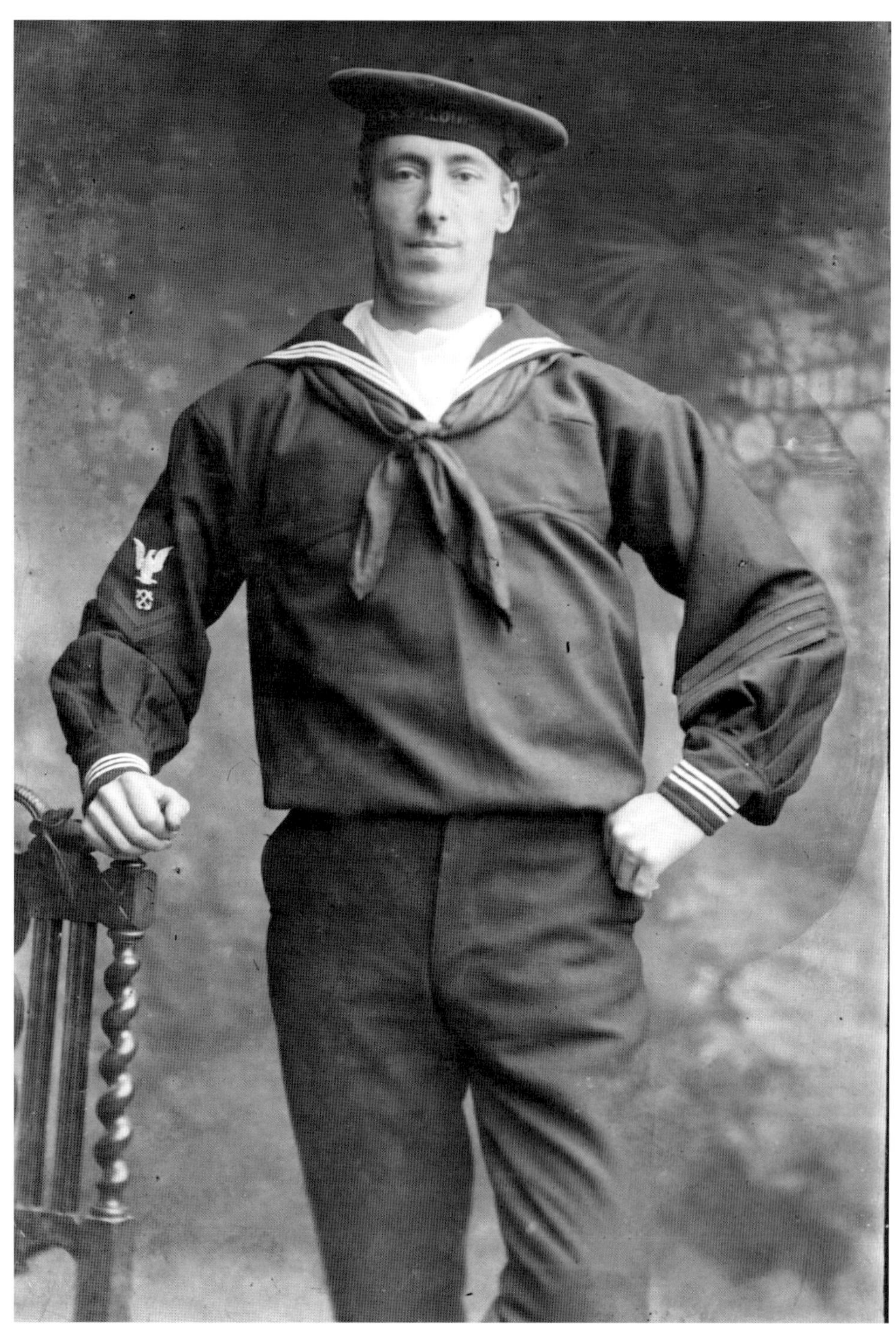

James as a sailor.

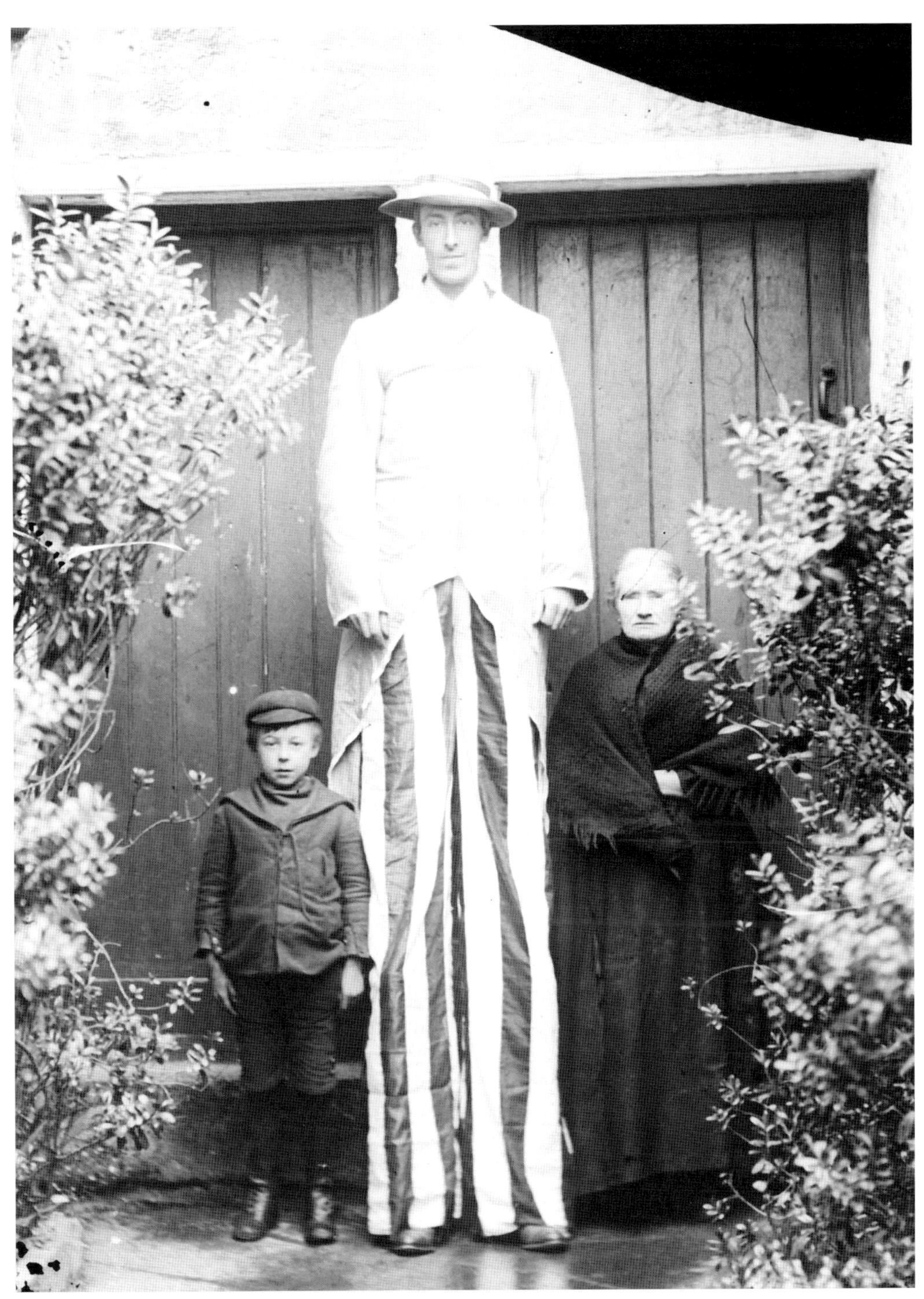

James on stilts.

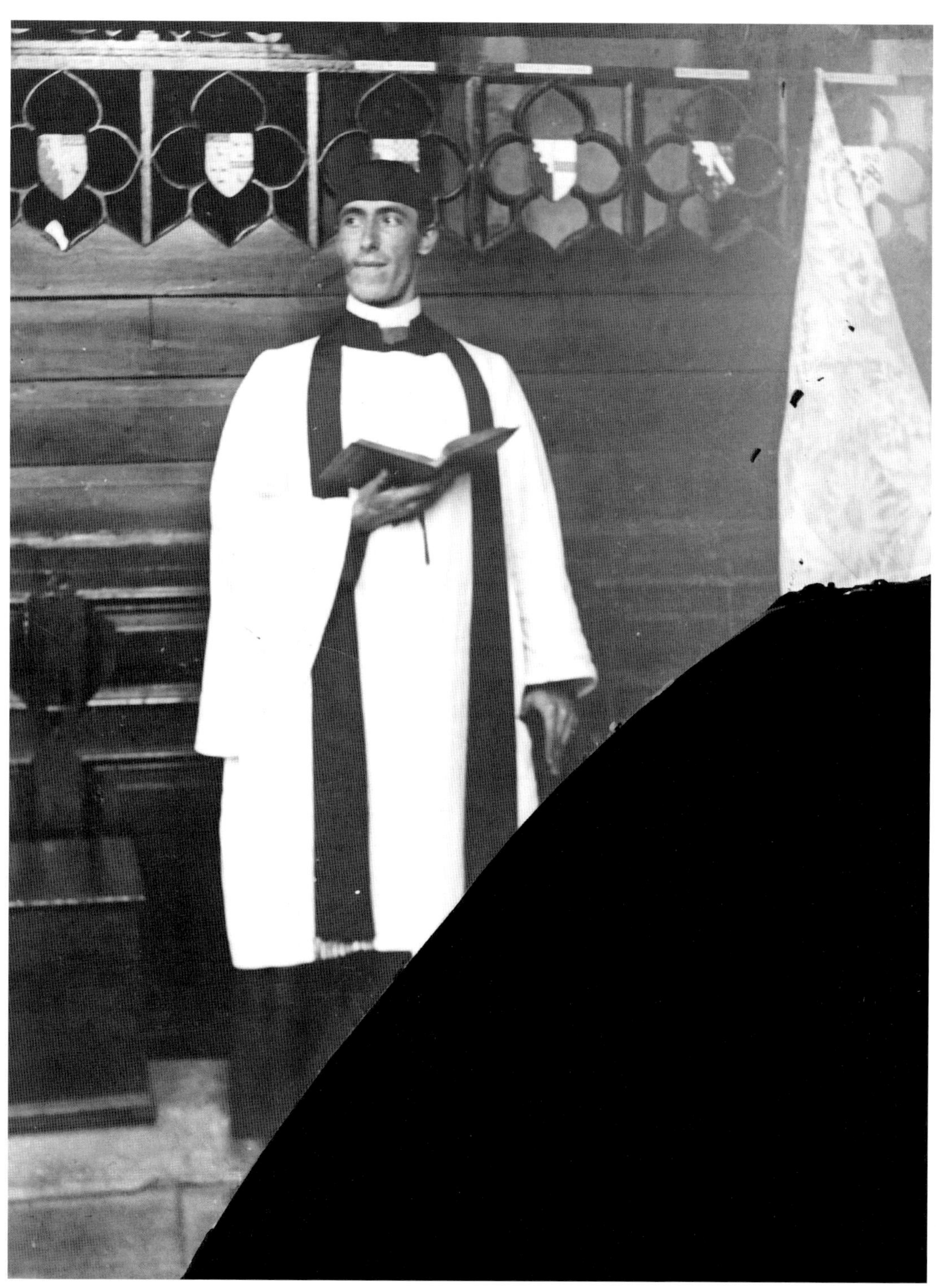

James as a priest.

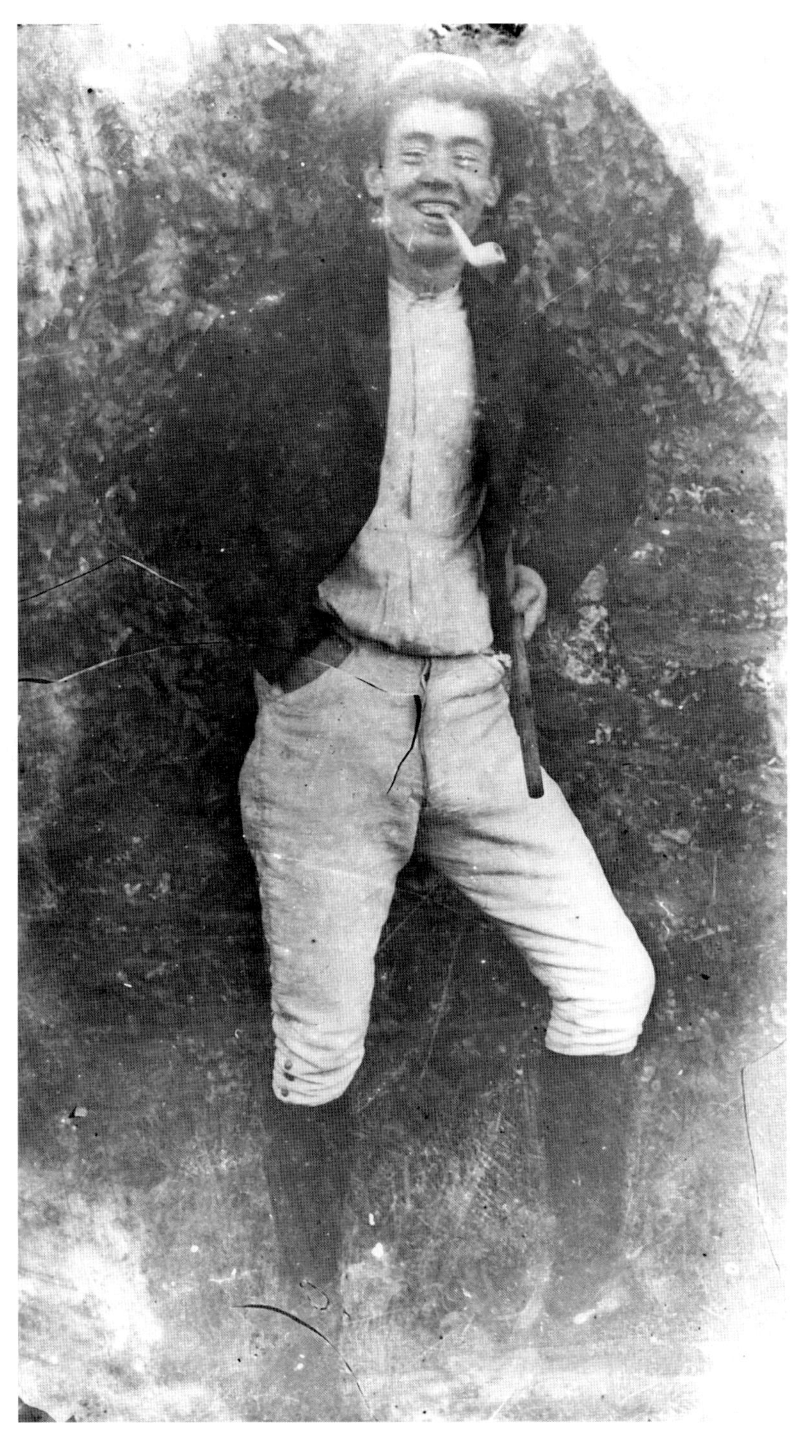

Phil dressed as a spailpin fánach *(a seasonal labourer).*

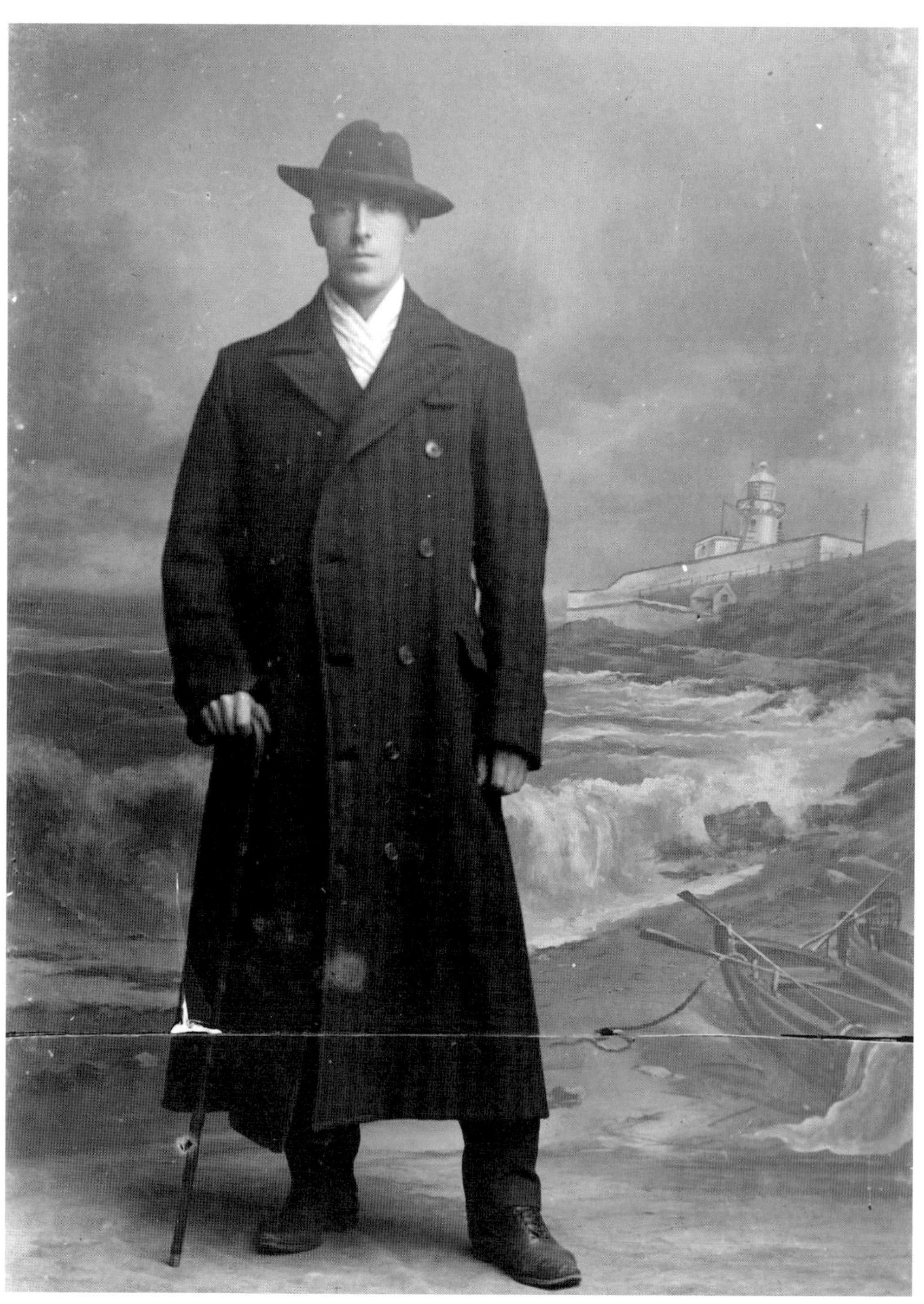

James in an overcoat against their lighthouse backdrop.

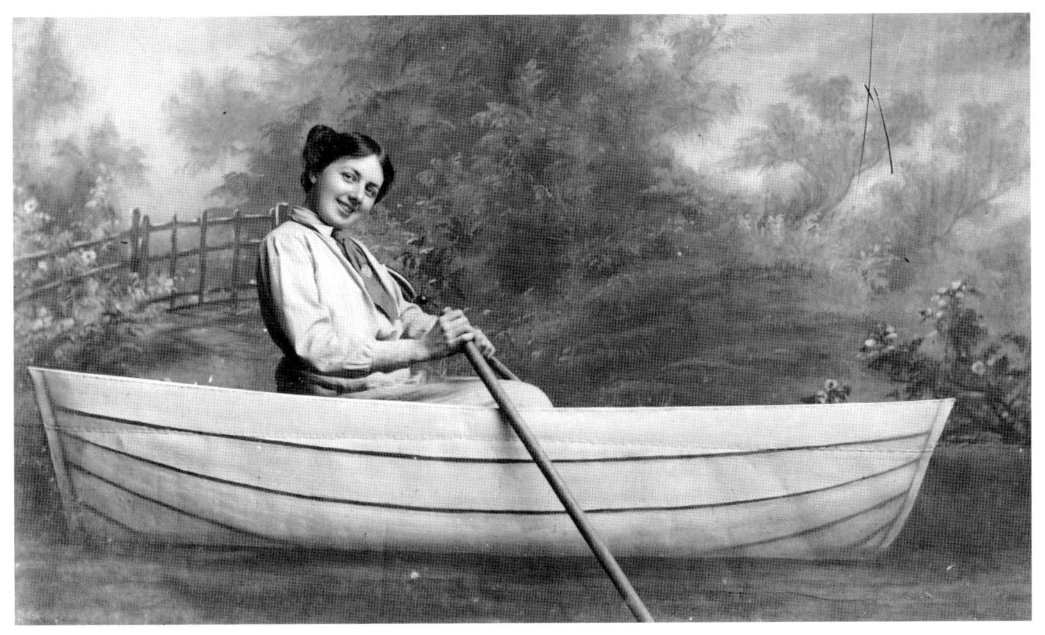

Marietta in a row boat set.

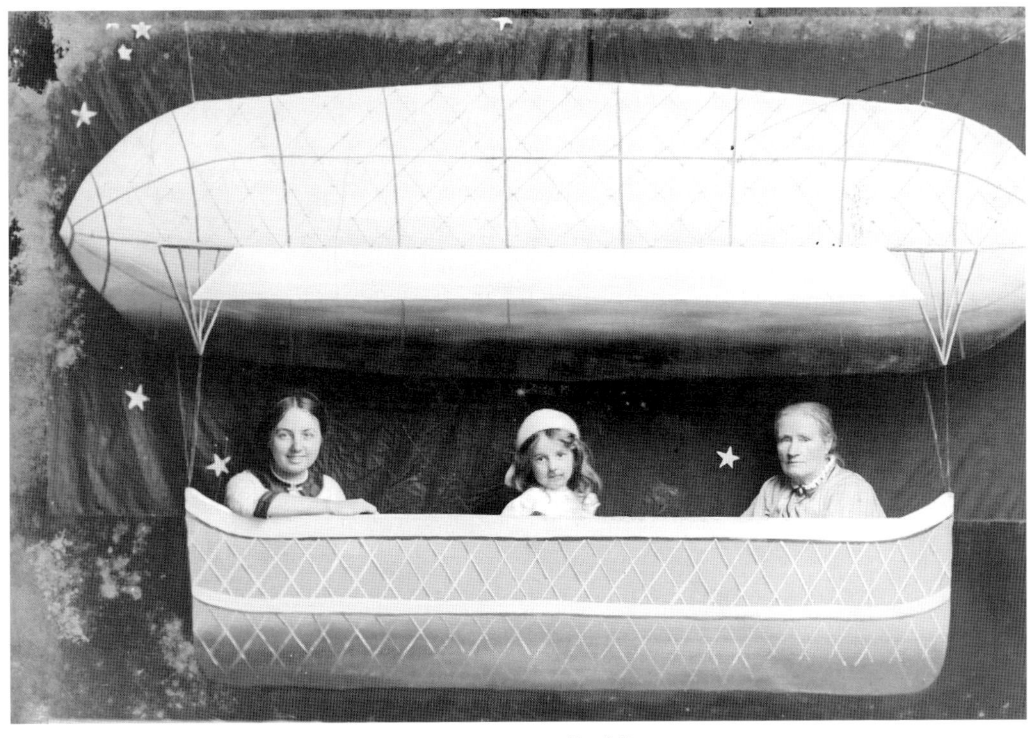

Horgan women in the blimp set.

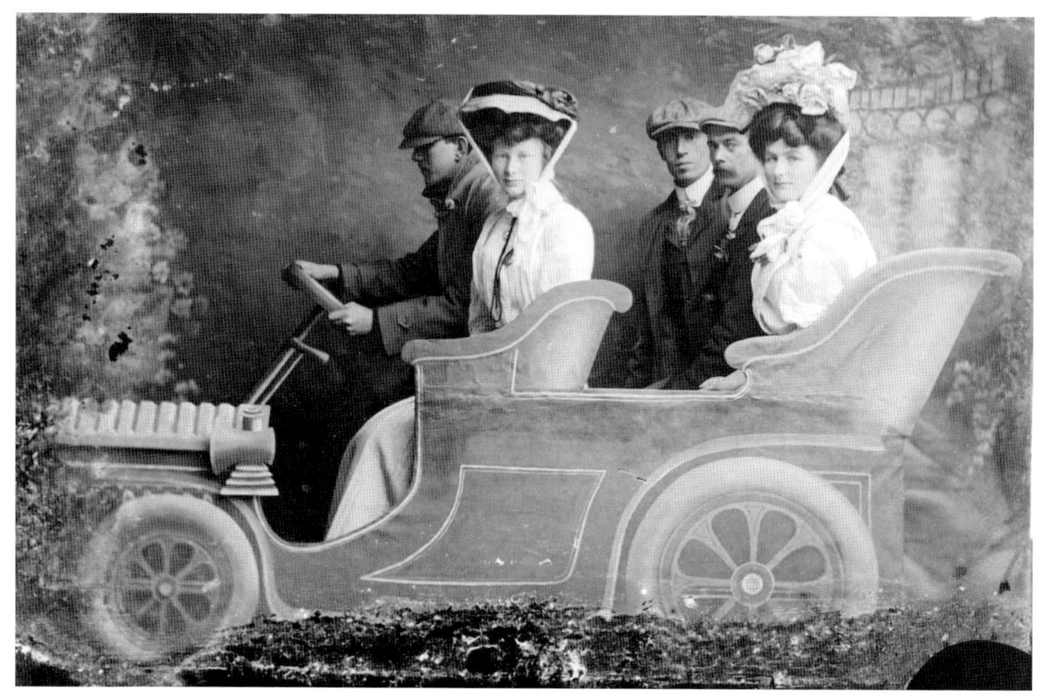

Horgan car set with ladies in bonnets.

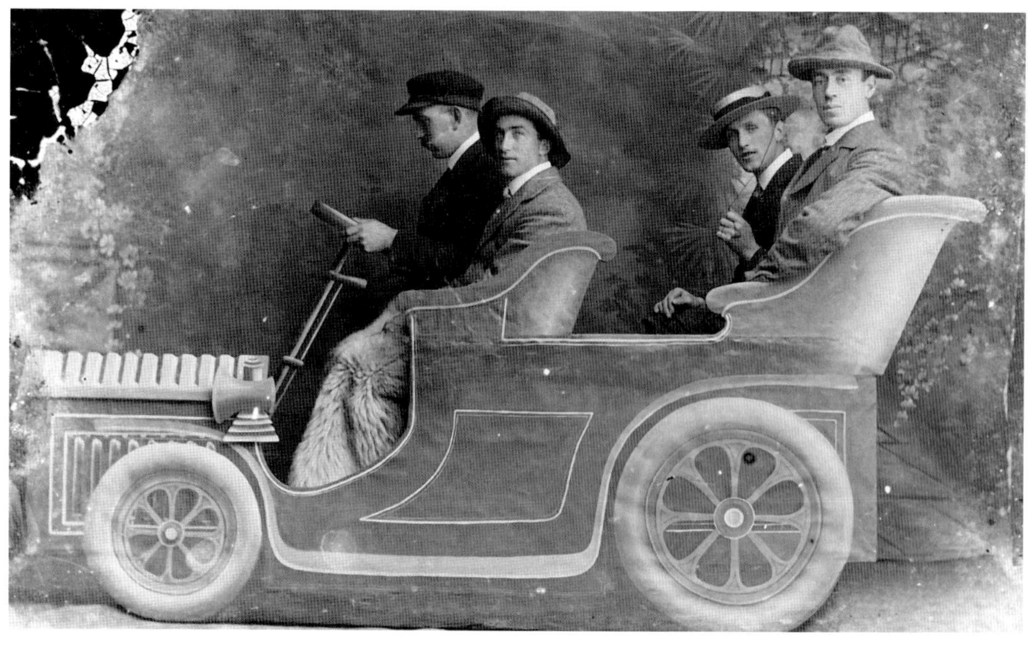

Another Horgan car set with male passengers and Philip in the back.

James and Marietta loved to dress the part and take their portraits, which were possibly used for marketing material and set the scene for the public to show what was possible.

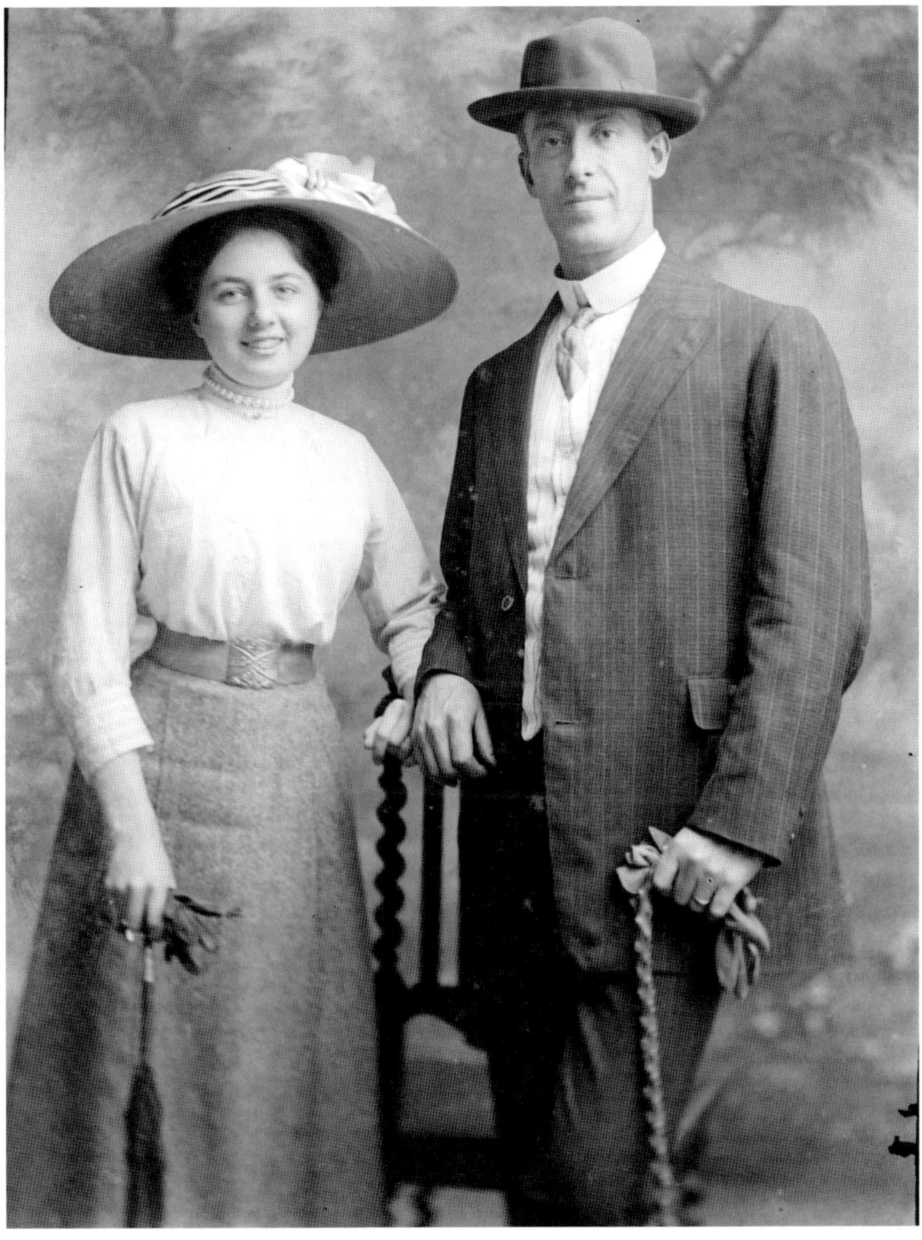

James and Marietta in the studio.

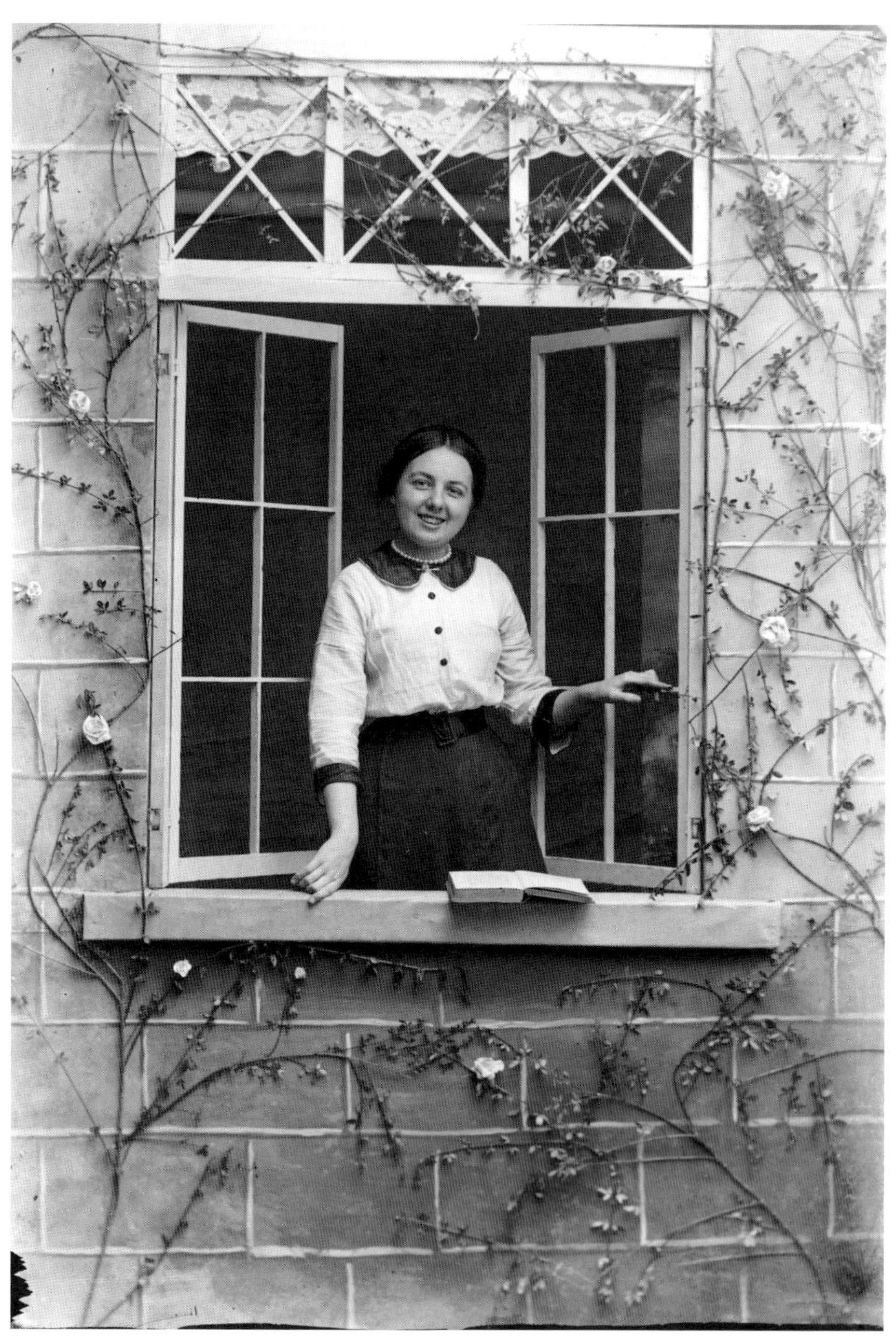

Marietta at a window.

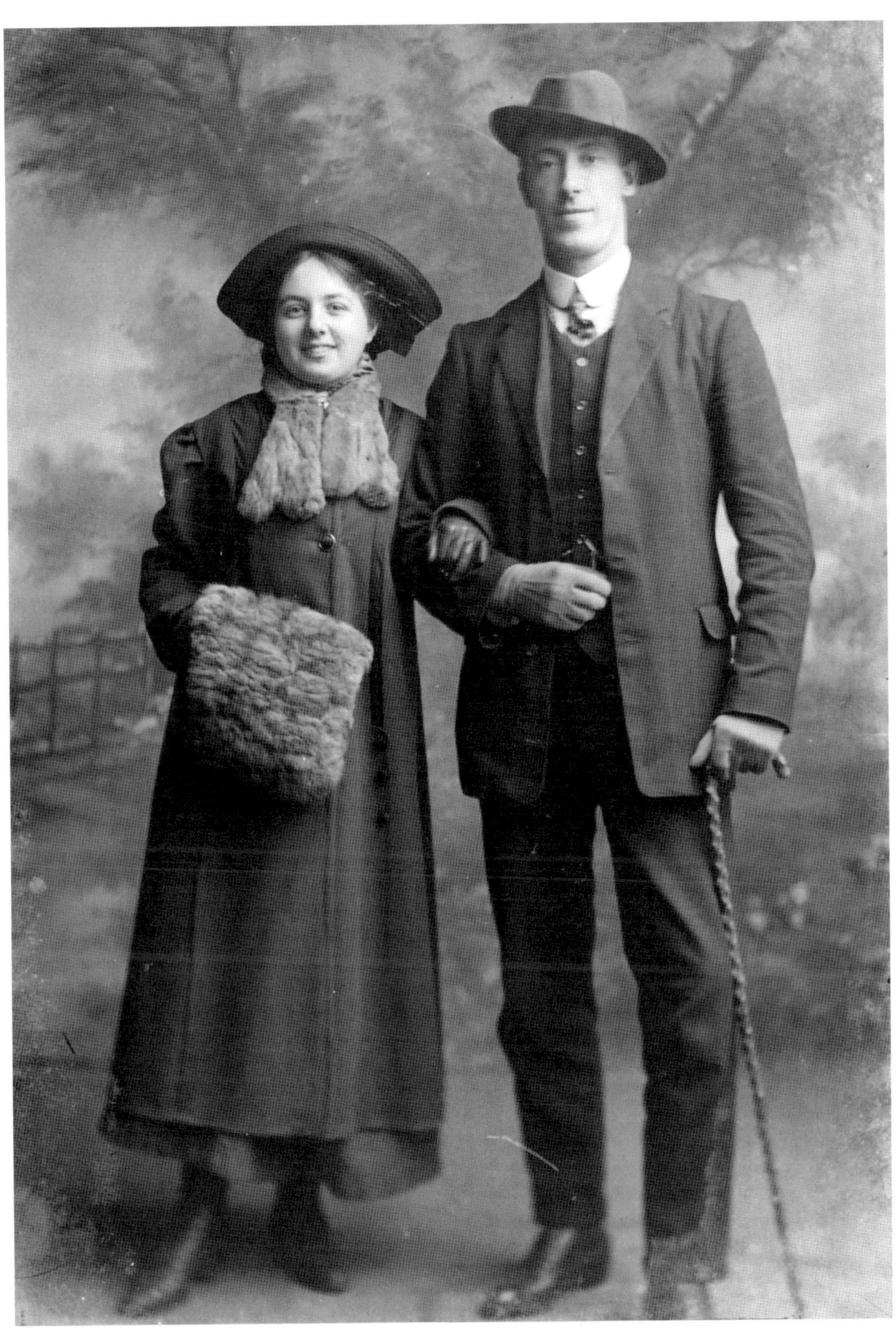

James and Marietta dressed in formal outdoor wear in the studio.

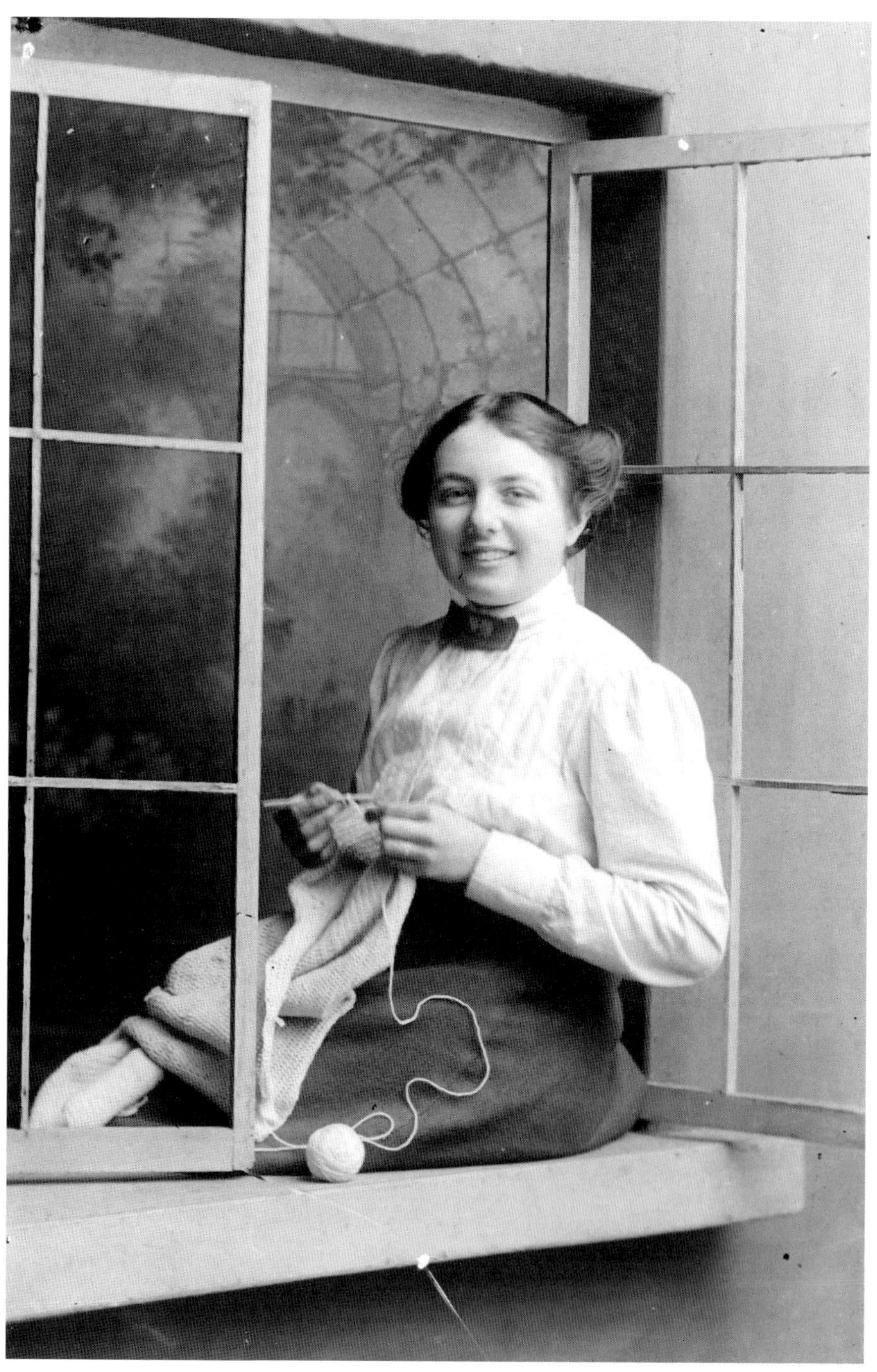

Marietta at window seat in the studio.

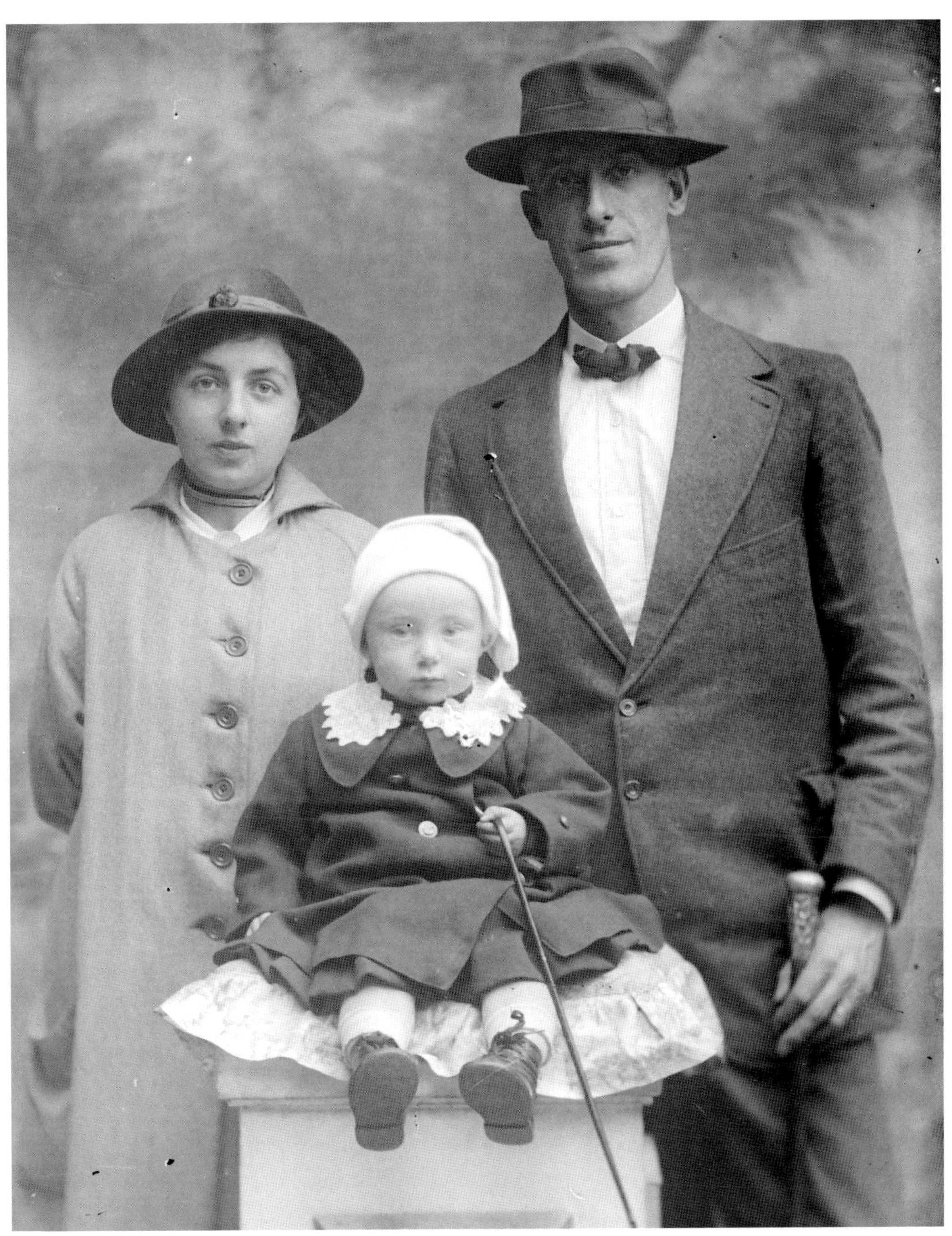

James, Marietta and their son Joseph.

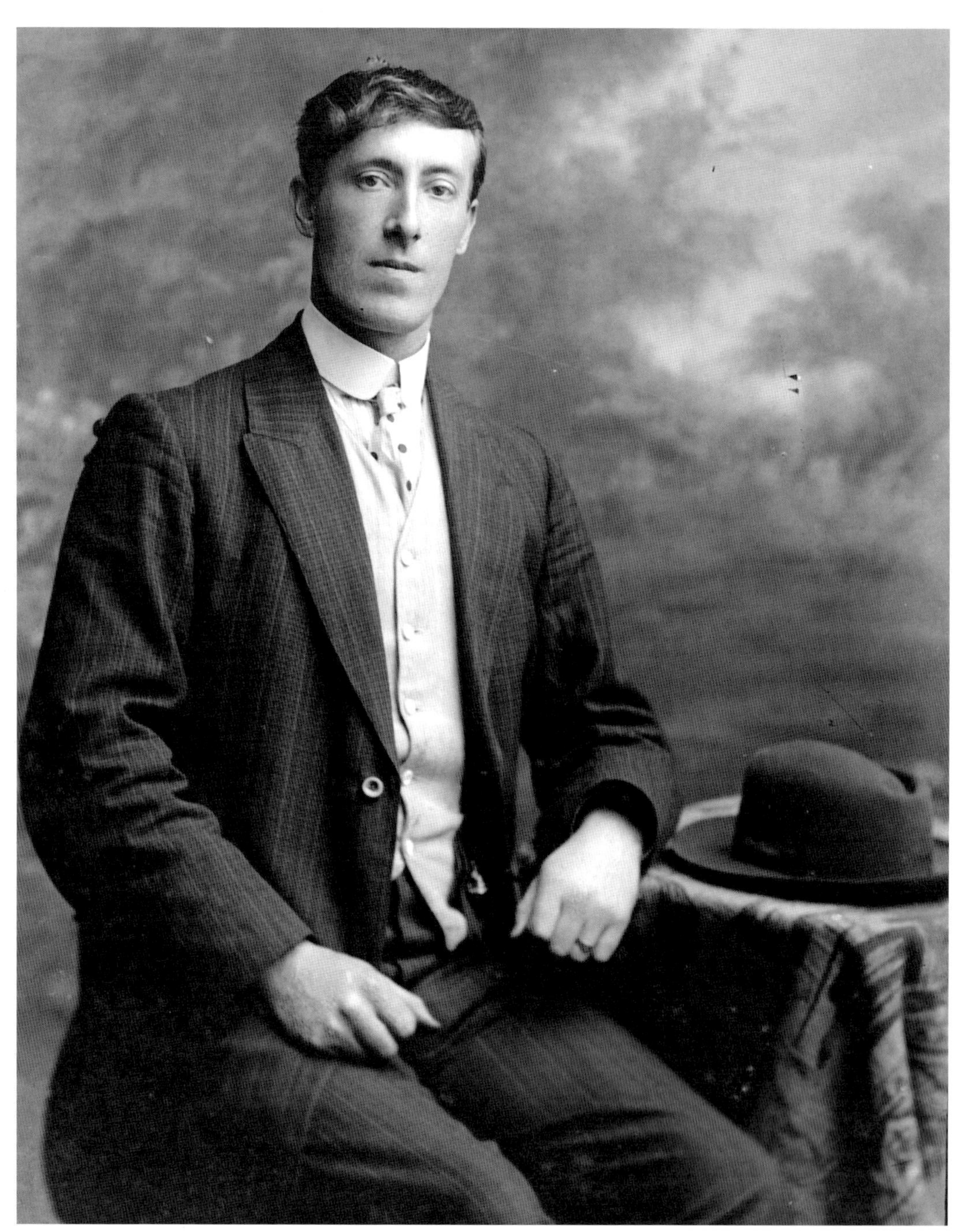

James with a bowler hat.

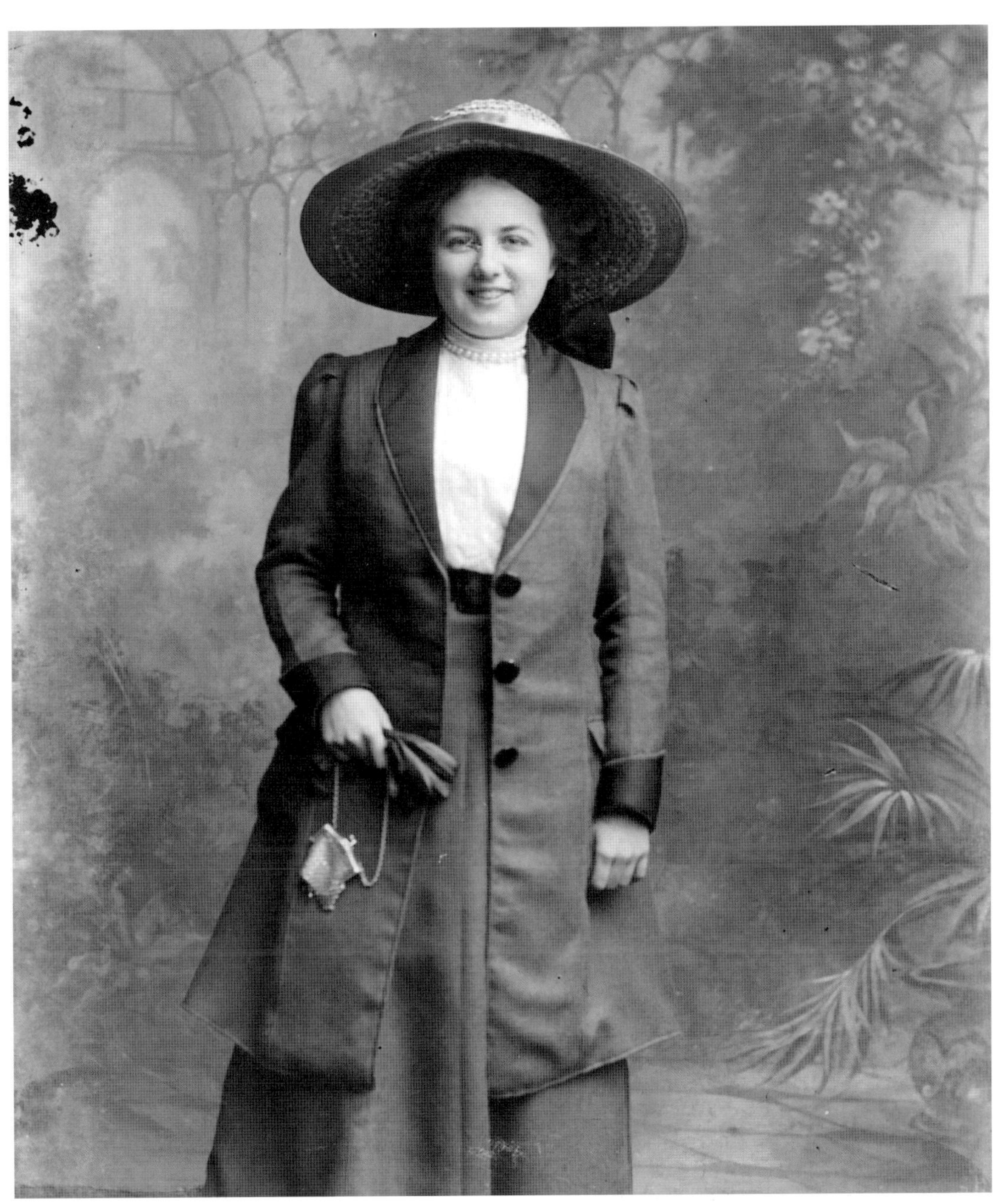

Marietta Horgan in formal wear.

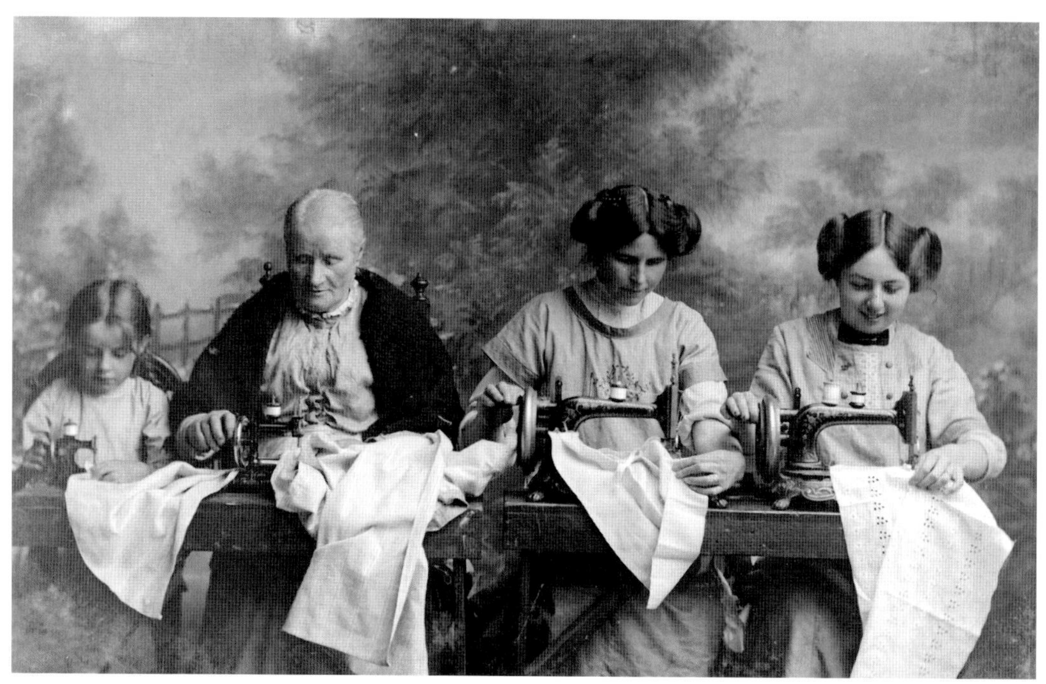

Four Horgan women in the studio, sewing at machines. More than likely Mary Ellen, with her grandmother Elizabeth, her mother Norah and Marietta.

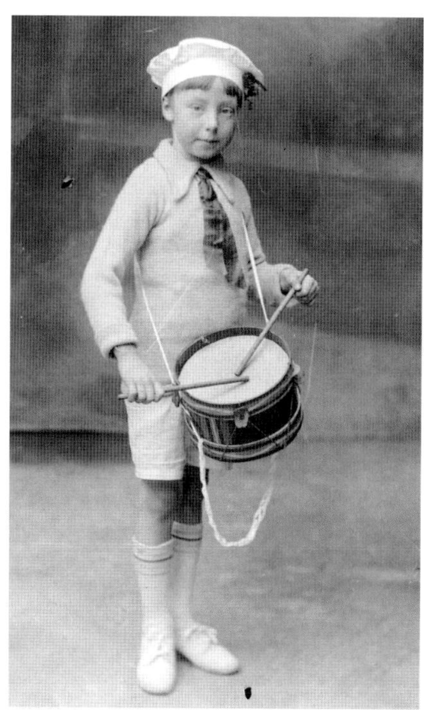

Joseph Horgan dressed as a drummer boy.

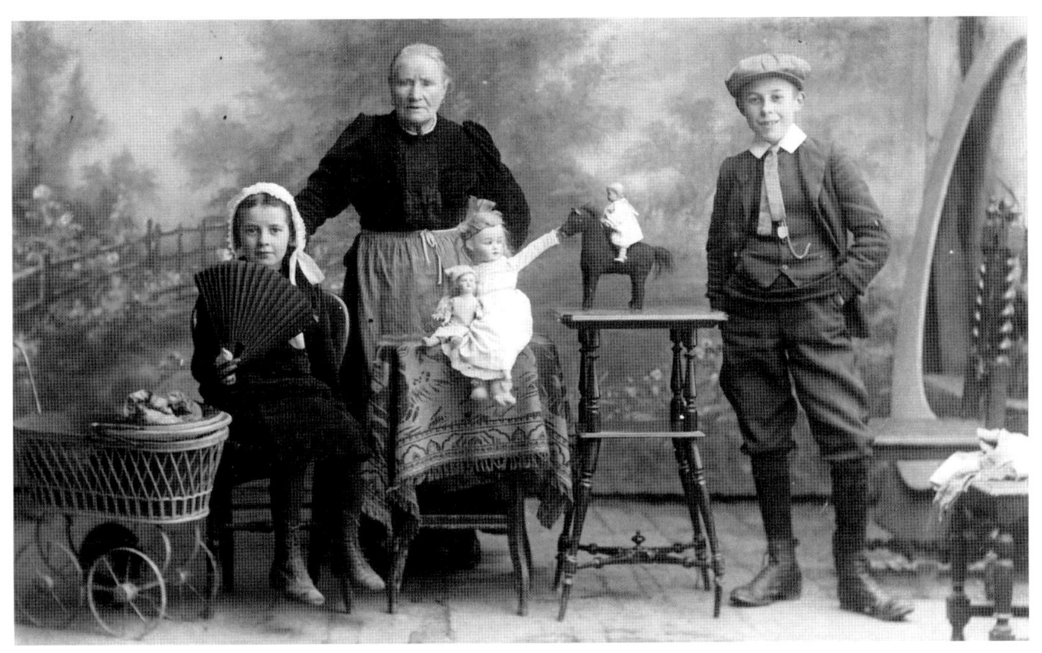

*Elizabeth Horgan, mother of the Horgan brothers,
with her grandchildren in the studio.*

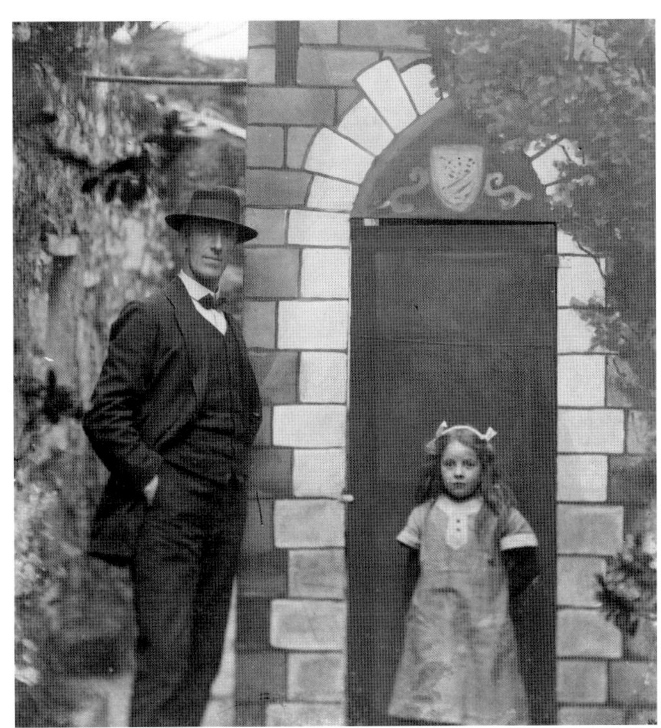

*James with one
of his children.*

Impromptu photographs of the family, generally taken in the Strand Street area of Youghal, show a very relaxed lifestyle.

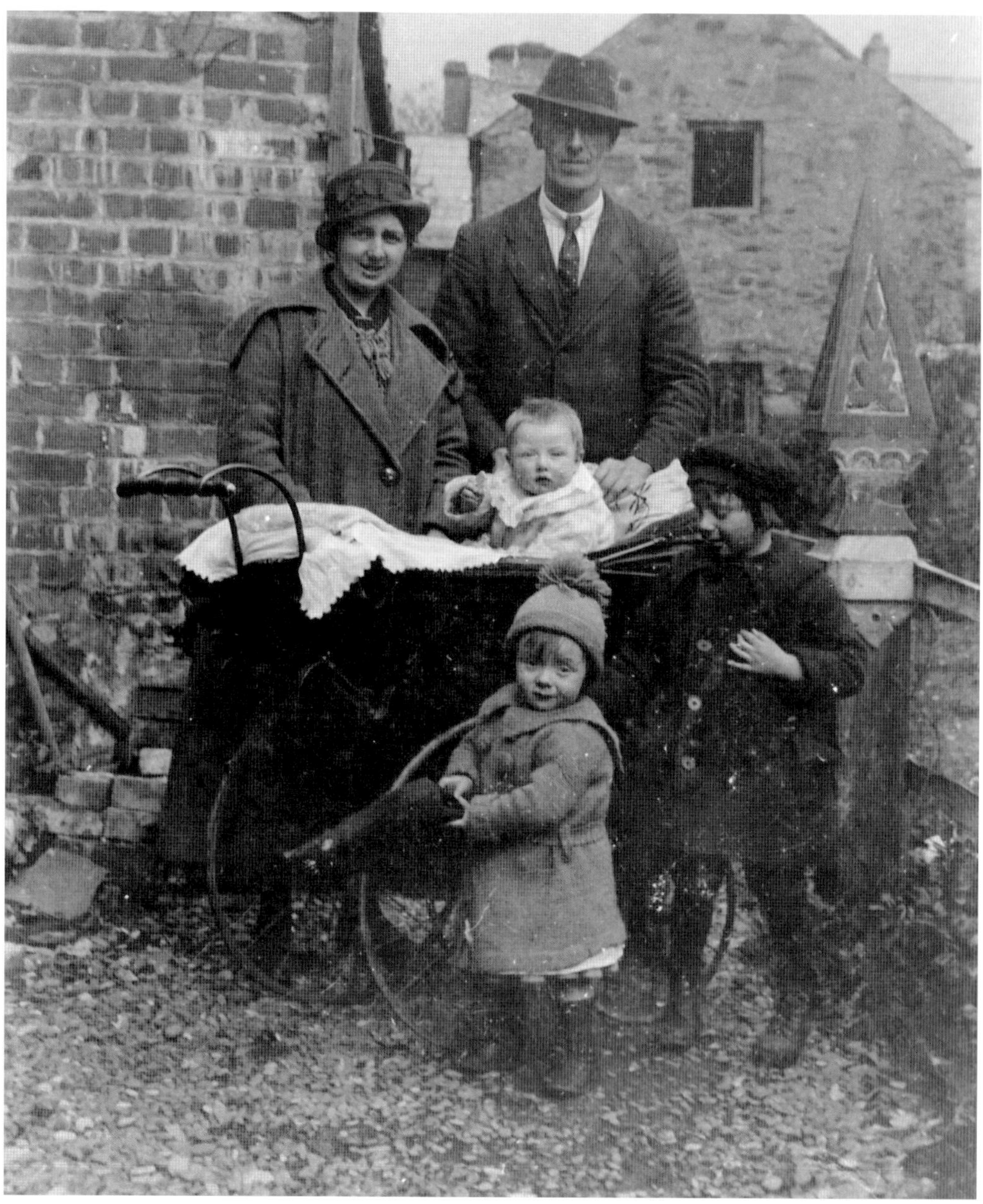

James and Marietta with their children Joseph, Augustine and Mary Theresa.

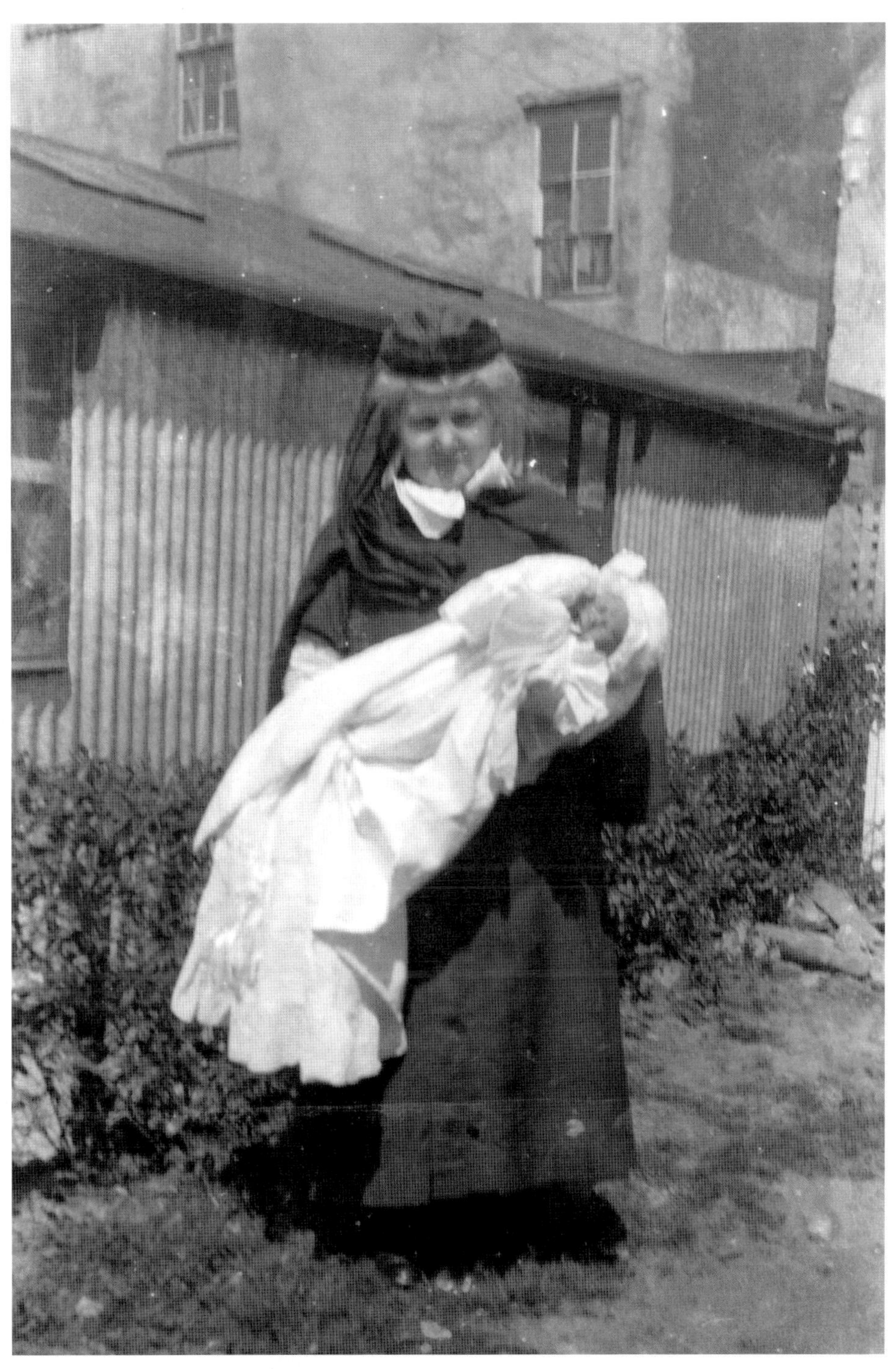

Midwife holding one of the Horgan babies.

Music was another of the Horgan brothers' talents. They created and played many instruments throughout their lives.

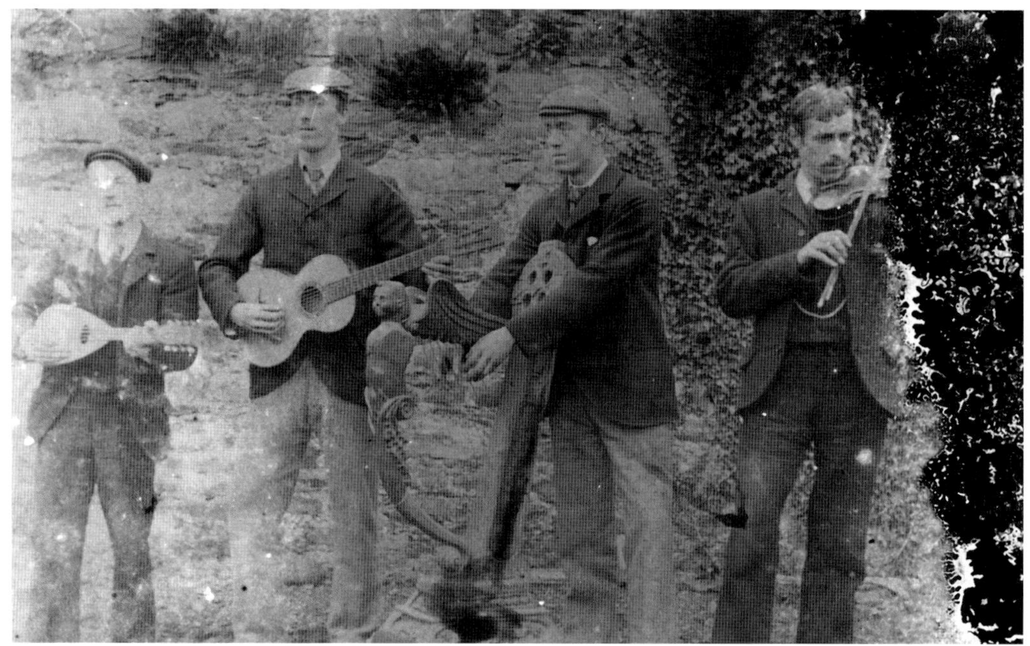

The Horgan brothers playing music with other musicians.

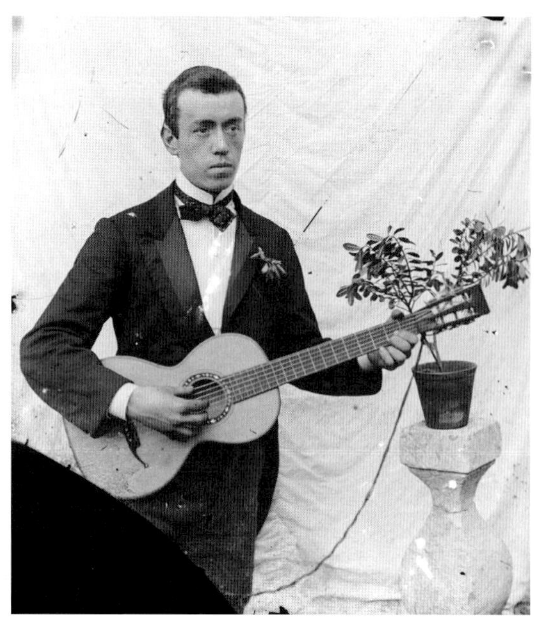

Philip Horgan with a guitar.

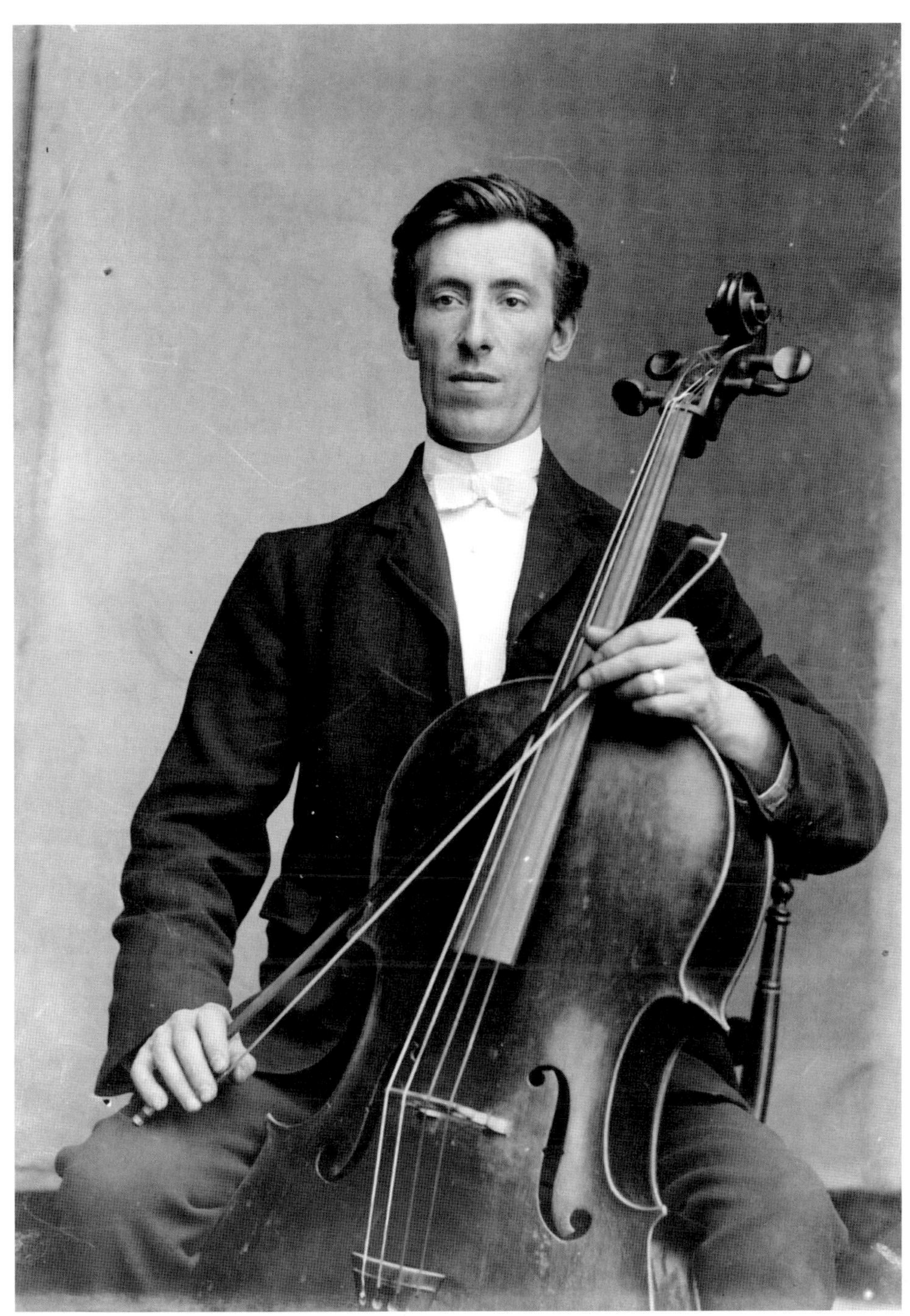

James Horgan with a cello.

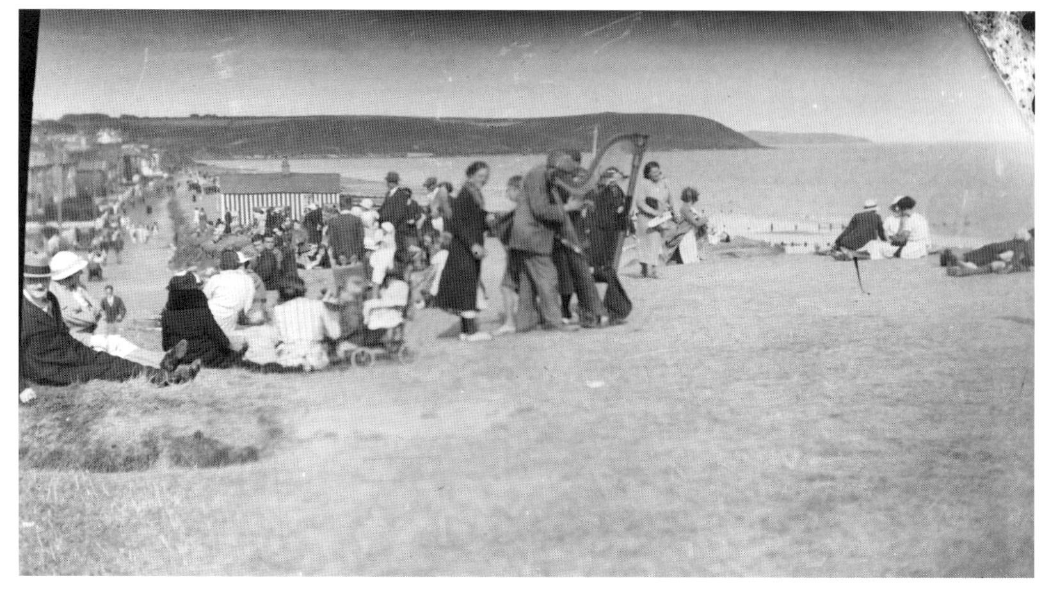

Harp playing on top of Claycastle at Youghal strand.

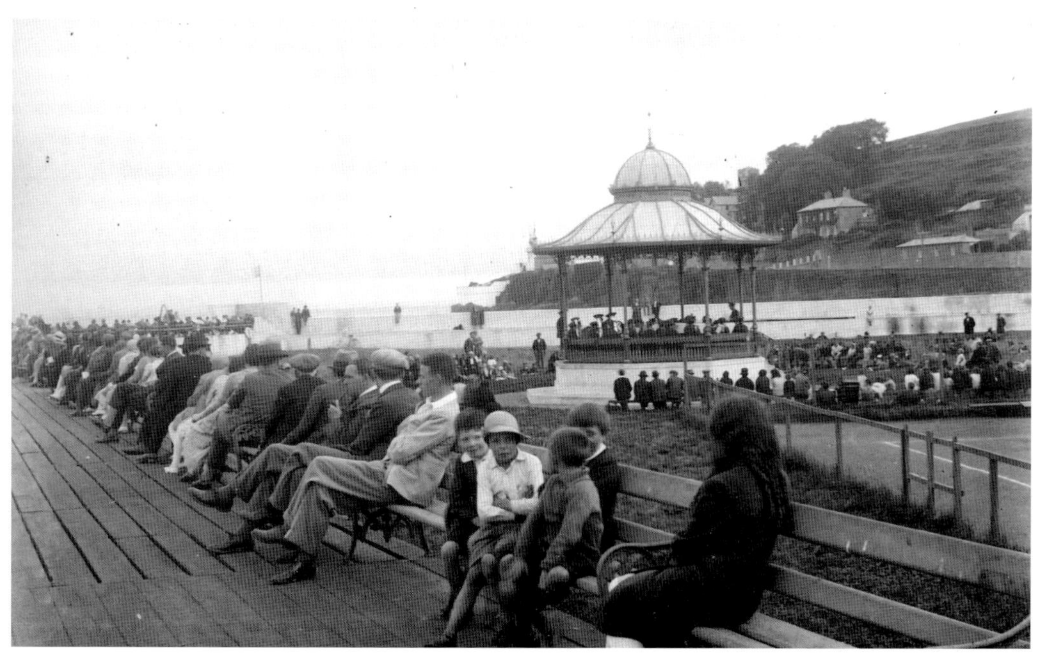

Crowds gathering at Green Park for the Corpus Christi blessing as a band plays in the bandstand.

THOMAS HORGAN

Where James and Philip were thought to be the more artistic of the three brothers, it was Thomas who was recognised as being business-like and kept all the finances and bookkeeping in order.

He married Hanora (Nora) Kelly, a native of Caliso Bay in Waterford, around 1900. They had a son, Ted, in 1903 and a daughter, Nelly, in 1905. Tragically, Nora died from tuberculosis, a condition that was not well understood until the mid-1940s.

Nelly contacted tuberculosis and died twelve years later. Thomas never got over the death and began to drink, which remained a continuous problem.

His son Ted married Mazie O'Sullivan from Cobh. She was a professional pianist who came to Youghal to play at the cinema as an accompaniment to silent films. She also played at 'all-night dances' in the Strand Palace.

Thomas lived with Ted and Mazie until his death in 1948.

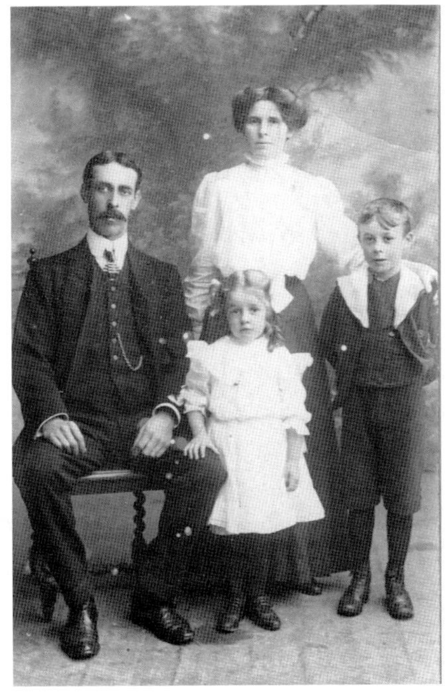

Thomas Horgan and his wife Nora with their children, Nelly and Ted.

Henry Ford

According to the Horgan descendants, Henry Ford, who was in Cork in 1912, visited the Horgan Brothers at their Photographic Studio and was an influential figure in their decision to open a cinema at that site.

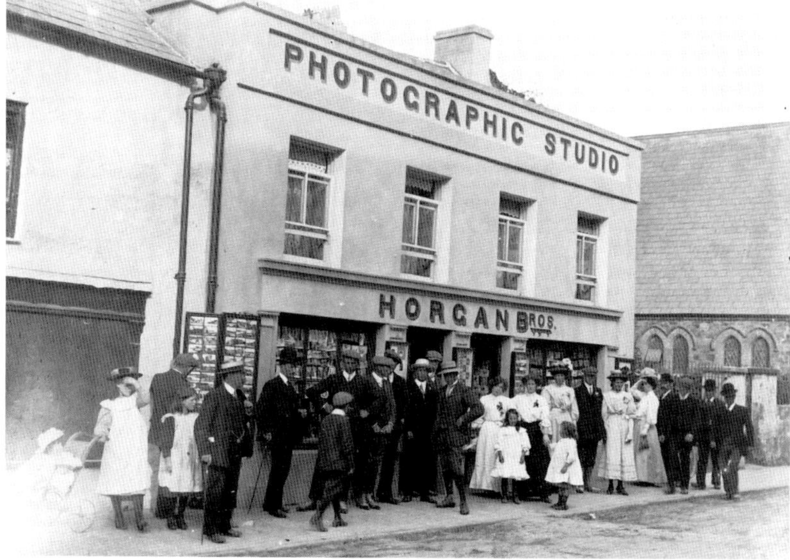

A group outside the Horgan Photographic Studio understood to feature Henry Ford.

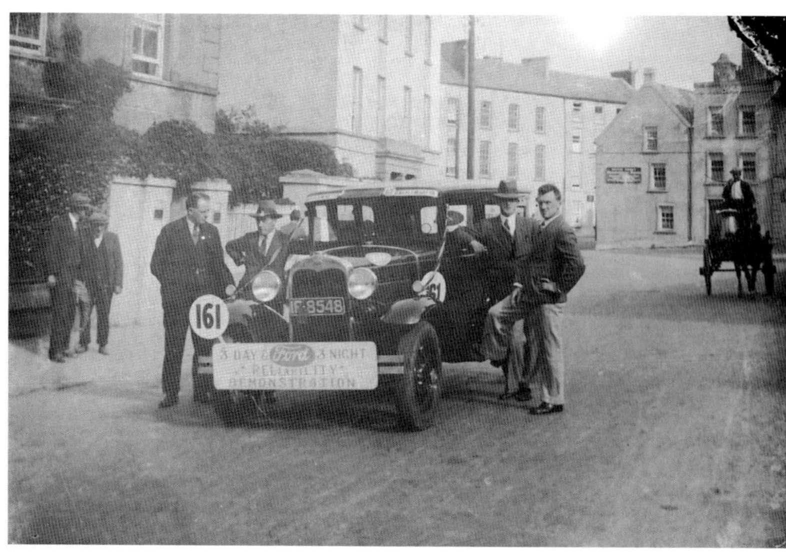

A later photograph of a Ford car being tested on Friar Street.

OPENING OF HORGAN PICTURE THEATRE

The Horgans purchased a cinema licence on 17 April 1910, and according to their descendants, Henry Ford advised them during a visit to Cork on how to finance their ambitions. However, the First World War broke out, and materials were extremely difficult to secure or afford, which may have caused the delay in building the cinema.

The Horgan Picture Theatre opened on Christmas week of 1917. It was a long theatre with over 600 seats and one of the first films the Horgan Brothers showed was one of their own from 'The Youghal Gazette' – The people of Ardmore, Co Waterford gathering at St Declan's Well for the Pattern.

There were two notable things about the Horgan cinema – the first was that it was a back projection screen. This meant that the projector was behind the screen, which ran into the Horgan family home. The screen needed to be

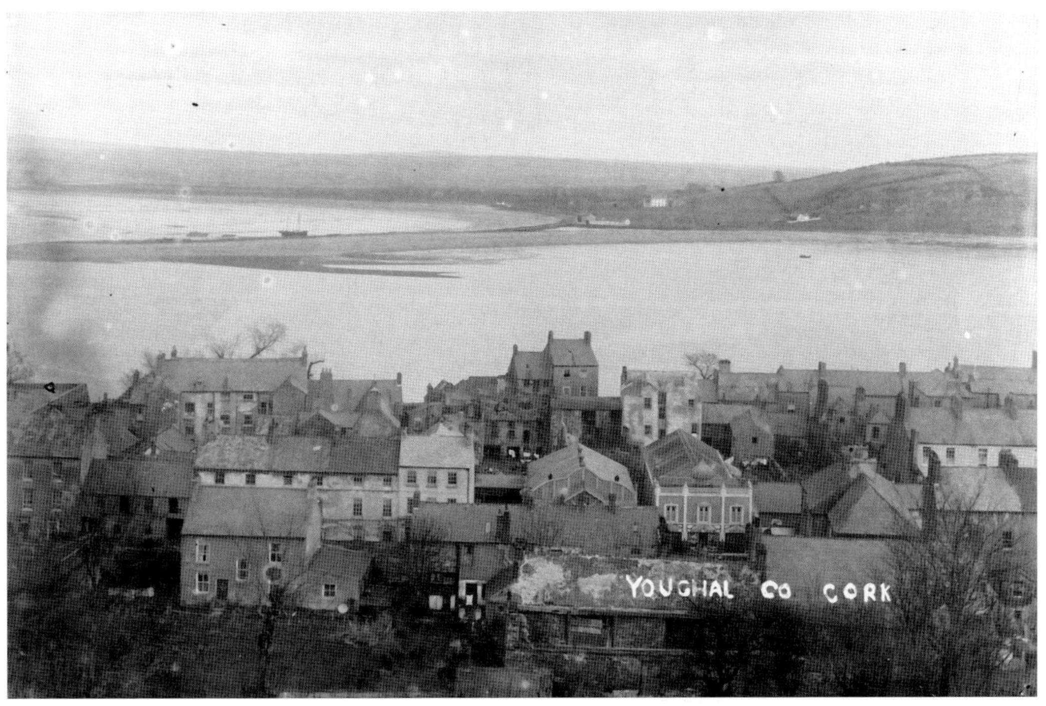

The Horgan Picture Theatre, the long building on the right,
and the Regal Cinema next door on the right.

dampened several times throughout the screening to improve the quality of the image on the screen, as well as to prevent fire.

The second notable feature was the intricate relief paintings by James Horgan, which lined the entire length of the cinema's walls, and these pictures show them.

The Horgan Picture Theatre would show a programme of films, including their own, which can be seen on the sample posters printed locally by Field's printers. The theatre was such a success that they continued to buy in films that arrived by train to Youghal and they stopped creating their own around 1921.

The projector from the cinema as well as many screening diaries are kept and preserved in the Irish Film Institute on Eustace Street in Dublin and can be seen there.

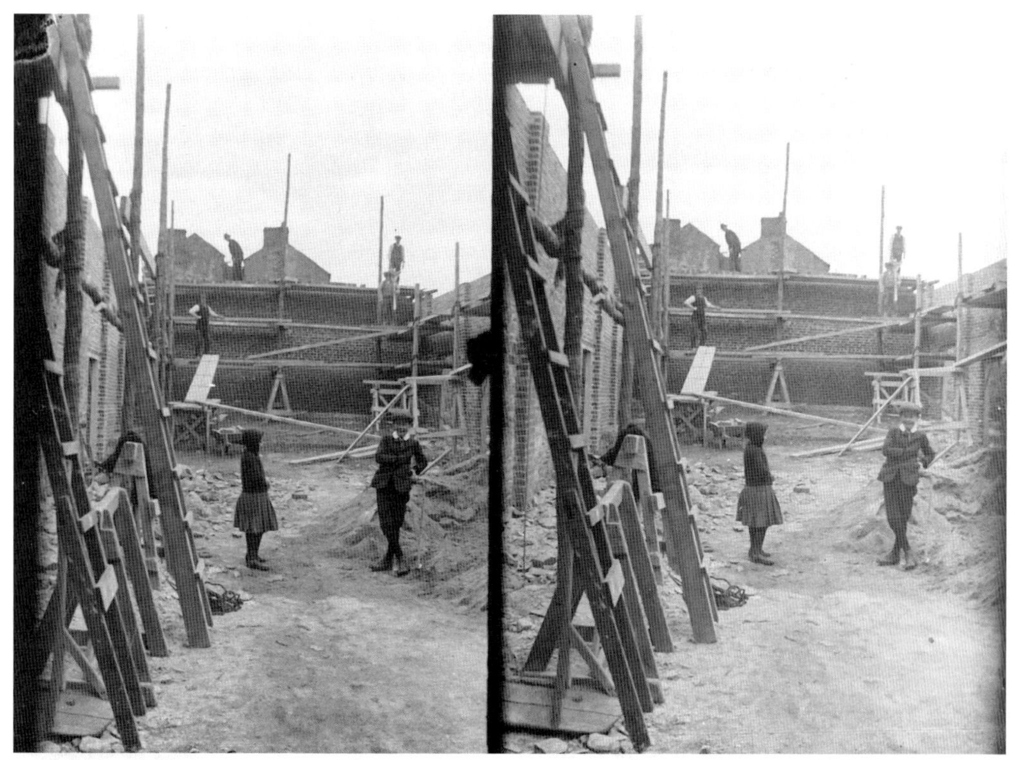

A photograph of the construction of the Horgan Picture Theatre in stereo pair format.

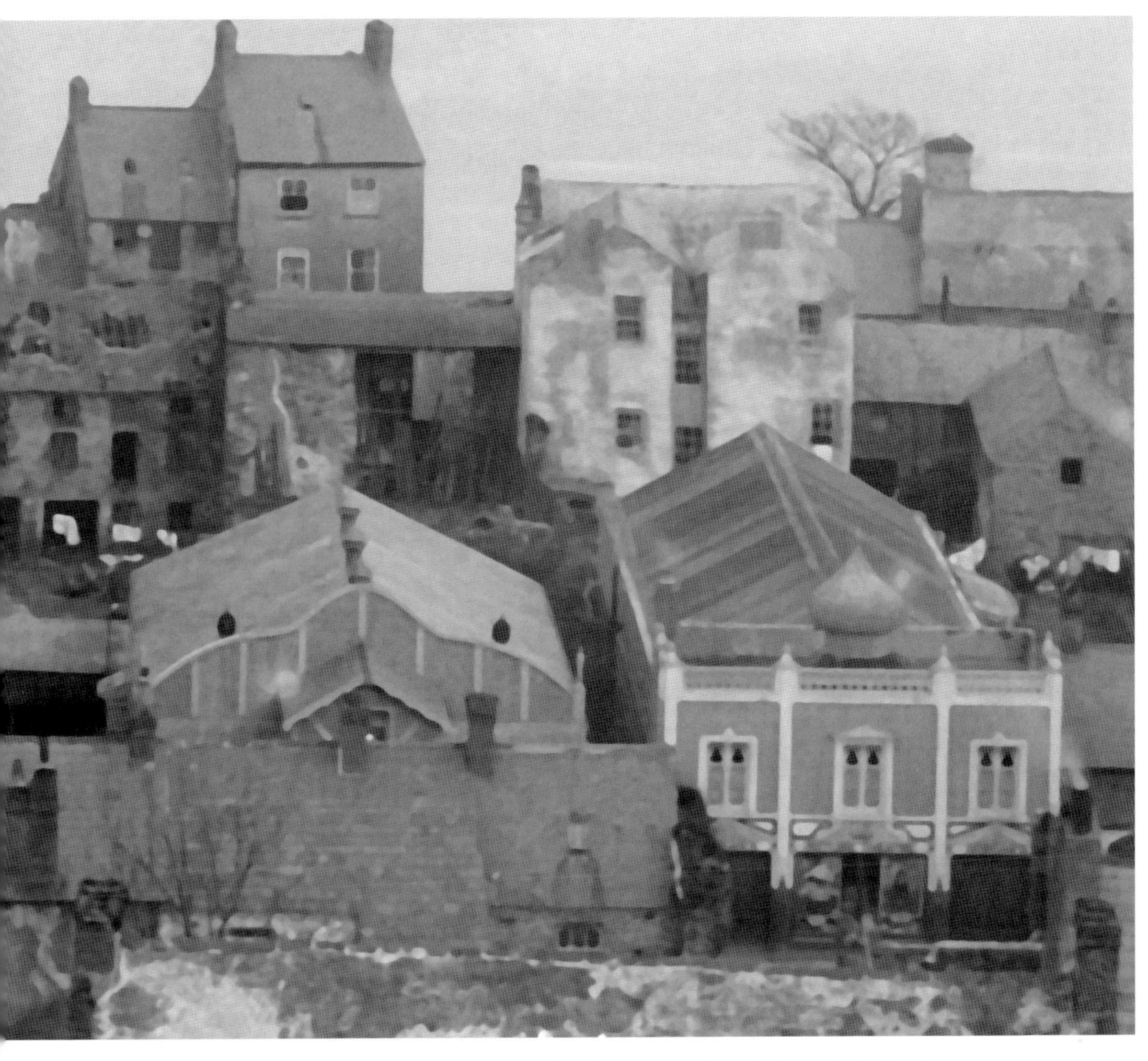

The Horgan Picture Theatre – the building on the right, with the dome.

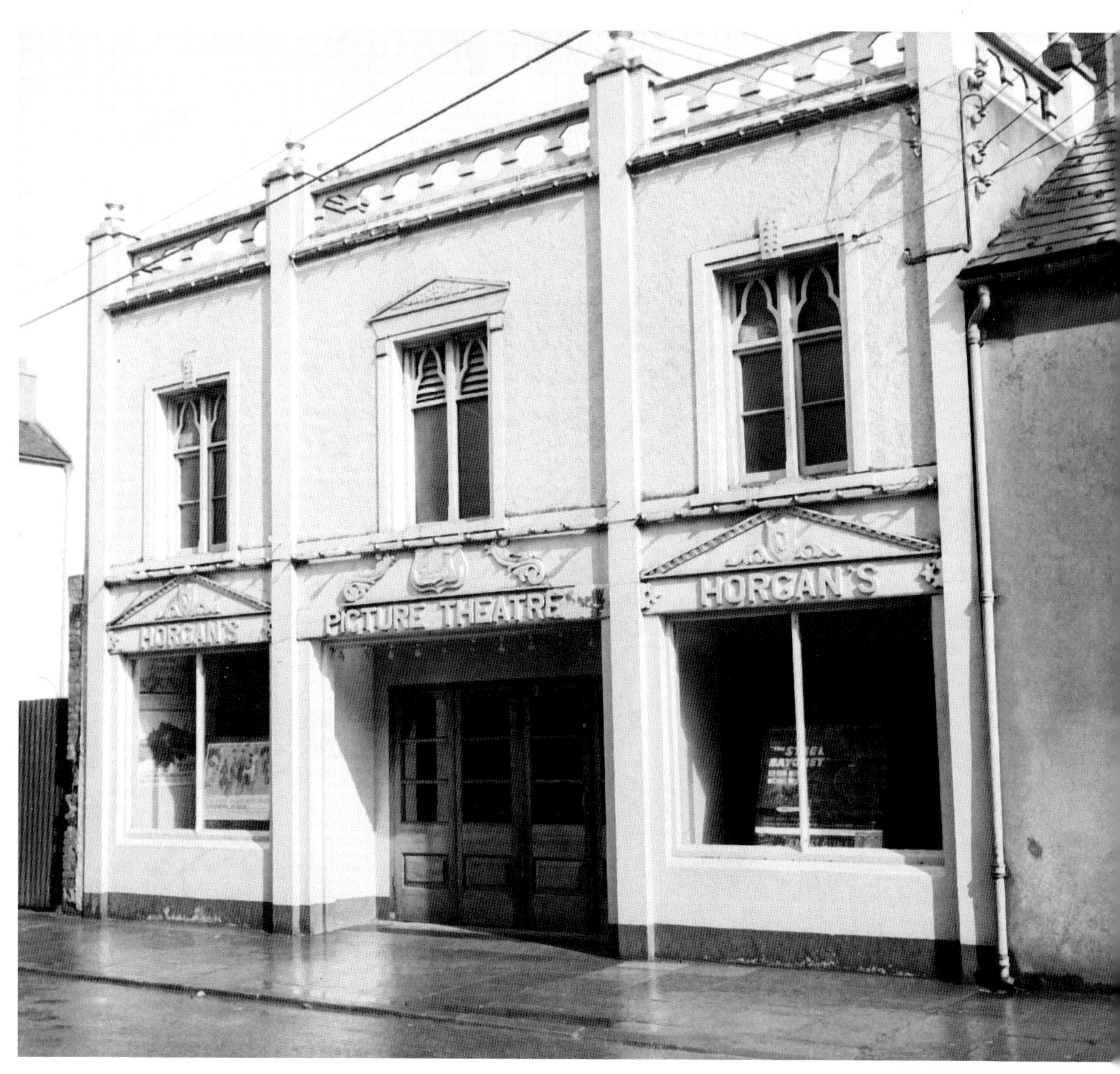

The exterior of the Horgan Picture Theatre on Friar Street.

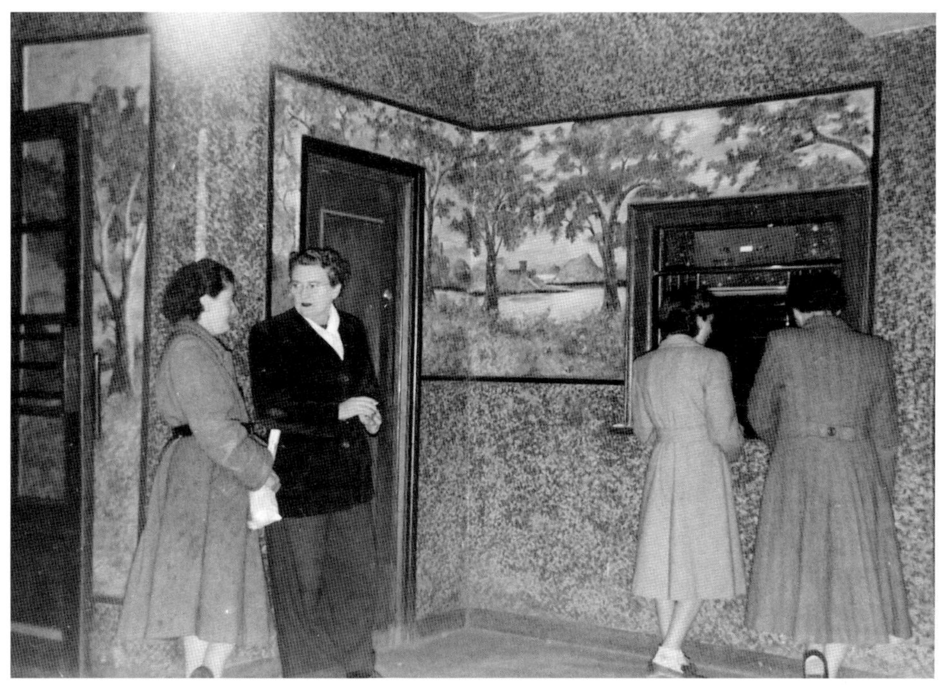

The cinema box office with some of James' paintings.

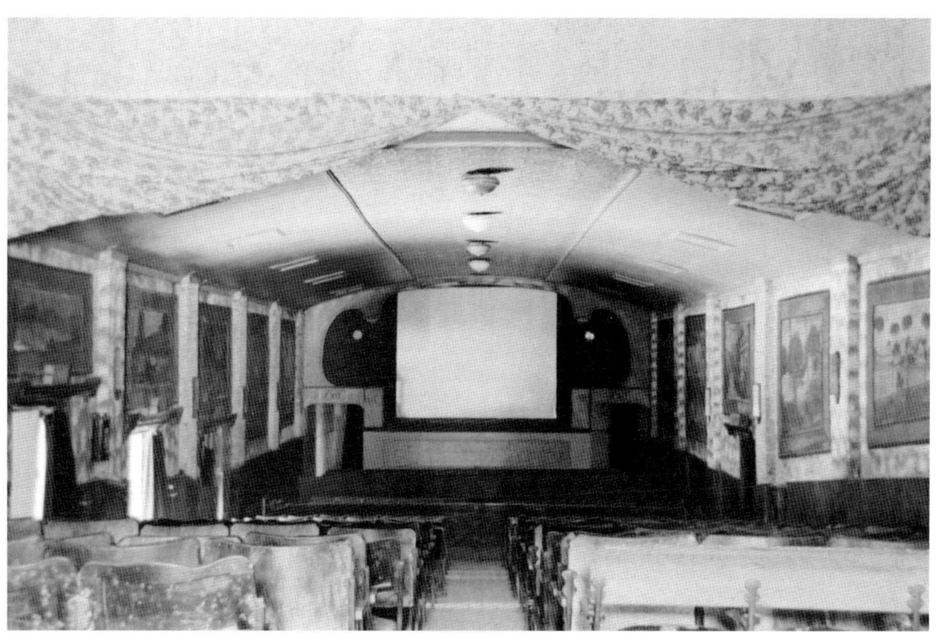

The interior of the cinema, with paintings by James on the walls,
looking at the screen which required rear projection.

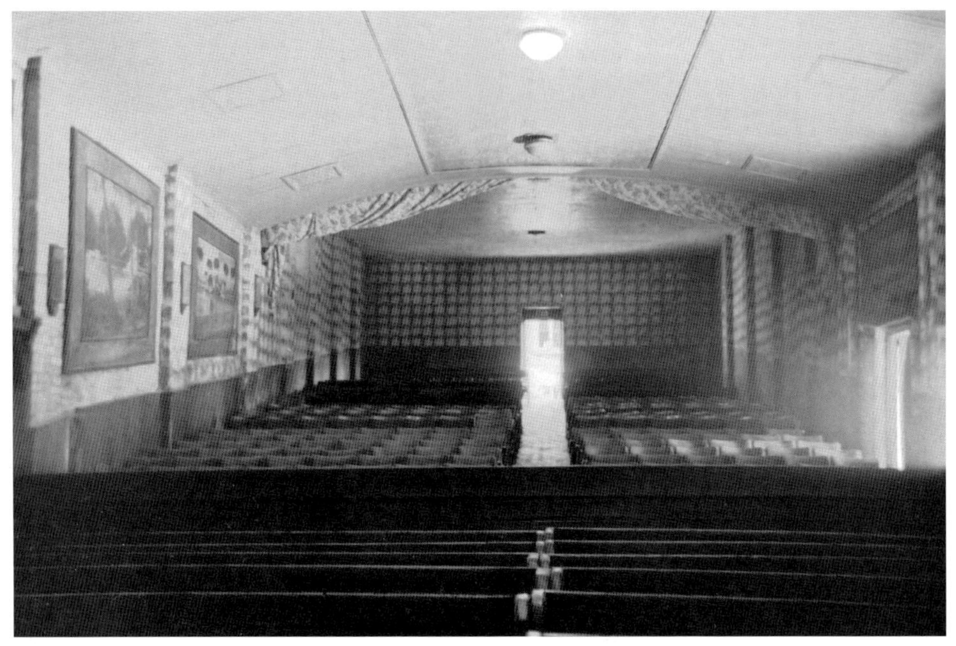

The interior of the cinema – looking at the entrance – different seating can be seen at the front of the cinema.

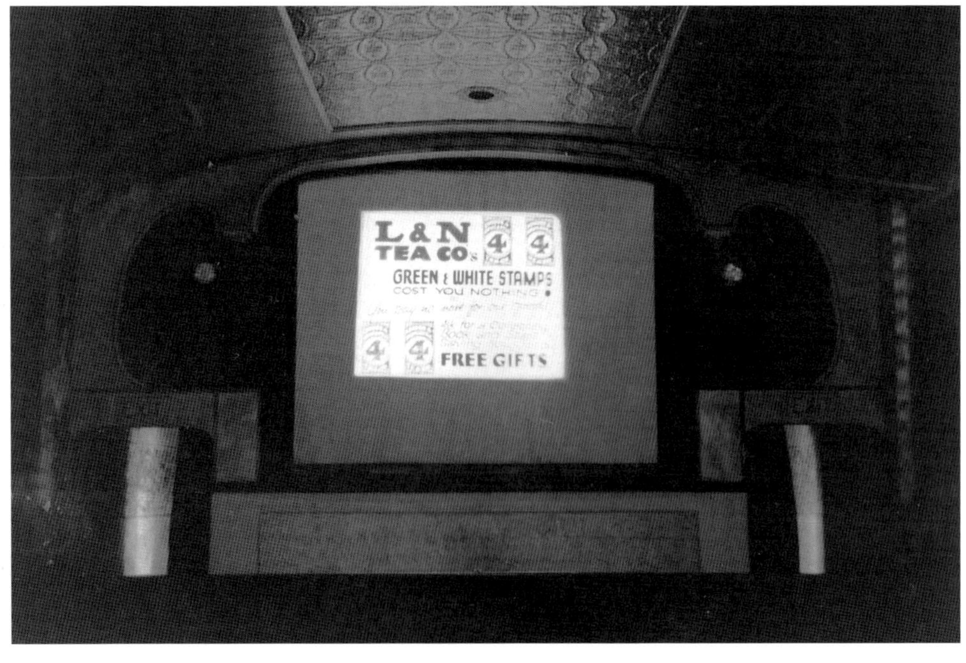

With a captive audience, the screen was an ideal place to advertise local businesses.

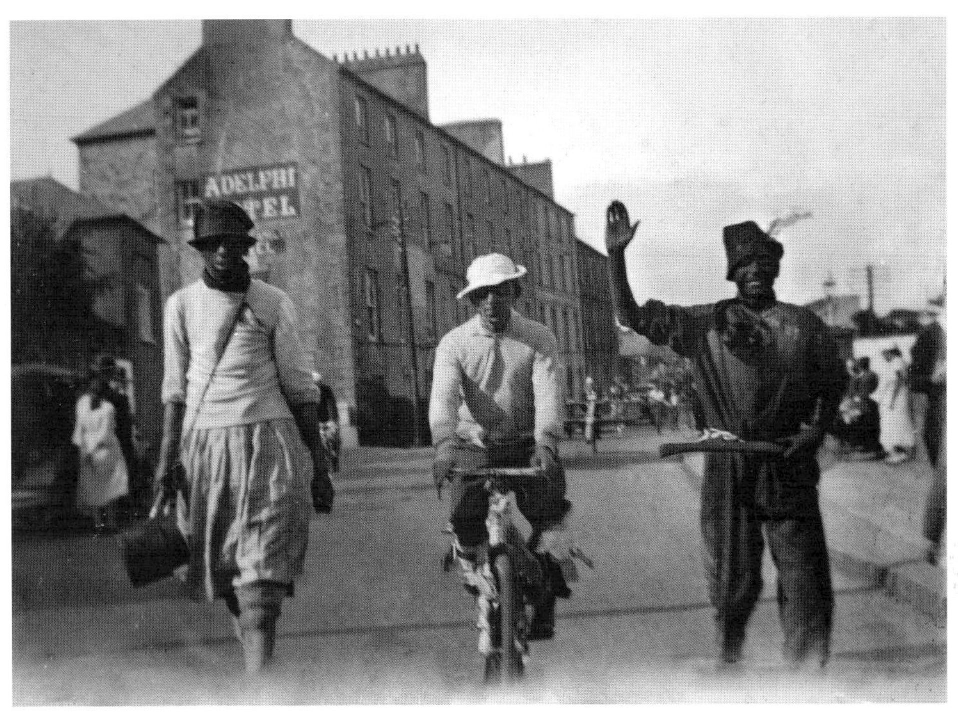

A photo of some actors who starred in the film Moby Dick *taken in 1954.*

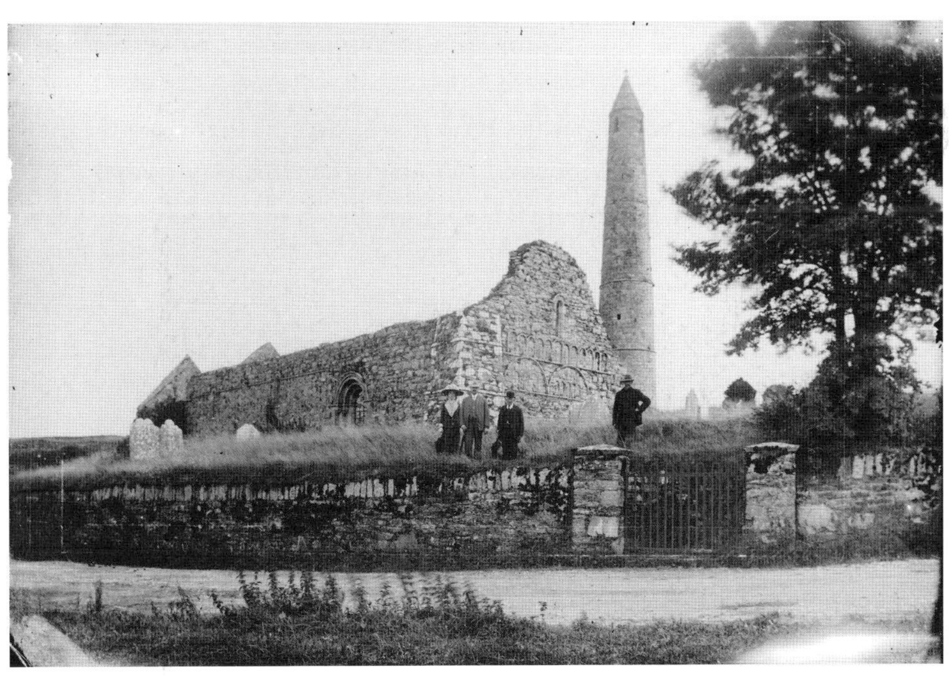

Ardmore Round Tower.

The Horgan Orchestra

In the early 1900s, when film developed from just being ten-minute novelties to one-hour dramas, music became essential. Background music was played to accompany the silent films on the piano to enhance the drama throughout the film. The piano was set to the side of the screen so that the pianist could see the screen and play appropriate music.

In 1916, the English government, keen to bolster its coffers during the prolonged war, imposed an entertainment tax on cinema. However, this tax did not apply if more than half the performance was live.

In this picture we see a full Horgan family orchestra, including James and his own hand-made cello.

The pianist for the Horgan Picture Theatre was Mazie Horgan, an excellent player, skilled at reading music and also at improvisation. The majority of the music was improvised to what was happening on screen. When she played at home, with the windows open, the music could be heard all over Strand Street, her long nails clicking on the keys before the note was played.

From the pages of her music book, the following tunes were marked with stamp edging:

'There is a flower that bloometh' – V. Wallace, 'Scenes that were brightest' – V. Wallace, 'Clementine' – P. Montrose, 'When other lips' – M. W. Balfe, 'The heart bowed down' – M. W. Balfe, 'Please let me like a soldier fall' – V. Wallace.

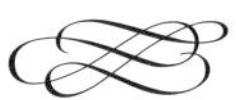

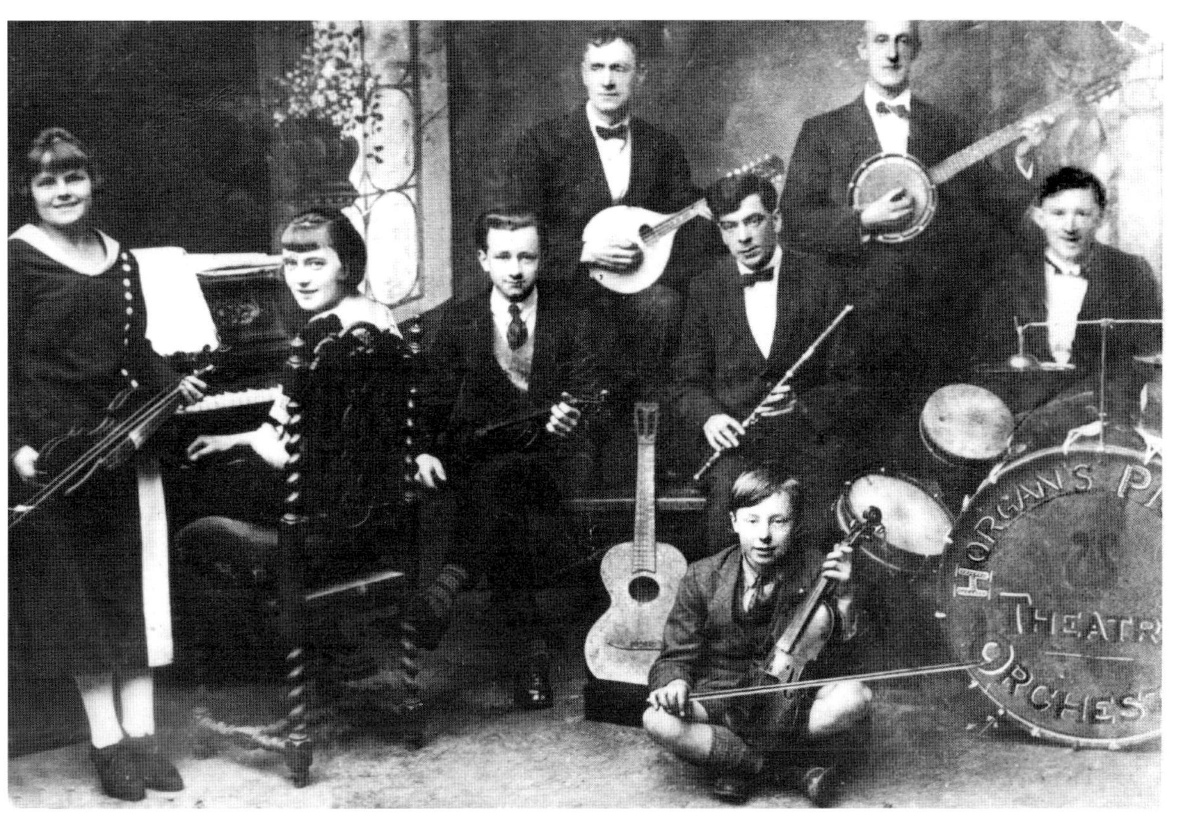

The Horgan Picture Theatre Orchestra.

Powering Projection

Films quickly evolved from just novelty items in a magic lantern show to full-scale dramas. In the early stages, these films were hand-cranked, and it was difficult to maintain an even speed over a whole show. Mechanical production was obviously required. Although Youghal had a good town gas system, gas could not drive a film projector. The Horgan brothers decided to use electricity, which was new to the town.

They set up a large petrol/paraffin engine that drove an electrical generator, which, in turn, drove the projector and lights for the cinema and all the family houses. This was preferable and much safer than using gas lights in the cinema, which would have to be ignited using a taper. The system, however, was not without its problems. The engine used very few strokes per minute, which gave a chugging effect and very uneven propulsion – unsuitable for cinema.

The problem was solved in two ways. First, a large, very heavy flywheel was added to the engine, building up enough momentum to counteract the chugging. Second, a pad was placed between the engine and the dynamo. This pad was made up of alternating layers of leather and monkey puzzle wood, which had a spongier texture and absorbed some of the chugging. The whole effect was quite satisfactory and worked for many years.

Next page top: *The Horgan cinema projection room.*

Next page bottom: *The Horgan Picture Theatre projector.*

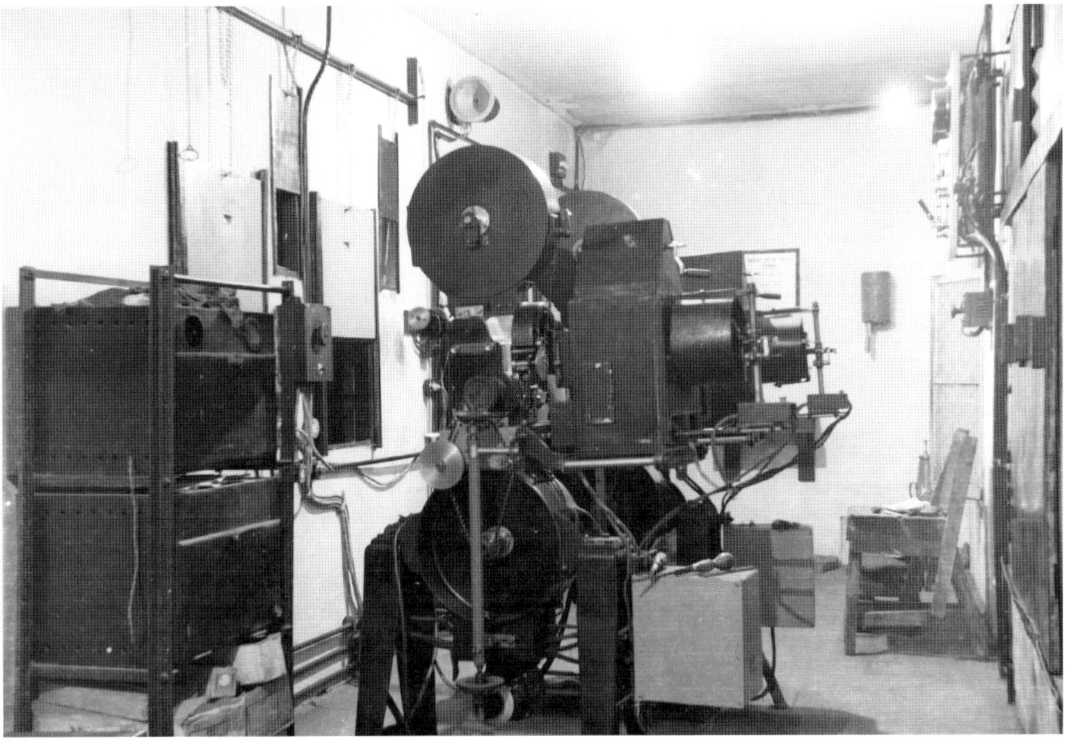

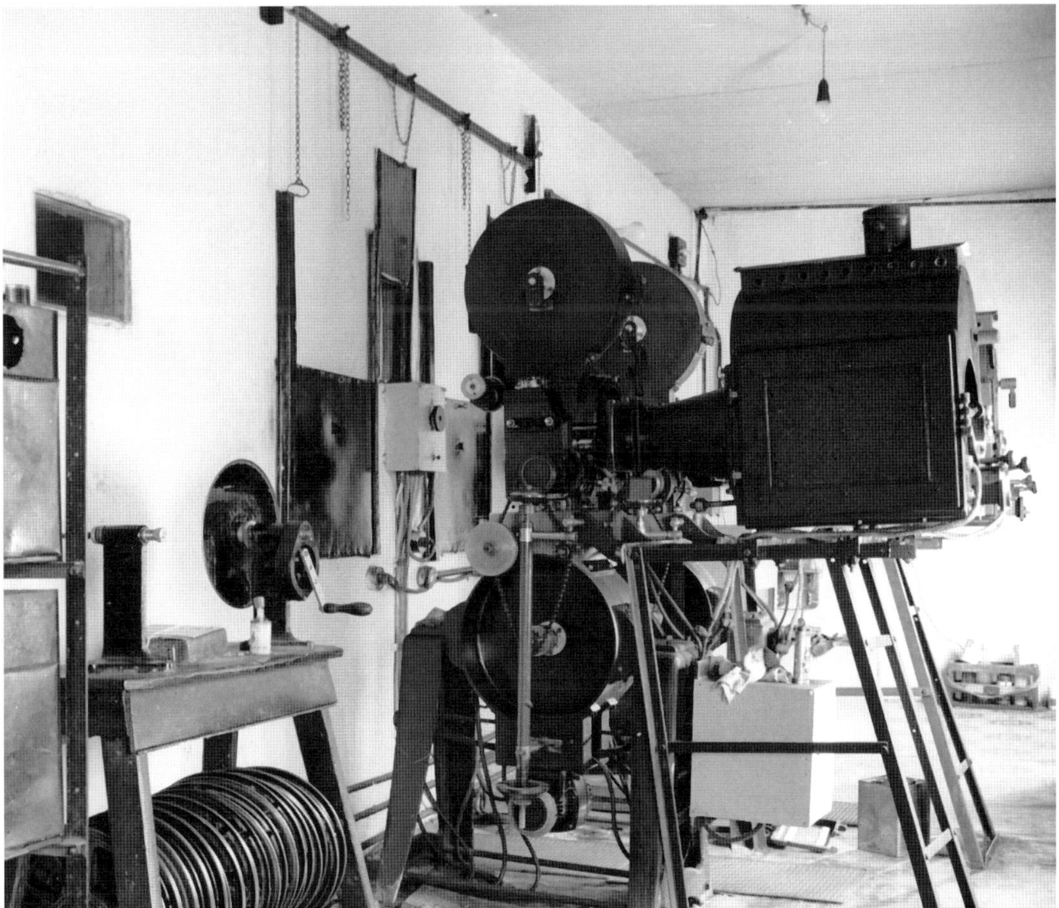

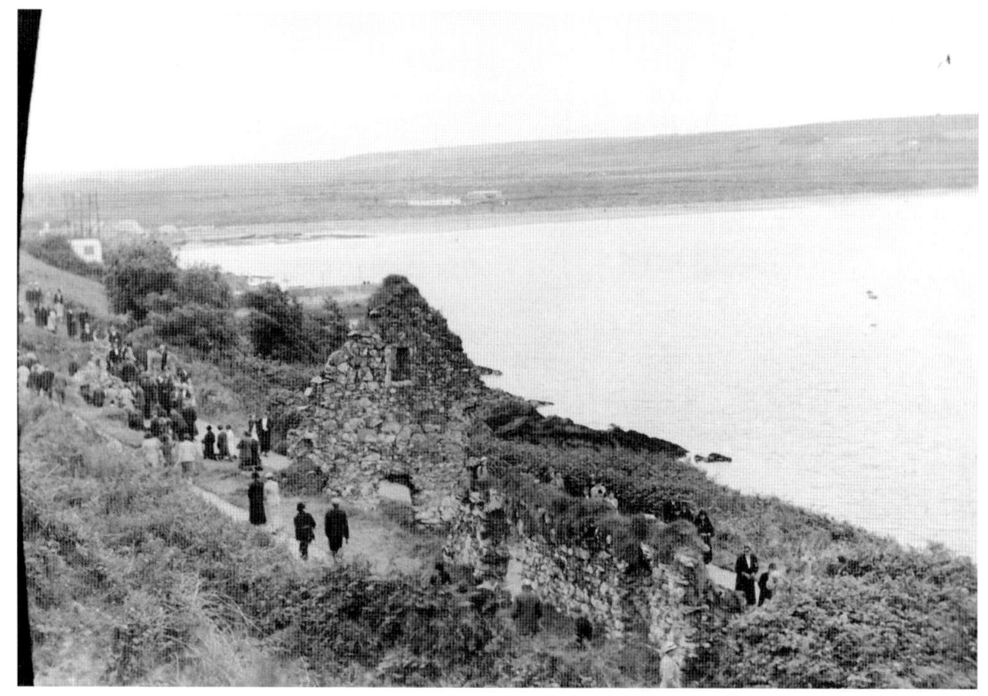

One of the first films shown in the Horgan Picture Theatre from the Youghal
Gazette, of pilgrims at St Declan's Well in Ardmore.

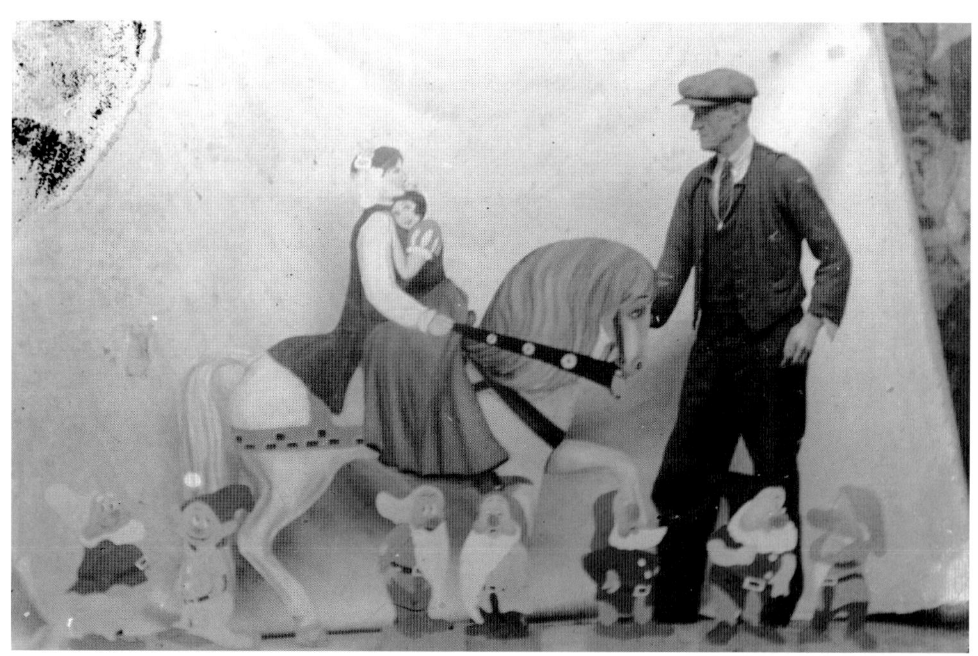

Thomas Horgan with promotional cut-outs for Disney's film Snow White and the
Seven Dwarfs in 1937, decades after the Horgans made their own animation film.

The Horgan Brothers cinema advertising posters were exclusively printed in W. J. Field's Printers in Youghal, a business that is over 200 years old and still in operation. Regular payments to Fields can be seen in the Horgan Brothers' account books kept by Thomas, which are stored in the Irish Film Institute.

Horgan poster.

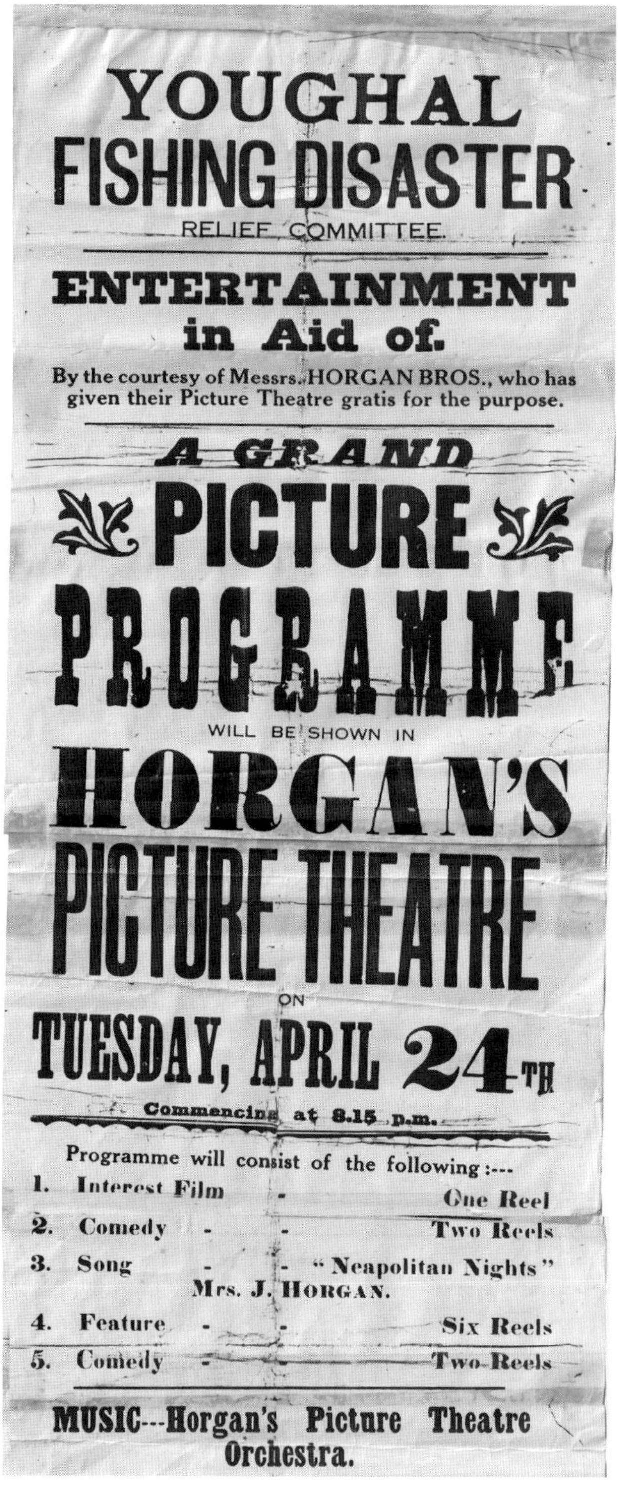

An advertising poster from the Horgan Picture Theatre from around 1920.

HORGAN'S PICTURE THEATRE YOUGHAL.

Commencing Each Night at 8.30 p.m. Matinees on Sunday, Wednesday and Saturday at 3.30 p.m.

WEEK COMMENCING SUNDAY, OCT. 18th, 1964

Sunday (One Day Only)

Dennis O'Keefe, John Payne, Arleen Whelan, Mary Anderson, in

PASSAGE WEST

Gripping drama of the —'Wagon Train.'
Full Supporting Programme.

Monday & Tuesday

Lana Turner, Hope Lange, Russ Tamblyn, Diane Varsi, Terry Moore, in

PEYTON PLACE

Love, hatred, murder, in this tense story in Tehnicolor & C/Scope.
Full Supporting Programme. Movie Tone News
N.B. This is the first time this picture is shown in Youghal—not to be confused with 'Return To Peyton Place.'

Wednesday & Thursday

Don Megowan, Silvana Pampanin, Silvo Loren, in

GUNS OF THE BLACK WITCH

Unconquerable barbarians of the sea, in Technicolor.

Also, Colleen Gray, Tony Dexter, Dean Fredericks, in

THE PHANTOM PLANET

Science shocker of the space age in Eastman Col.
Movie Tone News.

Friday & Saturday

20th Century Fox presents,

MARILYN

A film which features the story of Marilyn Munroe from her first film to her latest.   Also, Laurel and Hardy, in

THE BIG NOISE

Movie Tone News.

Next Week: 'Notorious Landy'

Prices of Admission— Night Performances   -   -   2/8, 1/4.
Matinees   -   -   1/7, 1/4, and Children 7d.

The Management Reserve the Right to Refuse Admi
and to alter the Programme.

The last remaining original Horgan Picture Theatre poster from Fields Printers.

THE END ...

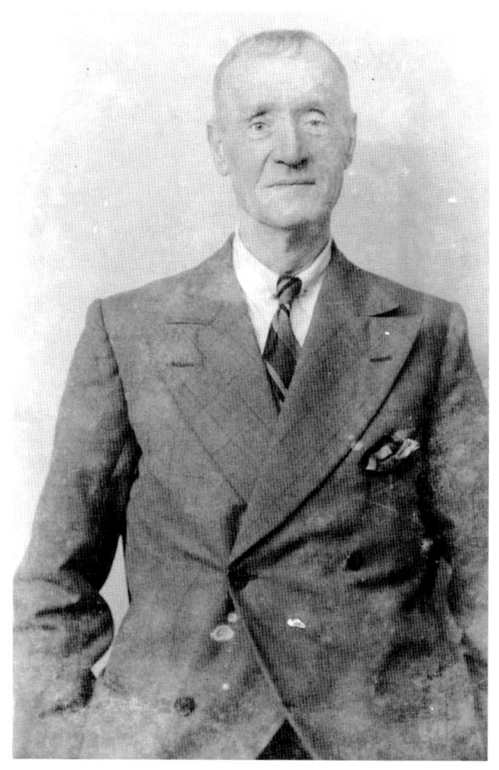

Thomas Horgan in advancing years.

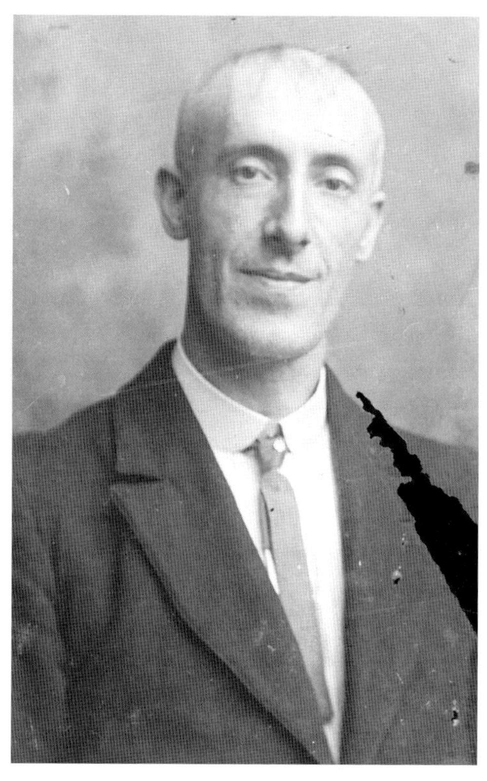

James Horgan in advancing years.

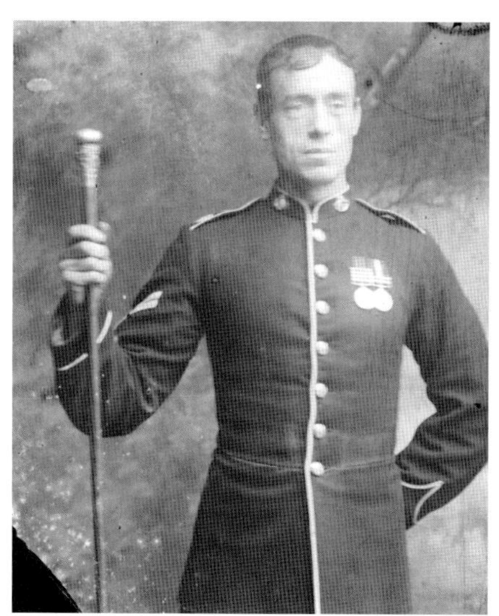

Philip Horgan, a little older.

Overleaf bottom image:
A Horgan family gathering.

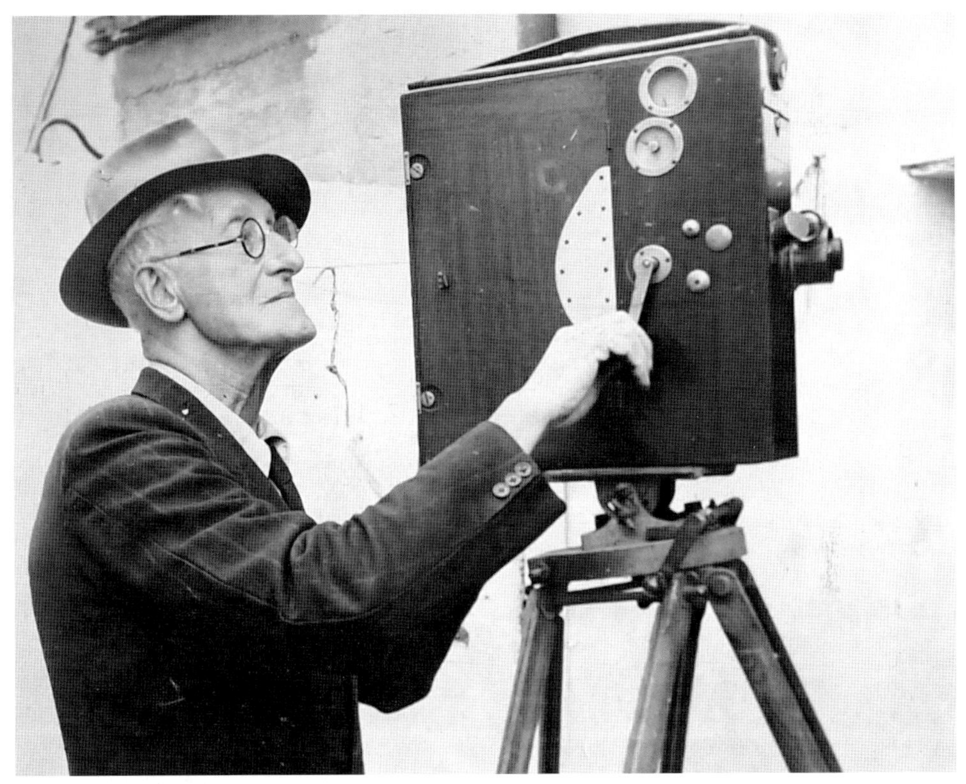

James Horgan with their film camera that now resides in the IFI in Dublin.

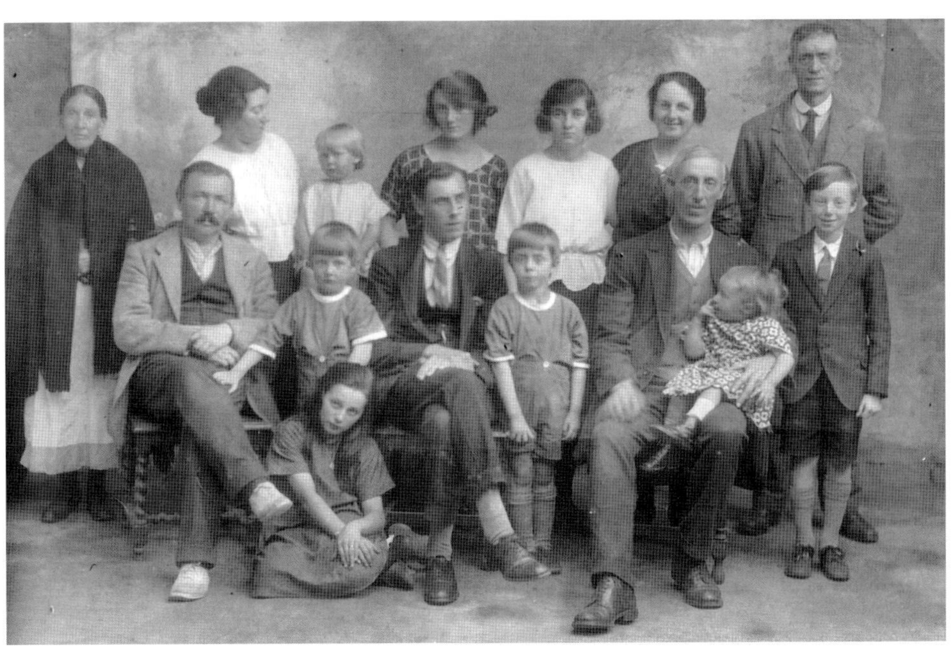

DEATH OF IRISH FILM PIONEER

The death of Mr. Thomas Horgan, senior partner of Messrs. Horgan Brothers, proprietors of Messrs. Horgan's Picture Theatre and pioneers of film exhibition and production in Ireland, occurred late on Monday night at his son's residence, Strand Street, Youghal, following a heart attack. He had been on duty as usual in the cinema during the night performance and retired, apparently in his usual health, but shortly afterwards, about 11.30 p.m. he became ill. Spiritual and medical aid were procured but he expired shortly afterwards.

A members of an old Youghal family of weavers, an industry now extinct, he became interested in photography in his youth and with his brothers James and Philip, pioneered the publication of picture post-cards in Ireland, which eventually attained world-wide circulation.

At the birth of the motion picture towards the end of the last century, he and his brothers pioneered film exhibition in Ireland and when the Cinematograph Act was passed in 1903 they were granted the first licence by the Cork Co. Council. At the end of the century the brothers constructed the first motion picture camera to be used in Ireland and with it they made some interesting films which they processed and exhibited. Portion of the mechanism of a film projector was used in the construction of this camera, but instead of the modern take-up spool, a black cloth bag was secured at its base into which the exposed film was "milked" by one of the brothers, through arm-holes in the bag, while another brother turned the handle and the third kept the lens in focus. With this strange-looking apparatus they photographed the late King Edward VII and Queen Alexandra when their Majesties visited Lismore Castle in 1903. When the brothers attempted to set up the camera outside the Castle entrance they were immediately surrounded by members of the R.I.C. and plain-clothers detectives, who questioned them at length.

Anarchists were very active at the time and the police, who had never seen such a motion-picture camera, feared that the strange apparatus might be an infernal machine. One herculean constable insisted on standing immediately in front of the lens and it was only possible to get the picture by pushing him aside suddenly as the Royal party passed. His helmet slipped over his face and the picture was taken before he could adjust it. However, as the Queen passed in her carriage, she apparently recognised the camera, as such, and bowing graciously, she

---

OBITUARY

The *Youghal Tribune* published an obituary for Thomas Horgan on 2 October 1948, where they describe in detail the Horgan brothers attempt at filming a live event, the visit of King Edward and Queen Alexandra to Lismore Castle. This is the first record of the brothers making films as early as 1904, but sadly no evidence of the film survives.

smiled into the lens.

A man of exceptionally quiet and retiring disposition, the deceased enjoyed the respect and friendship of many, not alone in his native Youghal and in the county, but in the international film industry which he had helped to established. He was a valued member of the L.S.F. during the war.

The funeral took place from the residence to the North Abbey Cemetery on Wednesday and was attended by a large and representative gathering. The chief mourners were: Mr. Ted Horgan (son); Messrs. James and Philip (brothers); Mrs. Maisie Horgan (daughter-in-law); Mrs. Ellen Kelly (mother-in-law); Mrs. May Horgan, Mrs. Mary O'Brien, Midleton, Miss N. Kelly and Sr. Mary Ellen, Winconsin (sisters-in-law); Messrs. Joe, Gus and Tom Horgan (nephews); Mrs. T. Watkins (niece), Mr. D. Watkins (nephew-in-law); Mrs. M. Horgan, Mrs. K. Horgan (nieces-in-law); Jas. and Augustine Horgan and Charles Watkins (grand-nephews); Joan, Nellie and Rosemary Horgan, Betty and Mariette Watkins (grandnieces); Mrs. E. Hodgeboom, Miss Alice O'Callaghan, Messrs. Rooney, Ardmore; Mr. and Mrs. T. Clohessy, Messrs. Henry, John, Thomas and Ml. Clohessy, Mrs. S. O'Connor and Miss Helena Clohessy, Mr. and Mrs. P. Comey (relatives). Immediate friends included Rev. Bro. Charles West, S.M.A.; Mr. T. Walsh, Miss M. O'Keeffe, Mr. and Mrs. O'Keeffe and family; Mrs. and Mrs. O'Brien and family; Mrs. S. Mangan, Mrs. George Dickenson and Mr. J. Russell. The officiating clergy were Rev. P. Barry, C.C., Rev. E. O'Callaghan, C.C., and Rev. Fr. Twohig, C.C.

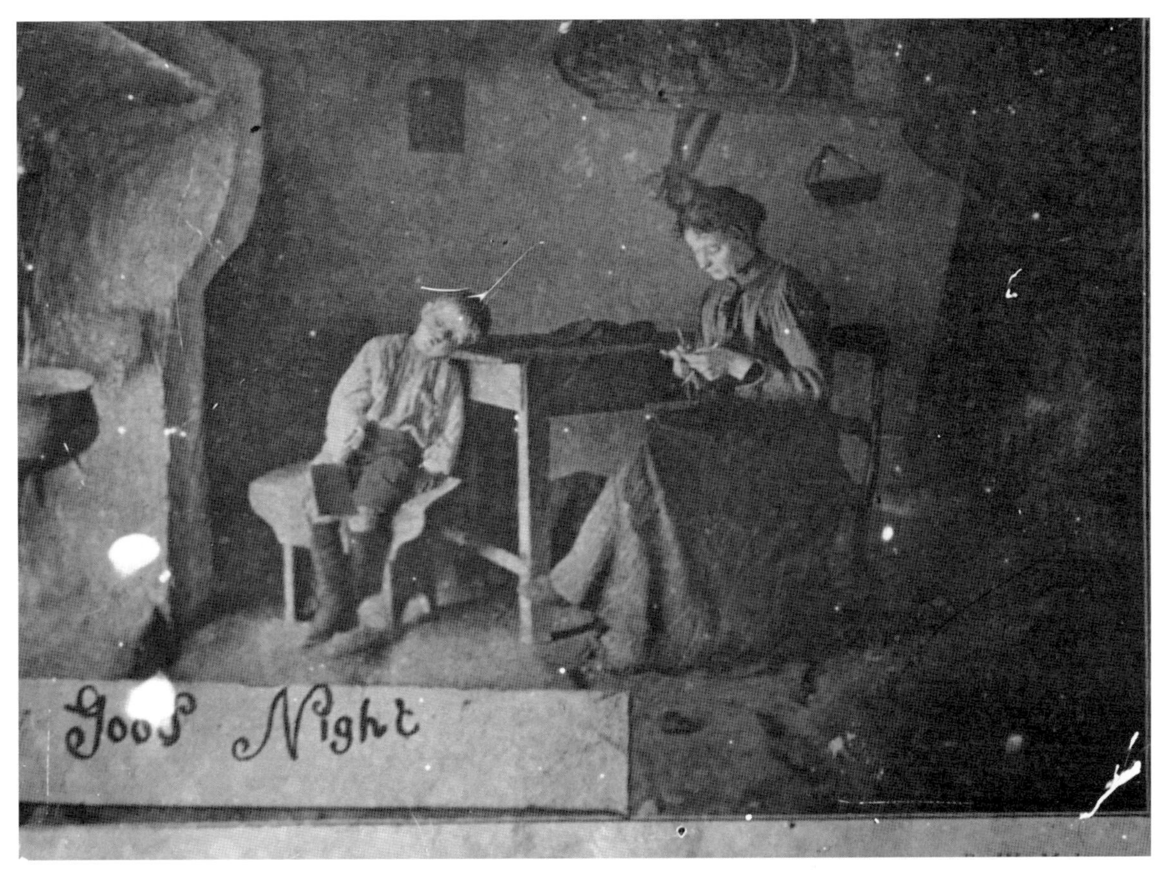

Good Night lantern slide from the Horgan Collection.

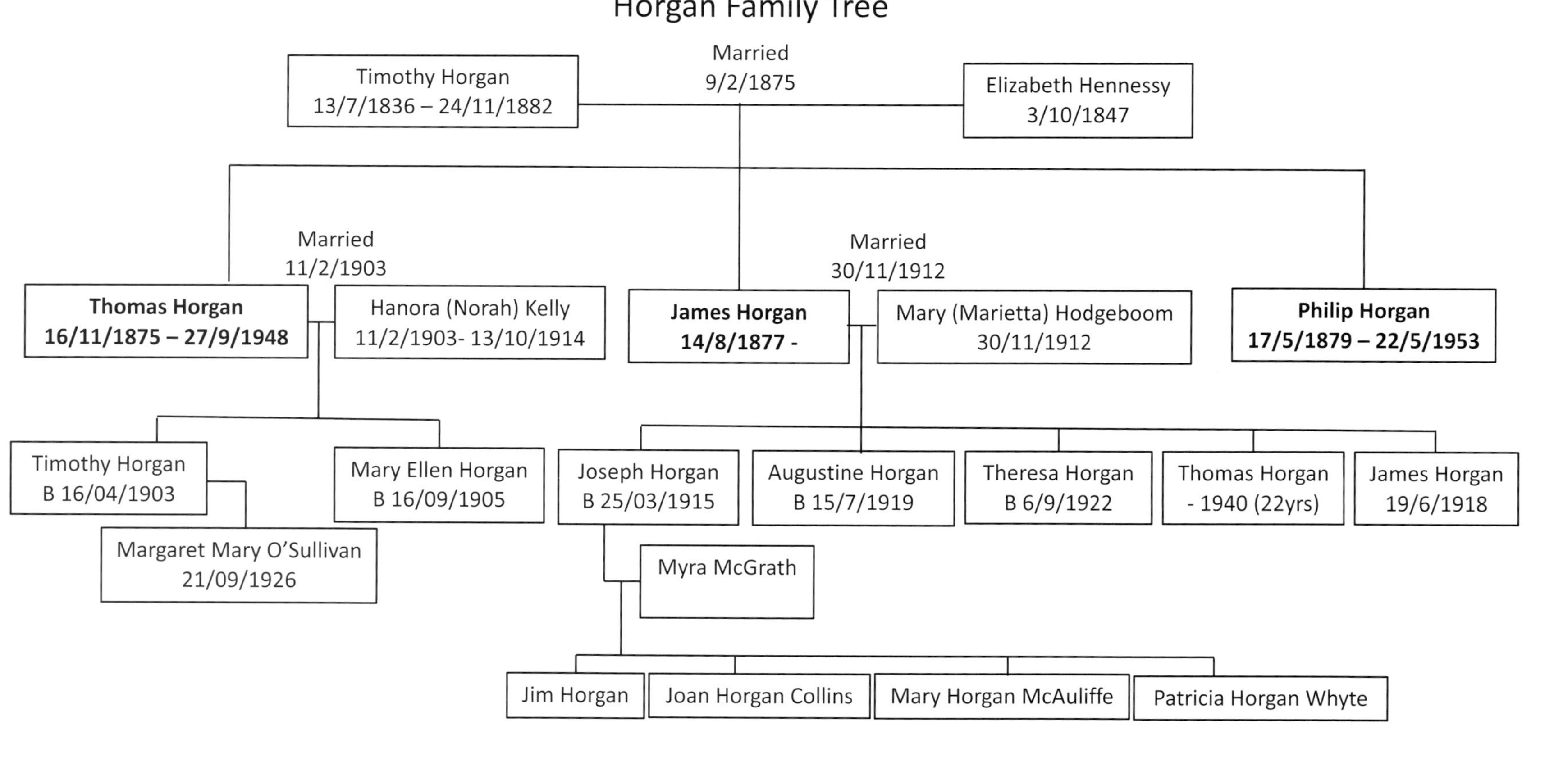

Horgan Family Tree
Timothy Horgan
13/7/1836 – 24/11/1882
Married
9/2/1875
Elizabeth Hennessy
3/10/1847
Married
11/2/1903
Married
30/11/1912
Thomas Horgan
16/11/1875 – 27/9/1948
Hanora (Norah) Kelly
11/2/1903- 13/10/1914
James Horgan
14/8/1877 -
Mary (Marietta) Hodgeboom
30/11/1912
Philip Horgan
17/5/1879 – 22/5/1953
Timothy Horgan
B 16/04/1903
Margaret Mary O'Sullivan
21/09/1926
Mary Ellen Horgan
B 16/09/1905
Joseph Horgan
B 25/03/1915
Myra McGrath
Augustine Horgan
B 15/7/1919
Theresa Horgan
B 6/9/1922
Thomas Horgan
- 1940 (22yrs)
James Horgan
19/6/1918
Jim Horgan
Joan Horgan Collins
Mary Horgan McAuliffe
Patricia Horgan Whyte

BIBLIOGRAPHY

'Death of Irish Film Pioneer', *Youghal Tribune,* 2 October 1948, p. 2.

Douglas Wiggin, Kate, 1901, *Penelope's Irish Experiences,* https://rnli.org/find-my-nearest/lifeboat-stations/youghal-lifeboat-station/station-history-youghal

E. A. Connell, Joseph Jr, November/December 2013, *HistoryIreland*.com, published in 20th-century/Contemporary History, Issue 6, Reviews, Volume 21.

Finn, Jack, 1936–1937, 'The Wreck of Annetta', Dúchas.ie, The Main Manuscript Collection, Volume 0492, p. 0286

Holohan, Bill, Solicitor & Senior Counsel,9 July 2020, '106 years ago today on 9 July 1914, the maverick 10th Lord Carbery, a pioneer aviator, performed aerial acrobatics for at the Mardyke in Cork Ireland.' Linkedin article.

https://www.ardmorewaterford.com/heroes-of-the-teaser/

https://www.ardmorewaterford.com/shipwrecks-of-ardmore-the-marechal-de-noailles-of-nantes/

O'Malley, Jim & Pardi, Richard, *Irish Post,* 19 January 2017: 'The names and remarkable lives of a group of set dancers captured by camera at a crossroads in Ireland over 100 years ago have been revealed thanks to the evidence of a 91-year-old man shortly before he died'.

Wesley-Smith, Peter 'The Kam Tin Gates', *Journal of the Hong Kong Branch of the Royal Asiatic Society,* Vol. 13 (1973), pp. 41-44.